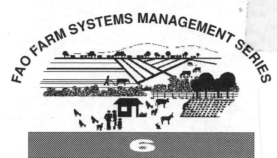

FAO FARM SYSTEMS MANAGEMENT SERIES

Farm management research for small farmer development

John L. Dillon
J. Brian Hardaker

Department of Agricultural Economics
and Business Management
University of New England
Armidale, NSW, Australia

FOOD AND AGRICULTURE ORGANIZATION OF THE UNITED NATIONS
Rome, 1993

PREFACE TO SECOND EDITION

The original edition of this bulletin was first published in 1980. Its popularity led to its being reprinted in 1981, 1984 and 1989. Since 1980, however, there have been a variety of methodological developments pertinent to farm management research for small farmer development. As well, some perspectives on small farmer development have changed. Thus, today, as compared to 1980, the role of women and the need for sustainability in small farm development are far better appreciated, as is also the potential contribution of farm management research to policy formulation and appraisal in the context of small farmer development. These methodological developments and changes in perspective provide the justification for this new extensively revised edition of the bulletin. As in the first edition, the orientation of the bulletin is to farm management research in the context of developing countries with an emphasis on small farms. Likewise, it is intended for use by farm management economists and farming systems specialists in developing countries faced with such tasks as assisting in the development, evaluation and introduction of improved technologies, enterprises or farming systems, the collection of farm management data and the monitoring of farm performance, the design and implementation of extension programmes, the planning, monitoring and evaluation of small farmer development projects, and the planning and evaluation of strategies and policies for small farmer development, agricultural marketing, rural credit, employment, etc.

As noted below, a variety of new methodological developments are outlined throughout this new edition of the bulletin. As well, however, the text now has an increased orientation to the perspectives generated by (1) a concern for sustainability of resources and the environment, (2) recognition of the role of women in small farm development and the need for gender analysis in farm management research, and (3) adoption of a farming systems perspective.

Major additions to the text include an outline of the farming systems research approach in Chapter 1, consideration of rapid rural appraisal methods and on-farm experiments in Chapter 2, the application of computers in farm management analysis in Chapter 3, integrated farm-household analysis in Chapter 4, the elicitation of probabilities and risk efficiency analysis in Chapter 8 and, in a new additional Chapter 9, the linkage between farm management research and agricultural policy with particular emphasis on the use of the policy analysis matrix aproach to policy appraisal and the use of farm management research in project planning and management as an element of development policy.

As in the first edition, in keeping the bulletin readable for farm management research practitioners, extension agents, planners and policy makers, we are conscious of the fact that we have sacrificed the full presentation of more complicated topics. For those who might need such further information, relevant references are provided at the end of each chapter.

For assistance and advice in the preparation of this second edition, our thanks are due to Messrs. Greg Daramola of Nigeria, Narciso R. Deomampo and John M. Dixon of FAO; and Ms. AnnaMaria Giorgi-Petrighi of FAO for final layout.

Armidale, 1992

PREFACE TO FIRST EDITION

The idea of this manual was conceived in the late 1960s through FAO's Regional Commission on Farm Management for Asia and the Far East.

Several economists from the region, including Dr Shao-er Ong, prepared a first draft of the manual at that time. However, the development of other commitments meant that no further work was carried out on the manual for a number of years. Very widespread interest and continuing expressed need for such a manual prompted FAO to give the work high priority in 1976/77, leading to production of an updated version of the manual which was reviewed and finalized at the Expert Consultation on Farm Management for Small Farmers in Asia and the Far East held in Bangkok, 11-15 September 1978. This consultation was attended by farm management experts from countries in the Region, FAO, A/D/C, APDI, ESCAP and other international agencies including donor organizations.

Revision and updating of the initial draft manual were coordinated and carried out by Professors John L. Dillon and J. Brian Hardaker of the Department of Agricultural Economics and Business Management of the University of New England, Armidale, Australia. They undertook this task drawing on the original draft, on comments made on that draft by Member Governments of the Region, and on suggestions and material provided by a number of economists in the region and other experts from FAO and elsewhere. Those who assisted included, in Bangladesh, Dr. M. Alamgir of the Action Research Project on Small Farmers and Landless Labourers and Dr. Md. Mosharraf Hossain of the Ministry of Agriculture; in India, Dr. I.J. Singh of Haryana Agricultural University; in Japan, Dr. Hiroyuki Nishimura of Kyoto University; in Korea (Rep. of), Don-wan Shin and Mr. Don Diltz of the Office of Rural Development; in Malaysia, Ti Teow Chuan of the Rubber Research Institute, Khoo Gaik Hong, Louisa Foh and Tuan Haji Osman bin Mohd. Noor of the Department of Agriculture, Kor Ah Kow of Selangor State Department of Agriculture, Mr S. Selvadurai of the Ministry of Agriculture, Dr. Hashin Nor and Fowzy bin Abdullah of MARDI, Dr. Donald C. Taylor, Mohd. Zainal Abidin Tambi and Eddie Chiew Fook Chong of University Pertanian Malaysia, Uzir Abdul Malek and Nik Hashim Mustapha of University Kebangsaam Malaysia, Abu Baker Hamid of FAMA, and Dr. Tan Bock Thiam of the University of Malaya; in Nepal, Dr. Ram Prakash Yadav of the Agricultural Projects Services Centre, Dr. Bharat Lal Karmacharya of the Department of Agriculture and Dr. Shao-er Ong of the A/D/C; in the Philippines, Jesus C. Alix of the Bureau of Agricultural Economics, Dr. Bart Duff, Dr. R.W. Herdt, Dr. R. Barker and Mrs. Esther Antonio of IRRI, and Dr. Ernesto P. Abarientos of the University of the Philippines at Los Baños; in Thailand, Dr. Kamphol Adulavidhaya of Kasetsart University, Dr Neal Walker, Boontam Prommani, Chamrus Ungkarpala-Ong, Dr. Somnuk Sriplung and Sa-nguan Bhananchai of the Ministry of Agriculture and Co-operatives, Dr. Ralph Retzlaff of the A/D/C, Mr. Pierre Laplante of ESCAP, Dr. J.H. Rhee of UNAPDI, Mr. A.R. Patten of UNDP and Dr. F. von Fleckenstein, Dr. Basilio N. de los Reyes, Mr. G.C.Clark, Dr. B.P. Dhital, Mr. H.G. Groetecke, Mr. B. Bruinsma and Dr. L.B. Marcelo of FAO; and in Sri Lanka, Dr. D.J. McConnell of FAO. In addition, assistance was also provided by Dr. N. Carpenter, Dr. H. Kunert, Dr. K.H. Friedrich and Mr. J.M. Dixon of the Farm Management and Production Economics Service, FAO, Rome, and by Mr. G. Allanson, Ms. A.M. Burrell, Dr. I.D. Carruthers, Dr. E.S. Clayton, Mr. M. Hamid and Dr. J.P.G. Webster of Wye College, England.

Most existing publications on farm management research methods are designed for developed-country agricultural conditions and assume a highly commercialized agriculture based on modern developed-country technology. Such publications seldom address the special issue of farm management research either as an instrument in development planning or as an element in the evolution of sound guidelines for agricultural development policy. By contrast, the present manual, through its focus on research methods appropriate for small farm analysis and its orientation to determining the needs of small farmer development, should better fulfil such functions. The manual is intended for use by farm management economists in developing countries (particularly those of Asia and the Far East) faced with such tasks as assisting in the development, evaluation and introduction of improved technologies or new enterprises, the monitoring of farm performance, the design and implementation of farm extension programmes, and the planning of strategies and policies for small farmer development, agricultural marketing, rural credit, employment, etc. Such problems are found throughout the developing world and the manual should find general application in farm management analysis pertinent to small farm development research. However, most of the case examples used relate to Asia and the Far East.

The manual is designed to be fully compatible with FAO's computerized farm management data collection, analysis, storage and retrieval system. Similarly, the manual is usefully supplemented by the FAO-sponsored AGRIPLAN manual.

Rome, 1980

TABLE OF CONTENTS

Page

1. INTRODUCTION

1.1 The small farm setting

Though the definition of *small farmers* has been the subject of much debate, it still remains fuzzy (Valdés, Scobie and Dillon, 1979; Wharton, 1969). Precise definition, however, is not required to recognize either the reality of the small farmers' plight or their importance in world development. In general, they constitute the bulk of the world's farmers, operate in a context of increasing local population pressure, have a very small resource base generating a chronically low standard of living either involving absolute poverty or verging on it, rely to a greater or lesser degree on subsistence production, and tend to be on the margin rather than in the mainstream of society in terms of political influence and the provision of health, education and other services.

Just how many small farmers there are in the world is not known exactly. Rough estimates are that about half of the world's population is dependent on subsistence agriculture, that about 40 percent of cultivated land is worked by small farmers, that 60 percent of all farmers are small farmers of whom a significant proportion are women, and that they account for less than 40 percent of all agricultural output. United Nations (1988) medium projection estimates are for an increase in the population of developing countries from 3.6 billion in 1985 to seven billion by 2025. Of these, about half will be living in rural areas, mostly on small farms. Rough as these estimates undoubtedly are, they indicate the immense significance of small farmers in world development. Moreover, the living conditions of small farmers and their families still remain largely as described by Umali (1978): "The bulk of the poor - 85 percent by World Bank estimates - are in the rural areas. They consist mainly of small farmers/fishermen, landless agricultural labourers, and shifting cultivators... These people are living truncated lives, suffering from disease and malnutrition. Some of them have no roof to cover their heads, no clothes to cover their bodies and no means, either to produce or buy the food they need for the bare sustenance of themselves and their families. Most of the small farmers are tenants and sharecroppers. They do not own the land they cultivate. Their lives - and their hopes - are dominated by those who own the land. They are often denied, both by design and circumstance, the basic human right to make their own decisions and the basic human right to an equitable share in the benefits of their toil. *Growth with social justice* will not result unless there is corrective bias in favour of the rural poor and unless the small farmers, who constitute the majority of the rural poor, are brought into the mainstream of development through purposive intervention."

No matter where they are found around the world, small farmers appear to constitute a subculture (Rogers, 1969). From an economic point of view, the most significant characteristic of small farmers is the small resource base on which they have to operate and their consequent low level of income. In general, they have control (often with very little security of tenure) over only a small area of land which is often naturally poor or depleted and often fragmented and subject to degradation; they have an extremely low level of human capital in terms of education, knowledge and health with which to work; and they suffer chronic indebtedness and lack accessibility to institutional credit and inputs. Concomitantly, their access to markets is often difficult and, when available, they face unstable markets and prices; they receive inadequate extension support; they have little share in the control and operation of rural institutions; and they lack the socio-economic power with which to gain access to public and other services that are available to other more powerful members of their national society. In consequence, the small farmer's existence is often precarious and the effect of poor weather or prices can be calamitous for the farmer and her or his family.

While small farmers have the common characteristics of limited resources and low incomes, their *modus operandi* around the world exhibits tremendous diversity. Contrast, for example, the farming systems of the pastoralist of semi-arid Africa, the shifting cultivator of the semi-humid tropics, and the small paddy farmer of monsoonal Asia. Just as great as these differences in ways of farming are the differences in culture that exist among small farmers from country to country and region to region. In consequence, small farmers cannot be thought of as a homogeneous group even within a relatively small region. Indeed, one of the major responsibilities of farm management research relative to small farmers is to detail their diversity around the world as a complementary step to the specification of priority problems for farm management research.

1.2 Farming systems research (FSR)

FARM MANAGEMENT RESEARCH AND FSR

There is significant overlap and commonality of interest between farm management research and what has come to be known as farming systems research (FSR) or the related FAO farming systems development approach (FSD) - see FAO (1989). This is because farm management research, carried out by agricultural economists, may often be conducted by them within the context of a multi-disciplinary FSR team. As well as one or more agricultural economists, such teams typically include other relevant agricultural scientists with training in soil, crop and animal sciences, rural sociology and extension. In such teams the role of the agricultural economist is to bring an economics perspective to the evaluation and improvement of the farming systems under study. This economics perspective relates not only to the farmer's management of her or his farm but also to farm-household interrelationships and the policy environment within which the farmer has to operate. Since such a broad perspective is the usual one followed in farm management research, in reality the involvement of a farm management researcher as a member of an FSR team better ensures the multi-disciplinary cooperation and farmer liaison that are necessary if farmers are to be best served by agricultural scientists.

DEFINITION OF FSR

FSR is a scientific method that focuses on farmers' circumstances and seeks to integrate farmers into the research process. Of particular relevance are the perceptions and expectations of small farmers and the constraints confronting them. Essentially, FSR adopts a farmer-oriented and problem-solving approach to agricultural research through appreciation of the production systems of farmers, their farm-household interactions, and the environmental variables - ecological, biological, socio-cultural, economic and political - which influence farmers' decisions. FSR thus recognizes that farming systems are dynamic and involve not merely the interaction of physical forces, but also expressions of free will arising from the purposiveness of farmer behaviour (Dillon, 1976).

The most significant difference between traditional disciplinary research and FSR is at the analytical level. While the traditional approach to agricultural research seeks a disciplinary goal or operates within a commodity framework, FSR takes a holistic view of the farm whereby physical, ecological and biological factors are integrated with the socio-economic environment as well as the expectations and preferences of the farmer. FSR is therefore highly complementary to the traditional disciplinary approach which investigates components of the farming system rather than the system as a whole. FSR provides an over-arching view of the agricultural system in addition to facilitating purposeful research management in terms of goal achievement and choice between research alternatives. In particular, FSR has been helpful in identifying major constraints to increasing farm output, and in providing improved understanding of farmers' circumstances and decision-making processes, thereby providing guidance for component research conducted on traditional disciplinary lines and for the formulation of agricultural policies better attuned to societal welfare (Tripp, 1991; Nagy and Sanders, 1990).

FEATURES OF FSR

Some of the distinguishing features of FSR are as follows (Dillon and Anderson, 1984):

- ◇ a problem-solving orientation to research;
- ◇ a holistic approach capable of capturing (or adequately understanding) the interplaying factors of a system for the purpose of improving performance;
- ◇ entails multi-disciplinary and interdisciplinary research: this feature has implications for coordinated use of base data, surveys, on-farm trials, on-station field and laboratory experiments, and modelling;
- ◇ focuses on the problems of identified and relatively homogeneous groups of farmers;
- ◇ dependent on farmers' participation with strong emphasis on bottom-up communication: this is in recognition of the farmer and her or his family as the core elements of the farming system;
- ◇ ensures effective links to, and influences upon, related component and basic research;
- ◇ emphasizes cyclical or feedback mechanisms: this implies a dynamic, action-oriented, adaptive approach wherein tentative solutions to identified problems are tested on both the experiment station and the farmer's field

and modified, to be redesigned or rejected on the basis of accumulating knowledge, understanding and experience (Tripp and Woolley, 1989);

◇ assessable by the extent to which it leads to (i) the development of cost-effective and socially desirable farming techniques that are readily adopted by its specified groups of client (usually small-scale) farmers and (ii) the introduction of socially desirable changes to policies influencing the farm system.

RELEVANCE OF FSR

From the above-listed features, FSR can be described as providing the framework for cooperation amongst agricultural economists, soil, plant and animal scientists, sociologists, extension specialists and other researchers. FSR also demands that each of the researchers works closely not only with other researchers but also with farmers so as to (a) ensure the relevance of the technology being developed and (b) recognize situations where institutional or policy changes are prerequisites to the adoption of improved farming methods either through the adjustment of existing farming systems or the introduction of new farming systems.

Another important dimension of FSR is the fact that it provides the opportunity of judging whether progress is being made towards the achievement of socially desirable objectives. Often, this involves tracing out the impacts of technical and other changes beyond the specific primary target group of farmers. Because of this consideration, FSR has been postulated to be an efficient approach to agricultural research which is especially suitable to national agricultural research systems where short- and medium-term goals need to be achieved within the requirement of government policies.

FARM-HOUSEHOLD FRAMEWORK AND ANALYSIS

Farm-household systems usually consist of three interlinked and interactive sub-systems. These are: the household as the decision-making unit; the farm with its crop and livestock activities as production elements of the farming system; and an off-farm component involving one or more of work, market or social relationships. The first of these sub-systems, which is the household as the decision-making unit, is particularly relevant because decisions taken at the farm-household level have far-reaching effects on agricultural production. The farm-household thus deserves special attention as the basic unit of analysis and development, especially in developing countries (Singh, Squire and Strauss, 1986). In this regard, it is important to understand the framework within which farm-household objectives are set and the methods by which these objectives are achieved. Particularly important characteristics of the farm-household system in the small-farm context are:

◇ its complexity due to the multiple objectives of the decision-makers involved;

◇ its dependence on indigenous knowledge developed over long periods of time;

◇ its flexibility due to the rational disposition of farmers in the face of compelling need for change.

The foregoing suggest that farmers' participation in the research process is essential, as is an understanding of the crucial factors influencing their decision-making. A good understanding of the dynamic processes involved in changes in the system is also essential in developing a workable framework for FSR analysis.

Another characteristic feature of the farm household in small-scale agriculture is the high proportion of family labour in the total labour input, as well as the high percentage of subsistence consumption relative to total output. Though the majority of farmers in the developing countries of Asia, Africa and Latin America are small-scale, they are responsible for the bulk of food production in their respective countries. Therefore, any attempt at boosting agricultural production needs to focus on improving productivity of small-scale farms. This realization has led to recognition of the importance of the farm household in the development of this type of agriculture, as discussed further in Section 4.9.

1.3 Definition of farm management research

By research is meant the orderly process of investigation by which we increase our knowledge of why the world is as it is and of how it might be changed. Applied research is research undertaken specifically for the purpose either of resolving a particular problem or of gaining the knowledge necessary to better achieve some goal. Generally, farm management research is applied research and has either or both of two broad aims:

- ◇ to provide information which will assist farmers in their farm management so that they are better able to achieve their goals whatever they may be; and
- ◇ to provide government with information on farmers and their management so as to assist in the better formulation of government policy and development planning.

These aims of the researcher differ from those of the farmer or of the farm management extension worker. From the farmer's view, farm management consists essentially of choosing between alternative uses of the available scarce resources of land, labour, capital, time and management so as to best achieve her or his goals given all the risks and other difficulties faced in the farming operation (Makeham and Malcolm, 1986). The role of the farm management extension worker is to give guidance to farmers by helping them to see their problems, to analyze them and to make soundly based recommendations about possible management decisions. In this work the extension worker relies heavily on her or his understanding of the relevant farming systems and their environments and on the knowledge generated by farm management research.

1.4 The need for farm management research on small farms

The overall need for farm management research on small farms lies in their importance as both a major component of the world's disadvantaged population and as potential contributors to the provision of adequate world food supplies. For virtually all the developing countries, development encompassing their small farmers is an essential element of national development. While ever they have a significant small-farm problem, countries cannot be regarded as developed. As outlined below, how farm management research can assist such development may be considered under the six headings of research contributions to: recommendations for small farmers, agricultural policy and adjustment, agricultural planning, project planning and appraisal, project monitoring and evaluation, and rural development.

FARMER RECOMMENDATIONS

It is generally agreed that small farmers use their limited resources and knowledge efficiently via their traditional farming systems. From a farm management point of view, to improve small farmers' welfare or incomes it is necessary to provide them with improved technology, greater security and, so far as relevant, better information of market trends and prospects. Farm management research can play a major role relative to all three of these needs.

The provision of improved market information implies farm management research which, in terms of both existing and potential farm enterprises, appraises likely market supply and demand so as to provide guideline price forecasts for dissemination to small farmers. Given such guidelines, small farmers can better respond to market needs. In such work the farm management researcher will often need to work in cooperation with commodity and marketing economists. Conversely, she or he will have a role to play in guiding national planners on the likely response of small farmers to price changes for farm inputs and products which might be promulgated as elements of national planning.

In terms of enhancing the security of small farmers, farm management researchers can contribute significantly both (a) by the appraisal of risks confronting small farmers and the assessment of strategies to meet such risks and (b) by consideration of the costs and benefits of alternative policies with respect to land tenure, farm size and other elements of resource access such as, for example, credit and irrigation policy.

At the other end of her or his professional work spectrum, the farm management researcher has a significant role to play in cooperative research with agro-biological scientists in the development, testing and evaluation of improved farm production systems. Such research on new technology, particularly in terms of its testing and evaluation, constitutes a major need to be met by farm management research. Only after adequate evaluation can soundly based recommendations about new technology be developed for dissemination to small farmers. There is also a liaison role to be played by farm management researchers. This is in providing feedback from farmers and guidelines based on real farm knowledge to agro-biological researchers so as to better ensure that their endeavours to develop new technology are well oriented to what is needed and feasible on farms. Too often in the past, research aimed at developing new technology for small farmers has been carried out without any recognition of what is feasible and appropriate in terms of the farmer's real-world situation. To avoid this problem, an FSR orientation is necessary.

AGRICULTURAL POLICY AND ADJUSTMENT

By agricultural policy is meant the specification by government of those laws, regulations and rules under which agriculture and agribusiness have to operate. Of course, not all aspects of the agricultural environment can be controlled by government. Nor will government wish to meddle with all those elements which it could control. Nonetheless, in all countries there tends to be a substantial government influence on agriculture via regulations and programmes relating, for example, to tenure, land and water rights, pest and disease control, prices, market arrangements, exports, labour welfare, credit supply and interest rates, etc. And many elements of national policy, such as exchange rate control, highway development, education and research funding, social welfare provision, etc. have a significant effect upon agriculture.

Farm management research involving the collection and analysis of farm-level data is needed in order to assess the impact on farmers and the general rural community of particular policies. Ideally this should be done *ex ante,* i.e., before the policies are actually introduced, so as to provide guidance on their likely efficacy and suggestions for their improvement. Politics being what it is, however, assessment is often not possible until after policies have been introduced. Frequently, farm management research will indicate quite untoward effects arising from policies which, at face value, seem only to have potentially beneficial effects. For example, in response to a severe weed control problem, government might introduce a subsidy on chemical herbicide so as to induce its use by farmers. The result, however, might be not only total weed control but also social unrest due to a significant loss of employment opportunities for those landless workers whose previous major source of income came from hand weeding. Prior farm management analysis of the effects of such a subsidy would have given warning of such a problem.

The aggregate effects of farmers' responses to agricultural policies can lead to significant changes in the economic structure of the agricultural sector. For instance, policy can influence production technologies as illustrated by the above example involving a herbicide subsidy. Market opportunities and prices are also important areas where policy can make farmers adjust their farm operations. In Nigeria, for example, when the federal government introduced its structural adjustment programme in 1986, many farmers responded to the signals this gave. Thus, due to the dissolution of export crop commodity boards and more realistic producer prices for export crops, there was a substantial shift of emphasis among farmers from food crops to production of the now more lucrative export crops. Such changes in economic structure, attributable to programmes and policies, can be analyzed with the use of mathematical programming models (Hazell and Norton, 1986) as discussed in Section 4.5. Sources of adjustments or changes in economic structure include the introduction of new crop varieties, land reforms affecting the distribution of farm size, and pricing and exchange rate policies.

Important in policy analysis is recognition of the difference between farm-level decision making and aggregate sector-level decision making. At the farm level, the responsibility for decision making rests on the farmer who formulates the goals to be achieved and decides on the technology and input levels to be used, within the limits of her or his resources and the prevailing policy environment. Attempts to model farm-level decision making thus result in normative studies, i.e., studies of the way in which farmers might best organize their resources to achieve their goals (rather than 'positive' studies of the way in which they do actually organize their resources). In such normative studies, the consequences of alternative decision rules and constraints on farmers' choices can only be simulated. At the sectoral level, decision making involves both policy makers and farmers. Many times their interests do not coincide, leading to difficulty in the achievement of desirable results in the economy. To handle this problem and maximize policy objectives, explicit specification of policy instruments with a corresponding set of relationships attempting to describe farmers' likely reactions to policy changes are of utmost importance. Again, farm-level data is crucial to such analysis.

In the analysis of structural change, care should be exercised so that parametric change is not mistaken for structural change. For instance, the removal of a subsidy on fertilizers following massive adoption by farmers, thus leading to higher input prices, constitutes a parametric rather than a structural change. The important issue is that the model to be employed proves useful for handling the effects of changes in parameters from their prior values. Two issues illustrate the difference between structural change and parametric change very clearly. While technological change in production, for example, an improved seed variety and its associated production package of inputs, leads to structural change with new resource levels as well as technical coefficients, land reform in the absence of complementary institutional reforms in credit, extension, etc., only results in parametric changes under the existing technology and production coefficients.

AGRICULTURAL PLANNING

As a basis for facilitating national development (by preventing bottle-necks in essential supplies, scheduling national budget receipts and expenditures, ensuring necessary supplies of credit, etc.) many developing countries now formulate national or sectoral plans for one or more years ahead. And even if there is no national or sectoral planning, there will often be regional agricultural planning as a basis for regional development. As discussed by Schickele (1966), in formulating such plans, farm management research is essential so as to adequately specify, firstly, the resource base available to farmers in the plan and, secondly, their likely investment, use of inputs and production over the period of the plan. All these quantities need to be estimated if the plan is to be realistic.

PROJECT PLANNING AND APPRAISAL

Project preparation and appraisal connotes an *ex ante* or prior evaluation of the biological, economic, social and logistical impacts of a project. To be able to prepare and appraise projects involving small farms a lot of intuitive considerations are involved in order to assess likely impacts within the socio-economic and ecological environment. Attention also needs to be paid to the possible influence of risk in the context of the project. Usually *ex ante* evaluation is conducted on the basis of hypothesized performance with the purpose of estimating the expected benefits and costs of the technology under test. The analysis seeks to evaluate the expected impact of changes in economic and biological terms. When applied to farming systems, it can be viewed as a simulation of the entire farm system. *Ex ante* analysis is particularly important, not only in estimating the potential benefits of new technology, but also in minimizing the risk of failure on the part of either researchers or farmers during the project implementation stage.

The evaluation of new technologies for small farms can range from intuition to analysis. However, analytical appraisal is essentially confined to work on models rather than on real systems.

Three approaches have proved useful for the collection of data to be used in *ex ante* project appraisal: case studies, representative farms and sample survey. In farm management research, when the *case-study approach* is considered appropriate, a few suitable farms, rather than representative farms, may be chosen for analysis. For example, farms with good records may be preferred to those with poor records. The logic in this approach is that in-depth study of some selected farms provides knowledge that aids understanding of the entire farm population, allowance being made for any peculiar circumstances of the selected farms. In a more thoroughgoing *representative farm approach*, efforts are made to select farms that adequately represent the population of farms in the target domain. The dearth of data on small farms in developing countries is a serious constraint to this approach as it makes it impossible to know whether or not the supposedly representative farms are truly representative.

Sample survey methods are usually employed to draw a random sample of farms from the population. Thereafter, necessary investigations are conducted leading to collection of data which are analyzed. Inferences can then be drawn, based on estimates obtained from the sample, about the characteristics of the population under study. However, this depends on the analytical method employed in relation to the reliability that can be put on the inference(s) drawn. This approach is similar in concept to the representative farm approach but requires a larger number of farms so as to achieve statistical precision of acceptable standard. The sample survey approach thus places a heavier demand on research resources.

In designing projects that involve improved technologies for small farmers it is important to draw a distinction between *in vitro* and *in vivo* analysis. This distinction depends respectively on whether the *ex ante* technology assessment is performed in abstract or in relation to actual farm circumstances (Hardaker, Anderson and Dillon, 1984). Difficulties with *in vivo* analysis arise from location specificity and diversity among target farmers in terms of their resource endowments, opportunities, skills, risk perceptions and attitudes, etc., as well as the inherent complexity of small farming systems themselves. In order to account for such diversity it is considered best to develop a portfolio or range of recommended technologies from which farmers can choose.

PROJECT MONITORING AND EVALUATION

Before implementation, any proposed public development project should be assessed to see if its likely benefits exceed its costs to a satisfactory degree. Such projects might be a dam to provide irrigation water, a levee bank to provide community flood protection, a road to give market access, a rural electrification scheme, etc. So far as the benefits or costs arise on farms, farm management research will be needed to determine these quantities. At the simplest level, the necessary appraisal following collection of relevant farm data may only involve budget analysis. Often, however, adequate appraisal will necessitate more sophisticated analysis using techniques such as linear programming to model and gauge likely project impact across the farm population affected.

A major contribution of farm management research to project appraisal can be the injection of realism into the assessment of possible benefits. Frequently, and especially so relative to projects oriented to communities of small farmers, projects are formulated by city engineers and planners who have little appreciation of farm realities and are far too optimistic in their assessment of potential benefits.

There are two objectives to be achieved by monitoring and evaluation: ensuring the efficient implementation of projects and improving the planning of similar projects. Monitoring affords project management the opportunity to assess performance against plan, while evaluation assists both management and national planners in gaining useful experience and knowledge. Through monitoring and evaluation it is also possible to compare performances across projects. The machinery for collecting the relevant data is usually set up within individual projects. The purpose more often is to inform managers and planners rather than comparison between projects. To this end, monitoring and *ex ante* analysis provide information which is germane to the attainment of project objectives. Many agricultural and rural development projects therefore include monitoring and evaluation units, especially when financed by international agencies such as the World Bank and UNDP. Such units have often revealed weaknesses in project design and implementation.

Through monitoring, information on project activity is made available to project management for the purposes of assessing progress and taking timely decisions to ensure progress is consistent with schedule. Such logistical aspects of project execution as input delivery, proper use of inputs and realisation of planned output are the central concerns of monitoring. Thus it is important to internalise monitoring in the project as part of effective management practice. It is necessary for a monitoring system to have the capacity to identify not only the deviations from targets but also the causes of these deviations so as to assist management in taking decisions for remedial action. By implication, only realistic targets should be set; otherwise detected shortfalls will be attributable to inappropriate projections rather than implementation deficiencies.

On the other hand, as discussed in Chapter 9, evaluation is an assessment tool which helps in determining whether planned objectives have been or will be achieved. It also involves measurements of outputs, effects and impacts. Some effects and impacts are not easily measurable, especially in the short run. Generally evaluation, unlike monitoring, requires a longer time span before firm conclusions can be drawn.

RURAL DEVELOPMENT

By rural development is meant the general development of the rural community in terms of such attributes as income, health, education, culture and infrastructure. Most often, rural development is attempted on a project basis relative to some particular region or target group community. Such projects are certain to need farm management research of all the types discussed above in relation to farmer recommendations, project evaluation, planning and policy. Such research will assist in determining the relative need for rural development programmes between different regions, what avenues of development are feasible, how they might best be undertaken and, by monitoring the developments over time, how successful they are.

1.5 Approaches to farm management research on small farms

The approach to be taken to farm management research on small farms might be discussed from many perspectives. We will emphasize the conceptual framework to be used, the role of models, the necessity for coordinated programmes, and the use of yield constraints as a guide to research priority.

CONCEPTUAL FRAMEWORK

Whether for farmer recommendations, project appraisal, regional development, national planning or policy purposes, all farm management research oriented to small farms is concerned with enhancing their development. To varying degrees such research will involve some focus away from individual farms to more macroeconomic considerations, but it will always involve a major element of work at the individual farm and local community level. If this farm-level work is to be successful, it must be based upon a correct conceptual framework and, as discussed below, will be greatly helped by the use of an adequate structural model of the farm situation.

The general methodology and principles of farm management research were developed in the context of commercial farms in the Western world. These principles of analysis are correct for small farmers in the developing world but the conceptual and situational framework in which they have to be applied is different. In particular, as discussed by Umali (1978), farm management research in Western developed countries emphasizes the individual farm and is based on private ownership of land. For much of Asia and Africa, however, traditional agriculture is based on a communal concept of land ownership and the farmer may often be best reached and assisted not as an individual but as a member of her or his local community group (Wong and Reed, 1978). Accordingly, compared to the situation in Western developed countries, farm management research for small farm development must generally be far more oriented to farmers as members of local community groups.

To further illustrate the kind of conceptual adjustments needed, it is fruitful to consider some of the everyday farm management research terms and concepts in the context of small farm agriculture.

The profit motive. This motive underpins most of the standard textbook presentations of Farm Management Economics. Its limitations for analysis and planning in the small farm context are too well known to need much elaboration but by way of example, the herdsmen of Africa (Masai, Somalis, Dinkas, etc.) regard their livestock as a walking bank, a measure of tribal status, or a social security fund, but seldom as an enterprise to be rationally managed to produce profit. To a lesser extent this applies also to some settled farmer tribes, e.g.,the Kinangop Kikuyu who manage dairy cows for profit, male cattle for status, and sheep and goats as a sort of family emergency fund. In these situations the profit motive is present, to varying degree, but it is seldom strong enough to furnish the sole necessary basis for farm management research and farm development planning.

Farm size. There are so many exceptions to the usual textbook meaning of this concept that pitfalls can easily occur. Consider the following examples.

◇ It is obviously not a very useful concept in the shifting small farmer agriculture of Sumatra, or Kalimantan, or the southern dry zone of Sri Lanka, etc.

◇ In the small farm areas of Kenya a nominally ten-hectare farm may be divided into four portions, one for each of three wives, which she operates as her farm, the residual land being used for a jointly managed livestock enterprise. In data collection this is important, because the farmer himself may not know much about any of the farming operations, leaving all that to his wives. Just which part of land we accept as defining the farm size will depend on our specific purpose and the kind of data we are collecting.

◇ In the Karangede Hills of Central Java no individual farmer owns or has permanent rights to a particular farm: periodically each farmer is allocated a parcel of land to cultivate, not necessarily the same piece or size in consecutive years. For planning purposes the relevant unit here would be all the village lands, not individual parcels.

◇ In the Tawangmanu farming system on Mt. Lawa, Central Java, vegetables and citrus are grown on family units of about a third of a hectare. The soil nutritive balance is maintained by carrying a green manure legume down from the mountain and incorporating this in the soil, and/or adding manure from cattle which are stall-fed with grass from government forest land on the mountain. Biologically and economically the farm would have to be defined as a third of a hectare of vegetables plus whatever forest area is needed to supply the nutritive additives.

◇ Finally, a Kenyan-Somali herdsman would not understand the concept of size at all, even of that land area needed to support his camels and cattle. The closest he could get to this concept might be to say that if the long rains come he will go north to the country of the Ogaden, and if they do not then he will follow the camels south to the wells at Mansa Guda. His farm is all that land between Moyale and Wajir.

These few examples illustrate the possible limitations of an apparently simple concept such as farm size. But if we cannot calculate, say, gross margin per hectare, net farm income per hectare, etc., cannot we substitute other measures of economic performance, say, return on total investment? It is not always easy to identify meaningful measures of performance. For instance, to a Somali herdsman, his camels are not an investment - they are his life.

Farmer decision making. This area of farm management research has developed rapidly in recent years. Main concern has been with how farmers arrive at their decisions, and with determining those factors which influence decision making. Relatively little attention has been paid to who makes the decisions because it is generally assumed (more or less correctly in the Western agricultural context) that they are made by the farmer. But this assumption can also often be wrong if applied indiscriminately to small farm situations, as the following examples show.

◇ The Kikuyu multi-family situation was noted above. If there are two or three wives each responsible for a piece of the land area, there will be three or four decision makers: each wife as maternal head of her family and as independent manager of her farm, and the husband making overall strategic decisions over the land in general and some or all of the livestock. There will also be group decisions made concerning the joint enterprises. The practical significance of this for data collection is that it would be a waste of time asking a Kikuyu man for data on cropping practices, disease and pest losses, yields, etc. Reliable data could only be obtained from the household member who actually does the work.

◇ To take an Asian example, just what does 'farmer decision making' mean in a Javanese paddy village? So standard are the farming practices and technology, so fixed by custom and routine are decisions as to when to plant, how to plant, when to weed and harvest, etc., that it is difficult to find any significant decisions left to the individual farmer. The significant decision makers are the village lurah (or chief, advised by village elders) and the whole community arriving at a sort of group consensus. Brave indeed would be the individual farmer who introduced radical changes in the accepted cropping technology or system, i.e., who actually made and implemented any but the most routine decisions. This has implications for the type of data to be collected, the source of such data, and the type of development plans we might formulate. For example, most data should relate to the village as a unit, would be obtained largely from the chief and other village officials, and any development plan would have to be acceptable to the whole village. In a sense, the research orientation would be toward village rather than farm development.

Multiple cropping systems. The explanations of farm management analysis in most text-books are based on the concept of separability and comparability of different crop and livestock enterprises. Individual farm enterprises are assumed to be largely separable and identifiable more or less in isolation so that measures can be made of their technological and economic efficiency on an individual enterprise basis, comparisons made among them, and recommendations made that some enterprises should be expanded and others contracted, etc. As emphasized by Ruthenberg (1976), this concept of separability and the methodology based upon it (enterprise gross margins, partial budgeting, linear programming, etc.) are quite valid for farms in developed countries and for many areas of Afro-Asian agriculture, but for others they are not. Consider the following examples.

◇ In the Tawangmanu farming system of Central Java noted above, there may be five or six different crops intermixed on the same land at the same time. The composition of the mix changes throughout the year. The degree of complementarity between some pairs of these crops is high: e.g.,beans and maize, where the beans give weed control for the maize and the maize later provides a trellis for the beans. Fertilizer applied to one crop has a spillover effect on associated and following crops. It is physically (and economically) impossible to make valid comparisons among single crops in the system. It is only possible to make comparisons between farms of the entire system, and between this and other systems. Indeed, as yet very little is known about mixed-crop (especially multi-tier) farming systems, from either the soil, biological, agronomic or economic points of view. The development of knowledge about these systems and particularly their contribution to sustainability is a major task for farm management research in cooperation with agro-biological scientists.

◇ In the Kandyan Hills of Sri Lanka, as in some other regions of South and Southeast Asia, multi-tier forest-garden farms constitute the dominant farming system. Typically these farms involve a diverse mix of perennial tree crops, under-planted with ground crops where shade and light permit (McConnell, 1992). These Kandyan forest-garden farms are typically of less than a hectare and support 10 to 12 (even up to 18) economic tree species. Tree density is very high at around 1 200 per hectare (up to 1 700 if kitui, areca and coffee are included in the mix). Yields of individual trees and species are generally low, but the overall economic returns (cash and food) per family for these small farms are surprisingly high. Almost all of the economic and agronomic data available on the crops grown in this system refer to them when grown in pure stands; practically nothing is known about them when grown as associations, i.e., as forest-garden multi-tier farm systems. Again the need for basic farm management information is obvious. For example, at first glance it might be thought that low yields of individual species in the mix are evidence of land use inefficiency, and that these farms could be further developed by thinning out the mix and concentrating on the more economic species. Such a judgement overlooks the fact that this system, far from being undeveloped, has been evolving over many centuries into what is now possibly one of the most botanically sophisticated systems known, a system moreover which is sustainable and provides a reliable and uniformly spaced stream of family cash income and food. Suffice to note that for present purposes, this system illustrates the danger that would lie in collecting data for and evaluating only one or two components of what would, on closer knowledge, turn out to be an already highly developed and complicated farming system.

Apparent versus real use-value of land. As a final example of the importance of having the correct concepts before we actually start collecting data or planning, it sometimes happens that the real use-value of land is not understood at either the data collection or planning stage. A good example is provided by a land development scheme in the southern Sudan which aimed at growing rice on a large scale in a series of dike-protected basins on the flood plain of a tributary of the Nile. Each September the river floods, water is released into the dikes, the crop is grown, then the water is drained out and the crop harvested. That is the theory and, to a considerably lesser extent, the practice. Agronomically and technically the scheme was feasible. However, there was one serious problem: the people did not want rice, they wanted fish. Fish are contained in the irrigation water released into the paddy basins and in years of high flood they come over the dike walls in the flood-waters. When the flood recedes, fish traps are set up outside the sluice gates. Where there are no gates, holes are (illegally) knocked in the dikes and traps set up there, and the fish crop is harvested as it drains out. In all this, as may be imagined, relatively little attention is paid to the rice. Had the planners been less fixed on their own agro-technical concepts, and made an effort to understand the land-use priorities of the people and their basic diet pattern, fish culture would have been planned for and incorporated as a significant activity in the scheme. Then a mutually acceptable fish/rice system might have emerged, instead of the unwanted foreign mono-crop technology which was imposed by the planners.

STRUCTURAL MODELS

A model is a simplified representation of reality which aims to capture the most important features of what is being modelled without the complication of all its less significant detail. Usually models of a farm, enterprise, process, etc. are developed as a research tool with which the operation and efficiency of a system under different operating conditions may be explored, for example, as outlined for linear programming models in Chapter 4 and production function models in Chapter 7.

There is a second role for models: they can be useful to outline the structure of the situation being studied and as guides to better problem identification and data collection. In this case they may first be constructed as preliminary/tentative/partial models to identify critical aspects in the farm situation and the kind of data needed, then elaborated upon and expanded to serve as research tools. Often this will be a very fruitful approach to farm management research with the steps of data collection, model building and better problem identification being taken more or less simultaneously. Thus the process may be that:

- ◇ a rough, tentative, first-stage model is constructed to describe what the farm situation or problem is thought to be, i.e., as an hypothesis;
- ◇ likely further information requirements are identified from this first-stage model;
- ◇ a tentative questionnaire is prepared for getting the necessary (missing) information and taken into the field both to pre-test the questionnaire in the conventional way and to get additional information or insights for amending and correcting the model;
- ◇ this additional information is incorporated into the model until it is sufficiently complete to allow positive identification of problems and data needs for their resolution; and
- ◇ the questionnaire is then modified preparatory to its use in the full field survey.

Obviously there are potentially as many kinds of structural models as there are different types of farms, enterprises or processes. Four broad groups can be noted:

- ◇ models of the agro-economic structure of whole farms;
- ◇ models of individual enterprises or cropping systems within the whole-farm system;
- ◇ models of processes (typically the handling of a commodity output from one enterprise); and
- ◇ models of an industry or industry sector.

Any such model might take the form of: (i) a verbal description or listing of all the factors involved in the problem; (ii) a systematic mathematical or algebraic statement of the problem (e.g., a linear programming matrix); or (iii) a simple sketch or flowchart of the relationship between steps in a process, processes in an enterprise, or enterprises in a farm system.

It is the latter type of flowchart sketch which is likely to be of greatest help in the preliminary stages of farm management research. Its construction forces the researcher to better appreciate and understand the system under study, provides a basis for further discussion with relevant parties, and immediately brings to light data needs for adequate specification of the system.

Figure 1.1 gives an example of a flowchart model depicting the structure of the process of harvesting and handling cardamom spice on a farm in a particular region of Sri Lanka. It was constructed using data from one estate for the purpose of clarifying for the research worker (who had no previous experience of cardamom):

◇ what sequence of steps or jobs was involved;
◇ the importance (cost) of each step;
◇ who did what in the process; and
◇ what data would probably be available and need to be collected if a survey of cardamom estates were to be undertaken.

Figure 1.2 presents a more elaborate structural model. It is for the annual operation of a mixed crop-livestock farm in the Sind province of Pakistan. The model was constructed to draw out the highly integrated nature of such Sind farms and to guide clarification of the complex relationship between crops. For example: dairy cows generate milk for direct family consumption as well as for conversion and sale as ghee, and they also generate manure for use on three of the five crops grown; four of the crops grown generate feed or by-products for the dairy and work cattle; and the work cattle supply both power and manure for the crops.

The five rectangles in the middle of Figure 1.2 respectively represent the crops grown - berseem clover, kharif fodder, wheat, sugar cane and cotton. Resource inputs into each of these crop enterprises are sketched as entering the system from above with cash expenses in the top row, then labour days, then bullock days and/or animal manure. Products from each enterprise are depicted as leaving from the bottom. Below each crop rectangle is shown total production of main and by-products, and the distribution of these between consumption and sales. For example, for wheat:

◇ area is 4.76 acres (1.93 ha);
◇ cash costs are Rs 297 (coming from the family);
◇ labour amounts to 115.9 days (all supplied by the family);
◇ bullock power inputs are 55.8 days of bullock work (coming from the bullock pool or total supply of 300 bullock workdays);
◇ animal manure input is 95 maunds (coming from the farm manure pool of 348 maunds);
◇ products consist of bhoosa (wheat straw) and grain;
◇ 104 maunds of bhoosa are produced (valued on the market at Rs 260) and are not sold but channelled into the total feed pool of the farm; and
◇ grain produced is 97.3 maunds (valued at Rs 1 556) of which 39 maunds are consumed by the family and 58.3 maunds sold (for Rs 932).

At the bottom of the model all produce consumed by the farm family and all produce sold are accumulated to the right and then top-right to give family farm cash income of Rs 7 790 and value of farm produce consumed by the family of Rs 1 464. Family cash income is later increased by Rs 359 from 119 days of work done by family members off the farm.

Figure 1.1

EXAMPLE OF A STRUCTURAL MODEL COVERING THE STEPS, WORK RATES AND VARIABLE COSTS PER 100 lb CURED OF HARVESTING AND PROCESSING CARDAMOM (McConnell, 1975)

Day	Operation	Worker	Work rate and costs per 100 lb cured	Materials per 100 lb cured	Variable costs per 100 lb cured (Rs)
1	Pick → Carry to dryer → Into sacks → Rub on floor / Spread on floor → Cut off tails → Pick out rubbish	Female Picker	In season: 20 to 50 lb green/day Off season: 7 to 10 lb green/day Mean picking cost: 30¢ per lb green		146
	Weigh	Field supervisor	1 man day @ Rs4 /day		4
2	Into dryer	Dryer attendant	1 man day @ Rs4 /day		4
3	Change tats				
4	Change tats			Woodfuel: 2yds/day @ Rs15 /yd	
5	Out of dryer				30
	If tails on, rub off → Winnow → Weigh → Grade	Factory labour	3 woman days @ Rs3 /day		9
	Grade → To packing boxes → Store → Dispatch / Grade → Storage boxes → Loose store → Bag → Dispatch	Factory labour	1 woman 1/3 day @ Rs3 /day	Bags: double gunny sacks, 65 lb net @ Rs 2.60	4 1
30	Dispatch			Total variable costs per 100 lb cured:	198

Figure 1.2

STRUCTURAL MODEL OF A SIND FARM SHOWING THE INTERDEPENDENCIES BETWEEN ITS CROP AND LIVESTOCK ENTERPRISES AS WELL AS ITS LABOUR COST AND INCOME FLOWS

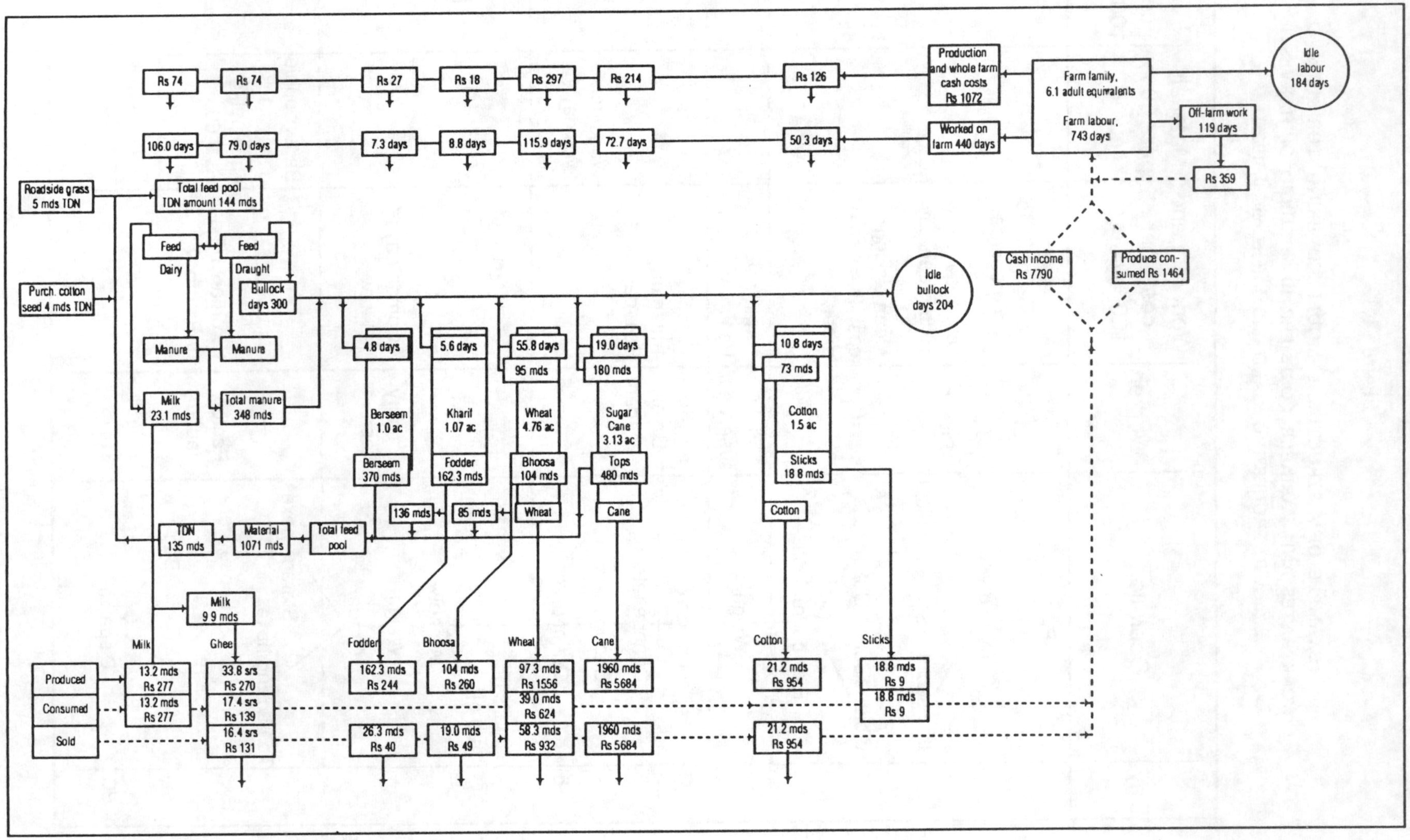

Family elements are shown in the top-right corner of the model. The average farm family consists of 6.1 adult equivalents. It receives Rs (7 790 + 1 464 + 359) = Rs 9 613 income. Part of the cash component of this income goes to pay annual fixed costs of the farm and direct livestock and crop production costs. These cash costs total Rs 1 072 of which fixed costs are Rs 242 not shown separately and the balance is incurred in livestock and crop production to the amounts shown for the individual enterprises.

While such average farm characteristics as the labour supply and its distribution between enterprises, costs and their allocation, total income and its sources, total land and its use, etc. could all be listed in a table, such a presentation would not be nearly so informative for research purposes as the model of Figure 1.2 This model shows at a glance that it would be very difficult to alter the structure of the farm without consequent repercussions throughout the whole farm system. Without such a model we might not adequately recognize the close and mutual dependence among enterprises and might, for example, set about collecting data for one enterprise in isolation, say sugar, without realizing that cane on these farms is structurally inseparable from cattle.

Using this Sind model for problem identification purposes, we might note that while the draught power supply is 300 bullock days, there are 204 idle bullock days. Dairy cows appear to be profitable (they produced Rs 547 of ghee and milk, and incurred only Rs (74 + 74) = Rs 148 in cash costs) and since both cows and bullocks produce manure required by crops, why not replace some bullocks with more cows? Such a change could be evaluated by linear programming as outlined in Chapter 4. A critical factor would be the peak seasonal demand for bullock power so that in further data collection we would need to pay particular attention to the crop calendar of operations.

Another possible research topic on these Sind farms might be to evaluate the economic feasibility of crop mechanization. The high degree of crop-livestock structural integration shown in the model of Figure 1.2 gives warning that such evaluation must involve a lot more than just simple comparison of the cost of bullocks versus the cost of tractors.

While structural models such as those illustrated in Figures 1.1 and 1.2 are of use for developed commercial farms, they are particularly important in guiding research on small farms. This is especially so in South and Southeast Asia. The bulk of Asia's small farms are very highly integrated. Compared to Western farms, more inputs are farm-produced (manure, animal power, seed, fuel); more products are wholly or partly processed on the farm before sale (gur, ghee, cottonseed, etc.); and a wider range of farm products is consumed by the family than is the case on most Western farms. Thus the farm planning and development problem is more complex and more care is required in identifying the chain of effects which would follow from an adjustment in any one enterprise or activity. In consequence, the introduction of new technology must be evaluated in terms of its system-wide implications and can rarely be considered simply in relation to a single product or enterprise.

NATIONAL PROGRAMME APPROACH

Farm management research topics have generally been selected on a case-by-case basis with research problems being chosen on the basis of (a) specific requests of government for work on problems of current interest; (b) topics of special interest to the researcher; or (c) topics selected because of the relative ease of data collection and low requirement for research resources. However, such an *ad hoc* and uncoordinated approach is inefficient relative to the critical needs of small farmers for farm management research. What is needed overall is a coordinated national programme approach where agricultural development planning is carried out from the farm and village level upward simultaneously with the implementation of national level policy and planning, the latter being guided by better understanding the reality of farm level needs and possibilities for change (Carpenter and Kunert, 1977; Schickele, 1966). Such a nationally coordinated approach implies farm management research which aims to:

- ◇ understand small farm systems and quantify the constraints to increased production and income which must be removed before small farm development can occur;
- ◇ identify additional local opportunities for remunerative employment and, as part of broader community development research, ameliorate the pressure for migration to large cities; and
- ◇ provide guidelines for improved formulation and implementation of national policy and planning by government.

A farm management research programme aimed to meet these needs in coordinated fashion would involve three aspects, as follows (Carpenter and Kunert, 1977).

The first aspect is the *identification of agro-economic zones* which are expected to have different types of constraints and development problems due to such factors as climate, soil resources, land use, distance from markets, traditions, ethnic groupings, etc. This identification would rely heavily on existing data sources (so far as they may be available) such as weather records, soil classification maps, land use maps, vegetation analyses, regional economic surveys, census records, etc.

The second aspect is the *surveying of a sample of farms from each zone,* perhaps stratified according to such criteria as size of farm, irrigated or non-irrigated, etc. The number of farms in each stratum would, of course, depend on survey resources. Regardless of sample size, sufficient information should be collected on each farm to give a good understanding of the farm system and its operation. To gain such understanding the survey data must be thoroughly analyzed so as to identify the overall constraints in each zone and the topics requiring in-depth research. In terms of both survey data collection and analysis, the FAO Farm Management Analysis Package FARMAP (Dixon *et al.*, 1986; von Fleckenstein and Gauchon, 1992) provides an excellent mechanism with the important advantages of being both systematic and standardized. Too, surveys in later years could expand the base sample size, in which case each survey would also serve as a benchmark data source for the ongoing evaluation of development.

Third, once the total problem complex has been better specified from the zonal survey data, detailed research programmes can be undertaken to systematically conduct *in-depth research on critical issues.*

These three programme activities of identifying agro-economic zones, conducting fact-finding surveys and researching critical issues are, of course, heavily interrelated and, once ongoing, not necessarily sequential. In-depth research may dictate further survey data collection or lead to a redefinition of zones, for example.

All three programme activities will also necessitate multi-disciplinary cooperation (Carpenter, 1975). Delimitation of agro-economic zones can hardly occur without the assistance of agronomists.

Likewise the advice of crop and livestock specialists will be important in guiding questionnaire specification (and any field measurements to be taken) for the farm surveys. Most of all, however, in-depth research will require a cooperative multi-disciplinary farming systems research approach. At one extreme, in order to provide guidance for policy makers and community development programmes, the farm management researcher will need to work with economists specializing in policy and marketing and with other social scientists concerned with sociology, education, public administration and politics. At the other extreme, cooperation with agro-biological researchers and also extension workers is essential for the development and testing of new production systems for small farmers. This will involve both experiment station and on-farm field research with a farming systems perspective.

The importance of cooperation in such research aimed at developing improved farming systems for small farmers cannot be overemphasized. New technology developed through agro-biological research will only be acceptable to the small farmer if it is based on recognition of the nature of her or his goals and an understanding of her or his present farming system. Such understanding of the farmer and the farming system, as well as evaluation of the research from the farmer's view, must come from the farm management researcher and the researcher's extension colleagues in their role as contributors to the research.

YIELD CONSTRAINTS

A particular activity requiring cooperative research between farm management researchers and agro-biological scientists (crop breeders, physiologists, pathologists, entomologists and agronomists in particular) is yield constraint research. This research is based on the conceptual model of Figure 1.3. This model recognizes:

- ◇ that due to non-transferable technology and environmental differences, there will always be a difference in yield per unit of area between the high yields obtainable on experiment stations and the best potentially achievable yield on farms - this difference is called Yield Gap I; and

- ◇ that the existing gap - called Yield Gap II - between actual current farm yields and the best potentially achievable yield on farms is caused by biological and socio-economic constraints.

Biological constraints refer to the non-application or poor use of needed production inputs. Socio-economic constraints refer to the social or economic conditions that prevent farmers from using the recommended technology. For example, a biological constraint might be that farmers are not applying enough fertilizer. An associated socio-economic constraint might be the lack of credit for farmers to buy such inputs.

Cooperative multi-disciplinary research methodology involving research station experiments, farm experiments and farm surveys has been developed to investigate and quantify the size of Yield Gap II and how much of it is caused by such particular biological and socio-economic constraints as listed in Figure 1.3 (De Datta *et al.*, 1978; Gomez, 1977). This methodology has been applied quite successfully relative to rice production in a number of Asian countries (IRRI, 1977). Its importance lies in the guides it gives to the relative physical and economic importance of the various constraints. This information, combined with estimates of the likely cost and chances of removing the different constraints, gives a rational basis for determining research priorities such as, for example, between plant breeding, disease control and water management. There are two difficulties with such yield constraint research, however. On the one hand, through its emphasis on physical yields, sight may tend to be lost of the influence of prices and personal goals on the individual farmer's decisions. On the other hand, while it has been relatively successful in relation to particular crops grown alone, the methodology has not yet been satisfactorily developed relative to multiple cropping systems. In such systems, what may be a constraint to one crop can be an advantage to another. Too, the farmer's purpose in using multiple cropping may be to satisfy multiple goals of food supply safety, cash income and food preference so that physical yield or its money value may be a very inadequate measure of system performance.

1.6 Conduct of farm management research

Four elements are crucial in conducting effective farm management research. They are:

- ◇ an adequate knowledge of theory;
- ◇ relevant practical knowledge and experience;
- ◇ an effective research strategy and adequate research resources; and
- ◇ satisfactory research administration.

Only if these requirements are met can the farm management researcher carry out research in satisfactory fashion using the techniques of data collection and analysis elaborated in the later chapters of this bulletin.

THEORY

The greater the researcher's command of theory, the better she or he will be able to orient the research and the more productive it will be. Theory ensures that the research goes beyond mere description and that it provides understanding as to (a) why things are as they are and (b) how they may be changed. Knowledge of theory also assists in guiding the selection of analytical techniques to be used in conducting the research analysis.

Since farm management is basically concerned with the ways a farmer obtains and organizes scarce resources (land, labour, capital, time and management) so as to achieve a set of goals, it is a process of economizing. Accordingly, the parent discipline of farm management is economics and the theory most directly relevant to farm management research is economic theory. At the same time farm management research must be recognized as multi-disciplinary in nature in so far as it must draw on and take account of information, principles and theory from such closely related sciences as sociology and psychology as well as the various fields of plant and animal science.

Figure 1.3

CONCEPTUAL MODEL EXPLAINING THE YIELD GAP BETWEEN EXPERIMENT STATION YIELD AND ACTUAL FARM YIELD

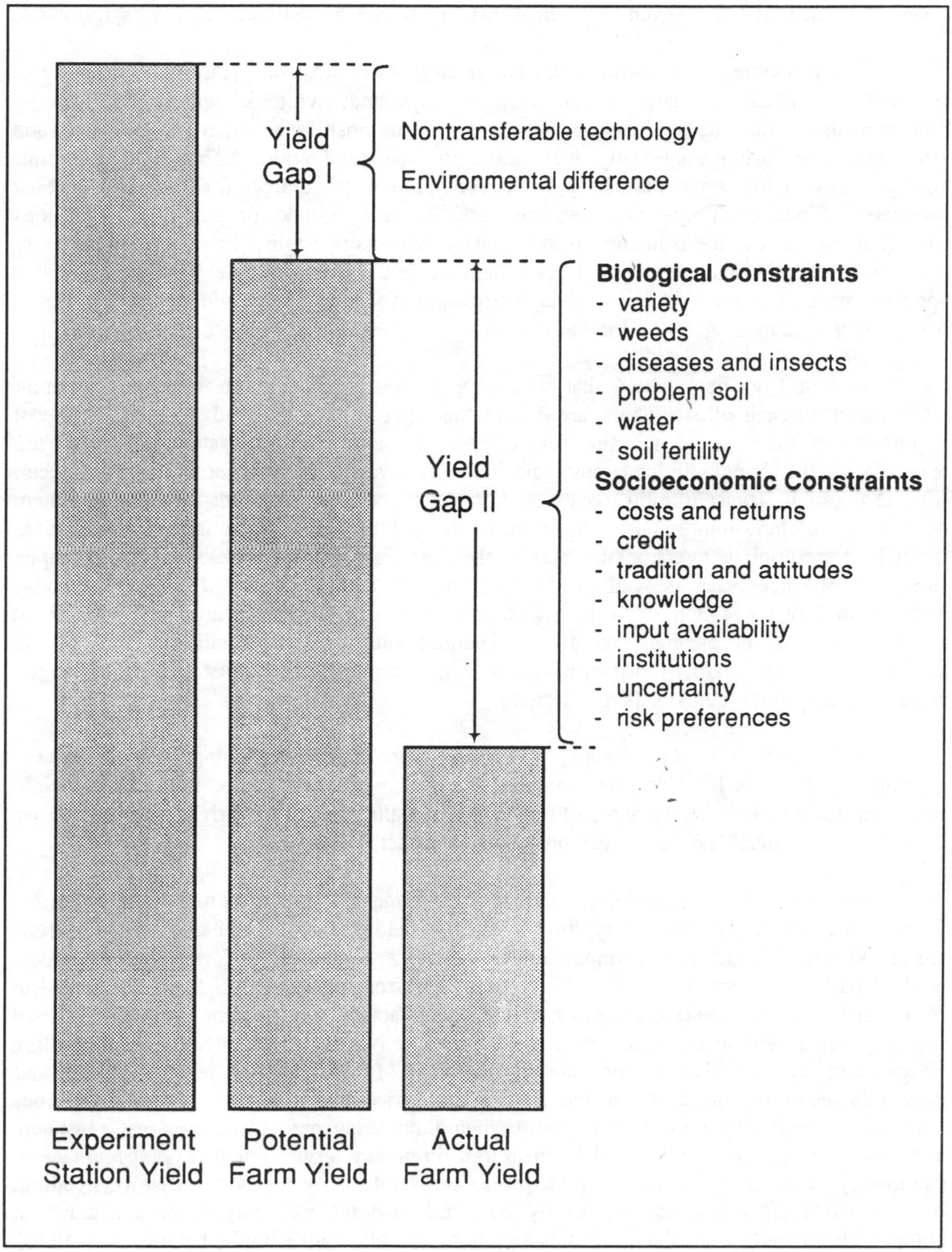

Perhaps the most important elements of economic theory relevant to farm management research are those encompassed by the principles of comparative advantage, diminishing returns, substitution, cost analysis, opportunity cost, enterprise choice and goal tradeoff. Leaving to later chapters such data-manipulation procedures as budgeting, linear programming, production function analysis, etc., by which these principles are applied, the essence of each of these seven theoretical principles can be outlined simply as follows.

The principle of *comparative advantage* largely explains the location of agricultural production. What it means is that various crops and livestock, with their differing requirements, should be produced in those areas or on those farms where the physical and other resources are economically best suited to their production. Thus even the most poorly endowed of farms may have some comparative advantage for some product or products. Since environmental resources are so variable, and production possibilities usually so numerous, the principle of comparative advantage applies on a world-wide basis, country-wide basis, and on a farm basis - field by field. This principle is so logical that it appears more like common sense than a principle, yet it has been violated many times, particularly in choosing crops for newly developed areas.

It should not be assumed that producing areas always maintain the same economic relationship to each other. There are factors that alter comparative advantage. The most important of these are: (a) the development of new farming systems or improved technology; (b) changes in input costs and in the relative prices of different farm products; (c) changes in transportation costs such as can occur when roads are improved or destroyed; (d) land improvement by drainage, irrigation, and so forth or land degradation through overcropping, overstocking, soil erosion, etc.; and (e) the development of cheaper substitute products such as synthetic fibres to replace natural fibres. Thus any area may improve or lose its economic position with respect to a given type of crop or livestock. It is the job of farm management research to evaluate such changing conditions and provide advice on needed farm reorganisation so that farmers can adjust to the changed circumstances more quickly than otherwise.

The principle of *diminishing physical and economic returns* is important because it determines the best level for any production practice. For example, it is this principle which guides a farmer on the yield of rice to aim for, the amount of irrigation water to use on a crop, how much labour to use on a particular activity, etc.

The principle is particularly useful in considering the level of output to be produced from a set of fixed resources as typified by a given field or farm. To these fixed resources are added variable factors (i.e., inputs under the farmer's control) in forms such as labour, seed, fertilizer, insecticides, etc. Diminishing returns come about from the physical relationship of these variable factors to the fixed factors. For example, in the case of weeding a rice field, as more and more units of labour (variable factor) are spent in pulling weeds from the field (fixed factor), the physical yield of rice increases, reaches a peak, and then may even decline through the trampling of rice plants as the task is overdone. Diminishing economic returns come about when diminishing physical returns are translated into value terms. Often value will be measured in money terms, but it is not necessary to use money values in order for the principle to be useful. Take the above case of weeding. In most cases the labour is supplied by the family and the rice may all be consumed at home with no money involved. In this situation the cultivator should balance any added physical labour in terms of its cost through other activities foregone against the added physical product, and decide how much weeding it is worthwhile to do. On the other hand, if because of the risk of insect attack the farmer applies an insecticide for which money has to be paid, ideally including a user-tax to compensate for adverse environmental effects, then she or he should balance the money cost of the insecticide against the expected money value of the increased yield or losses saved in order to decide whether or not the purchase of insecticide is worthwhile. This implies that the farmer should use insecticide up to the point where the last unit or application of insecticide is just expected to pay for itself.

The principle essentially is this: add the variable resource to the fixed resource as long as the added return expected from the last unit of variable resource used is just sufficient to cover the added cost of that unit. Given the many different variable inputs used by farmers, together with the fact that the extent of diminishing returns varies from region to region (and even within regions), a host of problem-solving studies could be done in this area of farm management alone, each of which would contribute to more efficient use of farm resources.

The third important principle is that of *substitution*. Since there are many technical possibilities of production, a farmer must choose the most economical method, measured in whatever terms (e.g., physical labour, time, or money) that suit her or his conditions. For example, a cultivator can prepare a seed-bed single-handed using only a hoe; or can hire additional hand labour; or can use a draught animal or a small tractor. Which of the alternative methods should be used? She or he will need to consider the physical performance of each production factor and the cost of each. The principle is this: in substituting one method for another, be certain that the saving in the method replaced is not less and preferably greater than the cost of the technique added.

Cultivators are constantly faced with problems of substitution even among resources that already exist on the farm. But the principle of substitution has an extremely useful application when farmers are considering the adoption of any new practice. If they are to progress, then old methods must be dropped and new ones added. But what to discard and what to adopt under various conditions of farm size, cropping patterns, capital availability and so forth, are genuine problems on which farmers need assistance. It follows that research should help find solutions to these problems.

It is also important to understand the principles of *cost analysis*. The reason for this is that each farmer does have some control over the costs of production on the family farm, but has little or no control over the prices received for products or the value that should be placed on them because these are determined by country-wide and world-wide factors. Other things being unchanged, a farmer must reduce costs per unit of output in order to increase net farm income.

The most important classification of farm costs is their division into those that are *fixed* and those that are *variable*. *Fixed costs* remain the same regardless of the volume of output. The farmer would have to pay them regardless of how much is produced on the farm. For example, while long-run rents for land generally are determined on the basis of quality, in any one year the rent paid is the same regardless of whether a farmer raises a bumper crop or a poor crop; the labour (or cost) of maintaining bunds remains the same regardless of the yield of rice; most of the cost of maintaining a bullock or buffalo remains the same regardless of whether or not the animal is fully used. Fixed costs become especially important when a farmer considers further investment in such things as tools, draught animals, machines or buildings. Any such investment can only be justified if it can be afforded and if, over the long term, it leads to a flow of benefits in excess of its cost. Benefits may arise either in terms of reduced variable costs (see below) or increased output at the same or a lower level of fixed cost per unit of output.

Variable costs are those which change as the size of operation changes. They occur only if the farmer decides to produce; they do not occur if the farmer decides not to produce. For example, much labour is required in vegetable production. If a farmer has to hire labour, then as production is increased the need for hired labour is increased and the outlay on labour increases. If no vegetables are produced there is no need for hired labour. Likewise, the fuel costs for a hand tractor increase as the use of the tractor increases; or the greater the area a farmer plants to rice, the greater the fertilizer cost. Because they vary directly with the size of operation, such costs are classified as variable costs.

The classification of a particular cost as fixed or variable depends partly on the nature and timing of the management decisions being considered. Some costs are fixed in relation to certain decisions but variable in relation to others. For example, land rent becomes a variable cost in relation to a decision by a farmer to lease more land; but for land already leased and being used, the rent is a fixed cost. In general, the time scale of decision making has an important influence on whether costs should be viewed as fixed or variable. In the long run, most costs are variable.

The principle of fixed and variable costs can be applied in many actual farm situations. For example, suppose that, due to drought, the yield of an upland rice field is so low that the farmer wonders if it is worth harvesting. At harvest time all costs so far incurred can be considered fixed since there is no way in which to recover them. If the farmer harvests the crop she or he will incur variable costs largely in the form of labour. But the rice will also add something to income. The farmer must decide whether or not to harvest the crop. If the value of the crop is worth more than the additional cost of harvesting, it should be harvested; otherwise it should not. Some might say that this principle would not apply where even very poor crops must be harvested in order to prevent hunger. But the yield of rice might be so low that more human energy is required to harvest it than there is energy in the rice if it is harvested and consumed. The situation is the same even if measured in physical terms. Any difference is in the units of measurements, and not in principle.

Another important consideration when it comes to choice between alternatives on a farm is the *opportunity cost* involved. This principle says that the cost of any choice, e.g., of using some resource in a particular activity, is given by the value of the best alternative use foregone. For example, if a farmer can earn a profit of $ 75 from a field of wheat and $ 95 by planting it to pulses, the opportunity cost of planting the field to wheat is $ 95. Since this exceeds the potential profit from wheat, she or he should plant pulses not wheat. And if the farmer persists in planting wheat, she or he should recognize that the profit earned is $ 20 less than could have been earned. In either case the farmer makes money, but the point is that she or he would have made more money from pulses. Of course, it is up to the farmer to decide in what terms to measure opportunity cost - it may be in money or leisure or some other form. What must hold is that each unit of land, labour and capital should be used where it will add most to income, however income may be measured (i.e., whether directly as money or in some other terms such as satisfaction or utility). This principle of resource allocation is extremely important in choosing enterprises, and hence in working out an efficient pattern of farm organization.

Stated more specifically, the principle of *enterprise choice* says that enterprises should enter the farm plan so long as their expected contribution to net farm income exceeds the opportunity cost of the resources they use.

In applying the principle of enterprise choice, allowance needs to be made for relationships between enterprises. Various enterprises on a farm may *compete* with each other for use of resources, as in the case when a farmer does not have enough labour to harvest two different crops at the same time. Conflicts of this kind need to be ironed out by adjusting cropping plans and the time of planting. Enterprises are *supplementary* when they utilize resources that otherwise would go to waste, such as ducks in Viet Nam which scavenge the fields for fallen rice after harvest. Enterprises can also be *complementary* by providing materials for each other, such as maize which utilizes the beneficial effects of a prior green manure crop or which provides a trellis for climbing beans. Complementary relationships can be especially significant between crop and livestock enterprises, and between crops in a multiple cropping system.

The overall goal of the small farmer as far as operation of the family farm is concerned is to make what she or he regards as efficient sustainable use of whatever resources are available - land, water, labour, tools, capital, goodwill, etc. The principles outlined above deal largely with the internal problem of allocation of these resources to those enterprises and activities that will maximize the net return (however the farmer desires to measure it) to the farm as a whole. It means putting to productive use those resources which are now idle part of the year, and making more effective use of those already employed. This, in fact, is often a significant problem in the developing countries where underemployment of labour in particular, and sometimes less than full utilization of capital and land resources, are often widespread through lack of opportunity at particular times of the year.

The principle of *goal tradeoff* recognizes that the small farmer has multiple goals that will often compete with one another. Such goals involve gaining cash income (to finance farm development, provide home amenities, educate children, etc.), ensuring family food requirements, having leisure opportunities, avoiding undue physical exertion, meeting social obligations, ensuring sustainable land use, etc. In managing a farm, the farmer will wish to achieve that mix of goal attainment which gives the best level of overall satisfaction (or utility) across her or his multiple goals. Inevitably, some of the different goals will be in conflict (e.g., cash income versus leisure). If they do not substitute for one another in both production (i.e., in their resource use) and consumption in constant proportions as their achievement varies so that one goal will dominate another, the farmer will have to achieve a satisfactory balance between them by trading one goal off against another. In doing this, the farmer should trade off one goal against another so long as the gain in satisfaction from the goal receiving increased emphasis is greater than the decrease in satisfaction incurred by decreasing the emphasis on the other goal or goals.

To a large degree, the successful conduct of farm management research involves the collection of data and its analysis and reporting in terms of the above seven economic principles. They guide the researcher in terms of the hypotheses to be tested, the opportunities for improvement and the data that are needed. Particularly in relation to small farmers, however, two facts must be emphasized about the application of these theoretical principles. These relate to the role of uncertainty and money.

Uncertainty. As elaborated later in Chapter 8, small farmers have to make their managerial decisions from year to year in the face of uncertainty about the climate that will prevail, the incidence of pests and disease, the prices they will confront, the performance of new technology and, often, their tenure status and the political environment under which they will have to operate. In consequence, the small farmer's decisions are risky ones; no farmer can ever be perfectly sure of the outcomes of her or his choices. This implies, on the one hand, that the small farmer has to exercise personal judgement about the risks that she or he faces in intuitive application of the principles outlined above and, on the other hand, that the farm management researcher must recognize in her or his consideration of these principles both the existence of uncertainty and the element of personal judgement about risk that will influence the small farmer's choices. Elucidation of the risks that the farmer faces, how they are perceived and her or his reaction to them are therefore a necessarily important part of farm management research. In turn, this implies that while the collection of data on farm systems in terms of enterprise mix, yields, costs, prices, cash flow, returns, technology used, timing of operations, etc., will provide a first step toward evaluation and understanding of farm performance and possible avenues of improvement in performance based on the economic principles outlined above, such historical data cannot tell the whole story. Management must relate to the future, not to the past, so that account must be taken of future possible yields, costs, prices and technology - about all of which there will be uncertainty and hence the need for exercising risky judgement.

Money. To a greater or lesser degree, small farmers operate in a mixed cash and non-cash environment. Some are completely market oriented and operate fully commercially in a money economy. Some are purely subsistence farmers and operate without any contact with a money economy. The great bulk of small farmers, however, are semi-subsistence, i.e.,part-subsistence and part-commercial, so that they have some contact with markets through which they receive money as part of their total income. It has sometimes been argued that, in so far as small farmers operate outside the cash economy, the principles of economic theory outlined above are irrelevant. This is not so. These principles are pertinent and applicable whatever the *numéraire* used to assess gains and losses, whether it be money or some other measure such as the farmer's or farm family's personal utility or satisfaction. What is true is that money, when applicable, is a very convenient measure because of its standardized exchangeable nature across farms, regions, and countries. As a result of this standardized exchangeable nature, a money-based analysis enables comparison between farms and the aggregation of individual farm performance to regional and national aggregates. What is also true is that money is a generally applicable measure for farm management analysis in the fully commercial cash-oriented farming found in developed countries.

However, the fact that money plays such a role in developed country agriculture provides no logical reason for dismissing the principles of comparative advantage, diminishing returns, substitution, cost analysis, opportunity cost, enterprise choice or goal tradeoff in the developing country context of small farm management. The difficulty is in specifying and quantifying the appropriate *numéraire* when - as in the case of most small farmers - the gains and losses from the farm operation are a mixture of money and non-money elements or involve no money returns at all. In the case of pure subsistence or barter situations, the quantity of food produced (measured in some standard terms such as weeks' supply of an acceptable mix and quality) or the production of some standardized units of barter may serve as a *numéraire*. More generally, however, when gains and losses involve both cash and non-cash elements, the tradeoff or exchange rates between them will be personal to the individual farmer (i.e., different from farmer to farmer) and for any one farmer may not be constant as their proportions vary. Since resources will never be available for farm management research on a farm-by-farm basis, some compromise is necessary. Generally, this will imply the use of some standard *numéraire* applied to analyze and evaluate all the farm population of concern and most often, because of its convenience and increasing relevance, this *numéraire* will be money. But just as with the need for judgement so as to allow for the influence of risk, farm management researchers using money as the *numéraire* for economic analysis of small farms should always be cognizant of the fact that, to a greater of lesser extent depending on the farm situation, money is a compromise measure. While it may be the best basis of analysis which is possible, it may also be a less than adequate approximation depending on the extent to which trading guides are available on the money value of non-cash gains (i.e., outputs both physical and psychic) and losses (i.e., inputs both physical and psychic).

Regardless of the *numéraire* used and the degree to which risk is relevant, all the principles of economic theory outlined above basically reduce to a single common sense maxim known as the *economic principle of marginality*. This is that whatever a farmer's set of goals may be, to achieve them as well as possible given the constraints of climate, resource availability and institutional-political structure under which she or he has to operate, the small farmer should always make choices so that use of resources (land, labour, capital, time and management) is such that the expected marginal gain from the slightest possible change in resource use is equal to the expected marginal loss (i.e., opportunity foregone) implied by the change. Gain, in the sense of this rule, is ideally measured as the extra satisfaction obtained; and loss is the satisfaction given up, however satisfaction may be measured, whether in money or other terms.

This rule of aiming to have resources used in such fashion that the expected marginal gain (or revenue) from any change in resource use is equal to the expected marginal loss (or cost) arising from the change is, of course, the rule which should be used by farm management researchers in appraising farm performance (and also in other work such as in developing farm plans and appraising the potential role of new or different technology and farm production systems). Particularly when blindly based on a money *numéraire*, such farm management research suggests not infrequently that small farmers are not following the principle of marginality and are therefore managing their farms inefficiently or, same thing, are using their resources and opportunities in a suboptimal way. Most often this conclusion will be wrong and the farm management researcher should resist the temptation of such a simplistic conclusion without further investigation.

Difference between how the farmer uses resources and what farm management research indicates should be done with them (assuming no change in technology) is inevitably due to the research being based on an inadequate representation of the farmer's goals, inadequate measurement of goal achievement and tradeoff rates between goals, inaccurate data on farm performance, false assumptions about the farmer's beliefs, inadequate accounting for risk influences, or some combination of all these factors. Assuming no gross errors in the farm data used, the message from such research should therefore be not that the farmer is inefficient, but that if her or his beliefs, goals and preferences were different and agreed with those assumed in the research, then certain changes in resource use would be needed.

While it is quite appropriate to attempt to change a farmer's beliefs about such things as the chances of success of new technology, likely future prices, etc., whether or not an attempt should be made to persuade the farmer to change her or his goals (and value system) is another question. It involves the philosophic and moral considerations well reflected in the humorist's comment that "Money only brings misery but it is nice to be able to choose your own misery". Suffice to note that the broad question of whether or not to try to change farmer goals and values will generally be a matter for government policy decision guided by farm management research bringing the possible benefits of such possibilities to the attention of policy makers. In this regard, as discussed by Umali (1978), farm management research is particularly relevant to policy decisions on the role of community groups and group action as instruments for the conscientization of disadvantaged small farmers so as to make them more aware of their circumstances and the possible opportunities open to them.

PRACTICAL EXPERIENCE

Just as crucial to farm management research as an understanding of theory is the need for the researcher to have practical appreciation, familiarity and experience with farming and rural people. Without such experience and appreciation, it is exceedingly difficult for researchers to understand the farming systems used by small farmers and to establish rapport and have empathy with them. Likewise, experience is necessary in order to appreciate and understand the physical and socio-economic environment under which small farmers have to operate, the decisions they have to make, the relative importance of these decisions, and the degrees of freedom they face in choices due to constraints of resources, market access, cultural norms, etc. At the most mundane level of data collection, without experience and acceptance the researcher will have no guide to errors of communication and misinterpretation that may occur. For such reasons, therefore, it is often crucial that women farmers or members of the farm household be interviewed by women for the collection of data.

Most importantly, without knowing something of the farmer's needs and the farming systems available to satisfy those needs, the researcher will have little basis on which to formulate researchable problems and their associated hypotheses for testing. In all, therefore, practical knowledge is a most important element for successful farm management research, particularly with small farmers. This is not to say that the researcher must at some stage have been a small farmer. What it does say is that the researcher will be advantaged by some training that has involved some period of practical farm experience actually doing farm work (rather than watching others do it) and if she or he has taken the opportunity to visit, talk, consult and establish rapport with small farmers in their fields and their homes so as to gain first-hand familiarity with their farming systems and way of life.

As well as practical experience with farming, it is important for the researcher to have (or to have access to) working knowledge of the research structure under which she or he has to operate. Such knowledge is important since farm management research, as with most applied research, has to be carried out under less than ideal conditions. In particular, institutional and budgetary constraints, logistical difficulties in the field and poorly trained personnel can have a very significant effect on research efficiency. Practical experience of the research structure and organization can be invaluable in helping to overcome or ameliorate these difficulties.

RESEARCH STRATEGY AND RESOURCES

Also essential to the conduct of successful farm management research are the use of an effective research strategy and the availability of adequate research resources. These aspects, of course, are interdependent in that a prime requirement of an effective research strategy is that it matches the resources available for research.

An important element of research strategy is that the research be oriented to the solution of a well-defined problem. This implies there will generally be a time constraint fixed by the need for some decision to be made on the basis of the research. There will also be restraints related to the availability of trained manpower, data processing facilities and financial support. Prior information of relevance will also usually be less than ideally available, as also will be physical resources such as transport and experimental facilities.

In attempting to match the research project to the resources available, three alternatives are possible (Andrew and Hildebrand, 1976). The resources may be expanded to fit the project if the sponsor is willing, or the project may be cut back to fit the resources available, or both these steps may be taken to some degree.

If resources cannot be expanded, the researcher has four ways in which the initially proposed project might be cut back. First, fewer variables might be studied, preferably those judged to be of greater importance. Second, variables might be aggregated into groups so that, while no relationships are excluded, the nature of the relationships is likely to be made less clear because of the loss of opportunity for detailed study implied by aggregation. A third possibility would be to change the nature of the analysis to be carried out. For example, without a professional statistician it may be infeasible to carry out sophisticated statistical analysis so that elegant and detailed data collection procedures may no longer be necessary. Of course, less complex analyses can usually be carried out more quickly and with fewer facilities, but the precision of the results will be reduced accordingly. Fourth and finally, the researcher may decide to compromise by making fewer observations. For example, she or he may elect to use a reduced sample size in a survey or collect less experimental data by reducing the number of treatments studied or replications used.

Research resource availability is an important determinant of the nature of the research product and its precision. The researcher must recognize the effect that resource limitations can have on what research is possible. Only by doing so, can she or he develop a research strategy that gives a desired probability of producing useful results. Projects designed without recognizing resource limitations can and do frequently run into difficulties such that even the limited resources are wasted. The result is that less effective information is made available for problem resolution (Andrew and Hildebrand, 1976).

In developing a farm management research strategy, a distinction can be made between the elements of research method on the one hand and, on the other hand, the administrative steps involved in the life of any particular project.

The essential *elements of research method* are:

- ◇ a problem statement accompanied by sufficient information to justify the need for research;
- ◇ a listing of the hypotheses to be tested;
- ◇ a listing of the objectives to be met;
- ◇ a decision on what theory is relevant and the analytical approach and procedures to be followed;
- ◇ a decision on the data requirements and how they are to be obtained;
- ◇ a detailed work plan showing the jobs to be done and their flowcharting;
- ◇ a decision on how the research results are to be reported and to whom; and
- ◇ a budget of the required resources.

All these elements of research method are interrelated. Theory, for example, will guide hypothesis formulation and data needs will determine the budget size (or vice versa!). The first three items listed above provide the orientation and focus of the research. It is through them that the requirement of specifying a researchable problem is met. Broadly, the selection of a researchable problem involves sharpening the focus on some particular aspect of a more general problematic situation present in the farm management field of interest to the researcher. Hypothesis formulation narrows the problem to tentative relationships whose validity is to be tested. Finally, the objectives specify the limits within which the research is to be conducted and describe the type of output to be obtained. Obviously, this is not a once-only process. The problem, the hypotheses and the objectives may each have to be amended and refined a number of times before finality is reached.

The essence of a problem is that it reflects a felt need. Relative to small farmers, this need may be felt by the farmers themselves or by some agency concerned with farmer or national welfare. To be relevant as a researchable problem, the need must be capable of being resolved as a result of information gained through research. Thus not all problems are solvable via research. Given agreement on the problem statement, hypotheses as to why the problem exists can be formulated for testing. These hypotheses will be formulated by the researcher on the basis of knowledge of relevant theory. Non-testable hypotheses are irrelevant since they cannot contribute to problem resolution.

Hypotheses, because they have to be tested, provide the guidelines for the type of data that need to be collected and the techniques to be used in analyzing the data. Formulation of hypotheses, therefore, should come before the collection of data. It is hypotheses that provide the link between the problem and the data collection and analysis stages of the research. The desirable characteristics of hypotheses have been well stated by Andrew and Hildebrand (1976) as follows:

- ◇ Hypotheses must be formulated as *if-then* clauses and stated in such a manner that their implications and relationships to the problem can be shown logically.
- ◇ Their statement should be as simple as possible both in terms of theory and number of variables involved.
- ◇ They must be capable of verification or rejection within the limits of the research resources available.

- ◇ They must be stated in such a way as to provide direction for the research, i.e., to suggest the data to be collected and the analytical techniques to be used for testing the data. In this sense they constitute a plan for action.
- ◇ Taken together, the hypotheses must be adequate relative to providing a meaningful degree of problem resolution.

Objectives describe what is aimed to be achieved by the research. In general, they will define the research project's limits, outline the means of conducting the research, identify for whom the research is being carried out, and specify the expected output of the research (which can then be used by the research sponsor to help resolve the problem studied by the research). It is the objectives which link the theoretical relationships implicit in the hypotheses to the analytical procedures and orientation needed to carry out the research.

The following statement provides an example of a statement of a research problem, hypotheses and objectives:

Problem: Farmers in the UVW district have low maize yields and this contributes to their low levels of net farm income.

Hypotheses:

- ◇ If farmers were to use nitrogen fertilizer on their maize then their yields and net farm incomes would increase.
- ◇ Farmers do not use nitrogen fertilizer because supplies are not available.
- ◇ The provision of a new road by which nitrogen fertilizer could be more easily brought into the district would be in the national interest.

Objectives: To determine for the UVW district (a) the yield and gross margin relationships between the use of nitrogen fertilizer and maize yield; (b) the contribution of maize to net farm income and how net farm income might change if nitrogen were used in maize production; (c) the availability of nitrogen fertilizer in the region and whether farmers desire its availability to be increased; and (d) if the construction of a road to the region would be worthwhile in benefit-cost terms. Overall, the aims of the project are to provide guidance on the possible role of fertilizer in increasing the net income of farmers in the district.

PROJECT ADMINISTRATION

Viewed in terms of administration, the life of any farm management research project passes through the three stages of formulation, execution and termination, each involving a number of steps for administrative action (Sitton, 1966).

Formulation phase. During project development or formulation, eight steps must be carried out:

- ◇ A need must be felt for information relative to some problem of research potential.

- ◇ Further information of a preliminary nature on the potential idea for research must be gathered.
- ◇ The problem must be narrowed to manageable limits for research and relevant objectives decided.
- ◇ Assessment must be made of the alternative ways in which the objectives might be achieved.
- ◇ Responsibilities must be determined as to who will perform what work and which agencies are to be responsible for different aspects and under whose supervision.
- ◇ A project outline must be written outlining the research project. This should cover the problem statement, hypotheses to be tested, objectives of the research, budget requirements and detailed responsibilities and procedures for achieving the objectives.
- ◇ Approval of the project outline (particularly in terms of budget provision) must be obtained from all the relevant individuals and agencies involved.
- ◇ A written record must be kept of everything pertaining to the project.

Execution phase. While project success is certainly dependent on proper formulation, the main effort of the project will be in the research execution period. From an administrative view, this can be divided into the following seven requirements:

- ◇ Activities must be coordinated.
- ◇ Necessary forms, instruction sheets, materials, etc., must be prepared.
- ◇ Personnel must be selected and adequately trained to gather data and/or record results.
- ◇ The data must be gathered, recorded and checked.
- ◇ The data must be summarized and analyzed via the appropriate analytical techniques relative to the hypotheses being tested.
- ◇ A report must be written giving the results of the research.
- ◇ Throughout, researchers must keep a written record of what is done and how it is done at each step.

Termination phase. Frequently, projects are left in an untidy state because this final administrative phase is ignored as personnel shift to new projects. Good research administration should not allow this to happen. Five terminating activities can be specified, as follows:

- ◇ The cooperation of all people who were involved should be acknowledged. This is essential for maintaining goodwill.
- ◇ The data collected should be reviewed to see if they suggest other problems for research or if, within the bounds of confidentiality as may be relevant, they may be useful for other purposes.
- ◇ All project material - correspondence, interview notes, preliminary data, field schedules or notes, tabulations, work sheets, reports, etc. - should be organized and filed for future reference if required, again with due regard to confidentiality as relevant.
- ◇ Budget expenditures should be summarized for easy reference in planning future projects.
- ◇ The results of the research should be disseminated in appropriate ways to relevant people. Unless this is done, the research might just as well not have been carried out.

1.7 Role of farm management research techniques

As illustrated by the wide-ranging variety of topics considered in this introductory chapter, the scope of farm management research is very broad and its range of contexts extremely varied. Unlike the specialist crop or livestock scientist, the farm management researcher has to be concerned with the whole farm in all its dimensions as a purposive system with agro-biological, economic, social and community elements (Dillon, 1992). This is particularly important for small farms which generally tend to involve complicated interdependent multi-product farming systems with a significant subsistence component. Undoubtedly, these characteristics make farm management research on small farms a difficult endeavour. It is for this reason that techniques of research analysis, as outlined in the remaining chapters of this manual, are important. These techniques, appropriately chosen for the problem and data at hand, enable the researcher to reach conclusions about how problems might best be resolved. In the case of simple tabular and budget analyses, the research data are drawn together in such a way that the researcher can apply his knowledge of theory to draw relevant conclusions: or, with more complicated techniques such as linear programming and production function analysis, the application of theory is carried out within the research technique itself to provide more direct guides to relevant research conclusions. Too, as shown in the final two chapters of this bulletin, the various techniques of farm management research can contribute significantly to the *ex ante* appraisal of risky choices by farmers and to the *ex ante* and *ex post* evaluation of agricultural policies and development projects.

1.8 References

ANDREW, C.O. & P.A. HILDEBRAND (1976). *Planning and Conducting Applied Research,* MSS Information Corporation, New York.

CARPENTER, N.R. (1975). 'Small Farmer Development: The Problem and the Programme from a Farm Management Perspective', *Farm Management Notes for Asia and the Far East* 1: 2-9.

CARPENTER, N.R. & H. KUNERT (1977). 'Farm Management Research - A Need for Rural Development', *Farm Management Notes for Asia and the Far East* 4: 1-15.

DE DATTA, S.K., K.A. GOMEZ, R.W. HERDT & R. BARKER (1978). *A Handbook on the Methodology for an Integrated Experiment-Survey on Rice Yield Constraints,* International Rice Research Institute, Los Baños.

DILLON, J.L. (1976). 'The Economics of Systems Research', *Agricultural Systems* 1: 5-22.

DILLON, J.L. (1992). *The Farm as a Purposeful System,* Miscellaneous Publications No. 10, Department of Agricultural Economics & Business Management, University of New England, Armidale.

DILLON, J.L. & J.R. ANDERSON (1984). 'Concept and Practice of Farming Systems Research', in ACIAR, *Proceedings of the Eastern Africa-ACIAR Consultation on Agricultural Research, 18-22 July 1983, Nairobi,* Australian Centre for International Agricultural Research, Canberra, pp. 171-86.

DIXON, J.M. *et al.* (1986). *FARMAP Users Manual, Vols 1-3*, Food and Agriculture Organization of the United Nations, Rome.

FAO, (1989). *Guidelines on the Conduct of a Training Course in Farming Systems Development*, Food and Agriculture Organization of the United Nations, Rome.

FRIEDRICH, K.H. (1977). *Farm Management Data Collection and Analysis: An Electronic Data Processing, Storage and Retrieval System*, FAO Agricultural Services Bulletin No. 34, Food and Agriculture Organization of the United Nations, Rome.

GOMEZ, K.A. (1977). 'On-farm Assessment of Yield Constraints: Methodological Problems', in IRRI, *Constraints to High Yields on Asian Rice Farms: An Interim Report*, International Rice Research Institute, Los Baños.

HARDAKER, J.B., J.R. ANDERSON & J.L. DILLON (1984). 'Perspectives on Assessing the Impacts of Improved Agricultural Technologies in Developing Countries', *Australian Journal of Agricultural Economics* 28: 87-108.

HAZELL, P.B.R. & R.D. NORTON (1986). *Mathematical Programming for Economic Analysis in Agriculture*, Macmillan, New York.

IRRI (1977). *Constraints to High Yields on Asian Rice Farms: An Interim Report*, International Rice Research Institute, Los Baños.

MAKEHAM, J.P. & L.R. MALCOLM (1986). *The Economics of Tropical Farm management*, Cambridge University Press.

McCONNELL, D.J. (1975). 'Stages in the Collection of Data for Planning Small-Farm Development', FAO, *Annex to Report of the Sixth Session of the FAO Regional Commission on Farm Management for Asia and the Far East*, AGS: FMX/75/ANNEX, Food and Agriculture Organization of the United Nations, Rome, pp. 51-68.

McCONNELL, D.J. (1992). *The Forest-Garden Farms of Kandy, Sri Lanka*. Food and Agriculture Organization of the United Nations, Rome.

NAGY, J.G. & J.H. SANDERS (1990). 'Agricultural Technology Development and Dissemination within a Farming Systems Perspective', *Agricultural Systems*, 32: 305-320.

ROGERS, E.M. (1969). 'Motivations, Values and Attitudes of Subsistence Farmers: Towards a Subculture of Peasantry', in C.R. WHARTON (ed.), *Subsistence Agriculture and Economic Development*, Aldine, Chicago, pp. 111-135.

RUTHENBERG, H. (1976). *Farming Systems in the Tropics*, 2nd edn, Clarendon Press, Oxford.

SCHICKELE, R. (1966). 'Farm Management Research for Planning Agricultural Development', *Indian Journal of Agricultural Economics* 21: 1-15.

SINGH, I., L.SQUIRE & J. STRAUSS (eds) (1986). *Agricultural Household Models - Extensions, Applications and Policy*, Johns Hopkins University Press, Baltimore.

SITTON, G.R. (1966). 'Essential Steps in the Life of a Research Project', in R.E. BORTON (ed.), *Selected Readings to Accompany Getting Agriculture Moving*, Agricultural Development Council Inc., New York, pp. 205-209.

TRIPP, R. (1991). 'The farming systems research movement and on-farm research', in R. TRIPP (ed.), *Planned Change in Farming Systems: Progress in On-Farm Research*, Wiley, Chichester, pp. 3-16.

TRIPP, R. & J. WOOLLEY (1989). *The Planning Stage of On-farm Research: Identifying Factors for Experimentation,* CIMMYT & CIAT, Mexico City and Cali.

UMALI, D.L. (1978). 'Opening Address: New Concept of Farm Management', in FAO, *Report of the Expert Group Meeting on Farm Management for Small Farmer Development in Asia and the Far East,* Bangkok, pp. 4-10.

UNITED NATIONS (1988). *Population Projections,* United Nations, New York.

VALDÉS, A., G.R. SCOBIE & J.L. DILLON (eds) (1979). *Economics and the Design of Small-Farmer Technology,* Iowa State University, Ames.

VON FLECKENSTEIN, F. & M.J. GAUCHON (1992). *The FAO Farm Analysis Package, FARMAP, Reference Manual*, AGSP, Food and Agriculture Organization of the United Nations, Rome.

WHARTON, C.R. (1969). 'Subsistence Agriculture: Concepts and Scope', in C.R. WHARTON (ed.), *Subsistence Agriculture and Economic Development,* Aldine, Chicago, pp. 12-20.

WONG, J. & E.P. REED (1978). *The Experience and Potential for Group Farming in Asia,* Teaching and Research Forum No. 17, Agricultural Development Council, Inc., Singapore.

2. DATA SOURCES AND COLLECTION

2.1 Introduction

Farm management is not an abstract science that can be conducted in isolation from the real situation on farms and from the actual circumstances of farmers. A necessary step in any farm management study must be to obtain information about the real farm situation. This chapter is concerned with some of the main methods by which such data are obtained.

It is useful to identify three stages in farm management data collection which should usually be implemented one at a time and in sequence. These are desk research, qualitative data-gathering, and quantitative data-gathering. The reason for following this sequence is to learn as much as possible about the problem at hand as quickly and cheaply as possible, and to avoid collecting unnecessary information. On some occasions just the first stage, or perhaps the first two stages, will provide enough information to enable the problem to be solved. Even if all three methods must eventually be used, it is important that the available information from the earlier stages is used to guide the data gathering in the later stages. Each stage will be reviewed in turn later in this chapter.

An important question to consider in relation to the collection of farm management data is the purpose for which the information is needed. Only by knowing the intended use of the information is it possible to assess which data are needed and to judge how adequately alternative ways of collecting the data may serve the particular needs. Once the purpose is established, it will be important to review what is already known about the problem at hand - the desk research stage. It may be that the farming systems that are the focus of attention are rather poorly understood, at least by the farm management analyst. (The farmers in those systems will know them very well!) If general knowledge of the target farming systems is poor, it will be unwise immediately to attempt to gather detailed quantitative information. Rather the analyst will need to start with collection of qualitative information about the system, using informal methods of enquiry of the type described later in this chapter. The aim in this stage is to define better the situation under study, and so to be better able to plan the quantitative data-gathering phase, if this is indeed needed.

When the time to begin the process of gathering quantitative data has arrived, it will be important to address issues about the needed levels of precision in data measurement. If the results of farm management analyses are to be of value, the data on which they are based must be both as accurate and relevant as economically possible. Accuracy relates to the degree of conformity between the data and the real facts the data are supposed to describe. Errors of observation, recording or reporting lead to inaccuracies in farm management data. Relevance is defined in relation to the intended use of the data. Data may be of little or no relevance if they are out of date or if they apply to a production system employing different resources or management skills to those employed by the farmers of concern. For example, as discussed below, experimental data may be of high accuracy but of low relevance to real farming conditions if the experiments are conducted under atypical conditions.

A high degree of accuracy and relevance in farm management data is not easily or cheaply achieved. Collection of data for farm management analysis always involves compromises. The judgement of the analyst in selecting data collection methods within the limits imposed by the resources available for the work is of the first importance. As discussed in the following sections of this chapter, different methods of data collection vary in reliability and cost. Moreover, there is a widespread tendency towards too much optimism about what levels of precision can be expected from a given data-gathering effort.

Because data collection is expensive, it is important to be careful in deciding what to collect. When a survey is to be undertaken, for example, there is a natural tendency to add more and more questions to explore various aspects of the farming systems being studied. Analysts should resist such tendencies by giving proper weight to the cost of collecting and processing the additional information, as well as to the risk that the collection of that part of the survey data of immediate importance may be compromised if too many questions are asked - both interviewer and respondent may suffer from fatigue so that questions get carelessly asked and answers carelessly given.

Finally, no data collection task should be attempted without at least considering the costs that will be imposed on farmer respondents and how these can be justified. What benefit will accrue to the cooperating farmers? If none, then it is important to be honest and tell them so, while explaining why their assistance will still be appreciated. Moreover, where there are opportunities to provide analyses of the information collected that will be of value to respondents, there is a moral obligation on the analyst to see that this is done.

2.2 *Desk research - the use of secondary data*

The best starting point in many cases where a need for data has been recognized will be to review the available secondary data, that is, information already collected by others and available in publications, reports or in the files of the relevant agencies. The types of secondary data to seek out obviously depend on the ultimate purpose of the enquiry. However, categories to consider include the following:

- ◇ *Climatic data*, for example on rainfall and its seasonal distribution and reliability, temperatures, radiation, incidence of climatic hazards such as cyclones, frosts.
- ◇ *Land capability data*, for example, land areas by type, soil type, slope.
- ◇ *Land tenure data*, for example, numbers of farms by size categories, tenure arrangements, prevailing rents.
- ◇ *Land use data*, for example, areas of the main crops grown, grazing and forest areas.

- ◇ *Population data*, for example, numbers of people by age and sex, average and distribution of household size, labour supply and employment information, education and skill levels in the work-force.
- ◇ *Investment data*, for example, levels of private investment in farming assets, transport assets such as trucks, public investment in infrastructure such as roads, market facilities, irrigation works, levels of credit availability and use.
- ◇ *Farming systems data*, for example, typical crop associations, livestock-crop or livestock-pasture associations, calendar of operations, extent of uptake of improved technologies.
- ◇ *Input-output data*, for example, levels of production and yields of crops and livestock, levels and rates of use of the main inputs such as fertilizer.
- ◇ *Gender task allocation*, for example, the division of farm and household work responsibilities between men, women and children.
- ◇ *Income data*, for example, sources, average and distribution of household incomes, wage rates.
- ◇ *Household consumption data*, for example, average expenditure patterns, levels and ranges of food consumption.
- ◇ *Welfare data*, for example, morbidity and mortality rates and causes, nutritional status of children and adults.
- ◇ *Price data*, for example, prices of main commodities traded locally, both inputs and outputs, seasonal variations in these prices, amounts going through the main marketing channels, cost and standard of living indicators.

Of course, to collect and assimilate all of the sorts of information listed above would be a large and difficult task, so it is perhaps fortunate that secondary data are often sparse or absent for many of these categories. It is nevertheless important to review such relevant secondary information as is available to make best use of what is already known and to see what gaps in knowledge remain to be filled by collection of primary data.

2.3 *Qualitative data collection*

Various largely informal methods of enquiry are commonly used to collect mostly qualitative information about a farming system. Some quantitative information may also be obtained using such informal methods variously known by names such as *field study*, *area familiarization* or *reconnaissance study* (Kearl, 1976). More recently, the term *rapid rural appraisal* has come into vogue (McCracken, Pretty and Conway, 1988; Molnar, 1989).

All these approaches involve familiarizing oneself with the area or problem, by direct observation and by talking to appropriate informants such as farmers, farm workers, storekeepers, moneylenders, officials, religious or social leaders. Because people from different backgrounds or with different disciplinary orientations tend to see the world differently, it is often helpful to use a team approach to the enquiries. Minimally, a farm management worker might need to collaborate with an agronomist or livestock specialist. Depending on the production system and the perceived problems to be addressed, the team might be enhanced by inclusion of, say, a nutritionist, soil scientist, ecologist, etc. However, large teams tend to be unwieldy and are generally to be avoided.

The justification of informal approaches is that they are usually the most effective ways of learning a good deal about a particular topic in a short time. For some problems the approach may provide all the information one needs (or has the time to collect) to be able to resolve the issue. In other circumstances, informal methods will be preliminary to the collection of quantitative data, perhaps by means of a formal sample survey. The mainly qualitative information gathered may be useful, even essential, in defining issues, formulating relevant hypotheses, establishing a suitable sampling procedure, drawing up a questionnaire, planning the logistics of the survey, and so on.

The obvious danger of the informal approaches is that one may obtain biased or incorrect information. The *key informants* who would usually be interviewed in such a study may all share a particular prejudice or viewpoint and it may be difficult for the researcher to meet other people, perhaps of lower social or economic status, who may express an alternative point of view. Government officers interviewed may espouse the official line or may paint a too glowing picture of reality to cover up their failures. Researchers need to be on guard against such possibilities. They should seek to interview a wide spectrum of people, not just local officials and key farmers. They will need to be on the look out for contradictions in the information supplied. When contradictions are found, it will be necessary to dig deeper to try to uncover the truth.

Combined with a modicum of common sense, informal methods can be very effective ways of gathering information. Apart from the dangers noted above, the chief disadvantage is that the information gathered tends to involve a substantial element of subjective interpretation and so lacks some of the authority of data gathered by means of a more formal survey. In truth, however, this reservation is somewhat artificial since all data require some interpretation and a badly conducted survey can be more misleading than a well-performed field study.

2.4 *Quantitative data gathering - farm surveys*

The survey method is probably the most widely used method of obtaining quantitative farm management data. It is also probably the most widely abused. To conduct a successful survey requires careful planning and close attention to detail in implementation. Some of the more important aspects of survey organization and management are reviewed briefly below. It is not possible to provide a comprehensive guide to the survey method in this short treatment and intending survey organizers should consult some of the excellent texts on the subject, a selection of which is listed at the end of the chapter.

DEFINING OBJECTIVES

No farm survey can be properly planned unless the objective or objectives are clearly defined (Kearl, 1976, Ch. 1). Proper design and conduct of a survey can be compromised by objectives that are too numerous, too ambitious or conflicting. In an ideal world, surveys would be purpose-specific, for only when a single specific purpose has been defined is it possible to resolve unambiguously such questions as what sampling method to use and what size of sample is needed. In reality, though, because research resources are limited, it is nearly always necessary to try to accommodate more than one objective in designing a survey. In this case, at least some ranking of objectives in order of importance should be made to help in resolving the conflicts between objectives that will almost inevitably be encountered.

DATA COLLECTION METHODS

There are three main methods by which farm survey data can be gathered. They are:

- ◇ direct observation;
- ◇ interviewing respondents;
- ◇ records kept by respondents.

Direct observation includes direct measurement by the research team of such things as crop areas, yields, disease incidence, etc. If done correctly, direct measurement should give data of high accuracy but the cost is often high and the procedure is not appropriate for many data categories.

Direct observation can also be used to collect information of a more behavioural nature such as allocation of time, rates of work, etc. The problem with such studies is that the mere presence of the observer can lead the person being studied to modify her or his behaviour. The observer must therefore try to be as unobtrusive as possible and should be prepared to discard data collected when it appears that bias may be present.

In anthropological studies the researcher often gathers information by actually taking part in the way of life she or he is studying. Although this method is seldom of direct use in farm management research, the researcher who has some direct experience of the social and economic system in the study area will often find this knowledge invaluable in interpreting the more quantitative farm management data (Srinivas, 1974).

Interviewing respondents is generally the simplest and cheapest method of gathering farm management data. Accuracy depends on the ability of respondents to remember the information requested and on their willingness to reply truthfully. When information is likely to be forgotten quickly, it may be necessary to interview the respondents at frequent intervals while the facts are fresh in their minds.

Most interview surveys are designed to be administered to one respondent at a time, usually the farmer or the head of the household. Of course, in some societies the notion of a single household head or farm decision maker may be inapplicable, and a number of individuals in each survey unit may have to be interviewed to collect all the data of interest.

In other cases, where important decisions are customarily made by discussion among a group of people, the individual approach may be inappropriate, even impossible. In much of the world, most of the farm work is done by women; yet, too often in the past, farm management surveys have been conducted by sending male enumerators to interview men. There is now a growing recognition that this can result in very biased and incomplete information. The women must be interviewed too and, whenever possible, this is best done by female enumerators.

In group interviews the researcher asks questions of the collected individuals who discuss the matter in an attempt to provide an answer, usually reached by consensus. The interviewer may or may not participate in the discussions. Usually some participation will be necessary to clarify the questions asked and to keep the discussion more or less to the point. The risk of bias introduced by the interviewer's involvement in the debate is apparent. Also, as anyone who has ever served on a committee or other such decision group will know, groups do not always function well as decision-making entities. The process of consensus formation may be slow and the decisions reached may not always be consistent. These are the realities the researcher must face if she or he wants to collect data from a group.

Records kept by respondents either as normal procedure or at the request of the researcher can be a very valuable source of farm management data. The method is appropriate for information easily forgotten but, of course, can be used only when respondents have the required level of literacy. The records may or may not be kept specifically for the purpose of the research study. For example, commercial or semi-commercial farmers may be required to keep financial records for tax purposes and these records can be a source of farm management data.

When special-purpose records are to be kept, the researcher must give very careful consideration to the design of the recording form and to the wording of instructions, headings, etc. Pilot testing of the record forms should be carried out before their general implementation. Unless respondents are experienced in record keeping, frequent checks of the information recorded may have to be made.

TYPES OF INFORMATION GATHERED BY SURVEYS

Both survey objectives and the environment of agriculture vary so much that it is almost impossible to provide any comprehensive list of the kinds of information to be sought in farm management surveys. However, there are certain categories of data that are commonly needed (CGPRT, 1986; RAPA, 1989). These are reviewed below. Many surveys embrace more than one of these categories.

Resource endowments. It is often useful to know what is the resource base of a particular region or group of farms. It may also be important to know how these resources are distributed among households, villages, or other groups of people including males and females. A survey can be conducted to determine the resource base of an appropriate sample of households or other survey units. Data would be gathered on such things as number, age, education and experience of workers, access to land, access to irrigation water, etc.

Resource utilization. It is usually somewhat more difficult to establish how the resources controlled by small farmers are used. Land use may be estimated by direct observation at the time of the survey, but estimating use of labour, for example, presents more difficulties, especially if information on year-round labour use is required. At best, such information can usually only be obtained by frequent visits to respondents; at worst, it may be unobtainable.

Input-output coefficients. For some purposes it is necessary to obtain data on such matters as yields per unit area of crops, yields per head of livestock, and use of labour and other inputs per unit area of crop or per head of livestock. The practicability of obtaining such information varies according to the type of farming and other circumstances. Sometimes it can be very difficult to obtain reasonably accurate information. For example, to estimate the yield of a subsistence crop one may have to either harvest and record the yield of a sample area, or else obtain a detailed record, perhaps on a day-to-day basis over several months, of household use of the product. Similarly, reliable data on rates of work may require a detailed diary to be kept of how labour time is spent. In some communities such information may be obtainable only by conducting daily interviews over the whole period of interest, with the very considerable attendant risk of both respondent and interviewer fatigue and hence of bad data.

Costs, returns and incomes. This is the kind of information that is most commonly sought in farm management surveys. The information is usually gathered either on a farm basis, or on a farm plus household basis. The data collected may relate only to cash items or an attempt may be made to measure and value non-cash items such as family labour use, subsistence output, etc. For some purposes it may be enough to know aggregate costs and returns, while for other uses the breakdown of these totals may be needed, perhaps on an enterprise basis so far as this is appropriate.

Information on knowledge, attitudes and beliefs. Because the behaviour of small-farm decision makers is so important for the success of various policy measures, it is common for surveys to include questions designed to elicit farmers' attitudes to such things as new techniques of production, research and extension programmes, climatic and price risks, etc. Special care is needed in phrasing questions to elicit such information if the responses obtained are to be reasonably reliable. Poorly worded questions will lead to biased results. In regard to certain sensitive topics, it may be impossible to obtain responses that are at all reliable.

Crop and farming systems. Particularly as a basis for cooperative work with crop and livestock scientists, and also so as to understand the production systems used by farmers, it is frequently necessary to catalogue and analyze the particular farming systems used by farmers. Data required include the crops grown, the type of cropping system used, either sole cropping or multiple cropping, and the calendar of operations. If the system is one of multiple cropping, more detailed information will be needed on the type of multiple cropping, e.g., intercropping, sequential cropping or relay cropping plus details of crop rotation and ratooning if relevant. Since the crop or farm system comprises all the components (physical and biological factors, labour, technology and management) required for crop or farm production and the interrelationships between them and the environment (climatic, economic, social and cultural), surveys involving crop or farm system specification can be very demanding of farm management research resources. In particular, such surveys may require not one but a series of visits spread over the year to the farms being surveyed.

Household consumption patterns. If the integrated nature of farm households is recognized, as discussed in Chapter 1, information relating to farm production will tell only half the story. For a comprehensive view of farm households, data will be needed on household consumption patterns, including consumption of food, whether home grown or purchased, other household cash expenditures, and the consumption of leisure (and hence the supply of family labour to farm work or to wage earning).

Gender-related information. In the small farm context, agricultural activities are undertaken by households which are complex decision making units. Differences between the roles of men, women and children, and patterns of intra- and inter-household relations, are embedded in farming systems and will both affect and be affected by changes in these systems. Each individual member in a household has a variety of responsibilities and activities, of which agricultural work may only be a part (Murphy, 1990). Gender analysis involves the study of farm-household responsibilities and activities relative to men, women and children in terms of (1) who does what? (2) who has access to or control of resources? and (3) who has access to or control of benefits? (Feldstein, Flora and Poats, 1990; Russo *et al.*, 1989). Such information can particularly assist agricultural researchers by indicating who should be included in the research as informants, as participants, as decision makers, as evaluators of new technology, as deliverers of services, as clients for service, and as beneficiaries of the research.

PLANNING THE ANALYSIS

Once the objectives of the farm survey have been specified, and the general type of information to be collected has been established, the next step is to plan the main analyses to be performed on the data after they have been collected. It may seem premature to worry about analyses before any information has been collected, but in fact many mistakes and omissions in the design and conduct of the survey can best be avoided by careful planning. The main tabulations of the data or other statistical analyses should be planned in detail beforehand. These analyses will obviously be structured in accordance with the survey objectives. These objectives may be formulated in the form of hypotheses to be tested using the survey data. Such an approach invariably assists in better specifying the type of data to be collected and the analyses to be applied to the data.

The main reasons for considering data analysis prior to collection of the data are to ensure that:

- ◇ all necessary data are gathered;
- ◇ no unnecessary data are collected;
- ◇ the data are collected in a form suitable for analysis.

DEVELOPING THE QUESTIONNAIRE

Once the survey objectives and associated data needs and analyses have been specified, a questionnaire can be developed to record the information needed for analysis. Usually the questionnaire will be designed to be completed by enumerators although, in some circumstances, simple questionnaires may be designed for completion by the respondents. Attention must be given to the general form of the questionnaire to see that the questions follow a logical and appropriate sequence. Questions that are to be answered by direct observation by the enumerator should be distinguished from those to be asked of the respondents. Care must be taken in wording questions to ensure that they are unambiguous, will not cause offence or otherwise lead to non-cooperation by respondents, and that the form of words used is not likely to prompt a particular answer. The spaces provided on the questionnaire for recording information should be arranged so that it is clear what is to be filled in and so that the data will be readily accessible for analysis. For instance, if answers are to be coded for computer analysis, as will often be the case, it will be necessary to leave space on the questionnaire for the appropriate codes to be entered.

In developing a questionnaire it is usually necessary to undertake a pilot survey. This involves conducting the survey on a trial basis with a small number of respondents who are broadly similar to those in the population of interest. The results of this pilot sample are not included in the final survey analysis. The purpose is simply to test out the questionnaire so that it can be revised in the light of trial experience. Often two or more cycles of pilot testing and questionnaire revision are needed.

The pilot survey will reveal how long each survey interview takes. Ideally this should be no more than about half an hour, and certainly not more than an hour. Both respondent and enumerator will become tired and liable to make errors if the interview lasts too long. When a questionnaire proves to be too time consuming, the analyst must try to cut out unnecessary or marginal questions and try to find more direct ways of obtaining the required information. If this fails, either the scope of the survey must be cut down, probably by curtailing the objectives, or it may be possible to ask some questions of sub-samples of respondents so that no respondents are required to answer the full set of questions, as discussed below under the heading of multiphase sampling.

Self-evidently, the questionnaire must be in a language well understood by the enumerators and respondents. In some countries this may mean that more than one version of the questionnaire has to be produced for use with different linguistic groups. Care must be taken in translation to preserve the intended meaning. It is a good idea to have the translated version translated back into the original language by a second, independent person to check if any meanings have been changed.

An excellent review of practical considerations in questionnaire design and development is provided by Kearl (1976, Chs 5 and 6).

DRAWING THE SAMPLE

Early in the planning of any survey the researcher needs to choose the sampling method to be employed. Many factors impinge on this choice, including considerations of the cost of statistical properties of different kinds of sample. Sampling techniques are comprehensively discussed in such texts as Cochran (1963) and Som (1973). A useful overview is provided by Parel *et al.* (1973). Here only a brief outline of the main aspects can be provided. There are two main types of samples that can be used in conducting a farm survey:

- ◇ probability samples; and
- ◇ non-probability samples.

The choice between the two depends partly on the sampling frame available and partly on the objectives of the study and the data needed. (A sampling frame is a list of those members of the population from whom the sample is to be selected.) Sometimes a combination of the two sampling methods may be appropriate, as discussed below.

Probability sampling is the term used to describe various ways of drawing a sample such that the probability of a particular individual being included in the survey is known or can be estimated with reasonable precision. It includes random, systematic, stratified and multistage sampling procedures.

Probability sampling has the important advantages that the risk of sampling bias is minimized and it is possible to draw inferences from the sample about the population from which the sample was drawn with levels of confidence that can be estimated statistically.[1] For these reasons, some form of probability sampling is usually to be preferred and the forms of non-probability sampling to be described later are generally used only when probability sampling is impracticable.

In *random sampling* each member of the population is assigned a serial number. Then the sample is drawn by reading from a list of random numbers of the appropriate range of values until the required number of individuals has been selected. This procedure ensures that each member of the sampling population has the same probability of being chosen.

A similar result, for most practical purposes, can be achieved by *systematic sampling*. In this method every *k*-th unit from the sampling frame is drawn, cycling through the population list from a random starting point. The sampling interval k is computed as N/n, rounded down to a whole number, where N is the number in the population from which the sample is to be drawn and n is the required sample size.

The main advantage of systematic sampling is that it is quicker and easier than simple random sampling. This may be especially important if the sample is to be drawn in the field. However, if the sampling frame is not in random order, and especially if there are periodic regularities in the list, systematic sampling can lead to bias.

With *stratified sampling*, the population to be sampled is divided into a number of strata or groups on the basis of one or more characteristics of interest. Then random or systematic sampling can be used to select the required sub-samples from each stratum. It is more efficient than simple random or systematic sampling in the sense that the selected sample is more likely to be representative of the population from which it was drawn.

In principle, stratification should be based on those characteristics of particular interest in the analysis. If several variables are of interest, this can lead to stratification that is too complex to be manageable. The same problem can arise if too many strata are defined for a single characteristic. In practice, however, these difficulties are seldom important. It is rare to have data on more than one or two characteristics of interest and specification of only a few strata is usually adequate to provide for the advantages of stratification without too much complication. Often the characteristics on which information is available are not those of direct interest, but if the available characteristics can be expected to be related to the parameters of interest, stratification will still be worthwhile. For example, geographical stratification will ensure a more efficient spread

---

[1] The formulae to use in drawing inferences about the population from a probability sample drawn using one or other of the methods outlined below are to be found in most texts on sampling methods, such as Som (1973). In addition, these formulae are normally embedded in statistical software packages used for analysis of survey data.

of farms across soil types, climatic conditions, etc., than would be given by a simple random sample.

For some purposes, stratified sampling may be almost essential. For example, suppose it is wished to compare certain characteristics of large and small farms and that the size distribution of farms is highly skewed toward small farms. Unless the sample size is very large, a simple random or systematic sample may well contain too few large farms to give meaningful results. By stratification into two or more size groups, the required number of farms of each size can be sampled.

The chief disadvantage of stratified sampling is that to apply the procedure it is necessary to have a sampling frame including the necessary information for stratification. Often such data on key parameters, such as farm size, are not available. Stratification also complicates somewhat the estimation of population parameters and precision statistics from the sample data.

Two or more steps are involved in *multistage sampling*. For example, in two-stage sampling a list of villages in the study area might first be obtained, and from these a sample of villages could be drawn. A list of the farmers within each sampled village can then be used to draw a sample of farmers for that village. In three-stage sampling, samples might be drawn of districts within a region, then of villages in the sampled districts, and finally of farms in the sampled villages.

One advantage of multistage sampling is that, when based on geographical units as illustrated above, it can lead to a substantial saving in travelling time and costs in conducting interviews. Secondly, it is not necessary to have a complete sampling frame of final-stage units. At the second and any subsequent stages the sampling frame can be constructed only for those units selected at the earlier stage. In other words, it is possible to build the sampling frame as the process of sampling proceeds.

The major disadvantage of multistage sampling is that the procedure is rather complex to apply and calculation of appropriate population estimates, including statistics indicating the precision of the estimates obtained, is more difficult than for some of the simpler sampling methods discussed above.

A special case of multistage sampling is *cluster sampling*. This is normally a two-stage procedure in which the population is first divided into groups or clusters from which a sample of clusters is drawn by random or systematic sampling. In the second stage all the individuals in these sampled clusters are included in the survey.[2]

The advantages of cluster sampling are those of multistage sampling, i.e., reduced travelling costs and the fact that a full sampling frame is not required. The important disadvantage is that the sample drawn is likely to be less representative of the population than, say, a simple random sample. Individuals in clusters may share similar characteristics to a greater degree than do individuals in different clusters. This disadvantage is reduced in ordinary multistage sampling by drawing more clusters with less than full enumeration

---

[2] The terminology here varies somewhat among authors. Some use the term cluster sampling even when only a sample of members of each cluster is taken.

of the individuals in each cluster. The cost of this greater representativeness is greater complexity in sampling and increased travelling costs.

Cluster sampling may be especially relevant when interest is focused on tracing transactions between all households in a village community such as for village studies as described below.

Non-probability sampling procedures are generally only used when probability sampling is not practicable. The reason is that the representativeness of the sample may be low and statistics that might be calculated from the sample data may be of dubious reliability. Some non-probability sampling procedures are more subject to bias than others. The major non-probability sampling procedures are accidental sampling, purposive sampling and quota sampling.

Using *accidental sampling* the researcher selects for a sample those individuals she or he happens to come across. If no sampling frame exists and if one cannot be improvised, perhaps for lack of time, this may be the only procedure that can be used. The risk of bias in such a method in obvious. For example, if the people encountered in a particular village are surveyed, the survey results cannot represent the characteristics of perhaps more industrious people who were at work in the fields or elsewhere at the time of the survey.

With *purposive sampling*, samples are drawn to illustrate or represent some particular characteristic in the population. For example, in studying some new technology not yet widely adopted, only those individuals known to have adopted the new method might be sampled. Most farm recording schemes, discussed below, are based on purposive samples of cooperative farmers selected for their capacity to supply the required information.

The procedure of *quota sampling* is used to try to minimize bias in non-probability sampling when probability sampling is not possible, perhaps for lack of a sampling frame. Quotas are established for different groups in the population and sampling proceeds, using accidental or purposive sampling, until the required numbers of individuals to fill each quota have been obtained. Alternatively, random or systematic sampling may be used to fill the required quotas, in which case quota sampling becomes a special form of stratified sampling.

A method of sampling that can be used in conjunction with some kinds of both probability and non-probability sampling is *multiphase sampling*. It is sometimes appropriate to collect some data from all units of a sample and other items of information from only a sub-sample of the whole sample. This method is known as *two-phase sampling* and the principle can be extended to three or more phases. The case for using multiphase sampling arises when it is difficult or expensive to collect all information from all respondents. For example, full enumeration may make the interview time too great so that response rate and data reliability would be adversely affected. In such a case, multiphase sampling might be used. Basic information would be collected from all respondents, but information of more marginal interest, or information for which a smaller sample size would be adequate to give the required statistical precision, would be collected only from sub-samples. A common scheme is to divide the questions dealing with the non-basic data into two and to arrange that each respondent is asked only half the questions relating to this part of the survey.

ORGANIZING THE FIELDWORK

If the information collected in a survey involving interviews of small farmers is to be reliable, it is obvious that good interviewing technique is essential. The first step in this direction is the development of a good questionnaire with questions suitably arranged and worded. But questionnaire design alone is only part of the story. Enumerators must know how to approach respondents to maximize the chances of willing cooperation. Enumerators must conform with the standards of etiquette of the people being interviewed. Specially selected enumerators may have to be appointed to deal with special groups of respondents, e.g., it is best for women to be interviewed by women and particularly so in the case of women members of particular castes or religions. It will usually be necessary to spend time reassuring respondents that they have nothing to fear by answering questions truthfully and that the information provided will be treated in confidence (which, indeed, should always be the case). Good enumerators will avoid prompting respondents and will know how hard to press for an answer when one is not immediately forthcoming. They will have an ability to detect when a respondent is not telling the truth and will know what to do about it.

Good interview technique is something that can be partly taught but which also depends on the personality and experience of the enumerator. For a more complete discussion of the special problems of interviewing small farmers, see Kearl (1976).

If the survey is too large for the analyst to undertakc alone, it will be necessary to select and train enumerators. Although obviously some minimum educational standard is required for enumerators, the emphasis thereafter should be placed on selecting reliable and well-motivated people, rather than on selecting by academic achievement. If the questionnaire has been thoroughly tested during a pilot survey, the enumerators should not meet unforeseen circumstances very often and it should be possible to train them to handle the normal spectrum of responses and to report any very unusual circumstances to the analyst.

Enumerators should be given some formal instruction in their task, followed if possible by some practice in administering the questionnaire to respondents who will not be included in the final sample. When working on the survey proper, close supervision is important, especially at first. Most good enumerators learn their skills on the job.

The flow of completed questionnaires from enumerators must be monitored. Each questionnaire should be checked for completeness as soon as possible (preferably on the same day) and should be returned to the enumerator if some items are missing. Often it is possible to devise certain technical checks on the internal consistency and general reasonableness of the information. Again, any anomalies that may be found should be referred back to the enumerator. By these means the need for care in obtaining and recording data is emphasized to the enumerators. Enumerators who persistently fall short of the required standard should be replaced.

There is not much that can be said about the logistical aspects of fieldwork in farm management surveys. Transport is commonly a major problem since it will often be necessary to visit farms in remote areas, perhaps widely scattered. As noted above, special sampling techniques can be used to reduce these difficulties. Apart from these procedures, the transport and communication problems likely to be encountered in a particular survey must be solved in the context of that survey. Good planning can minimize difficulties but the researcher must also be prepared to take swift and decisive action to resolve other difficulties as they arise.

DATA PROCESSING

Processing the results of a large survey can be a considerable task. The main option is between processing by hand, usually with the aid of electronic calculators, versus processing by computer. Of course, if access to a computer is not possible, no choice exists. Without a computer, very large surveys involving substantial data processing might not be practicable. For smaller surveys, however, the option is a real one. Subject to the provisos noted below, computers are fast and reliable. Computer analysis may or may not prove cheaper than employing clerks. There are a number of problems that can occur with computer analysis:

◇ Suitable software is needed, and the types of software needed for survey analysis can be quite expensive to buy. The proper use of such software requires a person or number of people appropriately trained and experienced. These resources may not be available. If they are not, there is a not inconsiderable risk that either the analysis will not be completed in a timely way, or that some errors will be made.

◇ The data must be keyed into the computer from the questionnaires. This can be time-consuming and errors can occur.

For these sorts of reasons, it is by no means a foregone conclusion that computer data processing is always best. Non-computerized methods of analysis can be useful for processing farm surveys with small samples and with substantial qualitative information. On the other hand, the greater flexibility and reliability that is attainable once the data have been entered to a database and verified usually means that computer processing is now used for most surveys.

FAO has developed a computer software package, known as Farm Analysis Package (FARMAP), especially for the rapid and flexible processing of rural survey data (Dixon *et al.*, 1986; von Fleckenstein and Gauchon, 1992). Processing includes all the operations performed on data in the course of generating useful summaries of results. In particular, the package provides excellent capacities for data checking and aggregation. It also offers a basis for a unified system of rural data collection, analysis, storage and retrieval. FARMAP can be installed on micro-computers, and is supported by FAO, including provision of training for users.

Whichever method of data processing is adopted, it is wise to build check procedures into the analysis. A little ingenuity will indicate many opportunities. For example, highest and lowest values for selected parameters may be determined and checked to see that they are reasonable.

The appropriate form of data analysis will depend on the objectives of the study. Some of the methods commonly used are discussed in subsequent chapters.

REPORTING

As explained above, surveys are expensive to do. It follows that, when a farm management survey has been undertaken, it is important that the results and findings are made available as widely as possible to potential users of the information. These may include planners and policy makers, research and extension personnel, people in the private sector dealing with agriculture, community organizations, and the farmers themselves. The means by which information is best communicated to such diverse groups will obviously vary according to circumstances. A variety of different approaches will usually be needed to get the message across. Presentations can be made to meetings of interested groups; radio, TV or print media can be used; and so on. However, although methods of communication are important to pass on the main findings and to make potential users aware of the results, there is usually no substitute for a full report that can be read by those needing more details of the work.

The preparation of the final report is a task that should be planned for from the very start of the enquiry. It is important that sufficient time and resources are made available for the writing up. The work involved is all too easily under-estimated. The result can be that a project is completed and staff are transferred to other duties before the report is finished. Chambers (1983, pp. 53-4) gives us a word-picture of what can then happen:

> "A report is required. It has to be written late, by dispirited and exhausted researchers who have already begun new tasks. Their families do not thank them for their absences, late nights and short tempers. They stare at print-outs and tables. Under pressure for 'finding', they take figures as facts. They have neither time nor inclination to reflect that these are aggregates of what has emerged from fallible programming of fallible punching of fallible coding of responses which are what investigators wrote down as their interpretation of their instructions as to how they were to write down what they believed respondents said to them, which was only what respondents were prepared to say to them in reply to investigators' rendering of their understanding of a question and the respondent's understanding of the way they asked it; always assuming that an interview took place at all and that the answers were not more congenially compiled under a tree or in a teashop or bar, without the tiresome complication of a respondent. The distortions are legion. But mercifully, however spurious their precision, 'findings' printed out by a computer have a comforting authority. The machine launders out the pollutions of the field and delivers of a clean product, which looks even cleaner and more comfortingly accurate when transferred to tables and text. These 'findings' are artifacts, a partial, cloudy and distorted view of the real rural world. But in the report they are, they have to be, facts."

Chambers is taking an extreme view here, but there is more than a grain of truth in what he says. Good planning from the start of a survey, proper monitoring of its execution, careful processing of the data, and an honest, realistic interpretation of the results will go a long way to avoiding the criticism of the survey approach in the remarks quoted above. But it is also important that the survey report is written up carefully, giving due attention to the limitations of the data collection methods. Results should be interpreted with caution, reservations noted, and spurious accuracy avoided. Yet the report must not be too long, or it will never be read by many of the busy people who would find its contents useful. A useful compromise is to prepare a fairly detailed executive summary of the main report, well cross-referenced to the main text, so that readers can get the main message easily and quickly, and can be directed to more detailed explanations when they need them.

None of the above provides much guidance on how the report itself should be written. Good writing is an art that it would be pretentious for us to attempt to teach here. Most of us find writing painful, and the goal of good style in written work is something for which we must constantly strive. A few principles are, nevertheless, worth mentioning.

First, plan the report carefully. Work out what is to be said and in what order. The chances are that the plans will evolve as the work of writing progresses, but the final product will be improved by good, adaptive planning. Second, have in mind the intended audience and try to write for them. The aim is to communicate, not to show how clever you are (nor to hide the deficiencies of what you have done under a camouflage of words). This usually means writing short, plain sentences. Third, be prepared to redraft what you have written in the light of reviews by yourself or others. Most well-written documents go through several drafts.

The report should describe the genesis of the study, the research aims, the methods used, such as the sampling procedure and the ways the data were collected, the results obtained (together with indications of their statistical reliability), and the conclusions that are drawn from those results. Implications of the results for farmers, the community, research and extension programmes, or planners and policy makers may be drawn out. The limitations of the work should be honestly appraised and the scope for further investigations pointed out. So far as possible, the basic data used should be included as appendices.

2.5 *Village studies*

Rather than sampling individual farms, it may sometimes be fruitful and relevant to conduct farm management surveys on a village basis. Data collection may then be undertaken, as relevant, for some items on a full village basis and for other items on a farm sample basis within the village. Further, the villages to be used may be selected by sampling after stratification so as to constitute a set of benchmark villages reflecting major characteristics of interest in terms of agro-climatic (climate, soil type, etc.) and socio-economic (farm size, infrastructure, etc.) attributes.

An excellent example, though rather more detailed than normal, is provided by the Benchmark Village Level Studies project of the International Crops Research Institute for the Semi-Arid Tropics (ICRISAT) (Jodha *et al.*, 1977). Aims of this project were to gain a thorough understanding of traditional farming systems in the semi-arid tropics of India, including identification of constraints on food production and development at the micro (farm and village) level, and to provide a basis for on-farm testing of new technology. Six benchmark villages were selected purposively taking into account 40 characteristics (climate, soil, location, land use, etc.) judged relevant on a benchmark basis. So as to ensure purposeful and efficient data collection, a set of eight prior hypotheses about traditional farming in the semi-arid tropics of India were formulated for testing

(Binswanger *et al.*, 1977). Socio-economic, farm management and agro-biological data were collected in each village. Table 2.1 shows the frequency with which agro-economic data were collected - based for most items on a stratified random sample of 30 farmer households and 10 landless labourers in each village. Analysis of the collected data is given by Walker and Ryan (1990). Obviously, studies of such a detailed continuing nature are very demanding in terms of research resources and would be beyond the means of most research institutions.

2.6 Farm recording schemes

Farm recording schemes may be divided into those schemes that are designed primarily as a service to participating farmers by providing them with information useful in decision making, and those schemes designed primarily as a source of data for more general farm management research purposes. Clearly, the latter kind of scheme is really a special kind of survey. It is usually distinguished from the typical survey by the fact that cooperators are likely to be specially selected on the basis of their willingness to cooperate with the research agency on a continuing basis. The distinction between the two types of recording scheme becomes somewhat blurred by the common practice of providing participants with management information from their records and from the records of other participants as a reward for their cooperation.

RECORDING SYSTEMS

Schemes vary in the extent to which the job of recording the required information is left to the participating farmers. Farmers may be expected to keep all the basic records, perhaps with close supervision from a field officer, or the field officers may visit the farmers regularly to collect and record the required information. Some schemes have been devised in which the records are kept by an agency such as a cooperative through which the farmers trade.

In order to monitor the recording process and to provide for rapid feedback of processed data to participants, regular submission of recorded data is normally required. Many so-called budgetary control schemes involve a regular matching of recorded progress against a budget. These schemes depend for their success on rapid processing of the recorded information and speedy return to participants of a statement of the processed data compared with the budget. Ideally this statement should indicate what actions the farmer should take to correct any faults or to exploit any opportunities revealed by the comparison.

THE INFORMATION RECORDED AND ITS USES

The information recorded may be physical information, financial information, or both. It may be on a whole-farm basis or may relate to some particular aspect of the farm, such as a specific enterprise, or may extend to the combined farm-household system. It may relate to task allocation by gender or to the timing of operations.

For small farmers, simpler recording systems are to be preferred. Records are more likely to be faithfully kept if participants can see their direct relevance to the decisions they face. Some very simple budgetary control procedures, based largely on

Table 2.1

DETAILS OF THE SCHEDULES USED FOR COLLECTING AGRO-ECONOMIC DATA IN ICRISAT'S BENCHMARK VILLAGE STUDIES

Type of schedule	Frequency	Remarks
Household census	Once	For all resident households; demographic, occupational, landholding and livestock possession detail.
Household member schedule	Annually	More details of above type for sample households; details about each member.
Plot and crop rotation schedule	Updated annually	Recorded physical and ownership status of farm plots; use status (fallow, cropped, double cropped, crop rotation during different seasons).
Animal inventory	Annually	Recorded sample households' position in terms of assets.
Farm implement inventory	-do-	-do-
Farm building inventory	-do-	-do-
Cultivation schedule	Every 15-20 days	Recorded plotwise input-output details for each crop for each season.
Labour, draught animal and machinery utilization schedule	-do-	Recorded actual utilization of these resources on the day preceding the interview; number of wage employment days, days of involuntary unemployment (for family labour and bullocks) during the period since last interview.
Household transactions schedule	-do-	Recorded type and value of every transaction involving inflow and outflow of cash, goods and services for sample households.
Price and wage schedule	Monthly	Recorded type and value of every transaction involving inflow and outflow of cash, goods and services for sample households.
Stock inventory, credit and debt schedule	Annually	Recorded inventory of stocks of food grains, fodder, consumer durables, savings, deposits, debt and credit position of sample households.

Table 2.1 (continued)

Type of schedule	Frequency	Remarks
Kinship and social exchange schedule	Every 15-20 days	Recorded details on the social networks behind exchange for sample households. (Incorporated with household transactions schedule.)
Risk investigation schedules	Sequence of six weekly interviews	Recorded farmers' preferences with respect to suggested weekly decision alternatives with varying degrees of gain and uncertainty of prospects; actual decisions and actions about farming; adjustment devices to meet consequence of drought, etc., for sample households.
Risk-attitude experiment schedule	-do-	Recorded farmers' actual choices resulting from their participation in risk game designed for the purpose.
Time-allocation studies schedule	Once every quarter	Recorded actual pattern of activities by all members of households of a subsample by constant observation for one day in each of the seasonal rounds.
Diet survey schedule	-do-	Recorded through actual measurement and observation of the items consumed by each member of the sample households.
Health status schedule	-do-	For all members of sample households, recorded nutritional deficiencies, disease symptoms and other issues related to health status using methods suggested by health and nutrition experts.
Demographic schedule	Once	Data to determine age-specific fertility of women and to indicate normal completed family sizes for all resident households.

physical records, can be very effective. For example, in intensive pig production, a budgetary control scheme based on records of breeding and fattening performance of the stock and of feed input, both measured in physical terms, and matched against target performance, tailored for individual farm circumstances, can provide a useful guide to action. The logic of such schemes lies in the fact that they target technical efficiency over which a farmer has most direct management control in the short run. Movements in the prices of inputs and outputs are generally beyond the farmer's control and it is not usually possible for immediate adjustments in farm organization or methods to be made in response to such price movements.

Budgetary control schemes based on financial data are normally operated on a monthly cash-flow basis. Actual net cash-flow each month is matched against some target and the reasons for deviations from the target are analyzed. For small farms there is much to recommend the inclusion of all domestic payments and receipts, including farm and non-farm items, in such records. The distinction between domestic payments, such as school fees, and farm payments, such as land tax, is an arbitrary one that has no real meaning to most small-farm families.

Some farm recording schemes do not incorporate the element of frequent feedback of information to participants. Instead the records are processed only at year's end. An annual summary for the farm may be prepared showing gross income and expenditure and some measures of profitability. This information may be given to the farmer, perhaps with some comparison between her or his own results and those of other participating farmers (see Section 3.4 below). Averages may be computed from the recorded data for groups of broadly similar farms and this information may be used for the comparisons noted above. It may also serve as a useful basis for farm planning work or for policy-oriented work relating, for example, to maintaining or improving rural incomes.

2.7 *Farm case studies*

Many issues in farm management can only be understood if the researcher has a detailed understanding of farm circumstances. To predict how farmers might react to specific policy changes may require intimate study of the realities of farm production and of farmers' attitudes. To collect such data from a large sample of farms might be too expensive. A case-study approach may be the only one possible in such circumstances.

The case-study approach involves intensive detailed study of only one or, more usually, of a few farms. The objective of this study is to learn, not only what is happening on the study farms, but why, i.e., to elucidate the cause and effect relationships that operate. This process of elucidation is often facilitated by studying more than one case. Two or three contrasting cases, by their very differences, may make it easier to identify important factors leading to the results observed.

Once an understanding of cause and effect relationships has been gained, the next step is to try to extrapolate to the population of interest. This extrapolation process is quite unlike the process of inferring from a sample to the population from which the sample was drawn. It is a process requiring judgement and experience. Obviously, a good knowledge of the relevant features of the farms in the population of concern helps in drawing inferences. For example, if the case studies reveal that the land/labour ratio is a critical factor influencing the profitability of adopting some new technology, it is very helpful to know the distribution of land/labour ratios in the population of farms if one is trying to draw conclusions about the probable extent of adoption of the technology. For this reason it is often useful to combine case studies with a simple survey to collect data on the distribution of key attributes in the population of concern.

2.8 Experiments

Experimentation in the social sciences may not be possible, or is at best difficult to organize. However, in the agricultural sciences experimentation is the main method by which knowledge is advanced. Farm management is located at the interface between the social and the biological sciences, and the farm management researcher should be able to cooperate with agricultural scientists in the design, conduct and interpretation of agricultural experiments to elucidate selected problems in farm production. No attempt is made here to review the complex issues of experimental methodology. Rather, a few comments are offered on experimentation from the perspective of farm management research.

As a source of farm management data, experiments have some important advantages. Input-output relationships can be elucidated by experiments in which the level of a selected input (or inputs) is varied while other inputs, so far as possible, are held constant. Inputs and outputs can be carefully observed and recorded to reduce recording errors to a minimum. By replication, statistical measures of the reliability of the results and of the significance of differences between treatments can be calculated.

Despite the above formidable advantages, experimentation has its drawbacks. In particular, it is usually expensive in terms of both managerial and physical resources. Most agricultural production processes involve the use of many inputs which interact one with another in determining the level of output achieved. Mainly for reasons of cost, and to avoid impossible complexity in experimental design, most experiments are constructed to elucidate the effects of varying only one or two input factors at a time. The danger in such work is that important interactive effects between the varied factors and others may not be revealed. Also, it is obviously important to select for experimentation those factors bearing most strongly on output and performance. There may be difficulties in identifying these factors or, once identified, they may not be factors amenable to investigation experimentally. For example, factors like quality of seed or standard of weed control may be difficult to measure quantitatively and to manipulate for experimental purposes. Likewise the effect of variations in climate over space and time may severely restrict the generality that can be attached to experimental results.

It has become clear that the chief limitation of most traditional on-station agricultural experimentation is that it is conducted under conditions quite unlike those faced by farmers. At least in the past, there was a tendency for experiments to be undertaken with very high levels of management by the standards of small farmers, and even with luxury levels of inputs not directly under study. Even today, it is not unusual to read of experiments in which the response to, say, nitrogen fertilizer is investigated with other soil nutrients not limiting, i.e., applied to a level of abundance that may be quite out of proportion to what is either normal or profitable on farms. The results of such an experiment may be almost useless for farm management purposes. Not only will the recorded yields be quite different to those achieved by farmers, but the marginal response to nitrogen may be quite different under experimental and farm conditions.

It was the growing recognition of the irrelevance of much on-station research to farmers' circumstances that led to the development of the farming systems research (FSR) approach, outlined in Chapter 1. The conduct of on-farm trials (OFTs) is one of the major distinguishing features of the FSR approach. Such trials provide the conduit that links researchers with reality. The scientists can try to test their ideas about improved ways of doing things under actual farm conditions. It is recognized in the FSR approach that the ultimate measure of success in a research programme is whether the technologies being developed are taken up by farmers. But a successful programme of OFTs may not lead directly to adoption - rather it will point up new problems that demand on-station work. By working with farmers, the research workers will come to a better understanding of the nature of the problems that have to be solved, thus making the whole research effort more relevant.

On-farm trials may be organized in different ways, according to circumstances (Farrington and Martin, 1987). Sometimes the trials are conducted by the researcher in farmers' fields; alternatively, they may be executed by farmers' themselves, with greater or lesser levels of supervision. Often (and usually desirably), extension personnel may be involved in the liaison with farmers. Sometimes, the FSR programme will meet any additional cash costs for the trial while the farmer is allowed to keep the produce. In some circumstances it may be necessary to guarantee the yield obtained.

Naturally, the OFTs generally need to be kept fairly simple. The number of treatments investigated must usually be restricted to two or three, and replication on the individual farmer's field is seldom possible. If replication is judged to be necessary, it must usually be achieved across several farms. However, it can be argued that the usual statistical arguments for replication are not relevant to OFTs. The aim, after all, is to develop a technology that will be taken up by farmers. If the improvement over the control is so small and uncertain that it can be detected only via a fully replicated trial, the new method is unlikely to be widely adopted.

As noted in Chapter 1, FSR requires a team approach and farm management workers are often needed as members of such teams. One role of the farm management worker in relation to OFTs is to assist in planning the programme. According to Tripp and Wooley (1989), this planning process involves:

- ◇ identifying problems limiting the productivity of the farming system;
- ◇ ranking the problems;
- ◇ identifying causes of the problems;
- ◇ analyzing interrelations among problems and causes;
- ◇ identifying possible solutions to the problems; and
- ◇ evaluating possible solutions.

The farm management worker may be involved in all these stages, but especially in the identification of problems through the analysis of the performance of the target farming systems. In addition, the farm management worker is likely to be responsible for the economic evaluation of possible solutions, including the results of OFTs.

Data obtained from OFTs are much more reliable as a basis for budgeting than similar data from on-station research. Evaluation of new technologies typically involves some budgeting, either in a partial framework, as discussed in Chapters 5 and 6 below, or, if the technology has far-reaching implications for the target farming systems, in a whole-system framework, using the whole-farm planning methods discussed in Chapter 4 below.

2.9 *Collecting other types of data*

The farm management researcher will often need to employ a wide variety of types of data, relating not only to farms and farm production, but to aspects of marketing, supply of agricultural inputs, the institutional framework of agriculture, and so on (Epstein, Gruber and Mytton, 1991). In this section a brief review of the main types of data likely to be useful for farm management research purposes is provided, together with a few comments on possible sources of such data.

Data on prices can often be obtained from published sources such as newspapers or from official market records. It is usually wise to investigate exactly what such data represent, how they are collected and how reliable they are. Price quotations in local markets may be higher than actual prices if bargaining is common. Similarly, afternoon prices may be different from morning prices if there is under- or over-supply. Farmers who sell to middlemen may get appreciably less than reported market prices and even when purchases are by a statutory body at a fixed price, transport and other transaction costs can mean that net farm receipts are far less than the quoted price.

If such price data do not exist, it may be the job of the farm management researcher to organize their collection. More commonly, the researcher will have to engage in collecting data from local suppliers on the prices of agricultural inputs such as fertilizer, sprays and stockfeeds. Most importantly, for farm management projects involving planning, the researcher will need to draw on and interpret outlook data to be able to make forecasts of future costs and prices.

Institutional information of importance in farm management studies can relate to such aspects as credit or land tenure; marketing arrangements such as quotas, contracts or purchasing schemes; the supply of irrigation water, electric power or other inputs; taxation; and so on. For some studies, information on regional demography, employment and income distribution may be needed. Because the farm management researcher is oriented towards problems at the micro level, not only may she or he need to employ these kinds of data in the analyses, but also the researcher is in a unique position to appraise the impact and effectiveness of institutional policies. Consequently, a part of the work can be to offer advice to, say, a credit agency or a statutory marketing body on how they can implement their programmes more effectively and on how their policies might be revised to better achieve specified development goals.

2.10 *Standardization in farm management data collection*

As should be clear from the preceding discussion, the types of data collected for farm management research purposes are highly variable. The data gathered will be dictated by the objective of the study. Although standardized data collection procedures have some advantages, discussed below, they also have some potential dangers. Standardization can lead to stereotyped thinking with information being collected for its own sake rather than as part of a process of solving relevant problems. When a particular research objective has been defined, standardized data collection formats may be found to be unsuitable because they omit certain relevant aspects, or include unnecessary aspects.

On the other hand, standardization has some important advantages. Much the same information is needed for many farm management research purposes and it is wasteful for each researcher to have to design a data collection questionnaire entirely from scratch. If a standardized form is available, much time can be saved and the risk of omitting necessary items can be minimized. Standardization can also be valuable in facilitating comparison of data collected by different researchers and in permitting routine processing of the information gathered. By ensuring compatibility of format of data, standardization permits the establishment of a national computerized farm management data bank which can be used as a source of reference data.

Standardized approaches to data collection and analysis can incorporate considerable flexibility in nature of data points collected and amount of detail recorded. For instance, the FAO FARMAP data and code structure is designed to be used at several different levels of aggregation, e.g., plot, crop or farm - see Dixon *et al.* (1986) and von Fleckenstein and Gauchon (1992). Yet the benefits of a standard code structure are retained. Because of the emphasis on matching the questionnaires to the particular purposes of the survey, and to local farming systems, no standard proformas are supplied.

A particular advantage of standardization relates to definitions of terms used in farm management research. There is an unfortunate tendency for proliferation of terms. Worse still, different researchers may assign different meanings to the same term. Thus opportunities for results to be misinterpreted arise and communication between researchers with similar interests is impeded. Some standardization of terminology is therefore to be strongly recommended. The glossary of farm management terms developed by the FAO (1985) is therefore recommended as an important aid to avoiding confusion.

2.11 References

BINSWANGER, H.P., N.S. JODHA, J.G. RYAN & M. VON OPPEN (1977). *Approach and Hypotheses for the Village Level Studies of ICRISAT*, Occasional Paper 15, Economics Programme, ICRISAT, Hyderabad.

CGPRT (1986). *Socio-economic Research on Food Legumes and Coarse Grains: Methodological Issues*, CGPRT Centre of the Economic and Social Commission for Asia and the Pacific of the United Nations, Bogor.

CHAMBERS, R. (1983). *Rural Development: Putting the Last First*, Longman, Harlow.

COCHRAN, W.G. (1963). *Sampling Techniques*, 2nd edn, Wiley, New York.

DIXON, J.M. *et al.* (1986). *FARMAP User's Manual, Vols 1-3*, Food and Agriculture Organization of the United Nations, Rome.

EPSTEIN, T.S., J. GRUBER & G. MYTTON, (1991). *A Training Manual for Development Market Research (DMR) Investigations*, BBC World Service, London.

FAO (1985). *Farm Management Glossary*, Agricultural Services Bulletin 63, Food and Agriculture Organization of the United Nations, Rome.

FARRINGTON, J. & A. MARTIN (1987). *Farmer Participatory Research: A Review of Concepts and Practices*, Discussion Paper 19, Agricultural Administration Unit, Overseas Development Institute, London.

FELDSTEIN, H.S., C.B. FLORA & S.V. POATS (1990). *The Gender Variable in Agricultural Research*, IDRC-MR225e, International Development Research Centre, Ottawa.

JODHA, N.S., M. ASOKAN & J.G. RYAN (1977). *Village Study Methodology and Resource Endowments of Selected Villages in ICRISAT's Village Level Studies*, Occasional Paper 16, Economics Programme, ICRISAT, Hyderabad.

KEARL, B. (ed.) (1976). *Field Data Collection in the Social Sciences*, Agricultural Development Council, Inc., New York.

McCRACKEN, J.A., J.N. PRETTY, & G.R.CONWAY (1988). *An Introduction to Rapid Rural Appraisal for Agricultural Development*, International Institute for Environment and Development, London.

MOLNAR, A. (1989). *A Review of Rapid Rural Appraisal Tools for Use in Natural Resource Management Planning and Project Design and Execution*, Forest Department, Food and Agriculture Organization of the United Nations, Rome.

MURPHY, J. (1990). *Women and Agriculture in Africa: A Guide to Bank Policy and Programs for Operations Staff*, World Bank, Washington D.C.

PAREL, C.P., G.C. CALDITO, P.L. FERRER, G.G. DE GUZMAN, C.S. SINSIOCO & R.H. TAN (1973). *Sampling Design and Procedures*, Agricultural Development Council, Inc., New York.

RAPA (1989). *Guidelines for Farming Systems Development Programmes*, Regional Office for Asia and the Pacific of the Food and Agriculture Organization of the United Nations, Bangkok.

RUSSO, S., J. BREMER-FOX, S. POATS & L. GRAIG (1989). *Gender Issues in Agriculture and Natural Resource Management*, USAID, Washington, D.C.

SOM, R.K. (1973). *A Manual of Sampling Techniques*, Heinemann, London.

SRINIVAS, M.N. (1974). *Village Living: A Source of Insights for the Social Scientist*, A/D/C Teaching Forum No. 35, Agricultural Development Council, Inc., New York.

TRIPP, R. & J. WOOLEY (1989). *The Planning Stage of On-Farm Research: Identifying Factors for Experimentation*, CIMMYT & CIAT, Mexico City and Cali.

VON FLECKENSTEIN, F. & J.M. GAUCHON (1992). *The FAO Farm Analysis Package, FARMAP, Reference Manual*, Food and Agriculture Organization of the United Nations, Rome.

WALKER, T.S. & J.G. RYAN (1990). *Village and Household Economies in India's Semi-Arid Tropics*, Johns Hopkins University Press, Baltimore.

3. SIMPLE DATA ANALYSIS

In this chapter some of the simpler ways of analyzing and presenting the types of data normally collected for farm management purposes are described. In many research studies, simple tabulations and comparisons of the data collected will suffice to meet the research objectives. Often such simple analyses will be all that are possible with the analytical resources available. At other times more advanced methods of interpreting and using the data may be needed, but even so, preliminary analysis along the lines described below will generally be an essential first step.

The chapter begins with a review of some general principles and methods relating to the presentation of data in an informative way. Though simple, these principles of data presentation are extremely important in order to ensure good communication in research reporting. The elementary material on tabular and pictorial representation of data in Section 3.1 can be skipped by readers already familiar with the topics covered. The following two sections then deal with generally applicable measures of farm performance. Section 3.4 contains some comments on the technique known as comparative analysis whereby farms' performances are compared either with a standard or with one another. Finally, in Section 3.5, the application of computers in farm management data analysis is briefly reviewed.

3.1 Tabular and graphical analysis

The first step in tabular or graphical analyses is the construction of a system of classification of the data. Appropriate criteria for classification will be determined by the nature of the research problem under study and by features of the data themselves. In the latter regard a distinction can be drawn between discrete and continuous variables.

TYPES OF VARIABLES

A discrete variable can take only a finite number of possible values. These values may be numerical, e.g., number of children, or they may be non-numerical, e.g., true or false, principal crop grown, gender, etc. On the other hand, a continuous variable, which for practical purposes is always numerical, can in theory take an infinite number of possible values within some (perhaps unlimited) feasible range. Examples of continuous variables are yield per hectare, farm size, age of household head.

In practice, continuous variables are treated as discrete, usually because of the limited precision of measurement. For example, yields may be reported to the nearest kilogram per hectare, farm size to the nearest 0.1 hectare and age may be reported in years only. Thus the distinction between discrete and continuous variables becomes blurred in practice. Nonetheless the fundamental difference between the two types of variable should be kept in mind since it is important in determining class boundaries in frequency distributions.

DEFINING CLASSES

Classification of data, by definition, requires segregation of the data into classes according to the value of one or more variables. For numerical variables, class intervals must be defined. It is usually desirable to make these intervals of uniform size. Moreover, the number of intervals must be sufficient to reveal any relevant patterns in the data, but there should not be so many intervals as to make interpretation difficult through unnecessary complexity and detail. If possible, intervals should be expressed in familiar and convenient numbers such as 5s or 10s.

In drawing up tables, class intervals must be mutually exclusive so that the data are expressed unambiguously. Thus it is not satisfactory to define intervals of, e.g.,0 to 10, 10 to 20, etc.; rather they should be, e.g., 0 to < 10, 10 to < 20, etc. which for a discrete variable implies 0 to 9, 10 to 19, etc. For continuous variables the class intervals should be consistent with the accuracy of measurement of the original data. If farm area was measured to the nearest 0.1 ha, class intervals should also be defined to one decimal place, e.g., 0.0 to 0.9, 1.0 to 1.9, etc. Not only should class intervals be mutually exclusive, but they should also, as far as possible, be collectively exhaustive of all possibilities. In particular, it is desirable to include a category *not ascertained* to accommodate any missing observations.

TYPES OF TABLES

It is useful to distinguish between general purpose or reference tables and special purpose or interpretative tables.

A *general purpose table* is constructed either to present a summary overview or to present a large amount of primary data in a convenient form. In the latter case, it will normally be included as an appendix to a report, its purpose being to provide users with access to the primary data so that they can make their own analyses and interpretations. A general purpose table may also be used by the researcher as part of the process of developing an appropriate form of analysis to meet the research objectives.

Special purpose tables, on the other hand, represent a more advanced stage in the analysis. They are chosen to illustrate some specific point or points about the data forming part of the logical investigation of the research objectives. The researcher will need to give careful thought to the format of special purpose tables to see that they convey the relevant information in the best possible way. The data in special purpose tables may be processed as averages, percentages, index numbers or in any other relevant way to meet the need for clarification or emphasis of specific aspects.

Table 3.1

EXAMPLE OF A GENERAL PURPOSE TABLE SHOWING THE DISTRIBUTION OF EXPENDITURES ON INPUTS FOR POTATO PRODUCTION IN VARIOUS AREAS

Area	Cost (US$/ha)	Distribution (%)					
		Seed	Labour	Fertilizers	Pesticides	Power, equipment fuel[a]	Total[b]
				Highland Areas			
Ruhengeri, Rwanda	300	38	62	0	0	0	100
Kenya	600	21	54	12	7	6	100
Sabana de Bogota, Colombia	1200	24	34	22	14	6	100
Benguet, Philippines	1900	55	16	17	10	2	100
Quezaltenango, Guatemala	1500	53	10	17	15	5	100
				Lowland Areas			
Cañete, Peru	1700	38	20	17	11	14	100
Dhaka, Bangladesh	2000	37	27	20	15	1	100
Punjab, India	na[c]	45	27	18	6	4	100
				Temperate Areas			
Puerto Varas, Chile	2400	33	15	21	31	0	100
South Korea	na[c]	32	38	3	26	1	100

[a] Includes draft animals, tractors, tools and implements.
[b] May not add to 100 due to rounding.
[c] Not available.

Source: Horton (1987, p.121).

Table 2.1 of Chapter 2 is an example of a general purpose table aimed at providing a summary overview. A further example, providing data of a more numerical nature, is given in Table 3.1. Examples of special purpose tables are provided in Tables 3.2 and 3.3.

In addition to their purpose - general or specific - tables can be classified according to their dimensions. The dimensions of a table specify the number of variables according to which the data in the table are classified. Thus, a one-dimensional or one-way table includes data classified according to only one variable, while in a two-dimensional or two-way table, two variables are used for classification, and so on. In practice, a four-dimensional table is about as complicated as one can expect most readers to grasp. Even so, it is usually better to break down tables involving three or more dimensions into simpler presentations whenever possible.

Table 3.2 is an example of a two-dimensional table, while a simple three-dimensional table (which also exemplifies an aspect of gender analysis) is illustrated in Table 3.3.

Table 3.2

EXAMPLE OF A TWO-DIMENSIONAL SPECIAL-PURPOSE TABLE SHOWING AVERAGE LEVELS OF INCOME BY FREQUENCY OF WAGE ACTIVITY OF SURVEYED HOUSEHOLDS AT KARIMUI, PNG

Wage activity	Low[a] K/ae/2w[b]	High[a] K/ae/2w[b]
Cash receipts:		
- wages	1.04	3.70
- cash crops	0.37	0.30
- animals	0.09	0.32
- food sales	0.53	0.45
- store revenue	0.51	0.38
- exchange received	1.90	2.72
Sub-total	4.44	7.87
Subsistence income	7.46	6.13
Total income	11.90	14.00

[a] The observations were categorised into two groups (each of 87 observations) according as the level of wage income per adult equivalent was below or above the median value.
[b] Kina per adult equivalent per two weeks.

Source: Adapted from Finlayson, McComb, Hardaker and Heywood (1991, p.127).

FORMAT OF TABLES

The general format of tables has been illustrated in the examples given above. This format is summarized in a generalized form in Figure 3.1 which also indicates the terms applied to different parts of a table.

All tables should be numbered, either consecutively through the report or using the notation *a.b* for the *b-th* table of chapter *a*, e.g., Table 3.1 is the first table in Chapter 3. Using this system, appendix tables would be numbered in the style *Ac.d*, indicating the *d-th* table in Appendix *C*, e.g., Table A1.4 would be the fourth table in Appendix 1.

The caption of the table should be as brief as possible but should clearly describe the contents of the table. Similarly, the headings in the boxhead and the stub should be brief but informative. The boxhead contains the headings of all the columns in the table and the stub contains the headings of all the rows.

Tables usually have a neater appearance if horizontal rules are used above and below the boxhead and at the foot of the table. In multi-dimensional tables, horizontal rules may also be used within the boxhead to indicate further levels of classification. (See Table 3.3 for an example.) Vertical rules should be used only if necessary for clarity.

Table 3.3

EXAMPLE OF A THREE-DIMENSIONAL SPECIAL-PURPOSE TABLE SHOWING LABOUR ACTIVITIES IN DAYS PER HECTARE OF MEN AND WOMEN IN BEAN PRODUCTION IN LA MERCED, COLOMBIA

Activity	Variety			
	Traditional		Improved	
	Men (d/ha)	Women (d/ha)	Men (d/ha)	Women (d/ha)
Land preparation	13.0	-	13.0	-
Planting and fertilization	12.5	0.5	11.5	0.5
Hilling, top dressing, weeding	25.0	-	21.0	-
Spraying	25.0	-	13.0	-
Harvest and postharvest	4.5	13.5	4.5	27.5
Seed preparation	-	3.0	-	5.0
Marketing	1.0	-	2.0	-
Total	81.0	17.0	65.0	33.0

Source: Adapted from van Herpen and Ashby (1991, p.9).

Footnotes are used to indicate sources of data, to record any qualifications or exceptions, or to convey any other essential information not incorporated in the table itself. Footnotes may be general (e.g., indicating the general data source) or may be tied to particular headings or entries by superscripts, as in Tables 3.1 and 3.2, or by bracketed lower-case letters (a), (b), (c), etc. Lower-case superscripts, e.g.[a], [b], etc., are recommended if feasible since they avoid confusion with powers of numbers when attached to numerical entries. Asterisks are conventionally used to indicate levels of statistical significance.

INTERPRETATION OF TABLES

While at least special purpose tables should be largely self-explanatory, it will always be necessary to provide some explanation of each table in the text. No table should be provided that is not specifically referred to and, except for appendix tables, discussed in the main text. The discussion should draw attention to the main points or relationships illustrated in the table. Sometimes the construction of the table itself may need to be described, while the main features can often be illustrated and explained by means of examples drawn from the table. Any relationships revealed in a table might be explored further in subsequent tables or other analyses.

Figure 3.1

GENERALIZED FORMAT OF A TABLE

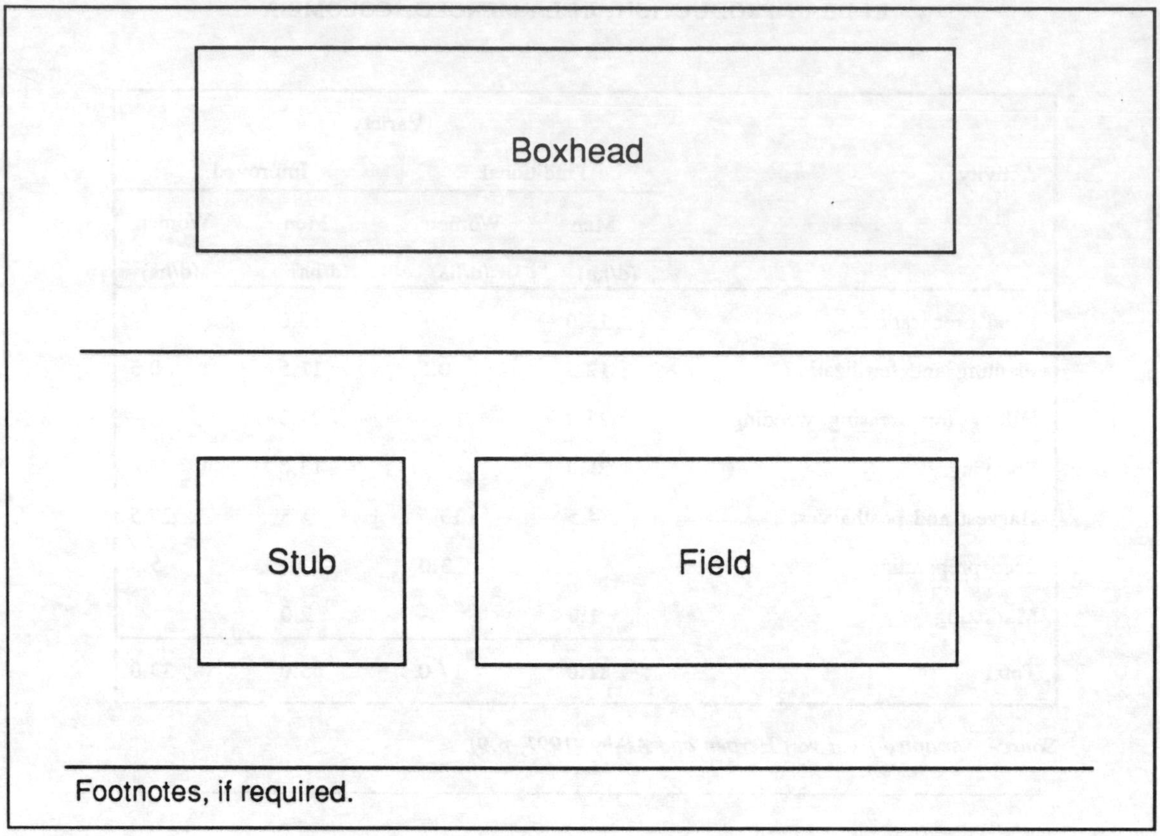

When using tables to analyze the results of a survey based on a probability sample, apparent differences in averages between classes in the data, or departures of observed frequencies from expected, should be tested for statistical significance. The t test can be used to compare means while the chi-square test is appropriate for comparing actual with expected frequencies. The methods of computing the necessary statistics for these tests and the application of these and other statistical methods to tabulated data are topics beyond the scope of this manual. Researchers engaged in such work who may need guidance on appropriate statistical methods are referred to any of the many good introductory texts on statistics such as Bishop (1983).

PICTORIAL REPRESENTATION OF DATA

It has been well said that a good picture tells a story better than a thousand words. Pictorial representation can also be used with equal advantage in place of a tabular analysis. Pictorial representation of data can often be used to clarify or emphasize relationships in the data and to provide the reader with a grasp of the data as a totality without she or he having to study all the individual values.

Producing graphs by hand can be quite time-consuming and requires a fairly high degree of skill if it is to be done well. However, as discussed in Section 3.5 below, modern graphical packages for PCs have greatly speeded up the process of preparing high quality graphs. These packages typically provide a wide range of options for the form of presentation. Among the most commonly used are graphs, scatter diagrams, histograms, bar charts, pie charts and frequency distributions. The examples in this chapter have all been produced using a PC-based graphics package.

A *graph* is drawn on two axes, representing two quantitative variables or dimensions. Graphical presentation is appropriate when there is a continuum in the data so that points representing paired observations of the two variables may be connected by a line. For example, a variable such as price may be plotted against time. Sometimes more than two variables may be included on the same graph, perhaps to show an association between two variables with a third. For example, Figure 3.2 is drawn to allow a comparison of trends over time in wholesale potato prices in Bangladesh. Note that it is usually unwise to include more than two or three variables on the same graph since the main advantage of pictorial representation is lost if a graph is made too complicated.

Figure 3.2

GRAPHS SHOWING THREE-YEAR MOVING AVERAGE OF WHOLESALE POTATO PRICES IN BANGLADESH (Horton, 1987, p.76)

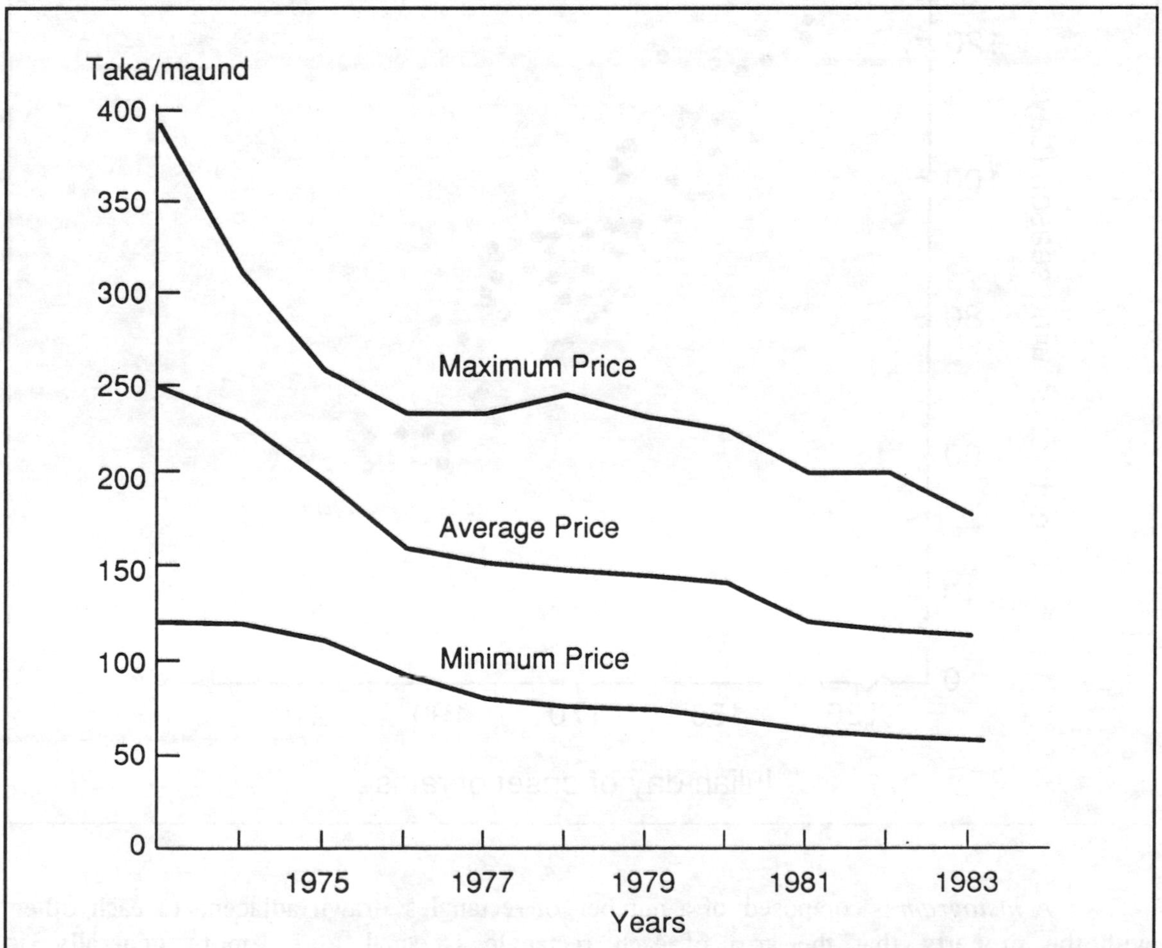

Scatter diagrams are appropriate when it is wished to show the extent of association between two variables in the data but when no clear continuum exists. The scatter diagram shows the effect of random and other effects in the data. It allows the reader to assess visually the extent to which the two plotted variables are associated. Often a statistically fitted regression line may be plotted as a graph on the scatter diagram. Alternatively, a straight line or curve fitted by eye may be adequate to emphasize an association between the variables in a scatter diagram. Figure 3.3, for example, shows the association between the length of the growing season and the date when the rainy season begins at ICRISAT's Sahelian Centre in Niger. Each dot represents one annual observation and a regression line through the points allows the nature of association to be quantified.

Figure 3.3

SCATTER DIAGRAM SHOWING ASSOCIATION BETWEEN SEASONAL RAINFALL AND DATE OF ONSET OF RAINS AT ICRISAT SAHELIAN CENTRE, NIGER

(Monteith and Virmani, 1991, p.186)

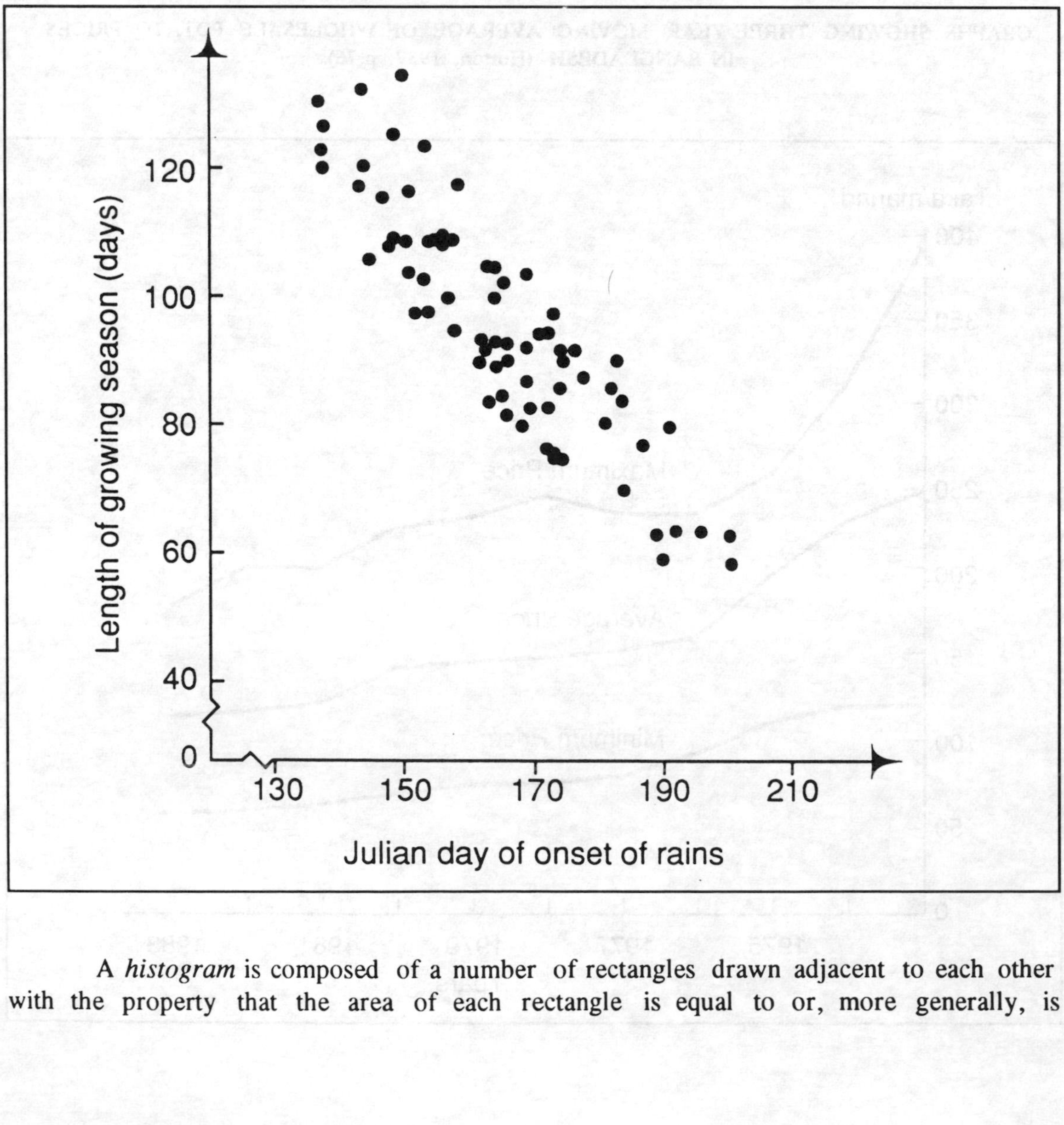

A *histogram* is composed of a number of rectangles drawn adjacent to each other with the property that the area of each rectangle is equal to or, more generally, is

proportional to the frequency of observations in the class interval represented by the width of the rectangle. Thus a histogram is useful in indicating the nature of the underlying frequency distribution. An example is provided in Figure 3.4.

Figure 3.4

HISTOGRAM SHOWING DISTRIBUTION OF HOUSEHOLDS ACCORDING TO FOOD COST, KINDA WATERSHED, MYANMAR (Thein *et al.*, 1990, p.30)

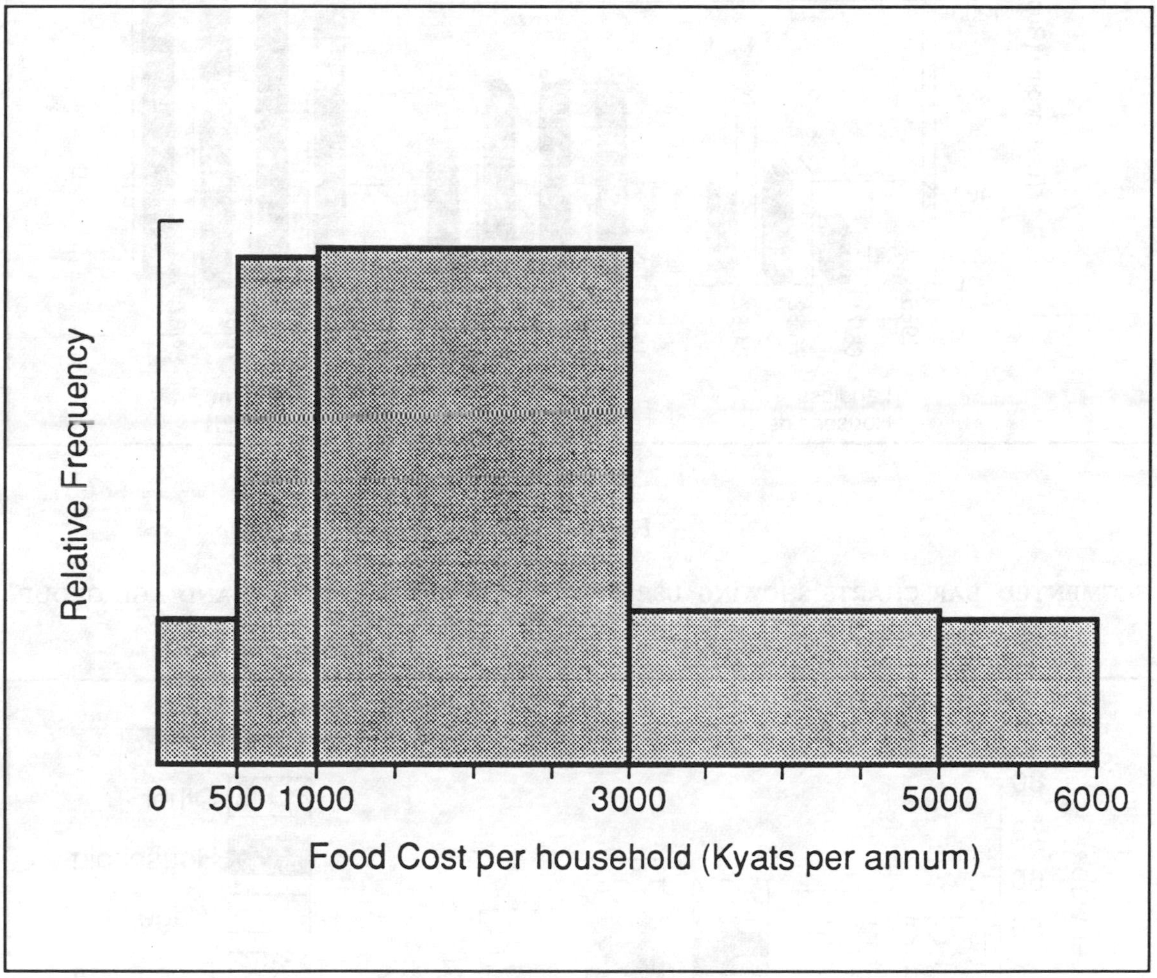

In a *bar chart* the sizes of different classes within the data are represented by bars of fixed width but of length proportional to the magnitude or frequency to be represented. This contrasts with the histogram where frequencies are represented by areas. When a bar chart is to be used to represent the magnitude of two or more variables, the bars may be shaded in different ways. Again, the advantages of pictorial representation can be lost if too many variables are included on the same chart. Figure 3.5 is an example of a bar chart in which shading has been used to differentiate three subgroups in the data. In this example, the capacity of the computer software used to represent the bars in three dimensions has been exploited.

Figure 3.5

BAR CHART INDICATING RELATIVE REAL INCOMES IN THE PAKISTAN PUNJAB, 1965-87 (CIMMYT, 1991, p.48)

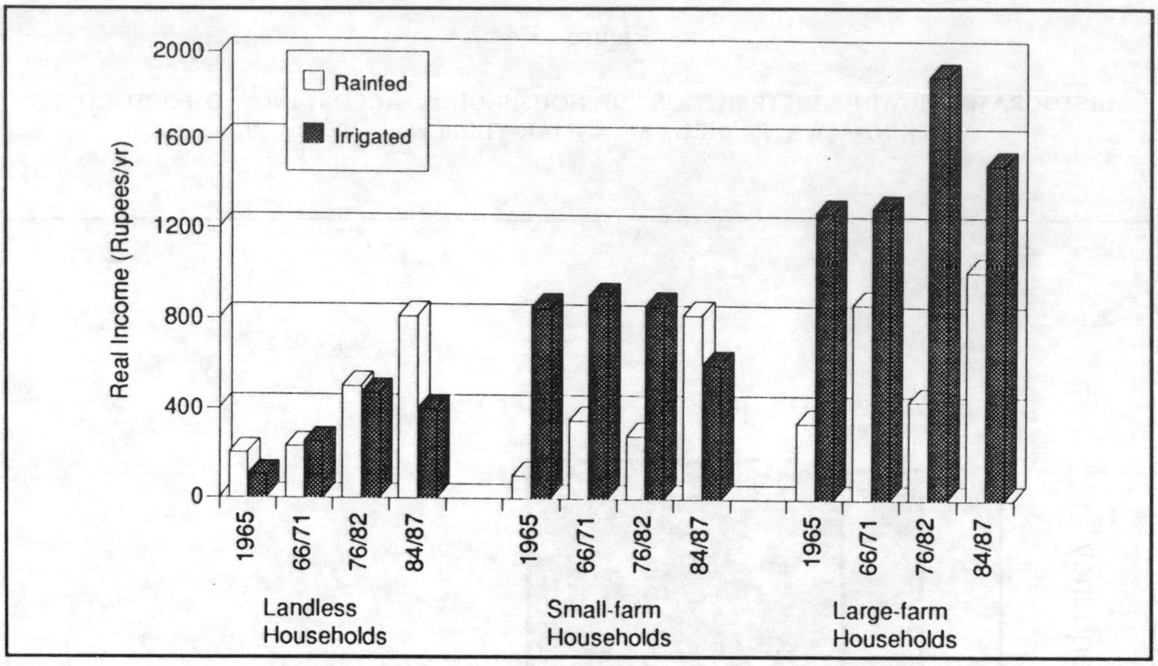

Figure 3.6

SEGMENTED BAR CHARTS SHOWING USE OF NON-LEISURE TIME BY SEX AND AGE GROUP IN TONGA (Hardaker *et al.*, 1988, p.35)

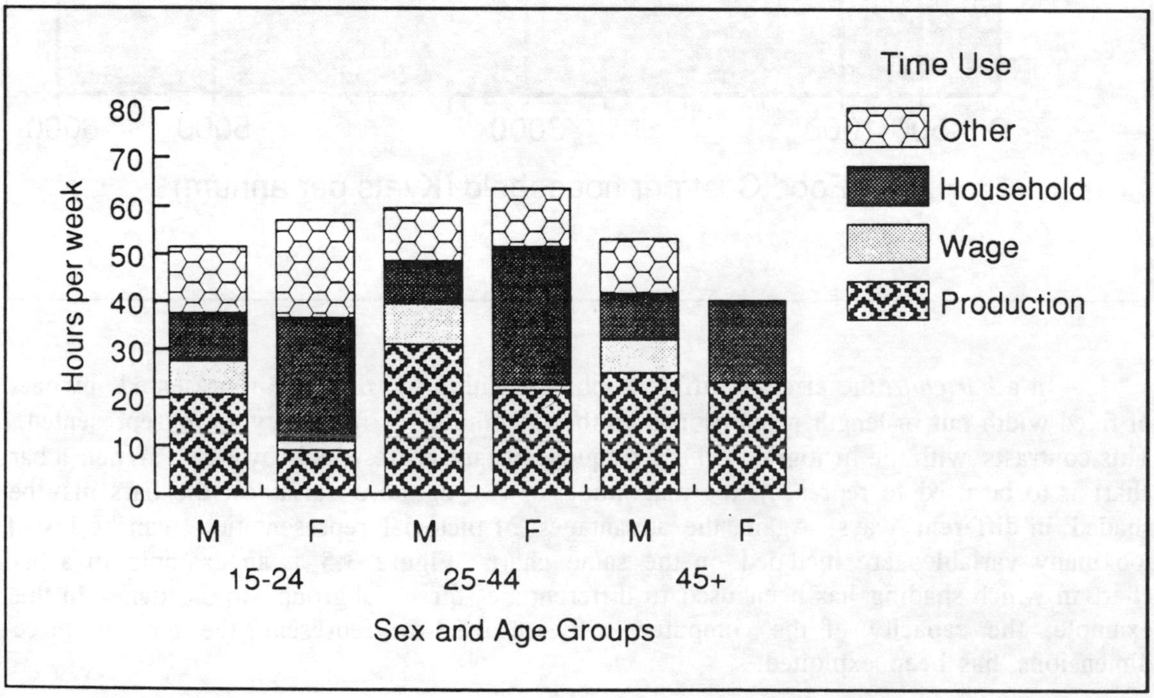

A bar chart can be extended to show the composition of the total magnitudes represented by the bars by segmenting each bar in proportion to the magnitudes of the different components. The component segments may be given a distinctive shading. Figure 3.6 is provided as an example.

A simple method of representing the contributions of the various parts to the whole, such as the percentage of an aggregate falling into different categories, is the *pie chart*. In a pie chart a circle is divided into segments such that the size of each segment (angle) is proportional to the frequency or magnitude of that class. Again, the various segments can be shaded or coloured in a distinctive way. An example making use of a comparison of two pie charts is shown in Figure 3.7.

Figure 3.7

PIE CHARTS SHOWING COMPARATIVE LAND USE FOR TWO VILLAGES IN KINDA WATERSHED, MYANMAR (Thein *et al.*, 1990, p.69)

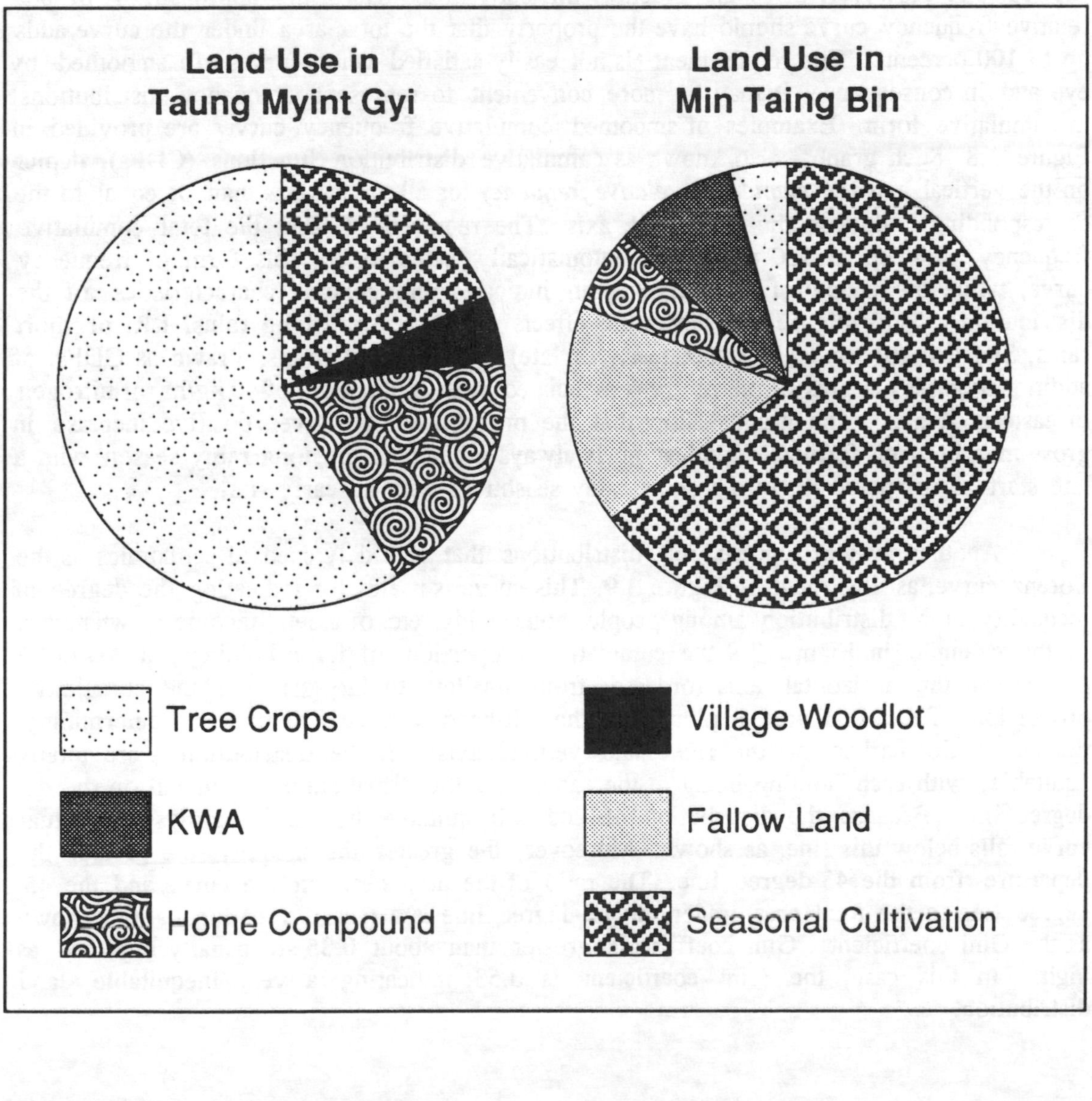

As noted above, *frequency distributions* may be represented pictorially by histograms. For some purposes, the histogram may be plotted using relative, rather than absolute, frequencies, i.e., by changing the vertical scale of the histogram from frequency to relative frequency (usually expressed as a percentage). Such a relative frequency histogram can alternatively be represented by a *relative frequency polygon*, which is the line graph obtained by connecting the mid-points of the tops of the rectangles of the histogram.

It is often reasonable to regard collected data as a sample drawn from a large population. It is theoretically possible (for a continuous variable) to choose very small class intervals such that the relative frequency polygon for a large population would closely approximate a smooth curve, known as a *relative frequency curve*. Moreover, it is reasonable to expect that such theoretical curves can be approximated by smoothing the relative frequency polygon of the sample, the approximation improving as the sample size is increased.

Smoothed relative frequency polygons are useful to indicate the general characteristics of frequency distributions, i.e., unimodal or multimodal, symmetrical or skewed, etc. However, there is a practical difficulty in the use of this approach. A proper relative frequency curve should have the property that the total area under the curve adds up to 100 percent. This requirement is not easily satisfied when curves are smoothed by eye and in consequence it may be more convenient to represent frequency distributions in cumulative form. Examples of smoothed cumulative frequency curves are provided in Figure 3.8. Such graphs, also known as cumulative distribution functions (CDFs), depict on the vertical axis the *cumulative relative frequency* for all values less than or equal to the corresponding value on the horizontal axis. The requirement that the total cumulative frequency adds up to 100 percent is automatically satisfied for this form of frequency curve, while the shape of the curve again indicates the general characteristics of the distribution. Thus Figure 3.8 shows the effects of (a) season (long rains, LR, or short rains, SR) and (b) timing of onset (early or late) on the distributions, drawn as CDFs, of additional gross margins of maize crops associated with application of 40 kg/ha of nitrogen in eastern Kenya. The graphs show that the probability of a given positive increase in gross margin from fertilizer application is always greater in the long rainy season with a late start as compared to in the short rainy season or with an early start.

Another way of representing distributions that is widely used in economics is the Lorenz curve, as illustrated in Figure 3.9. This curve is useful for indicating the degree of inequality in the distribution among people, households, etc. of assets, income or whatever. In the example in Figure 3.9 the cumulative proportion of farm holdings in Assam is plotted on the horizontal axis (ordered from smallest to largest), and the cumulative proportion of the total area is plotted on the left-hand vertical axis (thereby determining the size scale marked on the right-hand vertical axis). If the distribution were totally equitable, with each holding being of the same size, the distribution would fall on the 45-degree line. Because the distribution of land is inequitable between holdings, the actual curve falls below this line, as shown. Moreover, the greater the inequity, the greater the departure from the 45-degree line. The ratio of the area between the curve and the 45-degree line to the total area under the 45-degree line is a measure of inequality, known as the Gini coefficient. Gini coefficients greater than about 0.35 are usually regarded as high. In this case, the Gini coefficient is 0.53, indicating a very inequitable land distribution.

Figure 3.8

CUMULATIVE FREQUENCY CURVES SHOWING DISTRIBUTION OF ADDITIONAL GROSS MARGIN OF MAIZE UNDER LONG AND SHORT RAINS AND WITH EARLY AND LATE ONSET OF RAIN, KENYA (Keating, Godwin and Watiki, 1991, p.341)

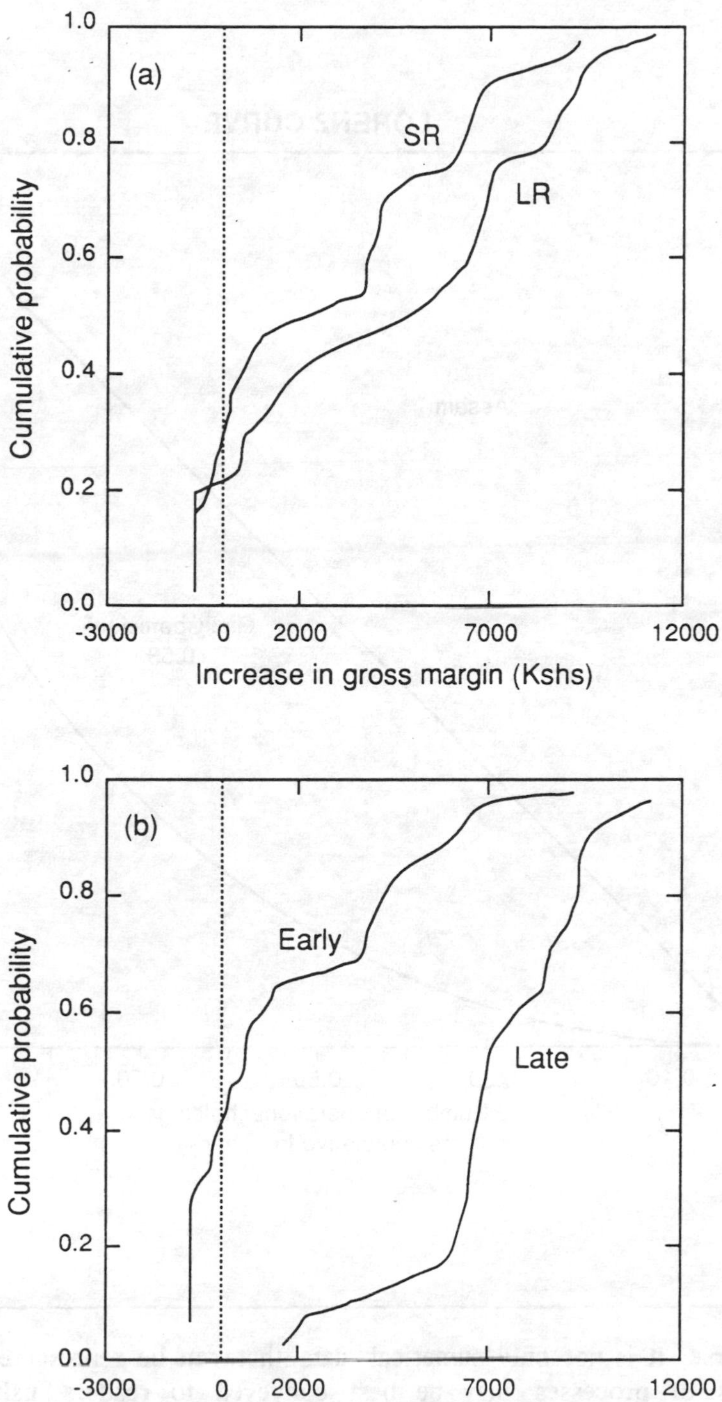

Figure 3.9

LORENZ CURVE SHOWING DISTRIBUTION OF LAND HOLDING IN ASSAM
(Das, 1988, p.63)

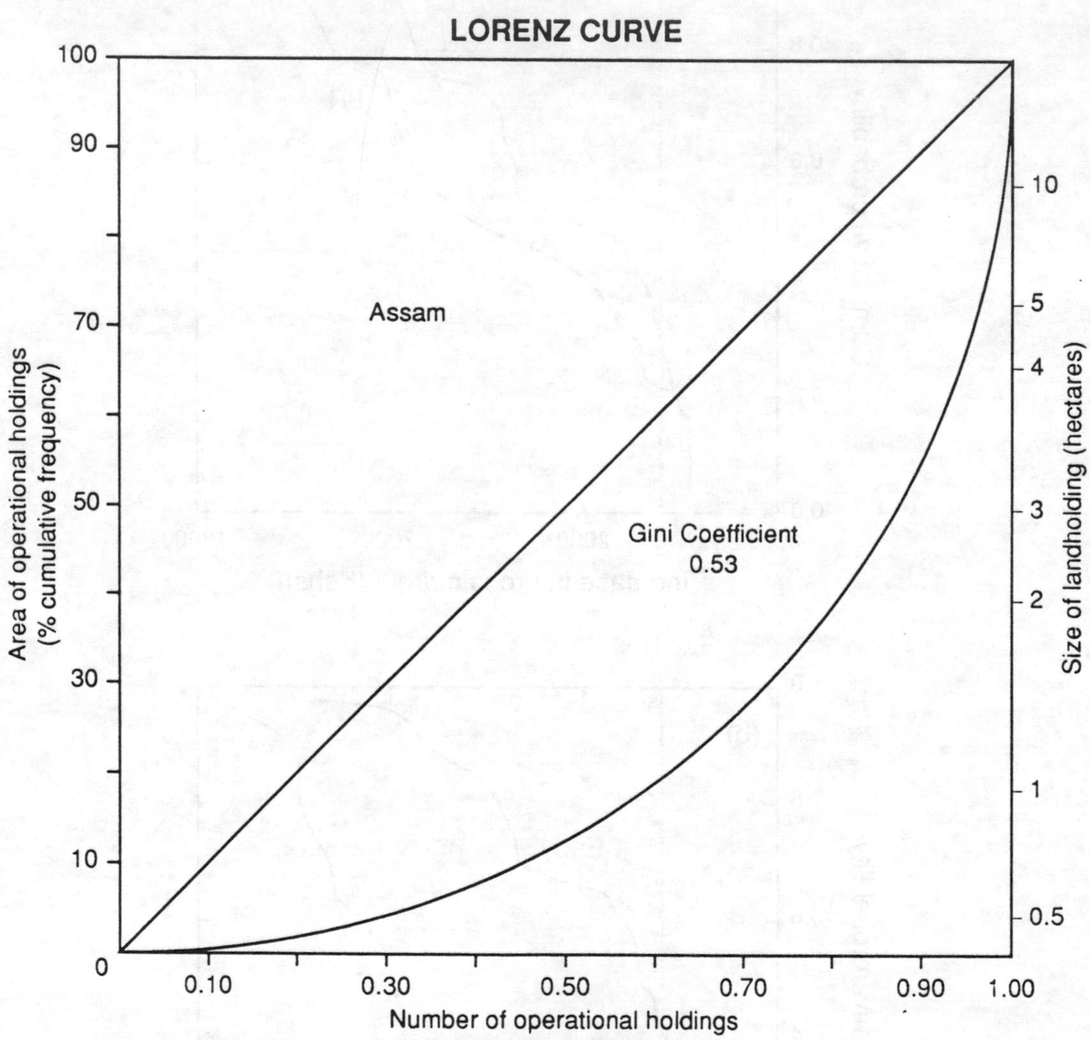

Of course, it is not only numerical data that can be represented graphically. A range of ideas or processes may be best conveyed to readers using graphics. An illustration is provided in Figure 3.10 in the form of a flow chart indicating the problems and causes of waterlogging in wheat. The use of such flow charts is often a very good way of indicating the relationships in a farming system. Figures 1.1 and 1.2 provide examples.

Figure 3.10

FLOW CHART SHOWING THE PROBLEMS AND CAUSES OF WATERLOGGING OF WHEAT
(Fujisaka and Harrington, 1989, p.22)

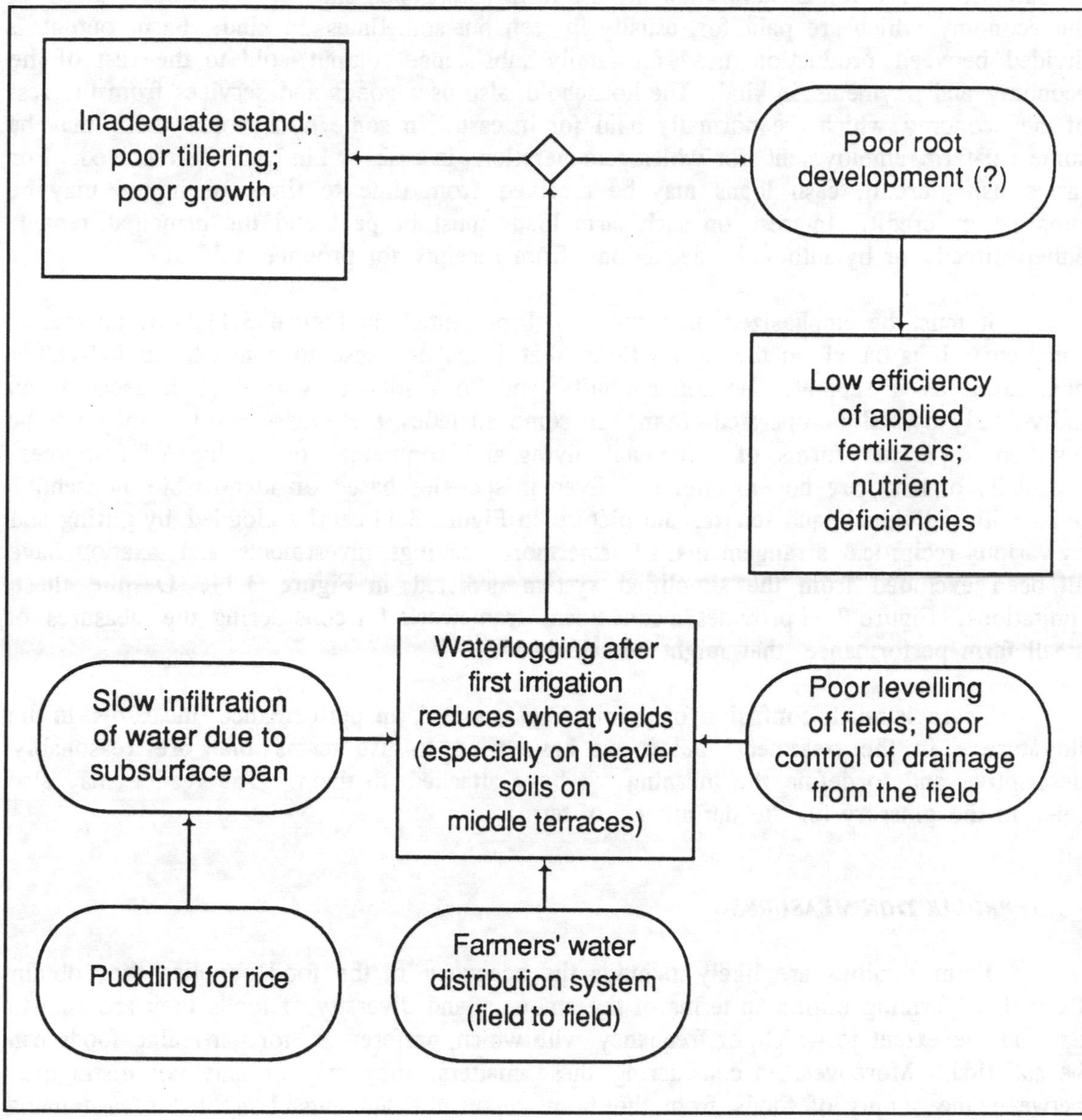

3.2 *Measures of whole-farm performance*

Small farms are distinguished from larger commercial farms by the closeness and importance of the links between the farm and the household. It makes sense in commercial farming to view the farm as a business and to gauge its performance by ordinary business criteria. The same criteria can be applied to small farms when the farm is being viewed as a business system, but different criteria are relevant if the farm is being considered as part of the support system for the household. Thus, in calculating measures of small farm performance it is necessary to be clear about the purpose of the analysis.

The main links between farm and household, and between these two entities and the rest of the economic system, including credit institutions, are indicated in simplified form in Figure 3.11. The household provides the labour for farm production. In return, the household receives income in the form of cash and as subsistence items for direct consumption. As well as family labour, the farm uses goods and services from the rest of the economy which are paid for, usually in cash but sometimes in kind. Farm output is divided between production used for family subsistence, output sold to the rest of the economy and payments in kind. The household also uses goods and services from the rest of the economy which are normally paid for in cash. In some households there may be some off-farm employment for which remuneration in cash or kind will be received. For farms using credit, cash loans may be received from time to time, or inputs may be supplied on credit. Interest on such farm loans must be paid and the principal repaid, either directly or by automatic deductions from receipts for produce sold.

It must be emphasized that the model presented in Figure 3.11 is by no means complete. It is based on the assumptions that it makes sense to consider an individual household as a separate economic entity and to associate with that household an individually owned or operated farm. In some societies these assumptions may not be justified. Various forms of communal living and communal ownership of resources, especially of land, are not uncommon. Even in societies based on identifiable household units with individual land tenure, the picture in Figure 3.11 can be clouded by gifting and by various reciprocal arrangements. Furthermore, savings, investments and taxation have all been excluded from the simplified system depicted in Figure 3.11. Despite these limitations, Figure 3.11 provides a convenient framework for considering the measures of small farm performance that might be calculated.

There is much confusion of terminology about farm performance measures in the literature. In the treatment below we have tried to use terms that are reasonably descriptive and to define the meaning we have attached to them. The reader may also refer to the glossary for the definitions of terms.

FOOD PRODUCTION MEASURES

Farm families are likely to judge the adequacy of the food supplies they obtain from their farming efforts in terms of the amounts and diversity of foods they are able to eat and the extent to which, or frequency with which, preferences for particular foods can be satisfied. Moreover, in considering these matters, they may or may not distinguish between the supply of foods from the farm versus the amounts bought for cash using income earned from the farm or in other ways. It is evident, therefore, that no single measure of food production or consumption is likely to capture all the dimensions of people's preferences. Nor is it likely to be possible to provide a comprehensive list of measures applicable in every case. Even from a nutritional viewpoint, where the focus is on the quantitative and qualitative adequacy of diets, there are many nutrients to be considered as well as the seasonal and intra-household distribution of these nutrients.

Evidently, then, any chosen measure of food production will at best give only a rough overview of farm-system performance. Typically, analysts have used food energy production (or consumption) expressed in Joules or calories per adult equivalent. Since adult equivalents are calculated for this purpose using some standards of energy requirements, the ratio of energy per adult equivalent is a measure of nutritional adequacy.

Figure 3.11

SIMPLIFIED REPRESENTATION OF FLOWS OF GOODS, SERVICES AND CASH IN A SMALL FARM SYSTEM WITH BORROWING

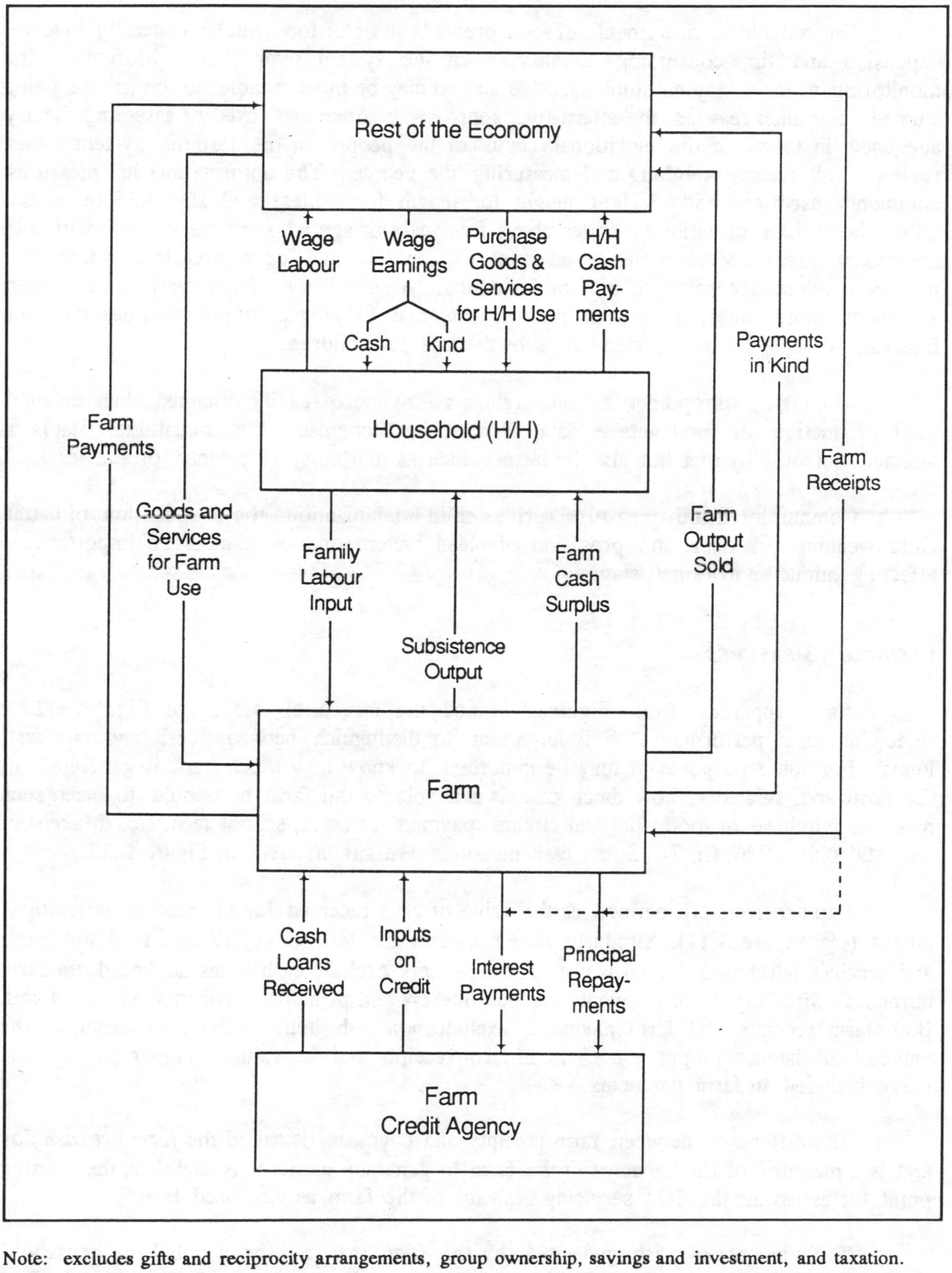

Note: excludes gifts and reciprocity arrangements, group ownership, savings and investment, and taxation.

Of course, alternative or supplementary measures can be calculated according to circumstances. For instance, if there are grounds for concern about dietary quality, it may be useful to calculate the protein to energy ratio, or to assess intakes of essential dietary components such as vitamins or minerals.

The reliable measurement of food production or of food intake generally involves expensive and time-consuming monitoring of the system over time. Moreover, the monitoring process may be quite intrusive and so may be unacceptable to the groups being studied. For such reasons, the alternative approach is sometimes used of assessing dietary adequacy in terms of the nutritional status of the people in the farming system under review. This means weighing and measuring the people. The anthropometric measures commonly used are body weight, height (or length for babies) and skin fold thickness. Often the focus is on children under about five years of age who are the most sensitive to nutritional stress. Measurements taken at a given date may be related to standards for healthy children according to age, or for adults. Alternatively, if observations are taken at two or more times, the system performance may be judged by growth rates over the interval, perhaps related to standard growth rates for children.

Although anthropometric measurements are more readily obtained than detailed food production or food intake data, it must be recognised that nutritional status is affected not only by diet but also by factors such as morbidity (incidence of sickness).

Community health measures such as child immunization, the introduction of better child weaning practices and provision of clean water supplies can all be important in affecting human nutritional status.

CASH-FLOW MEASURES

As is apparent from Figure 3.11 and the structural model of Figure 1.2, in reviewing farm performance it is important to distinguish between cash and non-cash items. For some purposes it may be important to know how much cash is generated by the farm and, relatedly, how much cash is available to the farm household to meet such needs as purchase of food, fuel and clothes, payment of taxes, school fees, etc. (Makeham and Malcolm, 1986, Ch.7). Some cash measures are summarized in Figure 3.12.

Farm receipts are defined as the value of cash received for the sale of agricultural output (see Figure 3.11). Similarly, *farm payments* are defined as the cash paid for goods and services purchased for farm use. Farm receipts exclude cash loans advanced for farm purposes. Similarly, farm payments exclude interest and principal payments on farm loans. Both farm receipts and farm payments exclude non-cash items. Thus, for example, the value of subsistence output is not part of farm receipts and the value of labour paid in kind is not included in farm payments.

The difference between farm receipts and payments is called the *farm net cash flow* and is a measure of the capacity of the farm to generate cash. It is useful as the starting point for assessing the debt servicing capacity of the farm as discussed later.

The amount of cash generated by the farm that can be devoted to household purposes can be calculated by making appropriate adjustments to farm net cash flow.

Farm receipts not arising from sale of produce, such as cash loans received, must be added; and farm payments not relating to purchases of goods and services, such as interest and principal, must be deducted. The balance is the *farm cash surplus* and is the amount of cash generated by the farm for household use. Clearly farm cash surplus must be positive if the farm is to be self-sustaining in terms of working capital.

Figure 3.12

CASH-FLOW MEASURES RELATED TO SMALL FARM PERFORMANCE

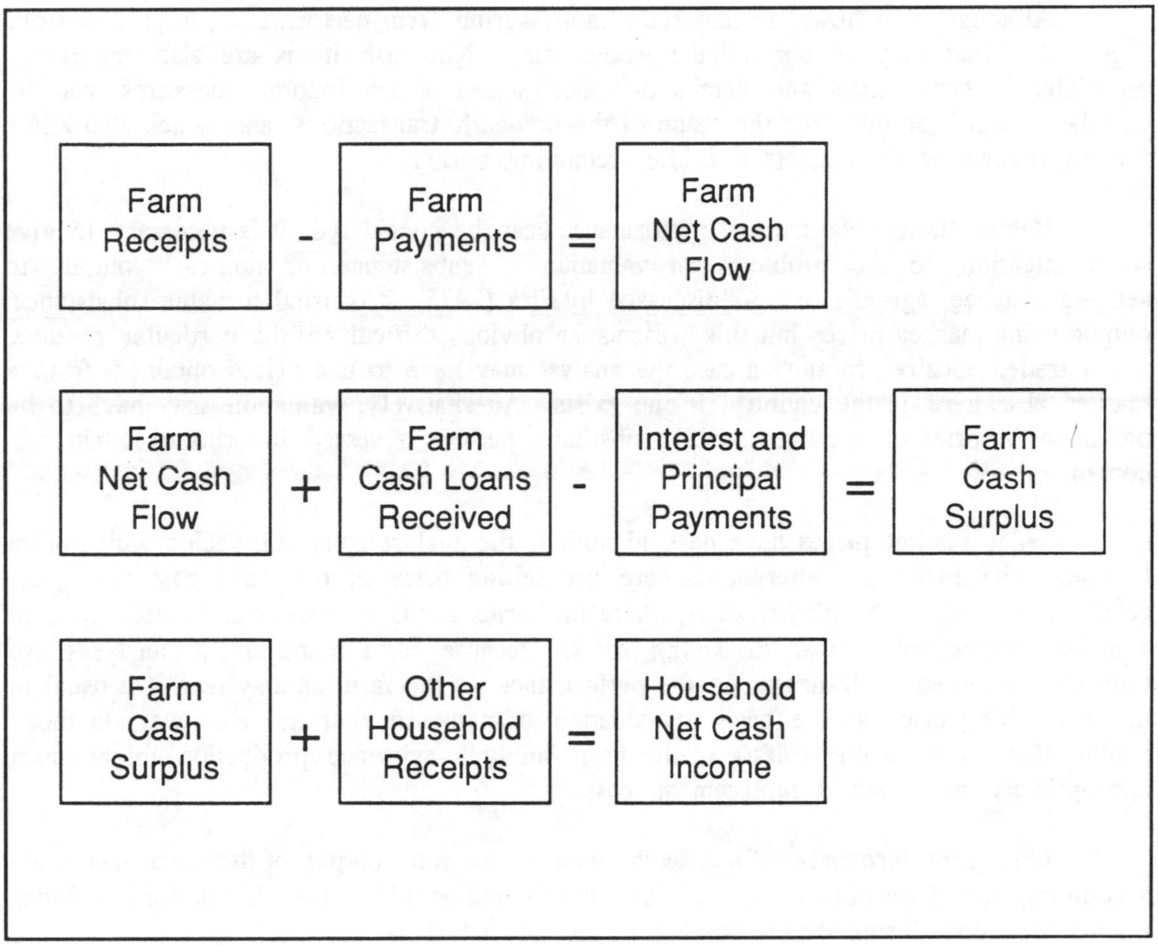

Finally, farm cash surplus, plus other household receipts such as wages for any off-farm employment or sale of cottage industry products, less any cash expenses incurred in productive activities within the household, is defined as *household net cash income*, which is the amount of cash available to the farm family for all payments not relating to the farm. It is then a partial measure of the welfare of the farm family. While subsistence consumption is not accounted for, a very low level of household net cash income can in some instances be an important indicator of poverty. In semi-subsistence agriculture it may be a reasonable approximation to assume that farmers have the ordered goals of first satisfying family subsistence needs and then of maximizing household net cash income. In this case the level of this measure reflects the degree of economic success achieved.

Cash flows may be calculated for any appropriate accounting period. For many purposes it may suffice to work on an annual basis. However, if the pattern of payments and receipts is somewhat seasonal, it may be necessary to assess the cash position more frequently, perhaps on a quarterly, or even a monthly basis. When a farm development programme is under way involving investments which take several years to yield income, long-term cash-flow budgets, calculated on an annual basis over, say, ten years, may be appropriate, These types of budgets are discussed further in Section 4.7.

INCOME AND PROFITABILITY MEASURES

Although cash flows are important in measuring farm performance, it is clear from Figure 3.11 that they do not tell the whole story. Non-cash items are also important, especially in subsistence and semi-subsistence agriculture. Income measures can be calculated which account for the value of the non-cash transactions and which also allow for any changes in farm assets over the accounting period.

Before these measures of performance can be considered it is necessary to give some attention to the problems of valuation of subsistence or non-cash output in semi-subsistence agriculture. As discussed by Fisk (1975), it is usual to value subsistence output using market prices but this presents an obvious difficulty if the particular product is not traded locally. In such a case the analyst may have to use prices obtained from a market elsewhere in the country, if one exists. Alternatively, valuation may have to be based on the price of some reasonable substitute, perhaps assessed in terms of nutritional content.

When market prices have been identified, the analyst must still decide which price to use. The two main alternatives are net selling price at the *farm gate* and gross replacement cost at the *kitchen door*, where the terms *net* and *gross* refer to deduction or addition, respectively, of all marketing costs. Because farm management analyses are typically concerned with measuring the performance of the farm as a system, it is usual to use net selling price as the basis of valuation of non-cash output. However, in those studies that focus on the welfare of the farm family, subsistence production might more appropriately be valued at replacement cost.

Gross farm income is defined as the value of the total output of the farm over some accounting period (usually a year), whether that output is sold or not. It therefore includes output produced during the accounting period and which is:

- ◇ sold;
- ◇ used for household consumption;
- ◇ used on the farm for seed or livestock feed;
- ◇ used for payments in kind;
- ◇ given to others; or
- ◇ in store at the end of the accounting period.

To avoid double counting, any output produced in earlier accounting periods but sold or used in the current period is excluded from the current gross farm income. Alternative terms for gross farm income include value of production, gross output and gross return.

In estimating gross income, those components of output that are not sold should be valued at market prices. The calculation is normally straightforward in the case of crops for which gross income is simply yield multiplied by net market price. Strictly, account should also be taken of any changes in the value of standing crops between the beginning and the end of the accounting period. Such changes can be important, especially for perennial crops. Where valuation of the standing crop is particularly difficult, some analysts use the costs incurred for the crop up to the time of preparing the account. Nevertheless, because of difficulties of valuation on costing, it is quite common to ignore such changes. For livestock, on the other hand, changes in the value of the stock of animals over the accounting period are usually taken into account. Purchases of livestock that are acquired for resale or home consumption are usually deducted from gross income since they can be regarded as part-finished output. Livestock gross income is therefore calculated as:

+	sales of stock
+	value of stock used for domestic consumption, payments in kind and gifts
+	value of stock at end of accounting period
–	purchases of stock
–	value of stock obtained as payments in kind and gifts
–	value of stock at beginning of accounting period
+	value of livestock produce (e.g., milk, eggs, etc.) produced.

Gross farm income is a measure of the total productivity of all the resources used on the farm. Ratios such as gross income per hectare or per labour unit can be computed to indicate the intensity of operation of the farm.

Total farm expenses are defined as the value of all inputs used up or expended in farm production, excluding family labour. An alternative term for total farm expenses is total farm costs. Ideally the expenses included in any accounting period should be those incurred in producing the output generated in that period. Sometimes, however, such segregation of expenses is difficult, partly for lack of appropriate farm records, but also because of the need to partition the joint costs involved in much agricultural production.

A compromise that can be adopted when the data are available depends upon the separation of total farm expenses into fixed and variable expenses. *Variable expenses* (also called *variable costs* or *direct costs*) are defined as those expenses that are specific to a particular crop or livestock enterprise and that vary more or less in direct proportion to the level of the particular enterprise (at least for small changes in level). *Fixed expenses* (also called *fixed costs*) are those farm expenses that do not vary in this fashion. If this division can be made, it may be possible to segregate for inclusion those variable expenses which relate to the production of the output generated in the current accounting period and to omit those variable expenses incurred in the current period but relating to production included in a subsequent (or earlier) period. On the other hand, because fixed expenses cannot logically be apportioned to output on any appropriate basis, they are generally measured as those fixed expenses incurred during the current accounting period.

Farm expenses include both cash and non-cash items. Thus, the value of goods and services for farm use paid for in kind or advanced on credit should be included. Similarly, farm production used for seed or animal feed which was included in gross farm income should also be included as a farm expense. Where capital inputs such as machinery are used, a depreciation allowance should be included so as to allow for the fall in value of the asset. There are many methods of estimating depreciation of farm capital items, but for most analyses of small holder farming, the straight-line method of calculation of depreciation is recommended. It should be noted, however, that interest on capital, whether owned by the farm family or borrowed, is not included in farm expenses.

The difference between gross farm income and total farm expenses is known as the *net farm income*. Net farm income measures the reward to the farm family for their labour and management and the return on all the capital invested in the farm, whether borrowed or not. It is therefore one measure of farm profitability that can be used to compare the performance of farms, subject to recognition that different farms may use different amounts of family labour. Because interest is excluded, comparisons are not confounded by differences in level of indebtedness. By deducting the value of various components of the resources rewarded by the net farm income, the return to the remaining resources can be calculated. Because of the difficulties of measuring and valuing managerial input, this factor is normally not costed but rather is reflected in higher or lower returns to the other resources.

Probably the most useful measure for appraising small farm performance is *net farm earnings*. This is computed from net farm income by deducting any interest paid on borrowed capital. It measures the total income earned from the farm for family purposes and is the reward to all family-owned resources used in farm production. Combining net farm earnings with any other household income, such as wage income or payments in kind from off-farm work, gives *family earnings* (or total household net income) which is the total income available to the farm family for all purposes. If assessments of poverty or of income distribution are needed for policy or planning purposes, these should usually be made in terms of family earnings.

In semi-commercial farming, return on capital is often a relevant criterion of farm performance. If a proportion of the capital is borrowed, two measures can be calculated. *Return to total capital* is calculated by deducting the value of family labour from net farm income. (For this purpose family labour is valued at prevailing wage rates. Note that this method does not give the true economic cost. The real value of labour is its opportunity cost, also called its marginal value product (MVP), i.e., the marginal value in the most profitable alternative use. This varies from season to season. At busy times the MVP of labour may be very high but at off-peak periods it may fall to almost zero. Moreover, the MVP is very difficult to determine. To obtain even an estimate requires budgets of all the main alternative uses of labour.) The resulting margin is normally expressed as a percentage of the *total farm capital* (i.e., the total value of the farm assets). *Return to farm equity capital*, on the other hand, represents the return to the family-owned share of farm assets and is calculated as net farm earnings minus the value of family labour. This measure, too, is usually expressed as a percentage, this time related to *farm equity capital*. Farm equity capital, also called farm net worth, is defined as total farm capital minus farm borrowings.

These two measures of return to capital can be used to assess the profitability of the farm investment. They can be related to the rates of return available on other investments. However, in making such comparisons the generally high level of risk attached to farm investment should be taken into account.

These two measures may have little application in less commercialized agriculture for two main reasons. First, unemployment and underemployment of labour are common in such agricultural economies, and thus the required valuation of unpaid family labour is difficult. Second, farmers in such an economy may have no alternative investments open to them, so that no comparative rates of return on capital are available.

Next, the *return to family labour* can be computed as net farm earnings less an imputed interest charge on farm equity capital. This profit measure can be divided by the number of family members working on the farm, expressed as *adult male equivalents* (see von Fleckenstein and Gauchon (1992, Ch.2) or Collinson (1983, Ch.11) for further discussion) to obtain an estimate of *return per person*, which can be compared with ruling farm and non-farm wage rates.

In rural economies where some farms are rented and some are owner-occupied, it may be desirable to treat both types in a similar fashion for purposes of comparing production efficiency between farms. In such a case the tenant farmer can be regarded as having 'borrowed' capital in the form of land from the landlord, the interest on this capital being paid in the form of rent in cash or kind. Thus, net farm income would be calculated without including rent as a farm expense, although the rent would be deducted along with any interest paid in calculating net farm earnings. Land tax can usually be regarded as a form of rent paid to the government.

If the purpose of the analysis is the estimation of household food security, some measures of nutritional efficiency may be useful. Output could be measured in terms of energy, either expressed directly in Joules (or calories), or in more familiar units such as equivalents in tons of wheat or number of adult equivalents sustained. These measures of energy production may be related to the land area used or to the amount of labour employed. Alternatively, the energy produced may be related to the energy consumed in production, either as purchased inputs alone, or also accounting for the labour energy expended.

MEASURES OF CAPITAL AND DEBT POSITION

Several measures have been suggested to describe the capital and debt position of a farm. Of these, the rates of return on capital have been discussed above. *Debt servicing capacity* can be assessed as farm net cash flow (Figure 3.12) less cash needed for family living expenses. This margin can be related to the annual interest and principal charges on a farm loan, these charges depending on the terms of such a loan. For example, with a farm net cash flow of $ 1 000 and assessed net family living expenses of $ 800, the debt servicing capacity is $ 200 per year. This would service a loan of $ 1 000 at 5 percent interest repayable over six years, or at 10 percent repayable over eight years. Of course, in determining actual borrowing capacity, account would have to be taken of possible variations in farm net cash flow over the period of the loan. In particular, account must be taken of the possible need to replace or purchase any capital items during the period of the loan. Such capital payments would reduce the farm net cash flow or, in the case of domestic items, increase payments for household expenses. Family living expenses may be treated as net of any wage income. Note that it is not generally good farm management practice to use such off-farm wage income to service farm loans, i.e., loans should not be taken if they cannot be repaid from the farm net cash flow.

Measures of the capital position of the farm obviously require some assessment of the value of the assets. This is never easy and may be especially difficult in semi-subsistence farming systems, for several reasons some of which are discussed below.

There are many ways of approaching farm asset valuation and choice between them can only be resolved by first considering the purpose of the valuation. In farm management analyses there are usually two related purposes:

(a) to assess the amounts of capital invested in the various assets in order to:

  (i) compare the efficiency of these investments with alternatives, or
  (ii) judge the financial security of the farm by assessing the values of assets against debts;

(b) to measure the changes in values of assets over time due to farming operations or price movements for the calculation of farm performance measures.

It is clear that, for (a)(i) and (ii), the net market values of the assets are the appropriate measures, provided that such values can be ascertained with adequate precision and at reasonable cost. Otherwise, values may be assessed from historical cost minus an estimate of subsequent depreciation, from replacement value, or as the capitalized value of the future income that could be earned from the asset.

A particular problem occurs in the valuation of assets that cannot in fact be sold, such as land held by the farm family but which is owned by the community. Here valuation may be meaningless, although the efficiency of the existing use of the asset can be assessed by considering what it could earn in the next best use (i.e., the opportunity cost). Only if the use value exceeds the opportunity cost is the existing use efficient. A lender assessing the value of such a non-marketable asset, such as a plantation crop on communal land, might value it in terms of the capitalized value of its earning potential, but only if the rights to the income flow could be acquired in the event of loan default. Not all land tenure arrangements in developing countries provide for such transfer of usufruct rights.

Changes in asset values through time, especially between the start and end of an accounting period, may be needed to estimate the depreciation costs of items such as farm equipment, or the contribution to farm income due to increases in the number or condition of farm livestock. Other changes, such as those due to changes in general price levels, are best treated as capital gains or losses that, while important in the overall assessment of farm business performance, should be viewed as unrelated to the profits earned from farm production. For further discussion of some of these issues, see Brown (1979).

In assessing value changes, net market values are again appropriate, although it is common in estimating, say, depreciation on machinery, to approximate these using the simplifying assumption of a fixed rate. Animals on the farm, crops in the ground or in store may similarly all be valued using standardized estimates for the sake of simplicity. Such standard values or depreciation rates need to be reviewed and, if necessary, revised from time to time.

A measure of the level of indebtedness of a farm that can be calculated is the *equity ratio*, defined as farm equity capital (total farm capital minus farm borrowings) divided by total farm capital (total value of farm assets). Equity ratio is usually expressed as a percentage and indicates the proportion of the value of the farm that is owned by the farm family. Critical levels of the equity ratio depend on such factors as the riskiness of the farming environment and the terms of farm loans. However, equity levels below about 60 percent probably indicate excessive borrowing.

AN ILLUSTRATIVE EXAMPLE

The example presented here is adapted from a hypothetical case farm developed by Friedrich (1977). For present purposes, some minor modifications have been made to the information presented by Friedrich. The analysis is based on a one-year period.

John Doe is a farmer in the Upper Region of country *XYZ*. He owns a farm of 12 acres (4.86 ha), divided into two parcels. He also rents a third parcel of 1.5 acres (0.61 ha) on a share-cropping basis, one third of the output being paid to the land owner. In addition, Doe is able to graze his cattle on communal land for a small rent.

The crops grown in the current year comprise 8.5 acres of mixed maize and groundnut, 3.5 acres of cotton and 1.5 acres of share-cropped rice. The groundnut and cotton are grown wholly for sale, while a portion of the maize and all the rice are retained for home consumption.

Cultivation of the crops is done with the help of a pair of oxen that Doe owns. He also employs a labourer on a permanent basis, as well as employing seasonal workers for selected jobs. In addition to the draught oxen, cattle are kept for milk and meat. The herd comprises three cows and a bull, together with young stock. Two calves were born during the current year and one heifer was purchased. No cattle were sold or slaughtered during the current year, but one cow was hand milked for six months, some of the milk being used in the house and the rest being sold. As well as his farm, Doe owns a shop which is run mainly by his wife.

Table 3.4 shows the net worth statement for Doe's farm. The statement comprises a list of the main farm assets owned by Doe and their value at the start and end of the accounting year. Debts are also shown on each occasion and Doe's net worth or equity in the farm is calculated as total assets minus debts. Equity ratios at the start and end of the year are also shown.

In Table 3.5 the farm income and expenses are summarized. A distinction is made in this table between transactions in cash, transactions in kind, and inventory changes. Variable expenses are deducted from gross income to obtain what is known as *total gross margin*. Then overhead expenses are deducted to give net farm income which in turn is used in calculating net farm earnings and family earnings.

Further amplification of the calculation of gross income is provided in Table 3.6 which shows the derivation of the gross income earned by the cattle. As can be seen, inventory changes adjusted for purchases (there were no sales) are included, as is the value of produce sold and consumed in the house.

The cash-flow measures described above are summarized for the case farm in Table 3.7. Adjustments to the cash components of gross income and expenses shown in Table 3.5

Table 3.4

NET WORTH STATEMENT FOR CASE FARM

Item	Opening value ($)	+ Purchases ($)	- Sales ($)	+ Appreciation /- Depreciation ($)	Closing value ($)
Farm assets:					
Land and improvements	7 467	0	0	-53	7 414
Buildings	650	0	0	-35	615
Tools and machinery	1 968	0	0	-153	1 815
Cattle	1 000	110	0	+90	1 200
Total	11 085	110	0	-151	11 044
Debts	515				0
Net worth (equity)	10 570				11 044
Equity ratio (%)	95.4				100.0

Source: Adapted from an example provided by Friedrich (1977).

are necessary because of the conventional treatment of livestock purchases as a deduction from gross income, rather than as an expense. Farm net cash flow is adjusted for interest and principal payments on the loan of $ 515 outstanding at the start of the year (see Table 3.4) to yield farm net cash surplus. Addition of net receipts from the store leads to a household net cash income for all domestic purposes of $ 5 176.

It is possible to use the information presented above to calculate a number of ratios of performance for Doe's farm. We consider first the return to total capital. This is calculated by deducting the imputed value of family labour used on the farm from the net farm income. Doe and his wife spent a total of 63 days on farm work, valued at $ 945. Thus, the return to total capital is 2 915 - 945 = $ 1 970. This margin can be related to the average value of total assets, i.e.,(11 085 + 11 044) / 2 = $ 11 064 (Table 3.4), so that the rate of return to total capital is calculated as 1 970 × 100 / 11 064 = 17.8 percent.

In a related manner, the return on equity capital is calculated from net farm earnings less imputed value of family labour, i.e., 2 863 - 945 = $ 1 918. This margin may be related to the average equity capital of (10 570 + 11 044) / 2 = $ 10 807 (Table 3.4) to give a rate of return of (1 918 × 100) / 10 807 = 17.7 percent. Both rates of return may be regarded as reasonably satisfactory in an environment where the cost of borrowed capital is of the order of 10 percent, as assumed in this case.

The return to family labour for John Doe and his wife may be found as the remainder after imputing a value to the equity capital invested in the farm. For an average equity of $ 10 807 (see above), interest at 10 percent amounts to $ 1 081. Thus,

Table 3.5

FARM INCOME AND EXPENSES FOR CASE FARM

Item	Cash ($)	Kind ($)	Inventory ($)	Total ($)
Gross farm income				
Crops[a]	5 160	715		5 875
Cattle[b]	283	428	200	911
Total	5 443	1 143	200	6 786
Less variable expenses	1 020			1 020
Total gross margin	4 423	1 143	200	5 766
Overhead expenses:				
Rent and land tax	60			60
Permanent labour	1 800	750		2 550
Depreciation of improvements, buildings and machinery			241	241
Total	1 860	750	241	2 851
Net farm income	2 563	393	-41	2 915
Less interest paid	52			52
Net farm earnings	2 511	393	-41	2 863
Plus off-farm earnings	3 180	500		3 680
Family earnings	5 691	893	-41	6 543

[a] Net of share to land owner.
[b] Net of purchases as per Table 3.6.

Source: As for Table 3.4.

the return to family labour is calculated from the net farm earnings as 2 863 - 1 081 = 1 782. When related to the 63 days of labour provided, equivalent to 0.315 labour years, this margin represents 1 782 / 0.315 = $ 5 657 per labour year equivalent.

3.3 Measures of partial farm performance

The farm management researcher will from time to time be asked questions about the economics of particular farm enterprises. She or he will encounter such questions as What does it cost to produce a ton of wheat? or Which is the more profitable, maize or beans? In a mixed farming economy and especially if multiple cropping systems are used, these questions cannot be easily answered. The reason is that farm resources such as labour are shared between the various enterprises on a mixed farm and it is usually

Table 3.6

CALCULATION OF LIVESTOCK GROSS INCOME FOR CASE FARM

Item	Cash ($)	Kind ($)	Inventory ($)	Total ($)
Closing value			1 200	1 200
Less purchases	-110			-110
	-110		1 200	1 090
Less opening value			-1 000	-1 000
	-110		200	90
Plus value of milk	393	428		821
Livestock gross income	283	428	200	911

Source: As for Table 3.4.

impossible (or very difficult) to work out the economic cost of the share used by a particular enterprise or crop within a multiple cropping system. However, the attempt is often made, valuing the resources at their average cost and using allocative rules-of-thumb.

Similar problems are encountered in valuing other resources such as draught animals or tractors, irrigation water, etc., and some products, such as cereal straw or stubble grazing, which are not directly saleable, may also present valuation problems.

The difficulties in such valuation (discussed above) mean that, except in a monoculture, estimates of the cost of producing a ton of wheat are only approximate at best. However, the central issue may not be the cost of production per se, but whether the current wheat price is sufficient to give wheat growers an adequate income. That question can be answered directly from farm survey data, if available. Similarly, the person who asks about the relative profitability of two crops probably wants to know whether a particular farmer or group of farmers should be advised to grow one crop rather than another. That question too can be answered by the budgeting methods described in Chapters 4, 5 and 6.

Although full enterprise costings are not generally recommended, it is often of value to calculate some measure of the performance of an individual enterprise on a farm. Provided its limitations are appreciated, the *enterprise gross margin* may be useful for this purpose. The gross margin of an enterprise is defined as the enterprise gross income minus the variable expenses attributable to that enterprise. (Variable expenses were defined above as expenses that vary more or less in direct proportion to the level of the enterprise.) The sum of all the enterprise gross margins on a farm is the *total gross margin*. Enterprise gross margins are usually expressed on a per unit basis, i.e.,per hectare for crops and per head for livestock.

Table 3.7

CASH-FLOW MEASURES FOR CASE FARM

Item	Flow ($)
Cash income	5 443
Plus livestock purchases	110
Farm receipts	5 553
Cash expenses	
Variable	1 020
Fixed	1 860
Plus livestock purchases	110
Farm payments	2 990
Farm net cash flow	2 563
Less interest and principal	567
Farm cash surplus	1 996
Plus off-farm receipts	3 180
Household net cash income	5 176

Source: As for Table 3.4.

An example of the calculation of an enterprise gross margin is presented in Table 3.8. The example relates to a cotton crop grown on the hypothetical case farm discussed above. The data in the table are taken, with minor changes, from Friedrich (1977). An enterprise gross margin is not a measure of enterprise net profitability since it takes no account of the demands the enterprise places on those farm resources represented by the fixed expenses. Rather, the gross margin measures the contribution the enterprise makes toward these fixed expenses and to the farm profit. However, gross margins find their main use as an aid in budgeting. The changes in gross income and variable expenses resulting from changing the level of a particular enterprise are automatically accounted for in the enterprise gross margin so that attention can be focused on planning the reallocation of the fixed resources or on adjusting their supply.

While enterprise gross margins provide a useful framework for presenting relevant data collected from a farm, there is a danger in placing too much emphasis on *historical* or *backward looking* performance measures. As noted above, gross margins are essentially planning tools and, while data on past performance may be a useful guide to the future, it is always necessary to consider what changes should be made to historical gross margins before they can be used in budgeting for the future. Thus, in using enterprise gross margins for planning purposes, the individual items of income and expense entering the calculation should each be revised so as to take account of any relevant or expected changes in price, yield and input levels.

Because gross margins are net of only variable expenses, it is always necessary when comparing enterprise gross margins per unit to assess the requirements for fixed resources of the farm. For example, crop A might have a much higher gross margin per hectare than crop B, but before we can deduce that it would pay to grow more of A and less of B, it would be necessary to consider, for instance, that crop B occupies the land for only four months compared with a full year for crop A, or that A places heavy demands on farm labour at a peak time and so could not be expanded without employing more labour.

Special problems may arise in calculating gross margins on small farms. For example, the common practice of multiple cropping can make it difficult (or inappropriate) to allocate variable expenses to individual crops within the cropping system. It may, however, still be useful to work out a gross margin for the mixed crop or cropping system as an entity, or even for the whole rotation. Comparisons with alternative crop mixtures or rotations on other farms can then be made.

The distinction between casual labour, normally regarded as a variable expense, and permanent labour, normally viewed as a fixed expense, may be somewhat arbitrary on occasion. For example, on some farms, workers are employed more or less year-round, but are paid on a task basis. Such wage payments clearly satisfy the definition of a variable expense. At other times, labour may be hired on a casual basis, yet may be allocated to tasks of an essentially overhead nature, such as maintenance work. In view of such ambiguities, it is important always to record full details of casual labour expenses included in an enterprise gross margin calculation. Moreover, the decisions made in distinguishing between fixed and variable expenses should always be kept in mind when reviewing gross margins.

3.4 *Comparative analysis*

Comparative analysis is a method of assessing the performance of an individual farm. It is important to distinguish between the special procedures of comparative analysis as developed in farm management and outlined below, and more general methods of comparison of results used, for example, in analysis of survey data. In the latter case the survey results may be set out in tables or figures, as described in the first section of this chapter, so as to facilitate comparisons between different groups of farms in the sample. The following remarks do not refer to such general methods of comparison of data.

Comparative analysis is the name given to the process of comparing the performance of a farm with some *standard*. The standard may be any one of:

◇ previous performance for the same farm;

◇ average performance for a group of broadly similar farms;

◇ some synthetic standard based on experimental and other data; or

◇ budgeted performance for the farm in question.

The differences between the farm being studied and the standard are noted, and an attempt is made to identify the reasons for these differences. The standards used may relate to technical performance, involving physical measures such as yields of crops, production of livestock, or use of inputs such as labour. Other standards may be measured in money terms, including such ratios as enterprise (or total) gross margins per hectare or per unit of some other resource, net income per hectare, return to total capital, etc. Some analysts (e.g., Blagburn, 1961) developed quite complex systems of comparisons of ratios against standards, designed to arrive by more or less logical steps at an identification of the specific strengths and weaknesses of a particular farm business. However, these systems are mainly designed for use on commercial farms, and would generally not be relevant for small, semi-subsistence farms.

Comparative analysis was more widely used by farm management specialists 30 years ago than today, and is essentially an extension technique, rather than a research technique. It thus tends to lie outside the main area of concern of this manual. Moreover,

Table 3.8

GROSS MARGIN FOR 2.5 ACRES OF COTTON ON CASE FARM

Item	Total ($)	Per acre ($)
Gross income		
1st crop 700 kg		
2nd crop 280 kg		
Total 980 kg at $ 1.22	1 200	480
Variable expenses		
Fertilizer: 100 kg DAP	115	46
Insecticide: 3 applications	50	20
Packing materials	50	20
Fuel and oil for irrigation pump	15	6
Casual labour		
Hoeing	80	32
Picking		
1st crop	250	100
2nd crop	80	32
Total variable expenses	640	256
Gross margin	560	224

Source: As for Table 3.4.

the technique can be criticized as lacking economic justification (Candler and Sargent, 1962). Since none of the standards normally used can be said to represent economic optima for the study farm, comparison with the standards may be of little value and may even be counter-productive, i.e., it may suggest changes that lead away from, rather than towards, the true (but unknown) optimum.

In a research context perhaps the main use for the comparative analysis approach is in regard to synthetic standards derived from experimental data. As discussed in Section 1.5, a valuable research approach is to study in detail the extent and causes of the *yield gap* between the yields obtained on experiment stations and those obtained on farms. The results of such study might be to emphasize the need for a more appropriate orientation of research to real farm circumstances.

3.5 *Application of computers in farm management data analysis*

The reduction in cost and increased availability of personal computers (PCs) have revolutionized the analysis of farm management data and the use of such data in planning.

These trends may be expected to continue so that, while today by no means every farm management analyst in developing countries who could use a PC has ready access to one, the proportion of workers with such access will increase in future.

The advantages of using PCs come from two main sources. First, there is the considerable increase in speed with which certain kinds of data manipulation or calculation can be performed. A task that would take hours to complete using pencil and paper and a conventional electronic calculator can be completed in seconds on a PC, once all the relevant information has been entered. Second, the storage of text and numerical information in very compact electronic form on a computer disk permits ready retrieval of the information and its rapid updating and editing as circumstances warrant. The exchange of information in electronic format among PC users is also greatly facilitated, either on floppy disks or, increasingly, using electronic transfer, frequently via the ordinary telephone system.

Unlike their mainframe ancestors, modern desk-top or lap-top PCs are reasonably user-friendly - some more than others. Nevertheless, to get the best from a PC a user needs two things:

◇ adequate access to a suitable machine and proper training in using it, and

◇ access to, and knowledge of, relevant software packages.

The increasing availability of PCs has been parallelled by an expansion in availability of software. These days the issue is seldom whether software is available to perform a given task; rather it is a matter of choosing amongst the available alternatives. It is also a matter of cost, since commercial software packages can be expensive, some perhaps prohibitively so. Fortunately, for many applications there are substitutes available that are almost as good as the widely promoted commercial products and cost considerably less - some are free. The following software packages are used in farm management analysis, in approximate order of frequency of use:

◇ Utility programs, such as menus, file management programs, etc., normally supplied with the PC.

◇ A word processing package for production and editing of reports.

◇ A spreadsheet package for certain types of data manipulation such as budgeting (see Chapter 4).

◇ A database package for the storage and manipulation of large amounts of information, such as the data of farm management surveys.[1]

◇ A statistical analysis package suitable for such tasks as cross-tabulation of survey data, regression analysis, etc.

◇ A graphics component or separate package to produce graphs and charts speedily and to a high standard.

◇ A set of special-purpose software packages for applications of use to the individual analyst, such as linear programming (see Chapter 4), stochastic dominance analysis (see Chapter 8), investment analysis, or project planning and control (see Chapter 9).

◇ A programming language (or languages) enabling skilled users to develop their own special-purpose applications. For example, most systems simulation models (see Section 4.5) are developed in this way.

The software that has done most to change the way farm management analysts go about their work is undoubtedly the electronic spreadsheet. The power of the spreadsheet lies in the fact that, not only can very detailed calculations, such as large development

[1] The FAO computer-based FARMAP system for farm management analysis is one such database system, especially adapted for farm management use (Dixon *et al.* 1986). Other general-purpose database packages are available that the user can tailor to suit a given application.

budgets (see Chapter 4) be set out in a systematic way, but also investigation of the effects on the calculations of changed data or assumptions becomes very simple and easy. Spreadsheet applications are therefore ideal for answering What if? questions, as in sensitivity analysis. They allow the analyst to do, reliably and quickly, calculations of a kind that previously would have been very time-consuming if not infeasible.

A similar expansion of capacity to handle data is also provided by other software such as database or statistical packages. Some of these applications will be discussed further in later chapters. However, it is the spreadsheet which most vividly illustrates the valuable role of PCs in the day-to-day work of the farm management analyst.

3.6 References

BISHOP, O.N. (1983). *Statistics for Biology,* 4th edn., Longmans, London.

BLAGBURN, C.H. (1961). *Farm Planning and Management*, Longmans, London.

BROWN, M.L. (1979). *Farm Budgets: From Farm Income Analysis to Agricultural Project Analysis*, Johns Hopkins University Press, Baltimore.

CANDLER, W. & D. SARGENT (1962). 'Farm Standards and the Theory of Production Economics', *Journal of Agricultural Economics* 15(2): 283-90.

CIMMYT (1991). *CIMMYT 1990 Annual Report. Sustaining Agricultural Resources in Developing Countries: Contributions of CIMMYT Research*, CIMMYT, Mexico City.

DAS, M.M. (1988). 'Structural Disability of Small Farming in Assam', in J. Hirst, J. Overton, B. Allen and Y. Byron (eds), *Small-Scale Agriculture*, Commonwealth Geographical Bureau and Department of Human Geography, Canberra, pp. 57-65.

DIXON, J.M. *et al.* (1986). *FARMAP Users Manual, Vols. 1-3*, Food and Agriculture Organization of the United Nations, Rome.

FINLAYSON, M.P., J. McCOMB, J.B. HARDAKER & P. HEYWOOD (1991). *Commercialisation of Agriculture at Karimui, Papua New Guinea: Effects on Household Production , Consumption and the Growth of Children*, Report of a Joint Project of the PNG Institute of Medical Research, Madang and the Department of Agricultural Economics and Business Management, University of New England, Armidale.

FISK, E.K. (1975). 'The Subsistence Component in National Income Accounts', *The Developing Economies* 13(3): 252-79.

FRIEDRICH, K.H. (1977). *Farm Management Data Collection and Analysis: An Electronic Data Processing, Storage and Retrieval System*, FAO Agricultural Services Bulletin No. 34, Food and Agriculture Organization of the United Nations, Rome.

FUJISAKA, S. & L.W. HARRINGTON (eds) (1989). *The Rice-Wheat Cropping Pattern in the Nepal Terai: Farmers' Practices and Problems, and Needs for Future Research*, National Agricultural Research and Services Center, Kathmandu.

HARDAKER, J.B., J.C. DELFORCE, E.M. FLEMING & S. SEFANAIA (1988). *Smallholder Agriculture in Tonga: Report of the South Pacific Smallholder Project in Tonga, 1984-85*, Project Report, South Pacific Smallholder Project, University of New England, Armidale.

HORTON, D. (1987). *Potatoes: Production, Marketing and Programs for Developing Countries*, Westview, Boulder.

KEATING, B.A., D.C. GOODWIN & J.M. WATIKI (1991). 'Optimising Nitrogen Inputs in Response to Climatic Risk', in R.C. MUCHOW and J.A. BELLAMY (eds), *Climatic Risk in Crop Production: Models and Management for the Semiarid Tropics and Subtropics*, CAB International, Wallingford, pp. 329-58.

MAKEHAM, J.P. & L.R. MALCOLM (1986). *The Economics of Tropical Farm Management*, Cambridge University Press.

MONTEITH, J.L. & S.M. VIRMANI (1991). 'Quantifying Climatic Risk in the Semiarid Tropics: ICRISAT Experience', in R.C. Muchow and J.A. Bellamy (eds), *Climatic Risk in Crop Production: Models and Management for the Semiarid Tropics and Subtropics*, CAB International, Wallingford, pp. 183-204.

THEIN, M., T.H. NU, L. NYUNT, K.P. OO, M. MAUNG & K. TUN (1990). *Pilot Watershed Management for Kinda Dam, Myanmar: Socio-Economic Study of the Pilot Demonstration Area*, United Nations Development Program and Food and Agriculture Organization of the United Nations, Yangon.

VAN HERPEN, D., & J.A. ASHBY (eds)(1991). *Gender Analysis in Agricultural Research*, Publication No. 204, CIAT, Cali.

VON FLECKENSTEIN, F., & M.J. GAUCHON (1992). *The FAO Farm Analysis Package, FARMAP, Reference Manual*, Food and Agriculture Organization of the United Nations, Rome.

4. WHOLE-FARM PLANNING

4.1 The context of farm-household planning

As described in Section 1.2, small-scale farming systems are characterized by close interactions between the farm, the farm household, and off-farm activities of household members. When possible changes in this system are being appraised, it is important to be aware of these interactions and to account for them. In this respect, planning for small-scale farming systems differs substantially from planning commercial farms. For example, many farm-households engage in other productive activities besides farming, such as fishing, hunting, gathering or handicraft manufacture. Some of these activities may be cash earning, and others provide for household consumption. However, many of these activities compete with crop and livestock production for scarce resources, e.g.,labour. A view of the farm as a business, which is the usual perspective when planning commercial farms, would mean that these important activities would be ignored. It is equally mistaken to regard such activities as child care or food preparation as unproductive while treating growing crops for food or sale as productive work. Both are vital for the continued survival of the household.

Taking the broader view of the farm-household system also emphasizes the importance of the *goals and objectives* of the household members. In commercial farming it is often a reasonable approximation to regard profit maximization as the relevant goal. But small farm-households clearly have quite different objectives, usually relating to the maintenance and reproduction of the household unit. The objective function is likely to include such dimensions as the provision of adequate levels of food and other necessities, both in the short and longer run, access to basic services such as health care and education of children to preserve or enhance the household stock of human capital, sufficient cash to buy a few extras above basic needs to make life more pleasant, and sufficient leisure time for adequate rest and for accepted levels of social activity. Planning of farm-household resource use that ignores these diverse but important objectives will be well wide of the mark.

Farm-household planning involves examining the implications of re-allocating household resources. The planner will be concerned to evaluate the consequences of some change or changes in what is produced by the household, and by what methods. Sometimes the changes being considered will be minor, involving perhaps a new variety of a crop or a new pasture type, and sometimes they will be quite radical, as when land of little or no agricultural value is brought into intensive production in some land-development scheme or when a new off-farm opportunity for wage employment arises.

The context in which farm-household planning studies are undertaken may vary widely. At one extreme, planning may be part of an extension programme wherein a specific plan is developed for an individual farm family. While the planning techniques described below are well suited to use in such an advisory context, the large number of small farm-households in most developing countries makes this individual approach impracticable as a means of achieving broad rural development objectives.

More plausibly, the extension use of planning methods will involve planning one or more case-study farm-households that can be regarded as to some extent *representative* of the target population of such households. The great diversity commonly found in rural populations in terms of resource endowments, management goals and abilities, etc. obviously limits the value of the *representative farm-household approach*. It is not usually possible to obtain a close match between the circumstances assumed for the representative farm-household and the circumstances of any large proportion of actual households. Rather, the representative case approach can be used to identify general guidelines about the economical use of resources for farm-households of particular types in a given area. These guidelines would then be promoted among the population in the region by the usual mass extension methods.

In a different context, the planner is concerned not so much with the question of what allocation of resources farmers should adopt to achieve particular individual goals, but rather with trying to predict what resource allocation farmers will adopt, given particular incentives, prices and available technologies. Again, attention may be directed to a number of representative farm-households and budgets drawn up for these cases would be scaled up to produce aggregated projections for development-planning purposes. Thus, this kind of rural planning is often part of the process of evaluating the feasibility and profitability of development projects.

Farm-household planning studies of the different kinds mentioned above may be conducted on either a whole-farm basis (including the farm-household), or a partial basis. In whole-farm planning, as the name suggests, the farm-household is considered as a complete entity. The whole crop and livestock production programme is reviewed and the use of farm-household resources (including any off-farm use) is considered on an overall basis. If profit budgets are to be prepared, they are constructed taking account of all income and expense items. In partial analysis, on the other hand, some aspects of the farm-household production system are taken as given and the budget analysis is conducted considering only those aspects that are directly affected by the proposal under review. Such budgets are called partial budgets. Their construction and use are discussed in Chapter 5.

4.2 The nature of the whole-farm planning problem

The integrated nature of small farm-household systems is such that it is often most appropriate to consider the system as a whole. Alternative enterprises or methods of production compete for the resources of land, labour and capital in its various forms. Time and other resources must be allocated between farming and non-farming activities. The various dimensions of the household objective function imply competition for resources. Moreover, there are often important inter-relationships among various components of the system. For example, livestock may depend upon crops grown for all or part of their feed requirements. The same animals may be used for draught purposes in the cultivation of these crops and the manure they produce may be an important source of nutrients for crop production. It is difficult in a partial analysis to account adequately for such interrelationships. For reasons of this kind, planning of small farms is often best undertaken on a whole-farm basis.

Whole-farm planning involves three main steps. The first is the development of a plan or programme. This plan will be specified in terms of both the levels to be adopted of particular farm enterprises and the methods of production to be used, as well as the details of other non-farm activities to be undertaken. Thus the plan will indicate not only what areas of various crops are to be grown and what numbers of livestock are to be kept, but also will specify which varieties of crops should be grown, when they are to be planted, what fertilizers and other chemicals should be applied, what intensity of weeding should be adopted, what time of family members is to be set aside for study or other work, and so on. In the case of livestock, such features as feeding methods and breeding programmes will be indicated.

The second step in whole-farm planning is to test the specified plan for feasibility in terms of the demands that the plan will place upon farm-household resources, and in terms of consistency with institutional, social or cultural planning constraints that apply. Thus the plan should be examined to see that it is feasible in terms of the land area available, that the implied rotation will be viable in both the short and the longer term without degrading soil fertility, that sufficient human labour, animal power or machine power can be made available to complete the work required in a timely manner, and so on.

The final step in whole-farm planning is to evaluate the particular plan and to rank alternative plans in terms of an appropriate criterion, with the objective of selecting the best plan. Clearly, as discussed, the criterion used should reflect the objectives of the farm-household. This is a complex task requiring detailed knowledge of human motivation that is generally not available. A common approach, therefore, is to add additional tests of feasibility to ensure that the basic standard of living of the family is assured, and then to rank plans in terms of some readily evaluated criterion such as net earnings. Provided adequate cognizance has been taken of the family's views in specifying constraints that ensure that enough food will be produced and enough cash generated to meet the essential needs, net earnings may be a reasonable surrogate for the actual but unspecified objectives.

In some planning methods, the three steps outlined above must be taken one at a time. In budgeting methods, alternative plans are usually developed intuitively, perhaps as modifications of the existing system or as adaptations of systems developed on other successful farms or in experimental work. These plans must then be tested for feasibility and, if necessary, modified further before they can be evaluated. However, in other methods the three planning steps are combined. Most linear programming and related procedures are designed to generate a plan that is both feasible in terms of specified constraints and optimal according to a defined criterion. Such programming methods are reviewed in Section 4.5 below. However, attention is first directed to the construction of activity budgets which are useful in whole-farm planning using either programming or non-programming methods. For further relevant discussion see Brown (1979) and Makeham and Malcolm (1986).

4.3 *Activity budgets*

Activity budgets are important because they form the building blocks used in all the farm planning techniques to be described later. They constitute a systematic listing of relevant planning information about nominated production technologies. They can be constructed for both farm activities and non-farm activities such as fishing. The information used may have been gleaned from farm-household surveys, records kept by farm-household members, experienced extension workers, experimental work, etc. An activity budget is a convenient means of summarizing such data regardless of its origin.

In discussing activity budgets it is first necessary to distinguish between an enterprise and an activity. An *enterprise* is defined as the production of a particular commodity or group of related commodities for sale or for use on the farm or in the farm household. Thus the term *rice enterprise* implies the production of rice (and perhaps rice straw) for sale or domestic use, without specifying the method of production employed. An *activity*, on the other hand, is a specified method of producing a crop, operating a livestock enterprise, or engaging in some other form of production. For example, dryland and irrigated rice are different activities but are part of the same enterprise.

The significance of the distinction between enterprises and activities lies in the fact that the whole-farm planning problem involves deciding not only what to produce but also how to produce it. That is, it involves selecting an appropriate mix of activities rather than merely a combination of enterprises. Of course, in principle, it would be possible to define an infinite number of activities representing all possible ways of producing various products. In practice, however, it is usually possible to define a relatively small number of activities which, individually or in combination, adequately span the range of production opportunities available to, and worthy of consideration by, a particular farm-household. The planning problem then reduces to selecting a mix of these activities that is at once feasible and optimal. In this context, an activity budget is a formal statement of the economic and technical characteristics of a particular activity, presented in a way that allows planning to proceed.

An activity budget comprises some or all of the following components:

- ◇ a brief but adequate definition of the activity, stating what is produced and how;
- ◇ a list of the demands placed on farm-household resources (e.g., land, labour requirements) per unit level of the activity;
- ◇ quantification of any interrelationships between the specified activity and other possible activities (e.g., grazing requirements of livestock or rotational attributes of crops);
- ◇ a listing of any non-resource constraints on the level of the activity either alone or in combination with other activities (e.g., marketing constraints or constraints reflecting the personal preferences of the farmer);
- ◇ a listing of variable inputs and costs per unit level of the activity;
- ◇ a statement of the output produced per unit level of the activity and, if the output is sold, an estimate of the net price received.

By way of an example, an activity budget for sweet potatoes in Tonga in the South Pacific is provided in Table 4.1.

Table 4.1

ACTIVITY BUDGET FOR SWEET POTATO IN TONGA IN 1989

(a) **Introduction**

English name	-	Sweet Potato
Scientific name	-	*Ipomea batatas*
Tongan name	-	Kumala

An important subsistence crop that is also sold on the domestic market. It has a short production period, with some varieties being ready to harvest four months after planting. Sweet potato is traditionally planted second to either yam or taro. It is used as a feast food. The leaves are frequently used as pig feed.

(b) **Production notes**

Climate. Although moderately drought resistant, the best yields are attained with an annual rainfall of at least 900 mm.

Soil. Friable soils produce the best yields, but sweet potatoes can also be grown in heavy clay soils if they are planted in ridges, mounds or other raised beds.

Scab-resistant varieties. The scab fungus is the most significant constraint on production. Some new varieties are scab-resistant.

Propagation. Planting material consists of vine tip cuttings which are 30-40 cm long; 3-4 cuttings are planted in each mound. Pest-free planting material must be used to avoid infestation by the sweet potato weevil.

Planting time. Sweet potato can be planted all year round, given adequate soil moisture. However, best yields are obtained from crops planted between March and July.

Planting density. Spacing ranges from 1.0m × 1.0m to 1.0m × 1.5m; an average of 1.2m × 0.9m is equivalent to 3 700 plants/ac.

Growth period. Sweet potato is harvested mostly after 4-5 months, but can be harvested from 3-8 months.

Disease and pest control. To avoid infestation by sweet potato weevil, treat affected planting material with Diazinon. Sweet potato scab can be controlled to some extent by treating the crop with Manzate 200 80% WP.

Storage. Sweet potato does not store well; only a few days in a dry area. It stores best in the ground as long as insect and pest levels in the soil are not too high.

Table 4.1

ACTIVITY BUDGET FOR SWEET POTATO IN TONGA IN 1989
(continued)

(c) **Economics of sweet potato production**

Basic details:

Spacing (m)	1.2 × 0.9
Density (plant/ac)	3 700
Average price, ($/kg)	0.33
Growth period (mth)	5
Average basket weight (kg)	22
Yield range (kg/ac)	1 500 - 10 000

Gross margin per acre:

Gross income	Yield (kg)	Price ($/kg)	Gross income ($)
Sweet potatoes	5 000	0.33	1 650(A)

Variable costs	Amount	Price ($)	Cost ($)
Land preparation			
- ploughing/slashing	1.5 h	18.00/h	27
- ploughing	1.5 h	18.00/h	27
- ridging	1.0 h	18.00/h	18
Planting material	10 500 cuttings		
Pest and disease control			
- Diazinon	1.75 L	8.00/L	14
- Manzate 200 80% WP	9.0 kg	9.00/kg	81
- mistblower operation	3 times	3.00/ac	9
Harvest costs			
- transport	5 trips	10.00/trip	50
- marketing	5 d	2.00/d	10
Total variable costs			236(B)
Gross margin (A) - (B)			1 414(C)
Return to variable costs ratio (C)/(B)			5.99

Table 4.1

ACTIVITY BUDGET FOR SWEET POTATO IN TONGA IN 1989 (concluded)

Effect of variations in price and yield on the gross margin:

Price	Yield (kg/ac)		
	2000	5000	8000
$/kg	$/ac	$/ac	$/ac
0.18	124	664	1204
0.33	424	1414	2404
0.53	824	2414	4004

Labour inputs:

Task	Labour h/ac
Manual land clearing	40
Preparing planting material	20
Planting	60
Weeding	100
Mounding	40
Spraying	24
Harvesting	50
Processing/packing	10
Selling	50
Total labour requirement	394
Gross margin per hour of labour	$ 3.95
Total labour cost (@ $2/h) (D)	$ 788
Margin after labour costs (C) - (D)	$ 626

Source: Adapted from Gyles, Hardaker and Verspay (1989).

4.4 *Planning farm-household resource use*

This section is concerned with the stage in farm-household planning relating to establishing the feasibility of a particular plan. Often this will prove to be the most important stage of a planning study of a small farm-household. Plans, defined in terms of activity levels, may often be strongly indicated by technical considerations. Thus the planner's main task is one of establishing that a proposed plan is indeed technically and economically feasible and acceptable to the farm family. The question of the merits of the proposed plan vis-à-vis alternatives either may not arise or may be a secondary issue to the question of feasibility.

The first requirement in planning farm-household resource use is for the planner to make an inventory of the resources available and of the constraints bearing on the choice of an activity mix. It is usually convenient to review resource and planning constraints under the following headings:

◇ land and rotations,
◇ irrigation,
◇ labour,
◇ draught animals and machinery,
◇ livestock feed,
◇ working capital and credit,
◇ family food and cash needs; and
◇ institutional, social, cultural and personal constraints.

In drawing up an inventory of these resource and planning constraints, the resource stocks or constraint levels should be quantified as accurately as possible.

A review is now provided of the quantitative information needed under each of the above headings and of some of the planning procedures that can be used to assess the feasibility of a plan with regard to each category of constraints.

LAND AND ROTATIONS

The objective of land and rotation planning is to establish whether a proposed plan is consistent with the land resources available, including the need to ensure that the implied rotation will not deplete the long-term productive capacity of the soil. As we shall see is the case in planning other resources, establishing feasibility in regard to land involves confirming that the resource supply is greater than or equal to the level of resources needed to operate the proposed plan.

In the case of land, the total resource supply is usually relatively easily established by determining the farm area. Account must obviously be taken of any areas that cannot be used for agriculture, such as land occupied by buildings, paths or roads, canals, etc. In most cases, it will be necessary to differentiate various classes of land such as arable and non-arable, irrigated and non-irrigated, etc.

Estimating the demand for land may at first sight also seem to be a simple task, but for some small-farm systems this is not necessarily the case. Crops may vary in both the length of time and the seasons during which they occupy the land. A proposed plan may incorporate both annual (short-duration) and perennial (long-duration) crops. In some areas and for some crops there is only one recognized growing season but in other places there are two or even three cropping seasons each year. In some parts of the tropics, there are no marked seasonal variations in weather and some crops, especially relatively robust species such as cassava for example, can be planted at any time of the year. Indeed, in some situations cassava shares with some other crops the property of having no clearly defined growing period. Thus cassava may be harvested some eight months or so after planting (less in favourable locations) or may be left in the ground for two years or more.

A further dimension of complexity in planning land use arises from the practice of many small farmers of planting mixed crops or of intercropping one crop with another.[1] Perennial crops such as coconuts may be intercropped with short-duration crops, especially before the perennial crop has matured. Two or more crops may be grown simultaneously to exploit differences in growth habit, etc. One crop may be planted as a previous one is maturing so that a sequence of mixed crops is grown.

In planning land use it is also necessary to take account of crop rotation and crop sequence considerations. Excessive production of crops that are demanding of soil fertility can deplete the productive capacity of the soil through such effects as removal of plant nutrients, build-up of pests and diseases, and loss of soil structure. Thus it may be necessary to ensure that any proposed crop rotation incorporates appropriate areas of legumes, pasture or fallow that will restore the fertility of the soil. The frequency with which crops that are vulnerable to soil-borne diseases may be grown may need to be restricted. Moreover, attention may need to be given to the sequence of crops. Crops demanding a high level of fertility may need to be included early in a rotation following a legume or other *break* crop. Some crop sequences may be more advantageous than others if, for example, there is a good match between the time of harvest of the preceding crop and the appropriate planting date for the succeeding crop.

---

[1] The terminology of multiple cropping systems is confused but some consistent definitions are given by TAC (1978). See also, for example, Dalrymple (1971) and Stelly *et al.* (1976).

All this can make the farm planner's task difficult. Ignoring for the moment the possibility of intercropping, land use planning involves:

- ◇ establishing the areas of each crop activity to be planted each year;
- ◇ establishing the planting dates and durations of these crops; and
- ◇ specifying the sequence in which the crops are to be grown.

A framework for planning land use is illustrated in Figure 4.1. Across the top of the figure the crop year is divided into appropriate *seasons*. In this case, six two-month seasons are used. The cropping sequence is represented in the body of the figure which shows the crops grown, their order in the rotation, and the period of time each occupies the land.

Figure 4.1

REPRESENTATION OF A CROP ROTATION

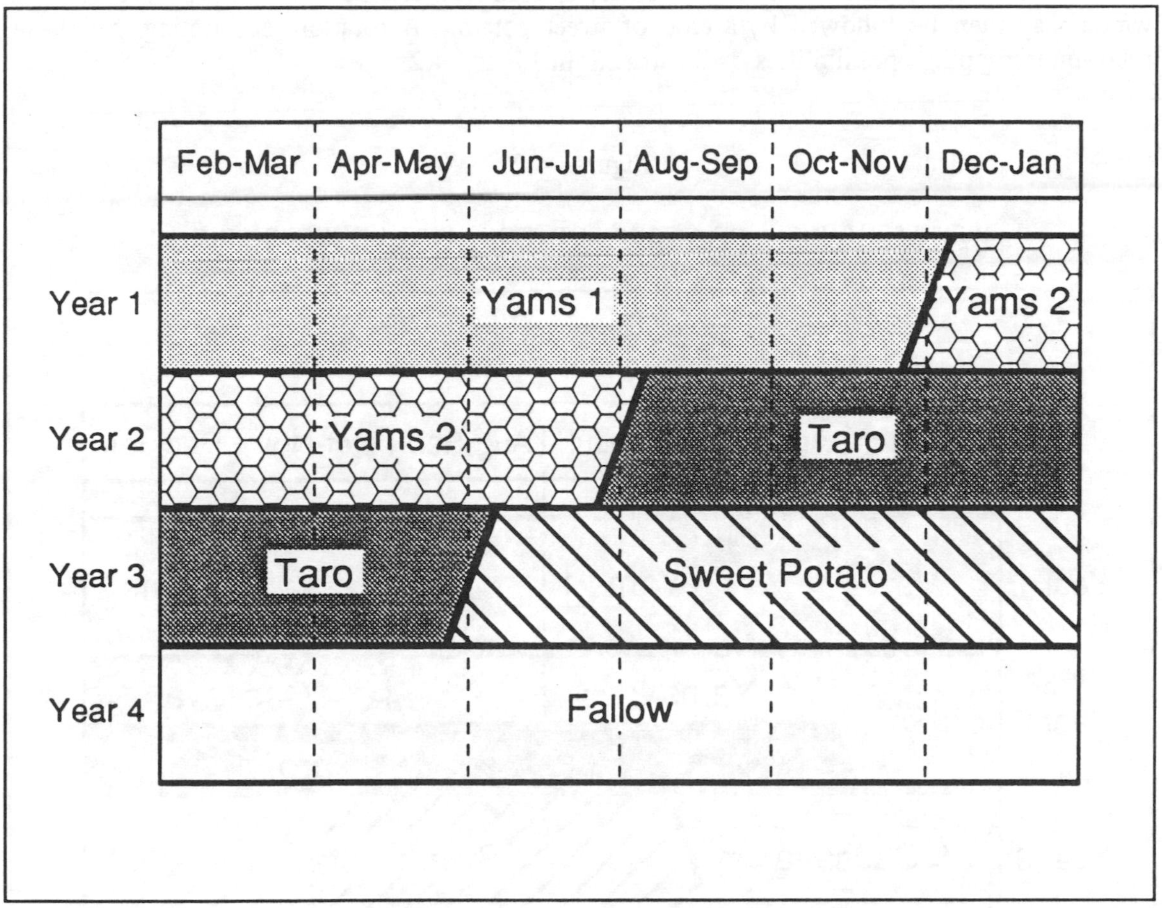

In the case illustrated the first crop planted is yams which occupy the land for about 10 months. The first yam crop is immediately followed by a second (taking 8 months) which is followed in turn by taro. Taro occupies the land for approximately 10 months and is followed in turn by sweet potatoes with a growing period of about 8 months. The rotation is completed by a 12-month fallow.

The area allocated to each crop in a rotation is called the *break*. If the break for the rotation illustrated in Figure 4.1 were 0.25 ha, the areas of crops planted in a *steady state* situation, in which 0.25 ha of first-crop yams were established annually, would be:

	(ha)
Yams	0.50
Taro	0.25
Sweet potato	0.25
Fallow	0.25

This adds up to 1.25 ha, but in fact the total area required is only 1.00 ha since, as Figure 4.1 shows, the rotation can be established on four plots of 0.25 ha, one for each *year* of the rotation.

The method illustrated can be extended to deal with relay intercropping. The rotation considered above can be modified to account for the fact that the second crop of yams can be interplanted with taro. Further, taro in turn can be interplanted with cassava which may then be followed by a crop of sweet potato. A rotation accounting for these relay-intercropping possibilities is illustrated in Figure 4.2.

Figure 4.2

REPRESENTATION OF A CROP ROTATION WITH INTERCROPPING

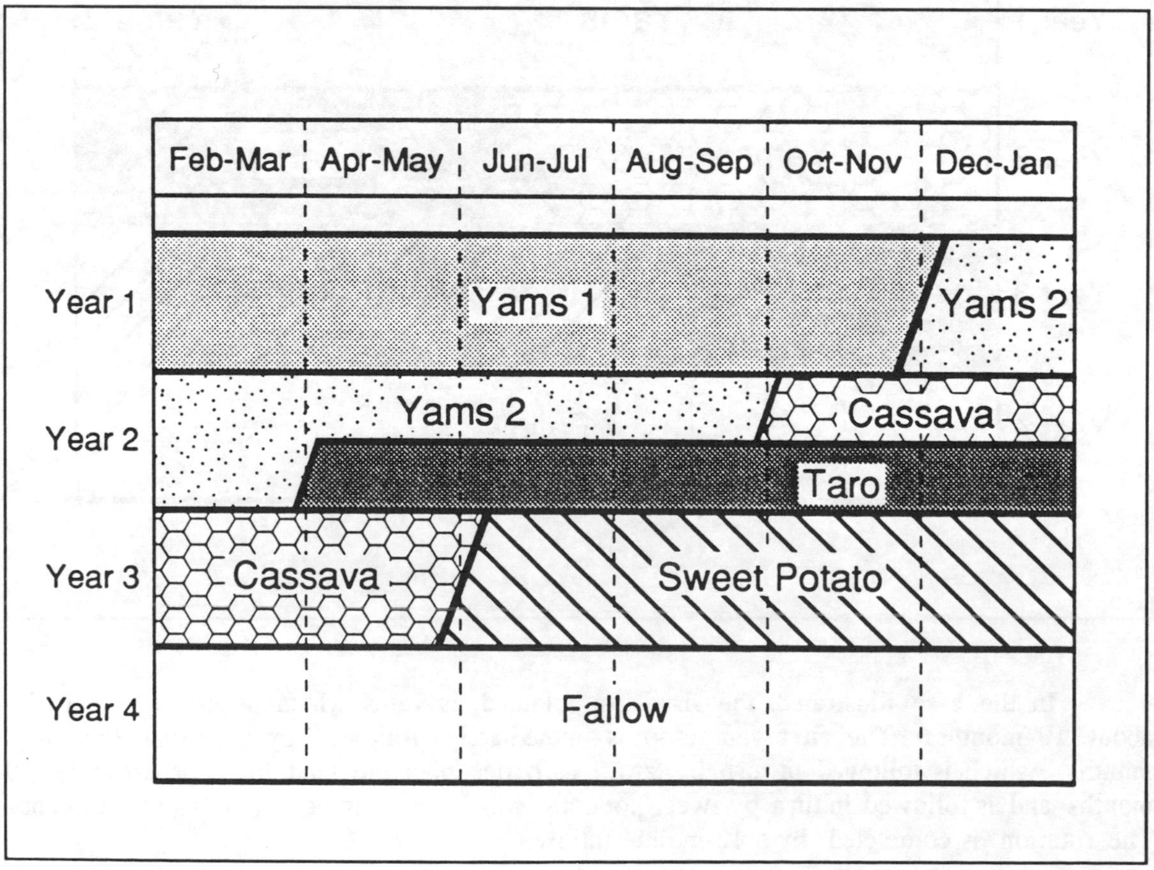

In the steady state, the new rotation comprises:

	(ha)
Yams	0.50
Taro	0.25
Cassava	0.25
Sweet potato	0.25
Fallow	0.25

The areas planted to the various crops are as before, except that 0.25 ha cassava has been added. Yet, because opportunities for relay intercropping have been exploited, the total land area occupied by the rotation in the steady state with a 0.25 ha break remains at 1.00 ha. Of course, the effect on overall farm performance of changing to a more intensive rotation in the manner illustrated will depend, *inter alia*, on the effect of relay intercropping on crop yields.

A rather different land-use planning problem arises in relation to intercropping of perennial crops. During the establishment phase of crops such as oil palm and coconuts, the young trees are sufficiently small to permit cash or subsistence crops to be grown between the rows. This practice not only provides a source of cash and/or food for the plantation owner and family, but can be valuable in controlling weeds that might otherwise compete with the young trees. Land-use planning in this case devolves to estimating the amount of land available between the trees. Clearly, this tends to decline as the trees grow until, when the overhead canopies of adjacent rows of trees meet, intercropping may cease to be practicable. Moreover, as the degree of ground shade increases, it may be necessary to select for intercropping only those plants that thrive under shady conditions.

To illustrate, if young coconuts are planted at 10 m × 10 m, and if it is deemed that, to avoid root damage to the trees, intercropping should not occur within 2 m of each tree, the area of land available for cultivation varies according to the planting system used for the intercrop, as illustrated in Figure 4.3.

It should, of course, be recognized that this somewhat theoretical approach gives only an approximate estimate of the potential for intercropping of tree crops. The approach hinges on making a good estimate of the root zone around each tree which should not be planted with an intercrop. Even if a reliable estimate of this area is available, the method provides no allowance for any competition between the two crops for light, soil moisture, soil nutrients, etc. Thus, the approach must be used with discretion, supplemented, whenever possible, with local data on crop yields under intercropping.

Mixed intercropping can be handled in one of two ways in land-use planning. First, the fact of mixed intercropping may be ignored. If 0.5 ha is to be planted with a mixture of maize and beans, it may suffice for planning purposes to treat this as, say, 0.25 ha maize and 0.25 ha beans or some other proportionate sole-crop equivalents. If such an approach is not practicable, perhaps because of complementarities between the two crops in, say, labour use, the second alternative is to define a new crop activity as mixed maize and beans. The production characteristics, input use, etc. of this activity would then need to be specified as for single crop activities.

Figure 4.3

INTERCROPPING POSSIBILITIES FOR A YOUNG TREE CROP

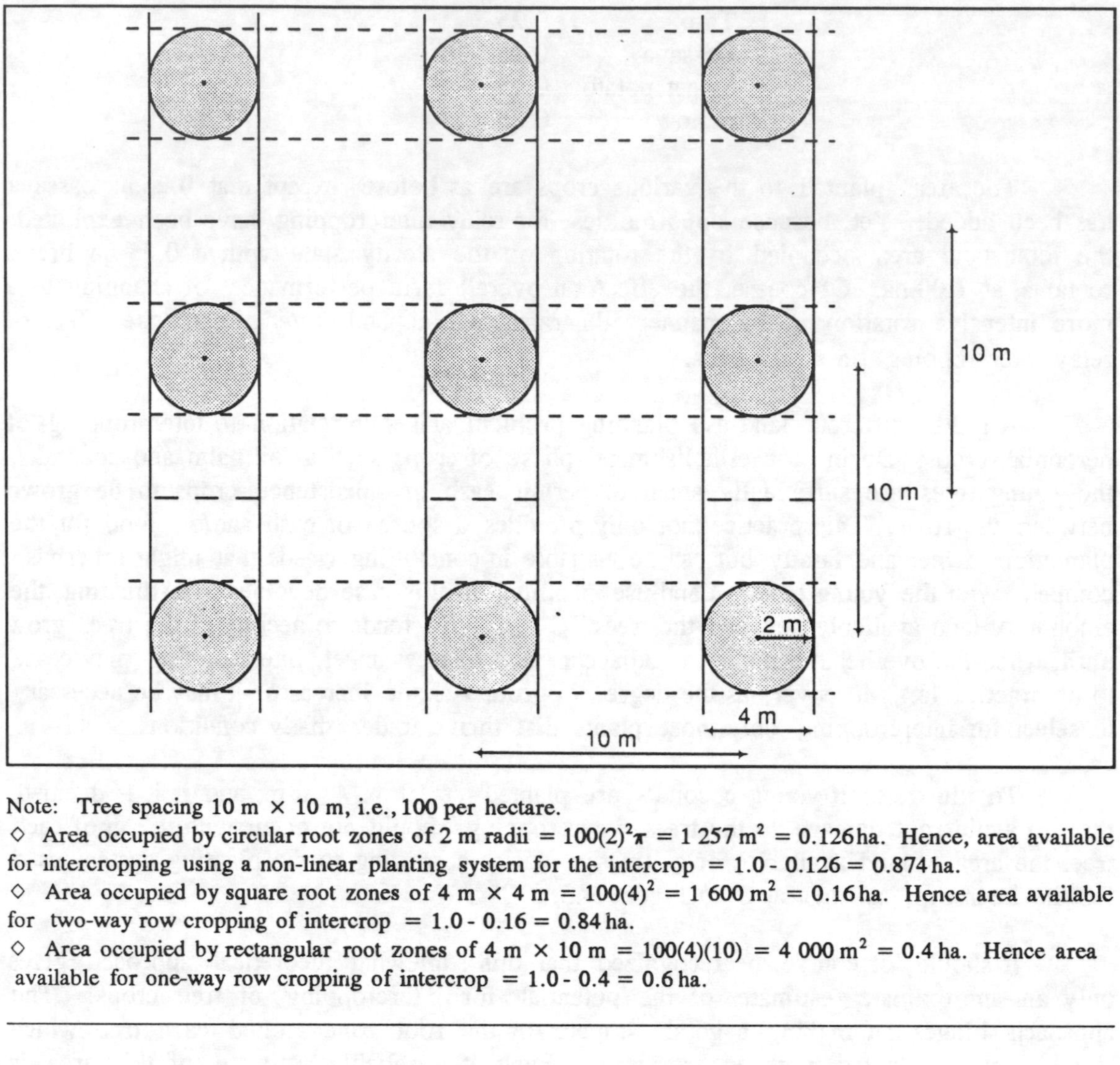

Note: Tree spacing 10 m × 10 m, i.e., 100 per hectare.
◇ Area occupied by circular root zones of 2 m radii = $100(2)^2\pi$ = 1 257 m^2 = 0.126 ha. Hence, area available for intercropping using a non-linear planting system for the intercrop = 1.0 - 0.126 = 0.874 ha.
◇ Area occupied by square root zones of 4 m × 4 m = $100(4)^2$ = 1 600 m^2 = 0.16 ha. Hence area available for two-way row cropping of intercrop = 1.0 - 0.16 = 0.84 ha.
◇ Area occupied by rectangular root zones of 4 m × 10 m = 100(4)(10) = 4 000 m^2 = 0.4 ha. Hence area available for one-way row cropping of intercrop = 1.0 - 0.4 = 0.6 ha.

IRRIGATION

Irrigation is an important resource in whole-farm planning for many farms. As with other resources, there are two related aspects of the irrigation planning problem - feasibility and profitability. The planner must establish, as conclusively as possible, that the farm irrigation resources are adequate to meet the demands imposed on them by the intended farm plan. She or he must also consider the profitability of the proposed utilization of the irrigation resources.

In regard to the feasibility question, the essential concern is to try to establish that, for the contemplated farm plan, irrigation supply is equal to (or greater than) irrigation requirement. However, in seeking to apply this test it is necessary to consider more than just the overall quantity of water. For example, it is necessary to consider the area of the farm that can be irrigated. Water may be available in abundance yet it may be impossible

Table 4.2

MEAN VALUES OF WATER BALANCE COMPONENTS FOR THE LAND PREPARATION PERIOD, LUZON, PHILIPPINES, 1969-70

Item	First-crop sites (mm)	Second-crop sites (mm)
Crop water requirement	500	171
Evaporation losses	223	198
Drainage	417	339
Total requirement	1 140	708
Less rainfall	289	182
Irrigation requirement	851	526

Source: Wickham (1973).

to irrigate some areas because of unsuitable topography, unsuitable soil type for irrigation or lack of an appropriate water delivery and control system.

Seasonality of water supply and requirements must also be considered. Rivers generally have periods of high and low discharge rates, and irrigation farming has to be adapted to the seasonal availability of water. On the demand side, the appropriate timings of waterings will generally depend on the crops grown, planting dates, and perhaps on cultural practices followed (e.g., direct sowing or transplanting). Similarly, in areas where crops are partly rainfed, seasonal differences in rainfall lead to seasonal variations in supplementary irrigation needs.

In the simplest case, farm planning for irrigation involves budgeting water demand for a given combination of crop activities and comparing this estimated demand to the estimated supply from the lift pump, tube-well, waterway system, etc. It is, of course, necessary to account for seasonality in such calculations, as indicated above, and to allow for the fact that, with some watering methods, the minimum amount of water that can be applied at any one occasion may be more than the optimal amount.

Methods of water balance budgeting have been developed (e.g., Burman, Cuenca and Weiss, 1983; Angus and Garcia, 1989; Perera, 1990) which, if the necessary basic data are available, permit the irrigation water requirement for a given crop activity to be determined. A water balance calculation for the land-preparation period only in Luzon, Philippines, is illustrated in Table 4.2. The data in this table are project-level averages and do not reveal the wide site-to-site variation that would have to be taken into account in planning individual farms. However, given such detailed data, a seasonal profile of total water needs can be found by adding up, on a seasonal basis, the calculated needs of all irrigated crop activities in the farm plan. The total profile obtained can then be related to the seasonal pattern of water availability, as dictated by such factors as pump capacity, flow in waterways, or institutional constraints. Figure 4.4 shows a water requirement profile developed for a rice production system planned for the Angat River Irrigation System, Bulacan, Philippines.

Methods of budgeting water need using the soil-water balance are usually based on technical, rather than economic, considerations. For example, it is usual to assume that, so far as practicable, each crop should be watered as soon as the soil moisture falls to a level at which the crop begins to exhibit moisture stress. If the marginal cost of water is not zero, as is often the case, it will pay to trade off a saving in irrigation costs against some yield loss by reducing the amount or frequency of irrigation. Similarly, if water is limited, it will generally be profitable to trade off some reduction in yield per hectare arising from a degree of crop moisture stress for the opportunity to grow a greater area

Figure 4.4

FARM IRRIGATION WATER REQUIREMENT, ANGAT RIVER IRRIGATION SYSTEM, BULACAN, PHILIPPINES (Julian, 1973)

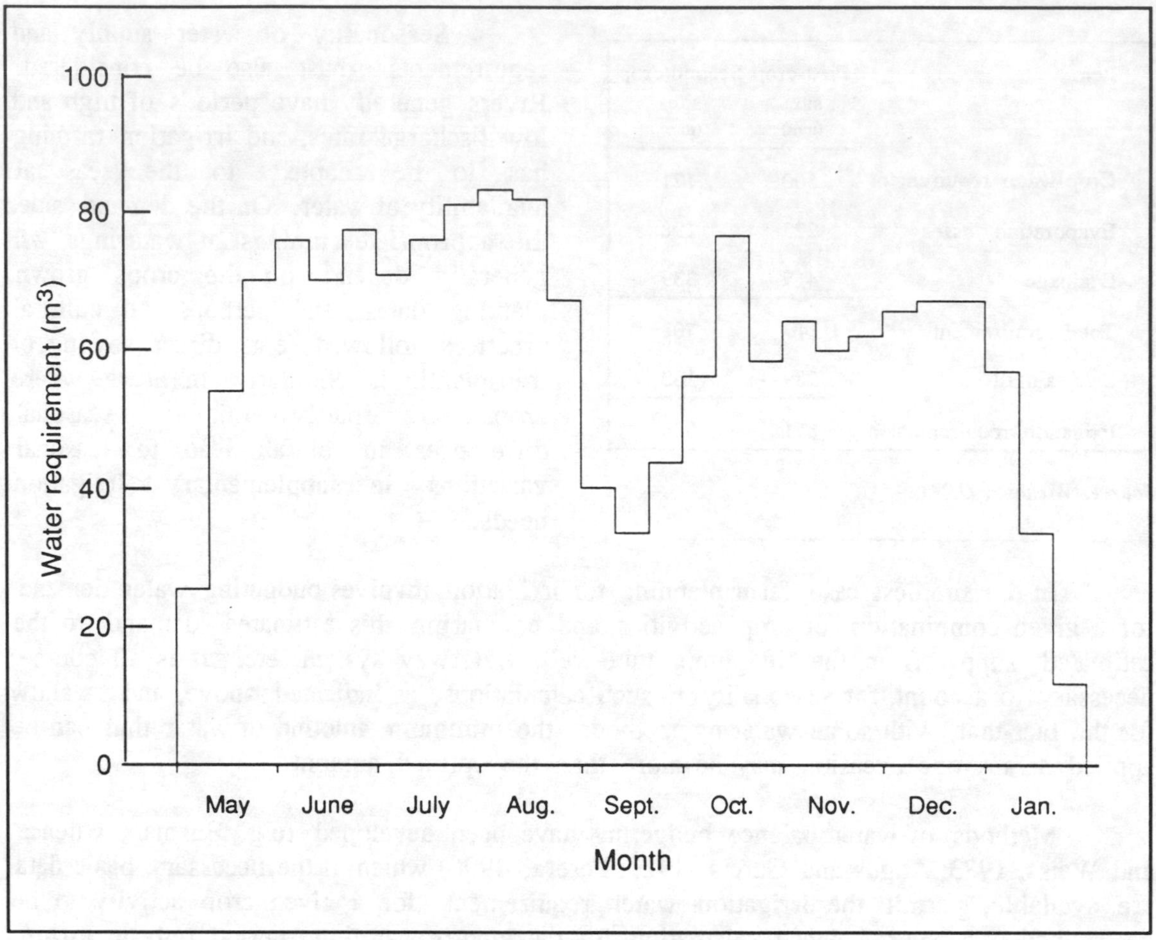

of irrigated crop. Finding the optimal rate of water application in such situations is akin to planning the optimal use of other inputs such as fertilizer. In principle, the methods of partial budgeting and analysis of response, discussed in Chapters 5 and 7, can be applied for all such planning problems. However, in the case of irrigation there is a dynamic dimension, not usually present for other inputs, i.e., the response of a crop to a particular application of water may depend on the amounts of water applied at earlier or later stages in the life of the crop. Methods of planning optimal water use recognizing the time-dependent nature of the response function have been developed (Matanga and Marino, 1979; Yaron and Bressler, 1983; Vaux and Pruitt, 1983; Dudley, 1988). However, in many real farm situations there may be a relatively small number of practicable alternatives to be considered, so that choice is simplified. For example, the choice may be between one, two or three applications of water to a given crop, and relatively simple budgets may reveal which is best.

Quality of irrigation water is also an important consideration. In many situations, management of water and salinity are interrelated. Extra water, over and above the crop water requirements, may be applied for leaching purposes. Irrigation water itself may be saline, requiring the consideration of the effect of salinity on crop and variety choices and yields. Various methods are available to model the dynamic effects of salinity on crop choice and profitability (Dinar and Knapp, 1986; Knapp and Wichelns, 1990).

Considerations of reliability are often important in planning farm irrigation. Water supplies obtained from the natural flow of streams, or by impounding water in dams, tanks or paddies, will vary from year to year. The supply of pumped water may be uncertain, for example, if power supplies for the pump are not assured (Pandey, 1989). In areas where water is distributed via a canal system, farmers on the network distant from the source may find themselves short of water if total water available is less than required or if the allocation procedures are inappropriate or incorrectly applied (Rosegrant, 1986). On the demand side, if irrigation is a supplement to rainfall, the amount of water needed will be uncertain, depending on variable rainfall.

In some areas, too much water can be as much a problem as too little. Inadequate flood control measures, poor drainage or poor layout of paddies, etc. can result in water that is too deep or too slow to drain away for optimal crop production. Improved, short-stemmed varieties of paddy, for example, may be risky to grow in areas where there is poor control of water depth during flood irrigation.

Irrigation planning which takes account of the reliability of supply or variability of demand is much more difficult than planning in a more certain environment. The methods of accounting for risk, described in Chapter 8, are appropriate. For the moment it is sufficient to note that accounting for risk will generally lead to a somewhat less intensive use of irrigation, since the penalties incurred when water supplies fall short of needs are generally quite severe. For this reason, a practical approach to irrigation planning under risk is to plan using conservative estimates of water availability and needs. Thus, one might base plans on a dry year, rather than on an average year. By this means, the chance of a serious shortfall in irrigation water supplies can be reduced to an arbitrarily low level.

LABOUR

As with other resources, the primary objective in labour planning is to establish that the supply of labour available to the farm will be at least equal to the demands imposed by a given plan, including allowances for labour time needed in the home and in non-farm work. If a labour surplus is found, planning may then centre on finding further productive employment opportunities. On the other hand, a labour shortage signals a need to plan an optimal strategy for making good the deficit.

Effective labour planning hinges on choice of a unit (or units) of measurement whereby the labour requirement of a particular farm plan can be assessed in relation to the potential supply of labour provided by the farm family, together with any hired labour. For most purposes, the use of labour-hour or labour-day units has been found satisfactory. It is usual to assume, regardless of actual work habits, that eight labour hours are equal to one labour day. The limitations of such a unit of measurement, however, are apparent. Workers vary in skill, strength and application, while jobs to be done in farm production also vary in the demands they impose on workers. The practice is sometimes adopted of measuring labour on a man-hour or man-day equivalent, applying conversion factors of, say, 0.8 and 0.5 to labour time supplied by women and children respectively. The weakness of this approach, however, is that for some tasks a woman or child might be at least as effective as a man and it would only be for tasks involving physical strength or endurance that such conversion factors might apply. In other words, conversion factors strictly need to be worked out on a task-by-task basis, and this is seldom practicable. If it is not, it may be reasonable to assume that workers will ordinarily be assigned to jobs either on a conventional basis or according to what work they do best. It is then reasonable to use a single uniform measure for labour measurement.

Special attention must be paid to cases in which cultural or other constraints dictate that only certain workers can perform particular tasks. In such cases it is necessary to consider not only overall labour utilization but also the supply of and demands on particular labour categories. Thus, if the custom is that females transplant rice and if it is taboo for males to assist with this work, the rice area may well be constrained by the available female labour force. Similarly, if, because of the strenuous nature of the work, land preparation must be done by men, the time of adult males may need to be accounted for separately.

Labour needs for a particular farm or non-farm activity can be established knowing the sequence of tasks to be performed and the labour needed for each task. Such data are usually collected by field survey involving either regular recording or time studies. With such information, seasonal labour profiles can be constructed for defined activities. The data on labour utilization for the sweet potato activity, presented in Table 4.1, are of the form needed to construct such a profile. A further example, developed from a survey of 35 plots of white sorghum cultivated by manual labour only in the Sahel zone of Burkina Faso is shown in Table 4.3.

Table 4.3

LABOUR UTILIZATION SCHEDULE FOR WHITE SORGHUM IN THE SAHEL ZONE OF BURKINA FASO

Operation	Labour h/ha (if done)					Percent area worked	Average h/ha grown
	Male	Female	Child	Non-hhold	Total		
Clearing	34.0	0.0	0.0	0.0	34.0	50.6	17.2
Soil preparation	127.9	34.4	93.4	0.0	255.7	6.1	15.6
Planting	31.9	6.2	3.0	0.4	41.5	100.0	41.5
First weeding	148.7	60.2	5.5	0.5	214.9	93.2	200.3
Second weeding	103.4	28.9	1.7	15.4	149.4	90.2	134.8
Harvesting	78.0	4.3	0.4	4.9	87.6	92.2	80.8
Total							490.2

Source: Matlon and Fafchamps (1988).

Seasonal labour profiles are based on division of the year into planning periods that may be chosen either conventionally, such as calendar months, or to correspond with the biological timetable of operations. Although conventional planning periods are often used, the latter approach is generally to be preferred. For example, if planting of a major crop must ordinarily be completed between early February and mid-March, it would clearly be appropriate to adopt these dates as the limits of a labour planning period, rather than to use calendar months. When using labour charts, as described below, the need to define specific planning periods is avoided.

Once seasonal labour needs for all the activities to be included in a particular plan have been estimated, attention must be directed to estimating labour supply. In principle, this is quite straightforward. The total labour time available in any period is found by adding for each available worker the time she or he can work in that period. In practice, however, while it is usually easy to determine the number of workers available, estimating the labour time of each can present some difficulties.

Since most farming operations cannot be performed in the dark, available working time is first of all constrained to the daylight hours. Further deductions must be made for personal needs such as mealtimes, rest and recreation. Time may need to be deducted for social activities, such as festivals, weddings, and visits to relatives, etc. Unless non-farm activities such as domestic tasks, work for the village, local government agency or church and, in the case of school children, for school work are explicitly included among the planned activities, the time needed must also be deducted from the time available. Commonly, some time is lost through illness, although obviously budgeting for this in advance is difficult.

Once available working times have been estimated, it may be necessary to make further deductions to account for environmental constraints on labour use. Many jobs require suitable weather conditions, so that a deduction must usually be made for bad weather. The extent of such deductions will usually vary from one season to another and may also be related to the kind of work to be done. For example, harvesting of grain crops usually requires dry weather, while planting might be possible in both wet and dry conditions. Relatedly, some jobs require suitable crop or soil conditions before they can be undertaken. For example, ploughing may be possible only within a certain soil moisture range, and grain may be put into store only when it is dry enough.

It should be evident from the above that estimating labour availability is not simple. Moreover, because the factors discussed above vary according to circumstances, no generally applicable standards can be provided. Estimates must therefore be made for each location, type of farming, etc. It is, however, worth noting that in village societies where the distinction between work and leisure is often somewhat blurred, it is easy to overestimate the time that people can allocate to farm work or other production.

Once the data for both sides of the labour planning relationship have been assembled, it is a relatively straightforward task to construct a budget of seasonal labour requirements compared with availability. Such a budget can be constructed in the form of a table, with a column for each labour period. Requirements in each period are obtained by multiplying the estimated per unit labour needs of each activity by the scale of that activity, followed by addition of the products. Comparison with the labour supply

Figure 4.5

SEASONAL LABOUR AVAILABILITY AND UTILIZATION ON A CASE-STUDY FARM

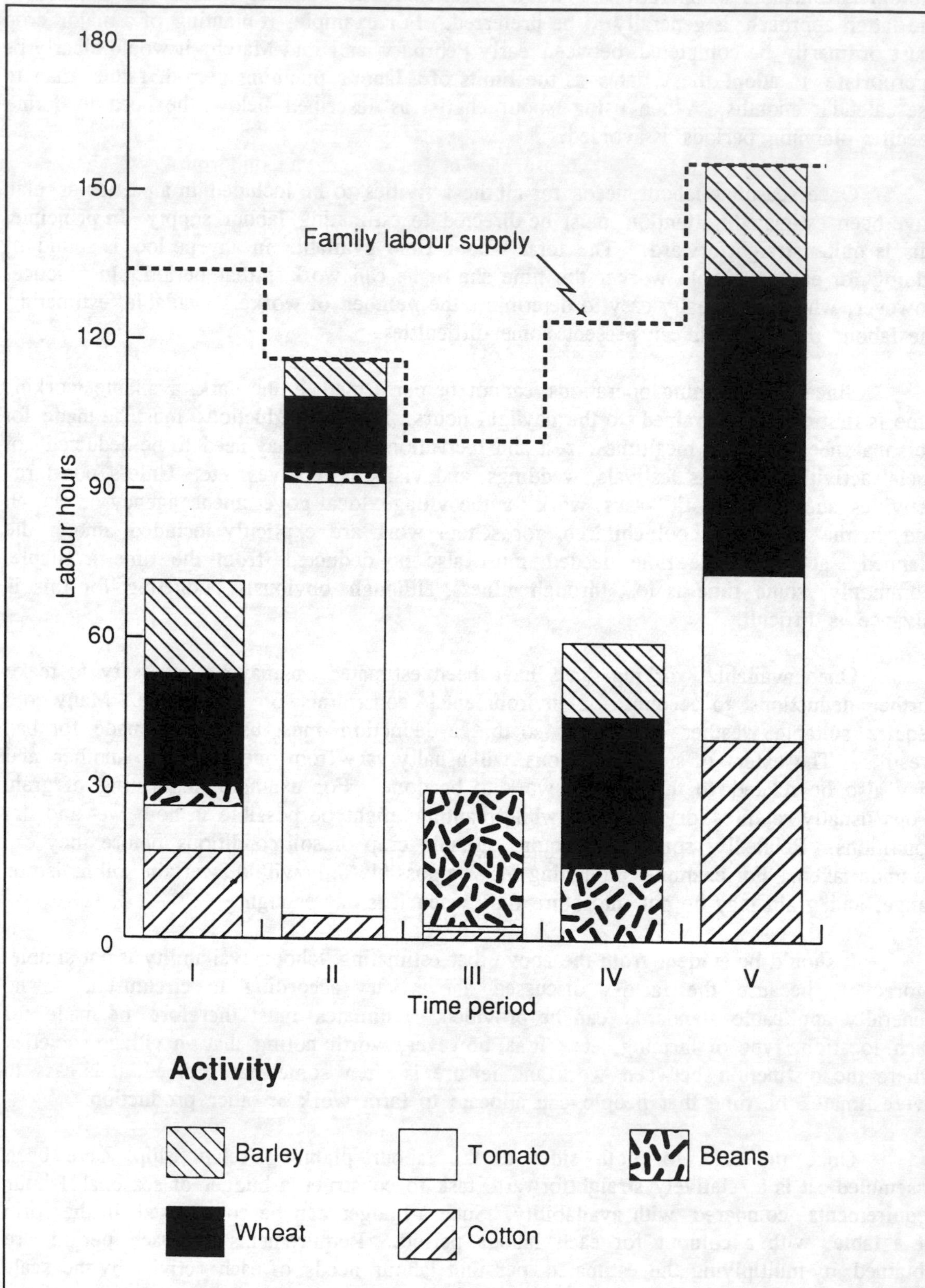

in each period will reveal the extent of any labour surplus or deficit. Figure 4.5 indicates in diagrammatic form the results of such a labour budget.

If the labour budget reveals a deficit of labour in some period or periods, it must be established whether casual or contract labour can be hired to the extent required to make good the shortage. Alternatively, the plan might be modified to reduce the labour requirement by including less of the labour intensive activity or activities. Partial budgeting (see Chapter 5) could be used to establish which alternative would be best.

In a related manner, a labour surplus might indicate an opportunity to change to a more labour intensive plan, if this is judged desirable, or for some members of the farm-family work-force to find off-farm employment.

An alternative, more flexible way of constructing a seasonal labour budget is by means of a labour chart. This is a figure with a calendar of working periods recorded on the horizontal axis and with number of workers recorded on the vertical axis. An example is shown in Figure 4.6. Note that the numbers of working days on the horizontal axis are

Figure 4.6

AN EXAMPLE OF PART OF A LABOUR CHART FOR A MIXED CROPPING FARM
(adapted from Hardaker, 1967, p. 174)

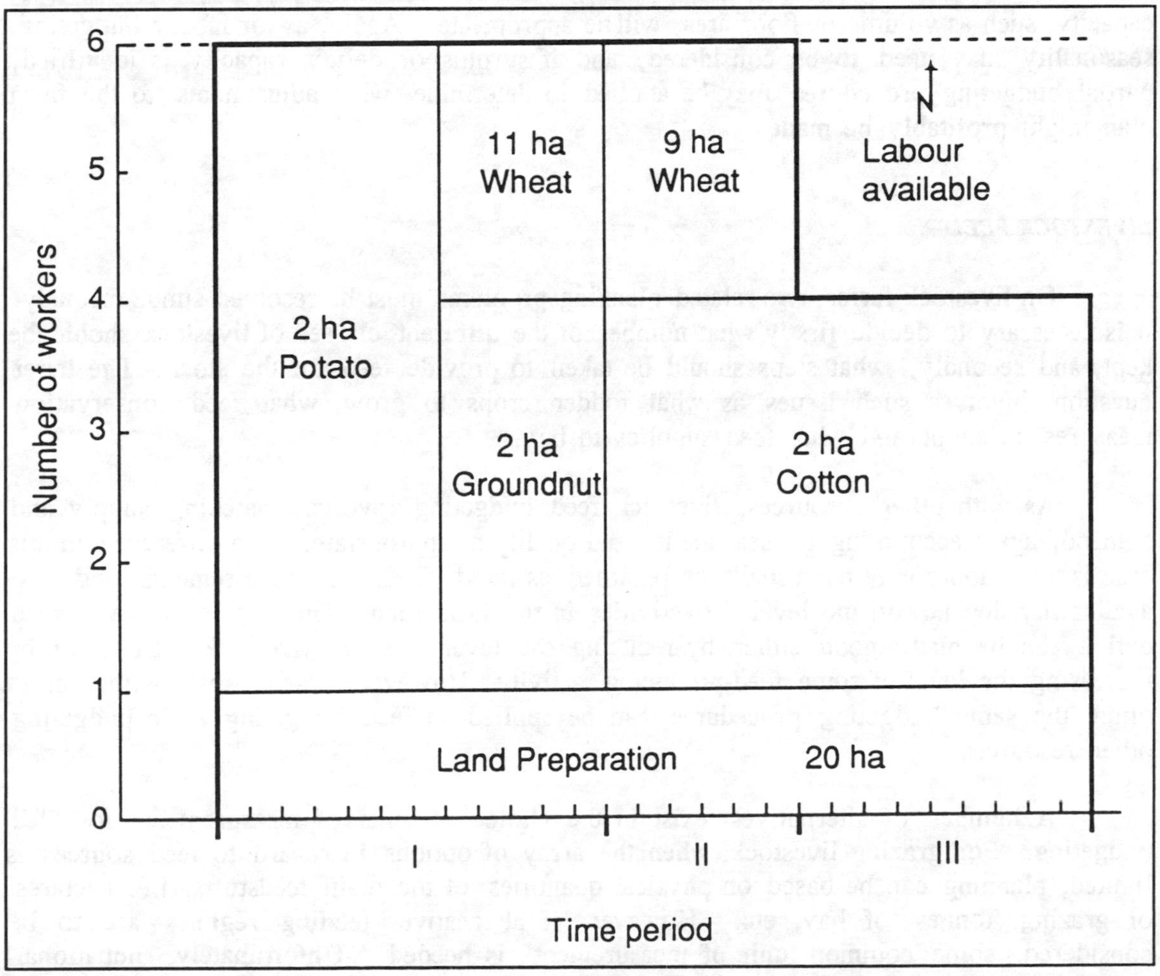

net of all lost time. The labour chart is completed, as illustrated in the example, by marking the number of workers assigned to each task and the duration of that task. A direct visual assessment can then be made of the adequacy of the labour supply available at any particular point in time in relation to needs at that time.

Labour charts of the type illustrated in Figure 4.6 have two main advantages over the tabular layout of labour budgets. First, the need to divide the year into discrete planning periods is avoided. Each task is represented on the chart in the period during which it is performed. Second, if some tasks demand teams of two or more workers, the chart will reveal the feasibility or otherwise of the plan in terms of the number of workers available, rather than solely in terms of total labour time, as with tabular budgets (Hardaker, 1967).

DRAUGHT ANIMALS AND MACHINERY

In some circumstances farm plans may be constrained by the availability of draught animals or particular items of machinery or equipment, such as tractors, ploughs, harvesters or stores. Methods of planning the use of such constraining resources are exactly parallel to the methods described above for labour budgeting, i.e., the demands on the resource for a given farm plan must be estimated and matched against the estimated supply. For draught animals and items of field equipment, demand and supply can be measured in hours, while for such items as grain stores or livestock pens, other units of capacity, such as volume or floor area, will be appropriate. Again, as for labour budgeting, seasonality may need to be considered, and if surplus or deficit capacity is identified, partial budgeting procedures may be applied to determine what adjustments to the farm plan might profitably be made.

LIVESTOCK FEED

On livestock farms, two related planning problems must be resolved simultaneously. It is necessary to decide firstly what number of the different classes of livestock should be kept, and secondly, what steps should be taken to provide feed for the stock. The latter question involves such issues as what fodder crops to grow, what feed conservation measures to adopt and what feed supplies to buy.

As with other resources, livestock feed budgeting involves matching supply and demand, again accounting for seasonality and quality as appropriate. The difference in this case is that supply may not usually be regarded as fixed. Both feed requirements and feed availability depend on the levels of activities in the farm plan. Thus, for example, a feed deficit can be made good either by reducing the level of some livestock activity, or by increasing the level of some feed-producing activity. However, bearing this distinction in mind, the same budgeting procedures can be applied in feed budgeting as in budgeting other resources.

A number of alternatives exist in the choice of units of measurement for feed budgeting. For grazing livestock, when the array of options in regard to feed sources is limited, planning can be based on physical quantities of the main feedstuffs, i.e., hectares of grazing, tonnes of hay, etc. However, if alternative feeding regimes are to be considered, some common unit of measurement is needed. Unfortunately, nutritional requirements of livestock are complex, involving several different nutrients, so that no one unit can be wholly satisfactory. Nevertheless, experience shows that adequate feed budgets can generally be constructed using metabolizable energy (ME) as the common denominator. Feeding standards are available from which the ME requirements of stock can be calculated (e.g., Corbett, 1990). These standards are an attempt to take account of the size of the animals, their rate of growth, level of production, etc. Similarly, published data are available giving the ME content of commonly available stock feeds. Applying such data to information on the yields of grazed crops or quantities of feed provided allows the ME supply to be calculated to a generally adequate level of approximation.

Because units of energy such as calories or Joules are not familiar to farmers and their advisers, it is sometimes found convenient to convert ME measures into *stock equivalents*. For example, a cow equivalent would be the amount of ME required by a cow at a defined level of production over a given period. The type of animal chosen as the basis of the stock equivalent system can be varied according to the predominating class of stock in a region. The system facilitates use of estimates of stock carrying capacities of pastures and fodder crops expressed in animals per unit area, e.g., 2 cows/ha.

With livestock such as pigs and poultry, when the animals are kept under an intensive system and are not permitted to forage, feed requirements cannot be adequately represented in terms of ME alone. Other nutrients, such as essential amino acids, minerals and vitamins, must also be considered. Recommended standards for the provision of these nutrients are available (e.g., Corbett, 1990) and the planning task becomes one of selecting a mixture of ingredients from the range available so as to meet the recommendations at least cost. While trial-and-error budgeting methods can be used for this purpose, the problem of selecting least-cost diets is well suited to solution by linear programming (LP). The use of LP for farm-household planning is discussed briefly later in this chapter. For a discussion of the application of the method to least-cost diet formulation, see Dent and Casey (1964).

WORKING CAPITAL AND CREDIT

As agriculture is transformed from a subsistence to a commercial orientation, capital constraints tend to become increasingly important. Planning in this regard relates to the seasonal patterns of cash payments and receipts. It is necessary to establish that cash will be available as and when required for family living expenses and to purchase the inputs required for the implementation of a given farm plan. If payments cannot be met from the farm-family's own cash resources, credit will be needed. Planning then involves establishing that credit needs are within the borrowing limits imposed by lenders or by the farmer's own attitude to debt, and that interest and principal payments on borrowings can be met from projected income flows.

The main planning tool used to account for capital and credit constraints is the *cash-flow budget*. This is a statement of projected payments and receipts associated with a particular farm-household plan. It is normally constructed on a period-by-period basis with cash balance being accumulated over the whole period of the budget. The planning horizon used and the length of the periods considered within that horizon vary according to the purpose of the budgetary analysis.

Table 4.4

EXAMPLE OF A SHORT-TERM CASH-FLOW BUDGET ($)

Item	Period					
	Feb-Mar	Apr-May	Jun-Jul	Aug-Sept	Oct-Nov	Dec-Jan
Receipts						
Banana sales	256	155	116	139	221	279
Cassava sales	-	-	-	117	212	128
Copra sales	11	6	16	27	24	21
Total receipts (A)	267	161	132	283	457	428
Payments						
Fertilizers	36	-	24	-	24	-
Sprays	12	12	12	12	12	12
Contract services	16	5	-	-	10	-
Paid labour	180	48	-	-	23	35
Total payments (B)	244	65	36	12	69	47
Farm net cash flow (A-B)	23	96	96	271	388	381
Less household payments	106	106	113	93	97	135
Surplus (+) or deficit (-)	-83	-10	-17	+178	+291	+246
Finance budget						
Opening balance	0	-83	-95	-114	+62	+353
Less interest accrued	0	2	2	2	0	0
Less deficit brought down	83	10	17	0	0	0
Subtotal	-83	-95	-114	-116	+62	+353
Plus surplus brought down	0	0	0	178	291	246
Closing loan balance	-83	-95	-114	+62	+353	+599

Short-term cash-flow budgets are normally constructed over a twelve-month planning horizon with the intermediate cash balance computed at monthly or bi-monthly intervals. Such budgets are useful for analyzing the seasonal use of cash and credit. An example of a short-term cash-flow budget on the basis of bi-monthly periods is provided in Table 4.4. As the table shows, net cash surplus or deficit is calculated for each period. Then, in this case, since borrowing is necessary, the cash surplus is transferred to a finance budget, wherein the level of indebtedness is computed on a period-by-period basis.

Medium-term cash-flow budgets are constructed in an exactly similar format to short-term budgets, but normally extend over a planning horizon of about three or four years, with divisions into perhaps quarterly or half-yearly periods. Medium-term budgets are appropriate when some change in farm organization or methods is contemplated which will take a few years to be fully implemented. Such budgets are also relevant when a loan is advanced that will be repaid over the period of a few years.

Long-term cash-flow budgets relate to a planning horizon of about ten years or more. Again, the budget format is as for short-term budgets, but with totals being accumulated for annual periods. The main role of long-term cash-flow budgets is in planning farm development, as described in Section 4.7 below.

FAMILY FOOD NEEDS

Small farms are generally (but not universally) characterized by a strong subsistence orientation. Commonly, a significant proportion of family food needs is produced on the farm. Thus the general level of health and welfare of the members of the farm family may be strongly dependent on the degree of success achieved in farm food production. Often, rural development programmes, of which farm management studies may form a part, have among their objectives the goal of raising the standard of nutrition of rural people. For these kinds of reasons, any farm management analysis dealing with small farms needs to give very careful consideration to the nature and extent of crop and livestock production for domestic use.

In principle, the nutritional aspects of planning family food needs are very similar to the considerations discussed above in relation to planning feed supplies for farm animals, and the same planning methods can be used. Thus it might be possible to specify family food needs either directly, in terms of so many tonnes of rice, kilograms of beans, litres of milk, etc. Alternatively, food needs may be specified indirectly using recommended nutritional standards (Passmore *et al.*, 1974). Family food intake can then be planned using the quantities of the different foodstuffs consumed and the composition of each in terms of essential nutrients. In performing such calculations it is, of course, necessary to consider losses of nutrients in storage, preparation and cooking.

It may also be necessary to consider the distribution of foods among the members of the household. For example, young children need diets with a higher protein content than adults and the fact that there is enough protein available in aggregate for all members of the household does not necessarily ensure the allocation of enough high protein foods to the children. A programme of nutritional education may be an essential co-requisite of any scheme to improve the availability and quality of food supplies to farm families.

An important difference between planning human nutrition and planning animal nutrition is that for people it is more necessary to take account of dietary preferences and customs. For example, if rice is the strongly preferred staple, a farm plan based on wheat as the main energy source will not be acceptable. Similarly, most people look for a degree of diversity in their meals, so that this aspect must also be allowed for in planning. Some degree of diversity of diets may be achieved by the purchase of certain food items that it is not possible or profitable to produce on the farm. In relatively few parts of the world do small farmers nowadays achieve total self-sufficiency in foodstuffs. Thus, in evaluating the adequacy of a given farm plan in terms of its capacity to meet family food needs, it will usually be necessary to also consider the availability of cash for food purchases. This aspect has already been reviewed above in relation to working capital and credit constraints.

INSTITUTIONAL, SOCIAL, CULTURAL AND PERSONAL CONSTRAINTS

Planning constraints falling into this class are so varied that it is difficult to propose specific methods for analyzing them.

Institutional constraints include such things as laws relating to labour, disease control, production or marketing quotas, etc. which must obviously be taken into account in farm planning. Similarly, there may be institutional restrictions on the availability of certain inputs such as fertilizer, which again will have an important impact on planning. In circumstances where a farmer or group of farmers is supplying a very small market, there may be no quota limiting sales, but the price received may depend upon the amount of production marketed. Planning must then account for the change in price to be expected as the volume sold is varied. Because of the estimational difficulties involved, it is fortunate that such situations are rarely encountered in small-scale farming.

Social, cultural and personal constraints are usually less clearly defined than are institutional constraints. Group pressures, cultural or religious taboos or obligations, and the personal attributes, beliefs and preferences of the farm-household decision makers can all have important influences on choice of farm-household organization and production methods. In so far as planning is concerned with change, some confrontation with traditional views is almost inevitable. The difficult task that the planner faces is to decide which of the constraints in this class can be ignored and which must be accommodated. It is almost a truism that, if all existing constraints, real or imagined, are accepted in farm-household planning, the best plan that can be found will be no different from the existing one. Progress can be made in planning only if the means can be found of convincing farm people that factors that have until now inhibited change can be circumvented or overcome. On the other hand, plans, however technically and economically sound, that require radical reform of the existing system may well be totally unacceptable to the farm families who are expected to adopt them.

The key to the solution of the planner's dilemma described above lies, first, in a careful analysis of all relevant aspects of the farming system, followed by an education programme. By careful collection and analysis of data, the planner must initially determine whether an improved system can be developed that is feasible and that will raise the standard of living of the farm family. Then, working either directly with the client farmers, or through the extension service, the planner must convince the farmers of the practicability and advantages of the proposed changes. However, the planner must always keep it in mind that, ultimately, the decision to change, or not to change, rests with the farm people. It is they, not the planner, who must bear the consequences of any decisions. Hence, nobody else can, or should, make such decisions for them.

4.5 Farm programming and systems simulation

The so-called *programming approach* to farm planning is directed toward the selection and combination of crop and livestock activities into a farm plan that is at once optimal, in the sense that it maximizes a defined objective, and also is consistent with the relevant constraints of the kinds discussed in the preceding pages. The objective usually considered is total gross margin (TGM). The programming approach to farm planning constitutes a particular type of farm-system simulation which, however, may also be conducted in other ways.

A number of methods have been developed to implement the programming approach. They can be classified according to their degree of formality. At one end of the scale lie the almost wholly intuitive gross margin budgeting methods, while at the other extreme are the computer-based methods such as linear programming. Various simplified programming approaches are located in the middle, combining formal rules with a large element of judgement. Simplified programming provides a convenient vehicle to illustrate the programming approach.

SIMPLIFIED PROGRAMMING

Simplified programming (SP), also called programme planning, is a method of selecting a farm plan in which the required calculations are performed by hand (perhaps with the aid of a calculator). For this reason, the application of the method is confined to relatively simple planning problems, involving only a few activities and constraints. If the real planning problem involves many activities and constraints, as is usually the case, the planner must use judgement to eliminate all but a few of the activities and to restrict the constraints to be considered to a few crucial ones. If this involves too great an abridgement of reality, SP may have to give way to the computer-based technique of linear programming to be described later.

In SP, the activities are selected and incorporated into trial farm plans according to certain rules. There are several variants of the method involving different rules (see, e.g., Clarke, 1962; McFarquhar, 1962; Weathers, 1964; Rickards and McConnell, 1967). None of the rules ordinarily used can be guaranteed to yield a plan that is optimal in the strict sense of earning the highest possible TGM. It follows that all SP methods require the planner to apply the selection rules with judgement, varying them as seems desirable.

The starting point for the application of SP is an initial table showing the activities to be considered, the gross margins per unit of these activities, the resource constraints to be accounted for, and the demands placed on these resources per unit level of each activity. Activity maxima and/or minima will also be noted. An initial table for an example problem is illustrated in Table 4.5.

Table 4.5 comprises the initial table for a 30 ha mixed cropping farm. The activities considered are cotton, tomatoes, beans, wheat, barley and rye. Constraints are

Table 4.5

INITIAL TABLE FOR SIMPLIFIED PROGRAMMING EXAMPLE[a]

Activity	Gross margin ($/ha)	Land (ha)	Cereal limit (ha)	Labour (days) I	II	III	IV	V	Maximum activity level
Cotton	450	1	-	15	4	1½	-	35	Quota 3.0 ha
Tomatoes	540	1	-	4	39	½	-	15	Labour II:3.0 ha
Beans	160	1	-	1	½	6½	3½	-	Market:6.0 ha
Wheat	320	1	1	1½	1	-	2	4	Rotation:15.0 ha
Barley	230	1	1	2½	1	-	2	3	Cereal limit:22.5 ha
Rye	200	1	1	2½	1	-	2½	3	Cereal limit:22.5 ha
Available resource:		30.0	22.5	154	116	100	124	156	

[a] The data shown are imaginary.

land, rotational constraints restricting cereals (i.e., wheat, barley and rye) to 22.5 ha and wheat to 15 ha, and labour in five seasonal periods. Cotton is limited to 3 ha by a production quota, and tomatoes and beans are limited by restricted local markets to 4 ha and 6 ha, respectively. The bottom line of the table shows the amounts available of land and labour in the five periods, while the columns above these resource supplies show the requirement of each resource type per hectare of each activity.

The first step in the particular SP method to be illustrated is to determine the maximum feasible level for each activity. These maxima are shown on the right-hand side of the table. The values shown are determined for each activity as the minimum of the individual activity limit and the most limiting resource constraint for that activity. For example, in the case of tomatoes, the marketing limit is 4 ha but the activity is limited by the labour constraint in period II to $116/39 \approx 3.0$ ha. The latter therefore becomes the effective maximum for the tomato activity. The sources of the maxima for the other activities are reasonably obvious.

The next step in the SP method is an important one since it can lead to a considerable saving in arithmetic. The activities and constraints should be examined to see whether any can be eliminated. For example, study of Table 4.5 reveals that barley will always be preferred to rye since it has a higher gross margin per hectare and imposes the same or smaller demands on farm resources. Thus, rye is *dominated* by barley and can safely be omitted from further consideration.

In a somewhat similar manner, it can be shown that some of the constraints can be dropped. For example, in labour period I, the maximum possible utilization of labour can be calculated by selecting the most labour-demanding activities in turn to their maximum levels.

The period III labour required under such an extreme farm plan is calculated as: cotton 1½ × 3 days; plus tomatoes ½ × 3 days; plus beans 6½ × 6 days; i.e., a total of 45 days, compared with 100 days available. In other words,labour in period III can never be limiting and the constraint is redundant. Similar considerations reveal that the labour constraints in periods I and IV are also redundant.

Table 4.6

TABLE OF RANKED GROSS MARGINS PER UNIT RESOURCE REQUIREMENTS IN SIMPLIFIED PROGRAMMING EXAMPLE

Activity	Gross margin per unit[a] ($)			
	Land	Cereal limit	Labour II	Labour V
Cotton	450(2)	[b](1=)	113(4)	13(5)
Tomatoes	540(1)	[b](1=)	14(5)	36(4)
Beans	160(5)	[b](1=)	320(1=)	[b](1)
Wheat	320(3)	320(4)	320(1=)	80(2)
Barley	230(4)	230(5)	230(3)	77(3)

[a] Ranking is given in parentheses.
[b] Infinity.

The next step in the SP method is to rank the undominated activities according to the gross margin of each per unit requirement of each resource. The purpose of this ranking is to provide a basis for subsequent selection of activities during the planning phase. The ranks for the reduced example problem are shown in Table 4.6. Thus, tomatoes exhibit the highest gross margin per hectare and so are ranked first in relation to the land resource, followed by cotton, and so on. In regard to the labour constraints, gross margins per day are found by dividing the gross margins per hectare by the corresponding day labour requirements per hectare.

Activity selection is now carried out by choosing one of the resources as a key constraint. Activities are then selected and included in the trial plan according to the rank of their gross margin per unit of this constraint. It does not matter very much whether the resource initially selected as a key constraint is in fact limiting, since subsequent analysis will reveal whether or not this is so. Moreover, it is unusual for there to be only one limiting resource, so that it is sensible to repeat the activity selection procedure using different assumptions about which constraint may be regarded as the key one.

In our example, we will begin by assuming that land is the key limiting constraint. Table 4.6 shows that tomatoes are ranked first in regard to land productivity. This activity is therefore incorporated into the trial farm plan to the maximum extent possible, i.e., 3.0 ha. The effects of this selection on the TGM and on the resource balances are calculated in Section A of Table 4.7. Inspection of the table after inclusion of tomatoes into the first trial plan shows that all the period II labour is used up. (In fact, there is a small deficit of 1 day.) As can be seen from Table 4.5, there is no activity with zero labour needs in period II, so that further selections are not possible. The trial plan including only tomatoes is designated Plan A in Table 4.7.

Table 4.7

ACTIVITY SELECTION FOR SIMPLIFIED PROGRAMMING EXAMPLE

Selection	TGM ($)	Land (ha)	Cereal limit (ha)	Labour II (days)	Labour V (days)
A. Select by GM/ha		30.0	22.5	116	156
1. Tomatoes to labour II					
limit: 3.0 ha	1 620	3.0	0.0	117	45
PLAN A	1 620	27.0	22.5	-1	111
B. Select by GM/day					
of labour II		30.0	22.5	116	156
1. Wheat to rotation					
limit: 15.0ha	4 800	15.0	15.0	15	60
	4 800	15.0	7.5	101	96
2. Beans to market					
limit: 6.0 ha	960	6.0	0.0	3	0
	5 760	9.0	7.5	98	96
3. Barley to cereal					
limit: 7.5 ha	1 725	7.5	7.5	7.5	22.5
	7 485	1.5	0.0	90.5	73.5
4. Cotton to land					
limit: 1.5 ha	675	1.5	0.0	6.0	52.5
PLAN B	8 160	0.0	0.0	84.5	21.0

The activity selection procedure can now be repeated using a different constraint as the basis of selection. Since labour in period II proved limiting in Plan A, selection according to this constraint seems sensible. Table 4.6 shows that beans and wheat tie for first place in terms of gross margin per day of period II labour. Both activities can be incorporated into the second trial plan to their maximum levels. Section B of Table 4.7 shows that no constraints are yet limiting, and activity selection can proceed down the list to the third-ranked activity which is barley. Barley can be included in the trial plan to the limit of the cereal cropping constraint, leaving enough of the other resources to permit 1.5 ha of cotton, which is next in rank order, to be included. The result is Plan B in which all the land is used and the cereal cropping limit reached, but with surplus labour remaining in periods II and V.

Further trial plans could be developed selecting on the basis of gross margins per unit of the cereal limit or of labour in period V. However, period V labour has not proved limiting in the analyses so far, so that it seems unlikely that selecting on this basis will be very rewarding. The cereal limit is only relevant for wheat and barley and Plan B already includes both these crops, with priority having been given to wheat which is ranked the higher of the two in terms of the cereal constraint. For these reasons, further selections based on returns to the other constraints do not seem to be appropriate.

Of the two plans so far developed, Plan B with a TGM of $ 8 160 is clearly superior to Plan A which has a TGM of only $ 1 620. However, before Plan B is accepted as the best that can be found, it is necessary to review the opportunities for substitution of activities at the margin of this plan. Land and the cereal limit are the two constraints that are operational in Plan B. Table 4.6 shows that tomatoes rank first in terms of return to these two constraints. The activity in Plan B ranked lowest in regard to the same two constraints is beans, and it is evident that more profit could be made by reducing the area committed to beans, substituting tomatoes. The extent of the possible substitution is restricted to 1.5 ha, at which stage all available labour in period V would be used up. The effects of making this substitution are shown in Table 4.8 in the shape of Plan C.

By similar reasoning to that used to justify replacing beans with tomatoes, it can be shown that Plan C can also be improved by substituting tomatoes for cotton. Substitution to the extent of 0.75 ha is possible, when period II labour becomes limiting. The result is Plan D, showing a TGM of $ 8 797, and comprising:

	(ha)
Wheat	15.00
Beans	4.50
Barley	7.50
Cotton	0.75
Tomatoes	2.25

Total	30.00

While Plan D cannot be said to be optimal (and in fact is not), there are no obvious opportunities via SP for further marginal substitution of activities to increase the TGM. This plan is therefore adopted as the end-point of the SP procedure.

As already noted, the particular SP procedure described and illustrated above is but one of many variants of the method. For example, the criterion used to select the activity to be included in the trial plan at any stage may be varied. One alternative is to select not the activity showing the highest gross margin per unit of a key constraint, but rather the activity which, when included in the trial plan, yields the greatest absolute increment in TGM. Other variants of the SP method place more emphasis on intuitive procedures, with the planner using judgement about the order of selection of activities, and also about the extent to which a particular activity should be introduced into the plan.

A particularly simple version of SP is known as *gross margins planning*. In this method, activity selection proceeds on the basis of one key constraint, usually land. However, the feasibility of the plan in terms of other constraints is evaluated only subjectively as the plan is developed. Thus, resource balances for these other constraints are not calculated at each stage. However, when a tentative farm plan has been arrived at, its feasibility in terms of other constraints may be checked by doing the necessary extra calculations. If the plan proves not to be practicable, it would then be modified as necessary.

Table 4.8

MARGINAL SUBSTITUTION IN THE SIMPLIFIED PROGRAMMING EXAMPLE

Substitution	TGM ($)	Land (ha)	Cereal limit (ha)	Labour II (days)	Labour V (days)
PLAN B	8 160	0.0	-	84.5	21.0
Remove 1.5 ha beans:					
(4.5 ha remaining)	-240	+1.5	-	+0.8	0.0
	7 920	1.5	-	85.3	21.0
Add 1.5 ha tomatoes	+810	-1.5	-	-59.5	-22.5
PLAN C	8 730	0.0	-	25.8	-1.5
Remove 0.75 ha cotton:					
(0.75 ha remaining)	-338	+0.75	-	+3.0	+105
	8 392	0.75	-	28.8	103.5
Add 0.75 ha tomatoes					
(total 2.25 ha)	+405	-0.75	-	-29.3	-11.3
PLAN D	8 797	0.00	-	-0.5	92.2

One advantage of SP, compared with some other programming methods discussed below, is that no computer is required. Moreover, within the limitations of the small numbers of activities and constraints that can be considered, the method can usually be guaranteed to give a plan that is at least close to the optimum. Formal rules are available to guide the inexperienced planner, while the more skilled analyst can use judgement to ensure that a satisfactory plan is quickly determined.

The disadvantages of the SP method are that it is relatively time-consuming to perform all the required calculations, while - at least in theory - the plan obtained may be far from the true optimum. Because of the tedious arithmetic involved, the numbers of activities and constraints that can be accommodated are limited. In consequence, the SP planning model may be a very poor representation of the real farm situation. Moreover, in SP, it is quite difficult to take account of interrelationships between activities, such as between pasture and livestock activities. By contrast, these types of relationships can be handled formally within the framework of computer-based programming approaches.

LINEAR PROGRAMMING

Although the various SP approaches outlined above are readily incorporated into PC-based spreadsheets, with considerable savings in tedious arithmetic and greater ease in testing alternative plans for feasibility and profitability, there is little point in such an approach. It is usually far better to make use of linear programming (LP), which is a computer-based procedure that can be used for farm planning. Within certain limitations to be described below, LP leads to the selection of that mix of activities which maximizes TGM. The initial information required for the application of LP is a table or matrix somewhat similar to that shown in Table 4.5 for the SP method. That is to say, the initial matrix will include all the available activities with their gross margins per unit and all the constraints on these activities. For each constraint, the level of the constraint will be shown, as will the per unit requirements of (or contributions to) that constraint for each activity.

Because the calculations are performed by computer, it is usually possible to include as many activities and constraints as seem appropriate to represent a given farm situation. Thus, initial matrices of the order of 50 or 60 activities and a similar number of constraints are quite common and much bigger matrices, involving even hundreds of constraints and activities, are not unusual.

The data for the initial matrix are fed into a computer that is programmed to perform the required calculations leading to the optimal activity mix. The method of calculation employed is somewhat similar to that illustrated for SP, except that the procedures for marginal substitution of activities are appreciably enhanced. A modern computer can usually complete the calculations for a realistic problem in a few minutes. LP models of reasonable size are readily solved on the increasingly ubiquitous personal computers (PCs). It would be virtually impossible to perform the same amount of arithmetic using an ordinary calculator in a reasonable time. Moreover, if the calculations were to be done by hand, the risk of error would be considerable. In contrast, a computer can be regarded as almost wholly reliable provided (a) that it has been correctly programmed and (b) that the correct data are provided as input.

It is not possible in this manual to give a comprehensive treatment of the use of linear programming for whole-farm planning. The topic is extensively treated elsewhere (e.g., Hardaker, 1979; Dent, Harrison and Woodford, 1986). The treatment here is therefore confined mainly to a discussion of the advantages and disadvantages of LP and related techniques for farm management research purposes.

The main advantage of LP for farm management research stems from the great power of modern computers to process large amounts of data efficiently. While the optimizing characteristic of LP is an important advantage over SP, a much more important consideration is that the LP model can be made as large as seems appropriate without worrying about the resulting computational burden. Moreover, most LP computer software provide facilities for efficient processing of variants of the basic model. This means that the effects on the optimal plan of changing key assumptions about prices, yields, or other rates of performance can be speedily investigated. Some LP packages incorporate parametric routines whereby selected coefficients in the initial matrix may be varied continuously over some chosen range and all relevant solutions in that range printed out.

LP also generates additional useful economic information about the optimal solution. For example, the *marginal value product* of each scarce resource is computed. This information is often useful in indicating where effort should be directed to relax operational constraints. Similarly, the *marginal opportunity cost* of each activity excluded from the optimal solution is generated by LP. This measure indicates the extent of improvement needed in the gross margin of each excluded activity before it could compete for a place in the optimal solution. Again, important policy implications may sometimes be drawn from such information.

By way of a simple illustration, the LP solution to the SP problem set out in Table 4.5 is shown in Table 4.9. It can be seen that the total gross margin of the optimal solution is somewhat better than that obtained by SP (viz., $ 8 904 as compared to $ 8 797 from Plan D of Table 4.8), illustrating the advantage of the optimizing nature of LP. Moreover, as shown in Table 4.9, some supplementary information is provided in the LP solution - e.g.,the computer output on the ranges of the gross margins of the individual activities for which, other things remaining unchanged, the optimal plan remains constant. Such information is useful in assessing the stability of the solution in the face of possible changes in costs or prices. These ranges are given for both the activities in the solution (i.e., the *basic variables*) and for the activities excluded from the optimal plan (i.e., the *non-basic variables*). Thus, other things remaining constant, the gross margin for cotton (currently $ 450/ha) could vary between approximately $ 195/ha and $ 975/ha without its optimal level moving respectively to something less than or more than 1.146 ha. Conversely, other things remaining unchanged, rye would need a gross margin of $ 230/ha (compared to its current level of $ 200/ha) before it would enter the optimal plan. The importance of the constraints binding the solution can also be assessed from the information on marginal value products. These results show the gain in TGM to be obtained from a marginal unit addition to the level of each individual constraint, again other factors remaining unchanged. Such information may be valuable in evaluating the feasibility and profitability of relaxing particular constraints.

The chief disadvantage of LP is the need for access to a computer. If a computer, together with the appropriate LP software, is not available close at hand, long delays and frustrations are likely in sending data away for processing. Moreover, self-evidently, a computer can only process the data presented to it. If the input data are incorrect or inappropriate, the answers obtained will also be wrong. It is easy to underestimate the considerable amount of work involved in constructing a medium-sized LP matrix and in transcribing the data for computer processing.

The utility of LP for farm management research may be limited in some circumstances by the assumptions on which the technique is based (though it must be noted that the same assumptions generally apply to SP). As its name implies, LP embodies an assumption of linearity in the calculation of TGM and total requirement of any resource for a given plan. One implication is that constant returns to scale and an absence of economies of size are assumed to apply for each activity, which may not always be a reasonable assumption. However, where non-linearities are held to exist, it may be possible to represent these adequately as a number of linked linear segments. For a more comprehensive review of this topic, see Hardaker (1979).

A more serious consequence of the linear character of LP is the implication that all activities and resources are infinitely divisible. This aspect of LP can lead to some unsatisfactory features in optimal solutions. There may be no difficulty in suggesting that a farmer should sow 1.53 ha of wheat, but it is obviously not sensible to suggest keeping 1.53 cows or buying 1.53 tractors. Usually these difficulties in LP solutions can be overcome by additional computing. For example, it would be possible to test the relative profitability of a farm plan with either one or two cows, or one or two tractors, but these additional calculations increase the cost and the amount of work involved in using LP. Although special integer programming methods have been developed to handle these difficulties directly, integer programming routines are less widely available than those for LP and are more difficult and expensive to use.

Table 4.9

LP SOLUTION TO SP PROBLEM OF TABLE 4.5

Basic variables [a]	Level [b] (ha)	GM range over which remain basic: Lower limit ($/ha)	Upper limit ($/ha)
Cotton	1.146	194.54	974.72
Tomatoes	2.227	284.29	3 350.00
Beans	4.127	4.65	208.02
Wheat	15.000	237.59	open
Barley	7.500	200.00	312.40
Non-basic variables			GM to enter
Rye			$ 230.00/ha
Binding constraints			Marginal value product($)
Land			156.54/ha
Cereal limit			43.76/ha
Labour II			6.91/day
Labour V			7.59/day
Rotation			82.40/ha
Non-binding constraints			Surplus units
Labour I			82.53 days
Labour III			70.34 days
Labour IV			64.55 days
Market			1.87 ha
Cotton quota			1.85 ha

[a] Basic variables in the LP solution are those activities which enter the optimal farm plan.
[b] These activity levels taken at the respective gross margins of Table 4.5 indicate the optimal plan has a TGM of $ 8 904.

A further major limitation of the LP method is that it is based on the assumption that all planning coefficients are single-valued, implying that, at least in ordinary use, no account is taken of risk. If risk is important, which is usually the case in small-farm production, this limitation is serious. However, as outlined in the next section, various programming methods have been developed to take some account of risk in farm planning.

RISK PROGRAMMING

As in the case of LP, a comprehensive review of risk programming methods in agriculture is outside the scope of this manual. For a more complete discussion of some of the methods outlined below and for an introduction to the literature, see Anderson, Dillon and Hardaker (1977, Ch. 7).

Risk programming methods may be appropriate for farm planning when yields, prices or other planning coefficients are appreciably uncertain. The importance of such uncertainty is enhanced in small-farm planning by the generally accepted fact that most small farmers are risk averse. Thus their choice of a farm programme is likely to be strongly influenced by uncertainties in their planning environment, particularly since they are generally poor and have no reserves of wealth to fall back on.

A variety of risk programming methods have been used in agriculture. These methods can be distinguished in several ways. An important distinction is between those methods that account for risk in the activity gross margins, and those that account for risk in other planning coefficients. Methods of the first type are better developed and more widely applied than are methods of the second type.

The most comprehensive method of accounting for risk in activity gross margins is by use of *quadratic risk programming*. In this method a matrix is assembled representing the variances and co-variances of the activity gross margins. This variance-covariance matrix is then attached to an initial farm programming matrix as would be used for LP, and the augmented problem is solved by quadratic programming. This is a computer-based procedure which allows the variance of the total gross margin to be minimized subject to the usual farm constraints, and also to a constraint on the average or expected value of the TGM. The latter constraint can be varied over its feasible range so that quadratic risk programming leads to the generation of the complete set of solutions, each of which represents a point of minimum variance of TGM for a given level of expected TGM.

It follows from the above that application of the quadratic risk programming method is based on the reasonable assumption that farmers are generally risk averse. The optimal plan for a particular farmer can be selected from the set of solutions in the so-called mean-variance or (E,V)-efficient set of farm plans, generated as indicated, according to the individual farmer's attitude to risk (Anderson, Dillon and Hardaker, 1977, Ch. 7).

An example of an (E, V)-efficient set is shown in Figure 4.7. For each point on the curve, the solution procedure would indicate the farm plan to be followed. Three points on the set are indicated corresponding to the plans that might be preferred by three farmers with different attitudes to risk.

Computer routines for quadratic risk programming are not widely available and are less highly developed than are those for LP. Mainly for that reason, several attempts have been made to use LP approximations to the quadratic risk programming approach to farm planning with risky activity gross margins (Anderson, Dillon and Hardaker, 1977, Ch. 7). Perhaps the best adapted of these methods for planning small farms is MOTAD programming. MOTAD is an acronym for minimization of total absolute deviation. Additional constraints are added to an ordinary LP matrix to estimate the absolute deviation of the TGM of any selected plan (Hazell, 1971). This measure of risk is then

Figure 4.7

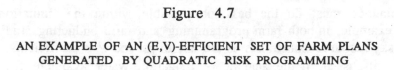

AN EXAMPLE OF AN (E,V)-EFFICIENT SET OF FARM PLANS GENERATED BY QUADRATIC RISK PROGRAMMING

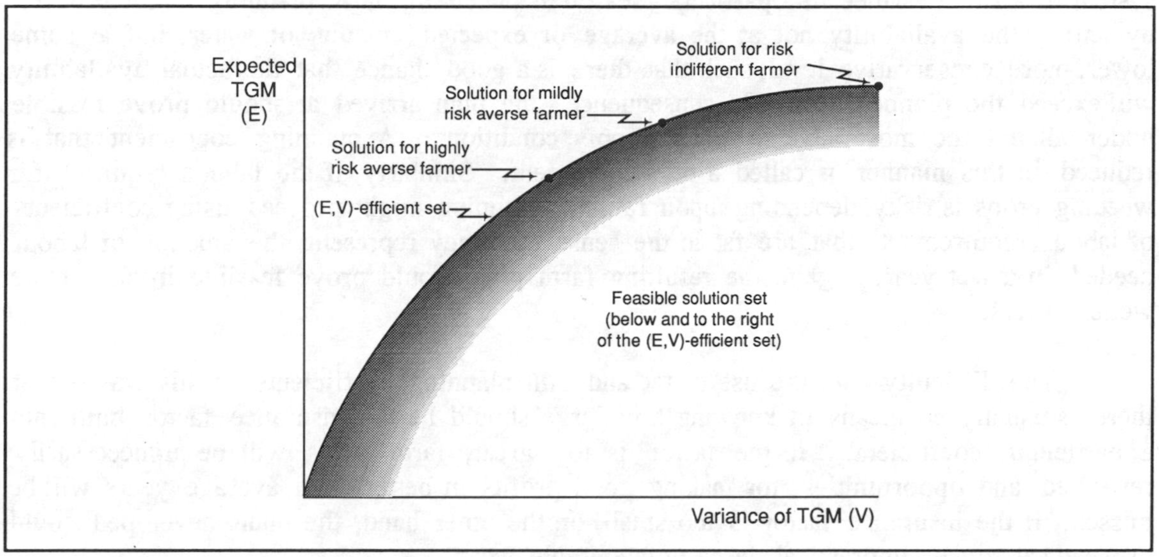

minimized subject to the usual constraints and to a constraint on expected TGM that is varied continuously over its feasible range. By this means a set of solutions is generated that approximates the (E, V)-efficient set. An example of the application of MOTAD to planning small farms in India is to be found in Schluter and Mount (1976). A further refinement of the MOTAD programming approach has been proposed by Tauer (1983). This method, called Target-MOTAD, reflects risk in terms of mean deviations in income below a specified target income level. It can be argued that such a treatment of risk more closely reflects the actual risk aversion likely to exist among small farmers.

The second type of risk programming problem distinguished above embraces those problems in which resource stocks or resource requirements per unit level of the activities are risky. Problems of this kind are inherently much more difficult to solve because an optimal farm plan cannot usually be specified unconditionally. The levels of at least some farm activities must usually be specified as functions of risky (i.e., stochastic) planning coefficients whose actual values do not become known until after some initial decisions have been made and some resources committed. Methods of stochastic programming, including chance-constrained programming, have been advanced as a means of at least approaching problems of this kind. The approach known as *discrete stochastic programming* (Cocks, 1968; Rae, 1971, a,b) is probably the best method so far developed but has the disadvantage of requiring a very large initial matrix to give even an approximate solution, so that it is expensive to apply. This and some alternative programming methods to deal with risky resource constraints are reviewed in Anderson, Dillon and Hardaker (1977, Ch. 7), and, because of their complexity, will not be discussed further here. It may be said, however, that farm planning problems with risky constraints are still largely beyond the scope of analysts in the field without access to the more powerful computers and software now available. Nor are such programming methods likely to be cost effective on an individual farm basis.

The problem of planning real farms with risky resource constraints cannot be ignored simply because wholly satisfactory methods of analysis are not yet available.

Instead, the planner must do the best job possible within the limitations of existing methods. For example, in both farm programming and farm budgeting studies, a common approach to risky resource constraints is the use of *fat* and *thin* coefficients. To illustrate, and as already discussed, if the amount of irrigation water available from a waterway system to a small farmer in a particular season is uncertain, farm planning might proceed by setting the availability not at the average or expected amount of water, but at some lower, more conservative level, such that there is a good chance that the actual availability will exceed the planned level. In consequence, the plan arrived at should prove feasible under all but the most adverse water supply conditions. A planning coefficient that is reduced in this manner is called a thin coefficient. Similarly, if the labour required for weeding crops is risky, depending upon rainfall, planning might proceed using coefficients of labour requirement that are fat in the sense that they represent the amount of labour needed in a wet year. Again, the resulting farm plan should prove feasible in all but the wettest years.

The difficulty with the use of fat and thin planning coefficients in this way is that there is usually no means of knowing how large should be the insurance factor built into a particular coefficient. If the factor is too great, farm plans will be unnecessarily restricted and opportunities for making good profits in better than average years will be missed. If the insurance factor is too small, on the other hand, the plans developed could prove disastrously impractical in an unfavourable year.

SYSTEMS SIMULATION

By farm system simulation is meant the mimicking of the farm operation via some type of model. The models used may vary from simple generalized budgets to detailed computerized one-off representations of the complex interrelated biological, economic and social processes making up a farm. As already noted, farm programming procedures constitute a particular mode of simulating farm performance so as to decide on an appropriate farm plan.

Another simulation approach is that of *Monte Carlo programming* (Carlsson, Hovmark and Lindgren, 1969). This is essentially a budgeting procedure. It has several advantages in the context of small farm planning. First, it permits the ready use of a complex objective function embodying several dimensions (e.g., cash income and subsistence food production). Second, integer constraints can be easily included. Third, it can incorporate risk considerations (Anderson, 1975). An application of the method to small farm planning is provided by Wardhani (1976) and the availability of packaged computer software (e.g., Anderson, 1976) makes it relatively convenient to use.

As outlined by Anderson (1974), farm systems simulation may also be carried out in many other ways. Applications to small farm situations are presented by Low (1975) and Zuckerman (1977).

4.6 Whole-farm budgets

Whole-farm budgets are drawn up to show the anticipated consequences, in terms of selected measures of performance, of some proposed farm plan. The plan may have been generated by SP, LP, Monte Carlo programming or by some more intuitive method, perhaps as a simple adaptation of an existing system on the particular farm or on some other farm.

The budget is constructed on a whole-farm basis to allow calculation of overall performance measures. It is usually measures of profitability that are of concern, such as net farm earnings, although cash-flow measures may also often be needed.

Whole-farm profit budgets are usually best prepared in gross margin terms. Thus, the levels of the farm activities and the gross margins per unit level of each are used to calculate the TGM. Then fixed expenses (including interest) can be deducted from the TGM to show the net farm earnings. This last step is important since it is usually the maximization of net farm earnings that is the goal in planning. Many farm planning procedures, including most of the programming methods, are concerned with maximizing TGM within fixed resource constraints. Often it will be worthwhile to seek means of relaxing constraints that are found to be limiting the choice of a profitable mix of activities. For example, a limiting labour constraint can be relaxed by hiring another worker, but this policy will obviously increase fixed expenses. A whole-farm budget can be used to test whether the increase in TGM which the extra worker makes possible is sufficient to more than offset the increased fixed expenses.

In fact, there are four routes to increased net farm earnings:

◇ changing the activity mix to increase TGM with fixed expenses constant;
◇ changing the activity mix to increase TGM with a lesser increase in fixed expenses;
◇ re-allocating resources so that fixed expenses can be reduced with no reduction in TGM; and
◇ re-allocating resources so that fixed expenses can be reduced with a lesser reduction in TGM.

The first two methods imply a move to a more intensive system, while the third and fourth methods represent a shift toward a less intensive system of production. Under most circumstances, increased farm profitability is usually most easily achieved by intensification. However, when farm costs increase or product prices decline, a reduction in intensity may be indicated.

An example of a whole-farm profit budget, drawn up for the best farm plan found for the example farm in the SP procedure of Section 4.5 above, is illustrated in Table 4.10. The whole-farm budget would be supplemented by activity budgets for the crops included, showing the assumed yields, prices and detailed variable expenses that make up the calculated gross margins per unit of each crop.

If appropriate, the whole-farm budget can be extended to calculate other measures of farm profitability, such as return on total capital. Similarly, if required, cash-flow measures, such as farm net cash flow, can be calculated. The calculations necessary to arrive at these measures have already been described and illustrated in Chapter 3 and so will not be considered further here.

Table 4.10

AN EXAMPLE OF A WHOLE-FARM BUDGET FOR THE BEST FARM PLAN FOUND BY SP

Activity	Area grown (ha)	Gross income ($/ha)	Variable expenses ($/ha)	Gross margin ($/ha)	Total gross margin ($)
Tomatoes	2.25	825	285	540	1 215
Cotton	0.75	610	160	450	338
Wheat	15.00	400	80	320	4 800
Barley	7.50	300	70	230	1 725
Beans	4.50	215	55	160	720
Total					8 798
Fixed expenses					
Labour					2 533
Rent					1 810
Machinery depreciation					590
General overheads					735
Interest					40
Total					5 708
Net farm earnings					3 090

4.7 *Farm development budgeting*

Development budgeting is appropriate when a change in farm organization or methods is being contemplated that will take some considerable time to implement. For example, development budgeting is appropriate when planning for the establishment of long-term crops, such as oil palm or rubber, or when planning to develop agro-forestry, or when planning to increase livestock production through a stock breeding programme and pasture improvement. Development programmes of these kinds usually generate relatively little cash during the early stages of the programme. Consequently, budgeting may be important to establish the amount of capital or credit needed for it to be feasible for the programme to be implemented. It may also be necessary to assess the overall profitability of a particular development scheme and to compare the costs and benefits of alternative methods of implementation. Development budgets can be used to make such evaluations.

Development budgeting, almost by definition, involves long-run planning, which is more difficult than short-run planning because of the increased uncertainties about prices, costs and rates of performance in the more distant future. Plans laid now relating to actions to be taken several years ahead are unlikely to be implemented in exactly the way, and with exactly the results, presently foreseen. Rather, planning is better regarded as an adaptive process, wherein current plans are used to guide current decisions, but where longer run decisions are made tentatively, and only in the degree of detail necessary to allow present decisions to be made. For this reason, very detailed long-term development budgets are generally not appropriate. Instead, such budgets should be seen as a means of setting out, in a systematic way, an overview of the main technical and economic features of the proposed development programme, as currently foreseen.

The first step in development budgeting is to establish a development target, i.e., to indicate what it is expected will have been achieved at the end of the planning period currently being considered. This target need not necessarily correspond to the position foreseen as the ultimate end-point of the farm development process. Instead, it may represent a convenient goal, adopted for the purpose of the analysis. Once this goal is attained, new plans could be laid for the next development study. By this means, unnecessary time and effort are not wasted in the preparation of detailed budgets for highly tentative plans relating to the more distant future.

Usually a useful step, once a target position has been established, is to draw up a rough and ready budget to make an estimate of the profitability of the target farm plan compared with the current farm system and to relate any increase in profit to the estimated amount of capital that must be invested to achieve the target position. In the event that the proposed development can be shown by this means to be quite unprofitable, the programme might be scrapped, or heavily revised, so that further efforts are not wasted in drawing up a detailed development budget for a venture that is unlikely to be adopted.

In development planning, there will usually be a number of technical questions to be resolved about how the programme is to be implemented. The methods to be followed, the priorities to be adopted and the rate at which development is to be attempted must all be decided before the detailed budget can be drawn up. Usually, many of these questions can be resolved on wholly technical grounds. For example, some methods may be clearly superior to others, either in yielding more output for the same inputs or in requiring less input to obtain a given level of production. Similarly, priorities are often unambiguously determined by technical considerations. For instance, it is clearly impossible for a new crop to be planted until after the land has been cleared and prepared. If important choices about the procedures to be followed remain unresolved, then, as already indicated, it may be necessary to draw up two or more budgets, one for each alternative, so that the best method can be chosen.

The next step in development budgeting is to set out the technical details of the selected programme(s) in a reasonably comprehensive way. It is necessary to specify the planned schedule of work so that the associated payments can be estimated. Similarly, the development programme should include estimates of what is to be produced and when, so that receipts can be predicted. With the aid of such a detailed technical programme, combined with forecasts of future prices for inputs and outputs, a cash-flow budget for the proposed development can be drawn up. The cash-flow budget, which may be constructed on an annual, quarterly, or even a monthly, basis, will show, for the planning period until the target position is reached, the anticipated farm receipts and payments, and hence the forecast farm net cash flows. An example of a development budget, showing the development programme and associated cash-flow budget, is shown in Tables 4.11 to 4.14.

The example shown in the tables relates to the development of a run-down coconut smallholding in Malaysia by rehabilitating part of the area, replanting another portion with an improved variety of coconut, and by planting coffee as an intercrop.

Table 4.11 provides an outline of the planned development programme and also indicates the anticipated crop yields. These yields are converted first into production estimates and then into gross incomes in Table 4.12. The capital and operating costs are detailed in Table 4.13 and the cash-flow budget, summarizing all the above data, is given in Table 4.14.

As the example illustrates, a cash-flow budget is useful to indicate the timing and amount of any cash deficits through the development period. Often such cash deficits will be made good by some form of credit arrangement. A finance budget can then be constructed, building on the results of the cash-flow budget, to represent the extent of borrowing and the manner in which interest and principal payments on loans advanced are to be met. For the example introduced above, we assume that a loan to meet the cash deficits is available at 8 percent interest per annum on the outstanding balance, the loan being repayable at will, i.e., as the farmer elects. The associated finance budget is shown in Table 4.15.

If development budgets are being prepared relative to a planning horizon within which appreciable inflation is expected to occur, some adjustments may be needed to the budgets to account for changes in the value of money over time. Should it be reasonable to assume that the various components of payments and receipts will be affected more or less equally by inflation, cash-flow budgets can be drawn up in terms of constant (Year 0) money values (i.e., inflation can be ignored). This has obvious advantages of simplicity and of avoiding the difficult task of forecasting the future rate of inflation. However, if inflation is expected to affect the budget components differentially, it will be necessary to account for changes in relative costs or prices, but again cash-flow budgets can be drawn up in constant money values.

It is necessary to take explicit account of inflation in a finance budget drawn up to represent the management of borrowed capital. Unless the rate of inflation is very high, it is usual for lenders to specify loan-servicing payments in current (inflation-affected) money values, rather than in constant (inflation-indexed) values. The cost of inflation to a lender is usually reflected through the charging of a higher interest rate. There are two alternatives the analyst can adopt to deal with this situation, both requiring a prediction of the rate of inflation. One possibility is to draw up the cash-flow and finance budgets in current money values. Alternatively, it may be simpler to draw up the cash-flow budget in constant (Year 0) money values and then to divide the cash surpluses or deficits by an index of inflation to convert them to current values before the finance budget is drawn up.

In assessing the economic merit of a particular development programme, the first question to be addressed is whether the programme is feasible, in the sense that any required loans can be obtained and repaid, and whether the farm family can maintain an adequate standard of living during the development phase. A finance budget of the form just illustrated will provide the means of testing the financial feasibility of the plan. However, in other cases the source and/or terms of finance may have not yet been established, and it may rather be a question of determining some measure of profitability of the investment. One or other of the investment appraisal techniques described below will then be relevant.

Table 4.11

MALAYSIAN SMALLHOLDER COCONUT DEVELOPMENT PROJECT: CROP AND YIELD DATA OF A SIX-ACRE FARM WITH ONE ACRE REPLANTED WITH MAWA AND 2.5 ACRES REHABILITATED AND UNDERPLANTED WITH COFFEE

	Pre-project	Yr1	Yr2	Yr3	Yr4	Yr5	Yr6	Yr7	Yr8	Yr9	Yr10	Yr11	Yr12	Yr13 on
Cropping pattern														
MAWA[a] replanting (acres)		0.5	1.0	1.0	1.0	1.0	1.0	1.0	1.0	1.0	1.0	1.0	1.0	1.0
Rehabilitation (Talls) (acres)		1.0	2.5	2.5	2.5	2.5	2.5	2.5	2.5	2.5	2.5	2.5	2.5	2.5
Old stand (acres)		4.5	2.5	2.5	2.5	2.5	2.5	2.5	2.5	2.5	2.5	2.5	2.5	2.5
Underplanting[b]														
- Tapioca (acres)		0.5	1.0	1.0	1.0	0.5	-	-	-	-	-	-	-	-
- Coffee (acres)		1.0	2.5	2.5	2.5	2.5	2.5	2.5	2.5	2.5	2.5	2.5	2.5	2.5
- Bananas (acres)		3.0	2.5	2.5	2.5	2.5	2.5	2.5	2.5	2.5	2.5	2.5	2.5	2.5
Yields[c] MAWA (nuts/acre)	-	-	-	-	-	342	3700	4882	5598	6375	8023	7526	8397	9174
Rehabilitated Talls[d] (nuts/acre)	-	1148	1148	1272	1406	1530	1545	1646	1760	1897	1965	2007	2035	1995
Old Talls (nuts/acre)	1148	1148	1148	148	1148	1148	1148	1148	1148	1148	1148	1148	1148	1148
Tapioca (piculs/acre)[e]	-	250	250	250	250	250	-	-	-	-	-	-	-	-
Coffee berries (piculs/acre)	-	-	-	6.75	13.5	20.3	27.0	30.4	34.0	34.0	34.0	34.0	34.0	34.0
Bananas (tons/acre)	0.53	0.53	0.53	0.53	0.53	0.53	0.53	0.53	0.53	0.53	0.53	0.53	0.53	0.53

[a] New coconut variety.
[b] Acreage equivalents.
[c] For coconuts and coffee, yields are shown according to years after planting.
[d] About 20 percent of the stand of rehabilitated Talls is new planting with Malaysian Talls.
[e] One picul is 133 lb or 60.33 kg.

Source: Adapted from an example provided by Koo Gaik Hong, Department of Agriculture, Kuala Lumpur.

Table 4.12

MALAYSIAN SMALLHOLDER COCONUT DEVELOPMENT PROJECT: PRODUCTION AND GROSS INCOME FOR A SIX-ACRE FARM

		Pre-project	Yr1	Yr2	Yr3	Yr4	Yr5	Yr6	Yr7	Yr8	Yr9	Yr10	Yr11	Yr12	Yr13	Yr14 on
Production MAWA (nuts)		-	-	-	-	-	171	2021	4291	5240	5987	7200	7775	7962	8786	9174
Malaysian Talls (nuts)		6 888	6314	5740	5864	6184	6509	6710	6834	7099	7407	7681	7825	7916	7918	7858
Tapioca (piculs)		-	62.5	125	125	125	62.5	-	-	-	-	-	-	-	-	-
Coffee berries (piculs)		-	-	-	6.75	23.63	40.55	57.45	70.9	79.6	85.0	85.0	85.0	85.0	85.0	85.0
Bananas (tons)		1.59	1.59	1.33	1.33	1.33	1.33	1.33	1.33	1.33	1.33	1.33	1.33	1.33	1.33	1.33
Gross income	Price (M$/unit)	M$														
MAWA	0.14/nut	-	-	-	-	-	24	283	601	734	838	1008	1089	1115	1230	1284
Malaysian Talls	0.17/nut	1171	1073	976	997	1051	1107	1141	1162	1207	1259	1306	1330	1346	1346	1336
Tapioca	0.44/nut	-	250	500	500	500	250	-	-	-	-	-	-	-	-	-
Coffee berries	15.50/picul	-	-	-	105	366	629	890	1099	1234	1318	1318	1318	1318	1318	1318
Bananas	168/ton	267	267	223	223	223	223	223	223	223	223	223	223	223	223	223
Total		1440	1590	1700	1830	2140	2230	2540	3090	3400	3640	3860	3960	4000	4120	4160

NOTES TO TABLE 4.13 (below)

[a] Based on replacement of 4 percent of coffee and coconut area each year.

[b] At M$ 20 per 1 000 nuts for picking and M$ 20 per 1 000 nuts for husking, splitting and carrying to the roadside.

[c] Contract rate for harvesting of coffee is M$ 5/picul. In the first and second years of bearing (Years 3 and 4 respectively) it is assumed that harvesting is done entirely by family labour. In the following years, however, about 50 percent of the harvesting is by hired labour.

[d] Land tax at M$ 1/acre and drainage charges (which are M$ 5/acre in the pre-project situation and in Year 1, and are M$ 10/acre from Year 2 onwards).

Table 4.13

MALAYSIAN SMALLHOLDER COCONUT DEVELOPMENT PROJECT: INVESTMENT AND OPERATING COSTS FOR A SIX-ACRE FARM (M$)

	Total	Yr1	Yr2	Yr3	Yr4	Yr5	Yr6	Yr7	Yr8	Yr9	Yr10	Yr11	Yr12	Yr13	Yr14	Yr15 on
Investment																
Development labour	454	203	251	-	-	-	-	-	-	-	-	-	-	-	-	-
Weed eradication	105	45	60	-	-	-	-	-	-	-	-	-	-	-	-	-
Land preparation	301	38	75	75	75	38	-	-	-	-	-	-	-	-	-	-
Planting materials																
- MAWA	176	89	87	-	-	-	-	-	-	-	-	-	-	-	-	-
- Malaysian Talls	25	10	15	-	-	-	-	-	-	-	-	-	-	-	-	-
- Tapioca	10	5	5	-	-	-	-	-	-	-	-	-	-	-	-	-
- Coffee	113	45	68	-	-	-	-	-	-	-	-	-	-	-	-	-
Fertilizer/lime	744	127	281	186	100	50	-	-	-	-	-	-	-	-	-	-
Contingencies	200	58	88	29	15	12	-	-	-	-	-	-	-	-	-	-
Replanting[a]	-	-	-	-	-	-	-	-	-	-	-	-	-	-	-	65
Total investment	2128	620	930	290	190	100	-	-	-	-	-	-	-	-	-	65
	Pre-project															
Annual operating costs																
Fertilizers	-	59	127	160	250	265	280	280	280	280	280	280	280	280	280	280
Plant protection	15	62	106	81	68	56	51	46	46	46	46	46	46	46	46	46
Harvesting																
- MAWA[b]	-	-	-	-	-	7	81	172	210	239	288	311	318	351	367	367
- Malaysian Talls	276	253	230	235	247	260	268	273	284	296	307	313	317	317	314	314
- Coffee[c]	-	-	-	-	-	100	140	175	200	210	210	210	210	210	210	210
Land tax[d]	36	36	66	66	66	66	66	66	66	66	66	66	66	66	66	66
Subtotal	327	409	529	542	631	750	886	1012	1086	1137	1197	1226	1237	1270	1283	1283
Miscellaneous	33	41	61	58	69	80	94	108	114	113	123	124	133	130	137	137
Total operating costs	410	500	640	650	750	880	1030	1170	1250	1300	1370	1400	1420	1450	1470	1470

Table 4.14

MALAYSIAN SMALLHOLDER COCONUT DEVELOPMENT PROJECT: CASH-FLOW PROJECTIONS FOR A SIX-ACRE FARM

	Pre-project	Yr1	Yr2	Yr3	Yr4	Yr5	Yr6	Yr7	Yr8	Yr9	Yr10	Yr11	Yr12	Yr13	Yr14	Yr15 on
								M$								
Receipts																
Farm sales[a]	1370	1520	1630	1760	2070	2160	2470	3020	3330	3570	3790	3890	3930	4050	4090	4090
Total receipts[b]	1370	1520	1630	1760	2070	2160	2470	3020	3330	3570	3790	3890	3930	4050	4090	4090
Payments																
Investment costs	-	620	930	290	190	100	-	-	-	-	-	-	-	-	-	65
Operating costs	410	500	640	650	750	880	1030	1170	1250	1300	1370	1400	1420	1450	1470	1470
Total payments	410	1120	1570	940	940	980	1030	1170	1250	1300	1370	1400	1420	1450	1470	1535
Net cash flow	960	400	60	820	1130	1180	1440	1850	2080	2270	2420	2490	2510	2600	2620	2555
Less household payments	960	960	960	960	960	960	960	960	960	960	960	960	960	960	960	960
Cash surplus	-	-560	-900	-140	+170	+220	+480	+890	+1120	+1310	+1460	+1530	+1550	+1640	+1660	+1595

[a] It is assumed that 6 percent of total production of coconuts at pre-project situation is retained for home consumption each year.
[b] Excluding subsidies.

Table 4.15

MALAYSIAN SMALLHOLDER COCONUT DEVELOPMENT PROJECT: FINANCE BUDGET FOR A SIX-ACRE FARM (M$)

	Yr1	Yr2	Yr3	Yr4	Yr5	Yr6	Yr7	Yr8	Yr9	Yr10	Yr11	Yr12	Yr13	Yr14	Yr15 on
Cash surplus[a]	-560	-900	-140	+170	+220	+480	+890	+1120	+1310	+1460	+1530	+1550	+1640	+1660	+1595
Plus loan advanced	560	900	140	-	-	-	-	-	-	-	-	-	-	-	-
Less loan repayment	-	-	-	170	220	480	890	771	-	-	-	-	-	-	-
Balance[b]	-	-	-	-	-	-	-	349	1310	1460	1530	1550	1640	1660	1595
Loan balance:															
Opening balance	-	605	1625	1906	1888	1819	1485	714	-	-	-	-	-	-	-
Plus loan advanced	560	900	140	-	-	-	-	-	-	-	-	-	-	-	-
Subtotal	560	1505	1765	1906	1888	1819	1485	714	-	-	-	-	-	-	-
Plus interest at 8%	45	120	141	152	151	146	119	57	-	-	-	-	-	-	-
Subtotal	605	1625	1906	2058	2039	1965	1604	771	-	-	-	-	-	-	-
Less loan repayment	-	-	-	170	220	480	890	771	-	-	-	-	-	-	-
Closing balance[c]	605	1625	1906	1888	1819	1485	714	-	-	-	-	-	-	-	-

[a] From cash-flow budget in Table 4.14

[b] Available for non-essential household payments, savings or investment.

[c] Closing balance in year *n* becomes opening balance in year $n + 1$.

INVESTMENT APPRAISAL

A number of investment appraisal methods have been advocated for use in agriculture. Some of the simpler procedures, such as payback period and rate of return on capital, may be used to give a rough indication of the merits of an investment, but the methods lack theoretical justification and can give misleading results. For these reasons, these methods will not be described here.

The more rigorous investment appraisal methods are based on the procedure of discounting. It is widely recognized that a dollar paid out or received today is more valuable than the same sum paid or received in the future. This difference in value need have nothing to do with inflation. Instead, it reflects the opportunity cost of capital. Thus, a dollar available today could be invested at the going interest rate of, say, 10 percent, so that in one year from now it would be worth $(1 + 0.1) = \$ 1.10$. In two years, if left invested at the same rate of interest, it would have grown in value to $1.10 (1 + 0.1) = (1 + 0.1)^2 = \$ 1.21$, and in n years the accumulated value would be $(1 + 0.1)^n$. This calculation is known as *compounding* and shows how a dollar available today can be converted to its equivalent value at some future time.

In general, the value at the start of year n, C_n, of some present sum P invested at an interest rate of i is given by $C_n = P(1 + i)^n$. By simple algebra, this equation can be turned round to give the formula for *discounting*. That is, the value of a sum C_n paid or received at the start of year n can be expressed in present value terms, when the interest rate is i, using the equation $P = C_n (1 + i)^{-n}$. For a more complete review of such interest rate procedures, see Chisholm and Dillon (1967).

The merit of the discounting procedure is that it allows payments and receipts occurring at different times in the future to be converted to a common standard in terms of their present value. They can thus be summed to determine the net present value of a project. *Net present value* (NPV) is a measure of the overall profitability of a project. If the NPV is positive the project may be said to be profitable, while if the NPV is negative it is not profitable. When comparing mutually exclusive projects, such as alternative ways of attaining the same development target, the one with the highest NPV is usually regarded as the best.

The NPV of the development programme illustrated above is calculated in Table 4.16 for two rates of interest. It should be noted that this application relates to a change in the organization of an existing farm. Thus only the increments or decrements in farm net cash flow are included in the appraisal. Moreover, the increase in the productive capacity of the farm at the end of the planning period must also be taken into account. This latter consideration is included in the form of the increase in the anticipated terminal value of the farm. Terminal values may be assessed either by reference to projected market values, or, more plausibly, by capitalizing the projected income stream from that date onward. An income stream of A dollars per annum into perpetuity may be converted to a current capital sum C using the formula $C = A/i$.

Table 4.16 shows that both the calculated NPVs are positive, indicating that the project is profitable, even at an interest rate of 12 percent.

The NPV method of investment appraisal is relatively straightforward to apply and gives a clear indication of the profitability or otherwise of a project. Its critics claim,

Table 4.16

MALAYSIAN SMALLHOLDER COCONUT DEVELOPMENT PROJECT: NET PRESENT VALUE CALCULATION FOR A SIX-ACRE FARM (M$)

	Yr1	Yr2	Yr3	Yr4	Yr5	Yr6	Yr7	Yr8	Yr9	Yr10	Yr11	Yr12	Yr13	Yr14	Yr15 on
Farm net cash flow[a]:															
With project	400	60	820	1130	1180	1140	1850	2080	2270	2420	2490	2510	2600	2620	2555
Without project	960	960	960	960	960	960	960	960	960	960	960	960	960	960	960
Difference	-560	-900	-140	+170	+220	+480	+890	+1120	+1310	+1460	+1530	+1550	+1640	+1660	+1595
Discount factor (8%)	0.9259	0.8573	0.7938	0.7350	0.6806	0.6302	0.5835	0.5403	0.5002	0.4632	0.4289	0.3971	0.3677	0.3405	3.9405[b]
Present value (8%)	-519	-772	-111	+125	+150	+302	+519	+605	+665	+676	+656	+616	+603	+565	+6285
Discount factor (12%)	0.8929	0.7972	0.7118	0.6355	0.5674	0.5066	0.4523	0.4039	0.3606	0.3220	0.2875	0.2567	0.2292	0.2046	1.5225[b]
Present value (12%)	-500	-717	-100	+108	+125	+243	+403	+452	+472	+470	+440	+398	+376	+340	+2428
Net present value (8%):	M$ 10 355														
Net present value (12%):	M$ 4 938														

[a] From Table 4.14.
[b] $(1+i)^{-15}/i$.

however, that it suffers from the disadvantage that the appropriate interest rate must be determined before the method can be used. Selection of the interest rate presents few difficulties if there is a well-developed capital market, for in this case the opportunity cost of capital may be taken as equal to the borrowing rate. However, if there is severe capital rationing, coupled with the use of institutional measures rather than high interest rates to restrict credit availability, the opportunity cost of capital may be appreciably higher than the cost of borrowing, and may be very difficult to determine. In such circumstances, the alternative investment criterion of *internal rate of return* (IRR) may be preferable to NPV.

The IRR is defined as that rate of interest which makes the NPV of a project exactly zero. It is normally found by extending the NPV calculation on a trial-and-error basis until the required interest rate is found. Interpolation methods can be used to speed the identification of the required rate. Application of the method to our example development project is illustrated in Figure 4.8.

The NPVs at both 8 percent and 12 percent interest have already been calculated, as shown in Table 4.16. Both are positive, implying an IRR greater than 12 percent. NPVs were therefore calculated for 15, 20, 25, 30 and 35 percent. The results are plotted in Figure 4.8 and it may be seen that the IRR can be estimated by interpolation to be about 31 percent.

Using the IRR criterion, a project is usually said to be profitable if it yields a rate of return greater than the cost of capital. In our example an IRR of 31 percent is considerably greater than the cost of capital, so that the project is worthwhile. In comparing mutually exclusive projects, the one with the highest IRR is normally regarded as the best.

The operational disadvantages of the IRR criterion are twofold. First, it is more difficult to apply than the NPV approach, and second, in certain circumstances, multiple solutions can exist. That is, there may be a number of interest rates that all yield zero NPV. Fortunately, multiple solutions are rarely encountered in practice, but the fact that they may occur is one of the reasons why NPV is generally to be preferred to IRR for appraisal of farm development projects.

In investment appraisal using either NPV or IRR it may be necessary to consider the effect of inflation. If the cash flows being discounted are in constant money values, the appropriate interest rate for discounting for NPV calculation or as the cut-off rate for IRR evaluation must be the opportunity cost of capital net of any inflation effect. For example, if the annual opportunity cost of capital is judged to be 25 percent and if annual inflation is expected to be 10 percent, the annual interest rate to be used in investment appraisal is approximately 15 percent[2]. Of course, if cash flows are expressed in current rather than constant money values, the rates representing the gross opportunity cost of capital should be used.

---

[2] The exact formula is $i^* = [(1 + i)/(1 + I)] - 1$, where i^* is the inflation-corrected rate of interest, i is the nominal rate of interest, and I is the inflation rate, all expressed in decimal form. In the above example i^* is equal to 13.64 percent.

Figure 4.8

RELATIONSHIP BETWEEN NPV AND INTEREST RATE FOR A SIX-ACRE FARM IN THE MALAYSIAN SMALLHOLDER COCONUT DEVELOPMENT PROJECT

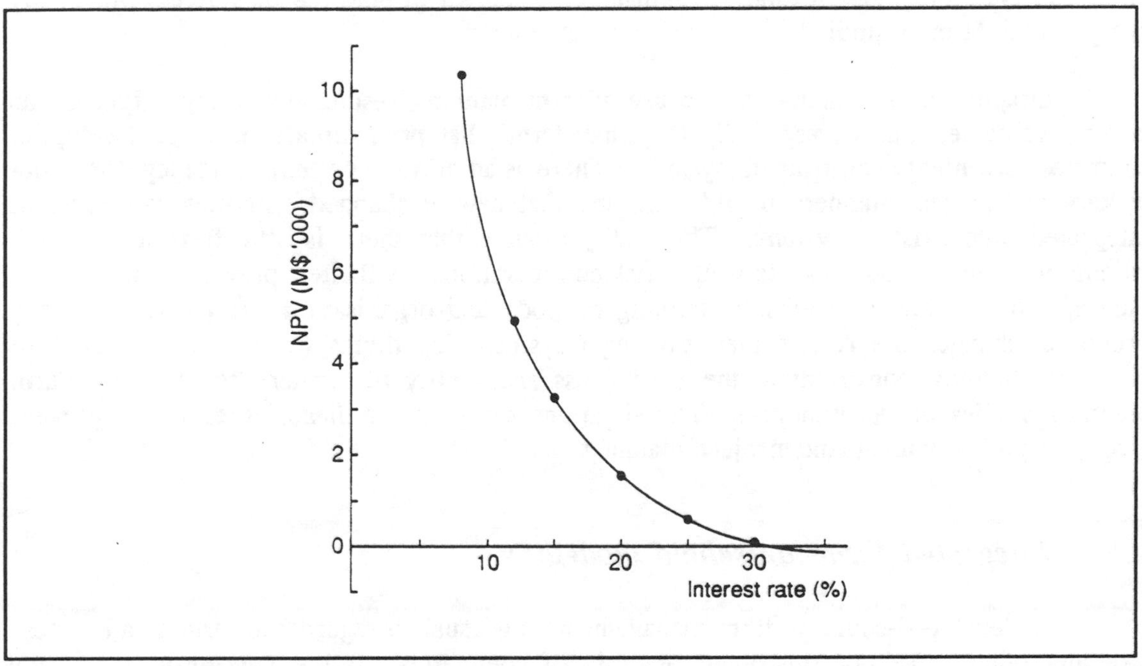

4.8 Aggregation of farm plans for policy purposes

In policy making, especially in project preparation and appraisal, as discussed by Brown (1979), it will be important to draw some inferences from farm planning work about the likely aggregated response of groups of farmers to new incentives or other policy-induced changes. Most commonly, this is done by the analysis of *representative farms*, followed by scaling up of the results according to the number of farms in the population that each such analyzed farm situation represents.

This method of predicting behaviour is subject to some important limitations. First, the analysis of the farm situations may not give a realistic estimate of what will happen. Perhaps the planning work has been done using overly optimistic assumptions of rates of performance or prices, or perhaps important constraints have gone unrecognized. Commonly, such analyses are based on the assumptions that farmers seek to maximize profits, when in reality they may have many other goals, as discussed in Chapter 1. Lastly, the derived plans may be based on information about technology or market opportunities that is not available to the target groups of farmers so that, at best, lags must be expected before the farmers are able to learn about the new information in order to take advantage of it.

A second limitation is known as *aggregation bias*. Even if the plans developed for the representative farm situations are realistic, there are dangers in scaling these plans up to the level of the population of farms. The reason is that farms vary in their resource endowments and other characteristics. A representative farm model may be truly representative of only a very small number of real farms. Actual farms that differ appreciably from the model situation may react quite differently from what is predicted for the model case. The risk of bias can be reduced by stratifying the population of farms and developing several representative models, but this obviously increases the work load on the analyst. Nor does it totally eliminate the problem of possible bias unless practically every actual farm is studied.

Despite these limitations, the use of farm planning results for policy purposes can be very valuable. Farms, especially the small farms that predominate in most developing countries, are highly constrained systems. There is an all too common tendency for policy makers and project planners to glibly assume that new or changed activities can easily be integrated into existing systems. The reality often is that there is little flexibility. Land, labour or capital constraints, as well as risk considerations, will often prevent farmers from moving too far from their existing farming methods and organisation. In particular, many proposed changes are riskier than existing ways of doing things (or are so perceived by farmers), thereby constraining the willingness and ability of farmers to change. Farm planning studies of representative farm situations can point up these issues and so prevent errors in policy making and project planning.

4.9 Integrated farm-household modelling

In developed-country farm management it is usual to regard the farm as a business like any other. Taking this view, analysis of commercial farms concentrated on the technical and economic efficiency of the production processes, with little or no attention being paid to the consumption behaviour of the farm household. Yet it is clear that, even in commercial farming, the distinction between farm and household is often somewhat artificial and misleading, particularly for family farms. For instance, the farmer must allocate cash income earned by the farm between farm and domestic uses. Should available funds be invested in, say, buying more land, or in educating the children? Both may enhance the future earning power of the family unit and so are legitimately regarded as competitive investments.

As discussed in Chapter 1, the inappropriateness of the division between farm and household is even more apparent in small-scale semi-commercial farming where most farm labour is typically supplied by the family and an appreciable part of the farm production is consumed in the farm household. In such situations a focus on production may give quite misleading results. For example, the response to a change in the price of a principal food crop in terms of quantity marketed is likely to be quite different on commercial and semi-subsistence farms.

A number of efforts have been made in recent years to model the production and consumption decisions of farm households in an integrated fashion. A good review is provided by Singh, Squire and Strauss (1986). Most empirical work has been based on what is known as the assumption of separability, as discussed below.

SEPARABILITY

We begin with the simplest case of a household producing only a single staple food using only labour inputs on a fixed land area and facing no risk. The household is assumed to have a set of preferences for consumption goods reflected in a household utility function defined in terms of consumption of leisure, staple, and cash goods. If it can reasonably be assumed that both labour and food crop can be traded without restriction in their respective markets, the value of these two commodities to the household will be reflected by their corresponding market prices. Under these circumstances, the optimal level of production of staple can be determined in the conventional way as the point where the marginal cost of labour used and the marginal revenue of staple produced are equated. Moreover, this optimum will be independent of either the characteristics of the household or its consumption preferences. In particular, it does not matter whether family or hired labour is used in production, or whether the staple is consumed in the household or is sold. The market prices measure the actual or opportunity costs in all cases.

Consumption behaviour, on the other hand, is clearly directly dependent on the household utility function. Moreover, the allocation is unlikely to be independent of the production decision made, since it affects the level of household income via the farm profit earned. This means that, under the assumption of effective markets, production decisions can be analyzed first and, once the level of farm profit is known, the allocation of the household income to alternative forms of consumption can be analyzed. Models of farm-household behaviour that are structured in this recursive way are said to be separable. Moreover, the principle of separability extends to more complicated cases where, for example, several products are produced, where other inputs are used in production and where consumption preferences extend over more commodities. All that is required for separability is that there be effective markets for labour and farm products (and no risk).

As explained next, separable models are much easier to analyze than models in which the required assumptions cannot be sustained. For this reason, most studies of integrated farm-household systems are based on the assumption of separability, even when the grounds for such an assumption are weak.

PROFIT MAXIMIZING MODELS OF PRODUCTION

As noted, the first step in analyzing an integrated farm-household system under the separability assumption is to determine the profit-maximising level of production, and hence farm profit. In general, two different approaches to this problem are available. The first is to use the methods of whole-farm planning described in this chapter (but dropping any constraints on household labour supply or any minimum household consumptions requirements). Mathematical programming methods probably offer the best option. Alternatively, and more commonly, a whole-farm production function may be estimated from cross-section data obtained by farm survey methods. The estimated average production function is then analyzed to determine the optimal level of output. Methods for the estimation of such functions are outlined in Chapter 7.

ANALYSIS OF CONSUMPTION

Once farm profit has been determined, the household *full income* can be determined, usually defined as farm profit plus the value of all household labour time (whether allocated to work or leisure), plus any unearned income. The allocation of this full income among alternative forms of consumption is usually achieved from sample-survey data from numbers of households by using well-developed econometric methods for the analysis of demand. The types of model used include the linear, log-linear and quadratic demand systems, or the almost ideal demand system. A discussion of these methods is outside the scope of this bulletin.

Once the demand system has been estimated, the two parts of the integrated farm-household system can be put together, in recursive fashion, to model behaviour of a representative household in response to various stimuli such as changed prices. It has been shown that the price and income elasticity of demand estimates from such integrated models are different from, and presumably superior to, estimates derived from models in which the integrated nature of the systems is not recognized.

SIMULTANEOUS TREATMENT OF PRODUCTION AND CONSUMPTION

As explained, most integrated farm-household models have been estimated making the assumption of separability to facilitate analysis. In reality, however, the assumptions of perfect markets and no risk are seldom realistic. Attempts to model integrated farm-household systems without these assumptions have generally taken one of two routes.

First, econometric approaches have been tried. They confront the difficulty that the number of equations to be simultaneously estimated is increased, since both production and consumptions aspects must be incorporated into the one model. Moreover, some of the required prices that would normally be part of the reduced form of such a system are not observable, since they are shadow prices, internal to the farm household. These difficulties together have been sufficient to discourage most attempts at such analysis.

Second, if some information can be obtained or plausibly assumed about the nature of household consumption preferences, an integrated planning model of the type discussed above can be used. Mathematical programming models with multiple objectives, or constrained to satisfy minimum household consumption standards, have been extensively and successfully used for such integrated modelling.

4.10 References

ANDERSON, J.R. (1974). 'Simulation: Methodology and Application in Agricultural Economics', *Review of Marketing and Agricultural Economics* 42: 3-55.

ANDERSON, J.R. (1975). 'Programming for Efficient Planning against Risk', *Australian Journal of Agricultural Economics* 19: 94-107.

ANDERSON, J.R. (1976). 'Risk Efficient Monte Carlo Programming: A Manual', *Miscellaneous Publication No. 6*, Department of Agricultural Economics and Business Management, University of New England, Armidale.

ANDERSON, J.R., J.L. DILLON & J.B. HARDAKER (1977). *Agricultural Decision Analysis*, Iowa State University Press, Ames.

ANGUS, J.F. & A.G. GARCIA (1989). 'Simulation Models of Water Balance and the Growth of Rainfed Rice Crops Growing in Sequence', in K.M. Menz (ed.), *Rainfed Rice Production in the Philippines*, Technical Report No. 13, ACIAR, Canberra, pp. 61-72.

BROWN, M.L. (1979). *Farm Budgets: From Farm Income Analysis to Agricultural Policy Analysis.* Johns Hopkins University Press, Baltimore.

BURMAN, R.D., R.H. CUENCA & A. WEISS (1983). 'Techniques for Estimating Irrigation Water Requirements', in D. Hillel (ed.), *Advances in Irrigation*, Vol. 2, Academic Press, New York, pp. 223-55.

CARLSSON, M., B. HOVMARK & I. LINDGREN (1969). 'A Monte Carlo Method Study of Farm Planning Problems', *Review of Marketing and Agricultural Economics* 37: 80-103.

CHISHOLM, A.H. & J.L DILLON (1967). *Discounting and Other Interest Rate Procedures*, Professional Farm Management Guidebook No.2, A.B.R.I., University of New England, Armidale.

CLARKE, G.B. (1962). *Programme Planning*, Documentation in Food and Agriculture 45, Organisation for Economic Co-operation and Development, Paris.

COCKS, K.D. (1968). 'Discrete Stochastic Programming', *Management Science* 15: 72-9.

CORBETT, J. (1990). *Feeding Standards for Australian Livestock*, Standing Committee on Agriculture, Ruminants Subcommittee, CSIRO Publications, Melbourne.

DALRYMPLE, D.G. (1971). *Survey of Multiple Cropping in Less Developed Nations*, Economic Research Service, U.S. Department of Agriculture and U.S. Agency for International Development, Washington, D.C.

DENT, J.B. & H. CASEY (1964). *Linear Programming and Animal Nutrition*, Crosby-Lockwood, London.

DENT, J.B., S.R. HARRISON & K.B. WOODFORD (1986). *Farm Planning with Linear Programming: Concept and Practice*, Butterworths, Sydney.

DINAR, A. & K.C. KNAPP (1986). 'A Dynamic Analysis of Optimal Water Use under Saline Conditions', *Western Journal of Agricultural Economics* 11(1): 58-66.

DONALDSON, G.F. & J.P.G. WEBSTER (1968). *An Operating Procedure for Simulation Farm Planning - Monte Carlo Method*, Department of Agricultural Economics, Wye College, Ashford.

DUDLEY, N.J. (1988). 'A Single Decision-maker Approach to Irrigation Reservoir and Farm Management Decision Making', *Water Resources Research* 24(5): 633-40.

GYLES, A., J.B. HARDAKER, & H.M.H. VERSPAY (1989). *Farm Management Handbook for Tonga*, (2nd edn), Technical Bulletin No. 8, published for the Planning Unit, Ministry of Agriculture, Fisheries and Forests, Tonga, by the South Pacific Smallholder Project, University of New England, Armidale.

HARDAKER, J.B. (1967). 'Farm Planning with Gang Size Restrictions', *N.A.A.S. Quarterly Review* 76: 166-76.

HARDAKER, J.B. (1975). *Agriculture and Development in the Kingdom of Tonga*, unpublished Ph.D. thesis, University of New England, Armidale.

HARDAKER, J.B. (1979). *Farm Planning by Computer*, GFM2, Ministry of Agriculture, Fisheries and Food, HMSO, London.

HAZELL, P.B.R. (1971). 'A Linear Alternative to Quadratic and Semivariance Programming for Farm Planning under Uncertainty', *American Journal of Agricultural Economics* 53: 53-62.

HEADY, E.O. & W. CANDLER (1958). *Linear Programming Methods*, Iowa State College Press, Ames.

JULIAN, S.I. (1973). 'Water Management Innovations in the National Irrigation Administration', in *Water Management in Philippine Irrigation Systems: Research and Operations*, International Rice Research Institute, Los Baños, pp. 97-112.

KNAPP, K.C. & D. WICHELNS (1990). 'Dynamic Optimisation Models for Salinity and Drainage Management', in K. Tanji (ed.), *Agricultural Salinity Assessment and Management*, American Society of Civil Engineers, New York, Ch 25.

LOW, A.R.C. (1975). 'Small Farm Improvement Strategies - The Implications of a Computer Simulation Study of Indigenous Farming in South East Ghana', *Oxford Agrarian Studies* 4: 1-17.

McFARQUHAR, A.M.M. (1962). 'Research in Farm Planning Methods in Northern Europe', *Journal of Agricultural Economics* 15: 78-100.

MAKEHAM, J.P. & L.R. MALCOLM (1986). *The Economics of Tropical Farm Management*, Cambridge University Press.

MATANGA, G.B. & M.A. MARINO (1979). Irrigation Planning: 1. Cropping Pattern', *Water Resources Research* 15(3): 672-8.

MATLON, P.J., & M. FAFCHAMPS (1988). *Crop Budgets for Three Agro-climatic Zones of the West African Semi-Arid Tropics*, Resource Management Program, Economics Group, Progress Report 85, ICRISAT, Hyderabad.

PANDEY, S. (1989). 'Irrigation and Crop Yield Variability: A Review', in J.R. Anderson and P.B.R. Hazell (eds), *Variability in Grain Yields: Implications for Agricultural Research and Policy in Developing Countries*, Johns Hopkins University Press, Baltimore, pp. 234-41.

PASSMORE, R., B.M. NICHOL & M. NARUYANA, in collaboration with G.H. BEATON & E.M. DEMAYER (1974). *Handbook of Human Nutritional Requirements*, FAO Nutritional Studies No. 28, Food and Agriculture Organization of the United States, Rome.

PERERA, B.M.K. (1990). Water Balance of Rice Fields', in K.M. Menz (ed.), *Rice Production in Sri Lanka*, Technical Report No. 17, ACIAR, Canberra, pp. 47-9.

RAE, A.N. (1971a). 'Stochastic Programming, Utility and Sequential Decision Problems in Farm Management', *American Journal of Agricultural Economics* 53: 448-60.

RAE, A.N. (1971b). 'An Empirical Application and Evaluation of Discrete Stochastic Programming in Farm Management', *American Journal of Agricultural Economics* 53: 625-38.

RICKARDS, P.A. & D.J. McCONNELL (1967). *Budgeting, Gross Margins and Programming for Farm Planning*, Professional Farm Management Guidebook No. 3, A.B.R.I., University of New England, Armidale.

ROSEGRANT, M. (1986). *The Impact of Irrigation on Area, Yield and Income Variability: A Simulation Analysis*, IFPRI, Washington, D.C.

SCHLUTER, M.G.G. & T.D. MOUNT (1976). Some Management Objectives of the Peasant Farmer: An Analysis of Risk Aversion in the Choice of Cropping Pattern, Surat District, India', *Journal of Development Studies* 12: 246-61.

SINGH, I., L. SQUIRE & J. STRAUSS (eds) (1986). *Agricultural Household Models: Extensions, Applications, and Policy*, Johns Hopkins University Press, Baltimore.

STELLY, M. *et al.* (eds.) (1976). *Multiple Cropping*, Special Publication No. 27, American Society of Agronomy, Madison.

TAC (1978). *Farming Systems Research at the International Agricultural Research Centers*, Technical Advisory Committee, Consultative Group on International Agricultural Research, World Bank, Washington, D.C.

TAUER, L.W. (1983). Target MOTAD', *American Journal of Agricultural Economics* 65: 608-10.

THOMPSON, S.C. (1970). *A User's Manual for Monte Carlo Programming*, Study No. 9, Department of Agriculture, University of Reading.

VAUX, H.J. & W.O. PRUITT (1983). Crop Water Production Functions', in D. Hillel (ed.), *Advances in Irrigation*, Vol. 2, Academic Press, New York, pp. 61-97.

WARDHANI, M.A. (1976). *Rational Farm Plans for Land Settlement in Indonesia: A Study Using Programming Techniques*, Thesis Reproduction Series No. 2, Development Studies Centre, Australian National University, Canberra.

WEATHERS, C.R. (1964). *Simplified Programming*, Circular 447, North Carolina Agricultural Experiment Station, Raleigh.

WICKHAM, T. (1973). Predicting Yield Benefits in Lowland Rice through a Water Balance Model', in *Water Management in Philippine Irrigation Systems: Research and Operations*, International Rice Research Institute, Los Baños, pp.155-81.

YARON, D. & E. BRESSLER (1983). Economic Analysis of On Farm Irrigation Using Response Functions of Crops', in D. Hillel (ed.), *Advances in Irrigation*, Vol. 2, Academic Press, New York, pp. 223-55.

ZUCKERMAN, P.S. (1977). Different Smallholder Types and Their Development Needs', *Journal of Agricultural Economics* 28: 119-28.

5. PARTIAL BUDGET ANALYSIS

Partial budget analysis is concerned with evaluating the consequences of changes in farm practices or organization that affect only part rather than the whole of the farm. The distinctive feature of partial budget analysis is that only factors contributing to changes in the measure or measures of whole-farm performance being considered are included in the budget. Thus partial budget analysis of the possible use of a new fungicide for one of the crops on a crop-livestock farm would be carried out by budget analysis encompassing only performance elements which would be affected by the introduction of the new fungicide; by comparing the situation with and without the new fungicide, the net effect of its introduction on relevant measures of whole-farm performance could be estimated.

The merits of a partial approach to budgeting are considerable. Partial analysis is less demanding of data than whole-farm budgeting. It is not necessary to have information on parts of the farm not affected by the change under review since the performance of these sectors will remain constant. For this reason, partial analysis is generally simpler than whole-farm analysis. Also, by their nature, partial budgets are typically applicable to a wider range of farm circumstances than is the case with whole-farm budgets.

Partial budget analysis can be used to evaluate the effects of a change in the way a farm is run on any of the measures of whole-farm performance discussed in Section 3.2. However, by far the most common type of partial budget is a partial profit budget, constructed to show the effect of the change under review on some measure of profit such as net farm income or net farm earnings.

5.1 Partial profit budgets

As already indicated, partial profit budgets - usually simply called partial budgets - are used to evaluate the effect on farm profit of a proposed change in the way a farm is operated and run. For this purpose, farm profitability can be regarded as being measured by net farm earnings (see Section 3.2).

Partial budgeting is most appropriate to evaluate the effects of relatively small changes in farm organization or methods. If large-scale changes such as a major reorganization in the enterprise mix are being contemplated, whole-farm budgeting (as described in Section 4.6) may be more appropriate, even though a partial approach is still possible. Partial budgeting is therefore a very useful farm planning method. In any farm management study it would be unusual not to encounter a number of alternatives relating to the conduct of a particular farm enterprise. Partial budgeting provides a convenient way of comparing the profitability of such alternatives. Moreover, as we shall show, partial budgeting is a relatively simple procedure. The method can readily be taught to extension workers, or even to farmers, provided they have a minimal level of literacy. For this reason, partial budgeting may be said to have the widest potential use of the planning methods discussed in this manual. The advent of micro-computers, and especially the development of spreadsheet packages, has greatly enhanced the scope for partial budgeting. Because the steps in the calculation can be built into the spreadsheet, the effects of changing assumptions about such things as cost, yields or prices can be evaluated practically instantaneously. Thus, sensitivity analysis of partial budget results is made very straightforward with access to a spreadsheet package.

The first step in partial budgeting is to describe carefully and exactly the change in farm organization or methods being considered. This is important because experience teaches that a common source of error in partial budgeting is confusion about the exact nature of the change under review. To minimize the risk of such error, the proposed change should be spelt out in some detail, and should be written down at the head of the budget which should also show the date of the analysis. These steps will also minimize possible confusion if the budget is referred to again at some later date.

Next, the gains and losses resulting from the specified change should be listed and quantified. Losses may be classified under two headings. First, there are the extra expenses or costs that occur because of the proposed change. Second, to these must be added any gross income or revenue foregone in consequence of the change; that is to say, any revenue which would be received under the present farm system, but which would no longer be received if the change under review were to be implemented.

On the other side of the budget, the gains also can be classified into two categories. First, any expenses or costs saved as a consequence of the proposed change should be detailed. These are costs that would have been incurred under the existing system, but that would be avoided if the proposed change were to be adopted. Second, to these gains (if any) should be added any extra gross income or revenue that arises in consequence of the proposed change.

The change in farm profit associated with the budgeted change can now be calculated quite simply as total gains minus total losses. If total gains are greater than total losses, the budget obviously indicates that the proposed change is profitable. If the converse is true, the indication is that the change is not profitable. Of course, this assessment of the change in farm profit is contingent upon the correctness of the technical and financial data used in the budget.

In partial budgeting it is not always possible to quantify and include in the budget all the factors bearing on the decision as to whether or not a proposed change should be implemented. It is therefore a good idea, as the next step in the analysis, to list any important non-pecuniary factors bearing on the choice. These factors will include such considerations as the degree of risk associated with the change, the implication of the proposal for the farmer and her or his family in terms of the amount and nature of the work to be done, and the management skill required to operate the proposed new farm system successfully. Any prerequisites for the successful implementation of the proposed change should also be noted. An example is where additional capital which must be borrowed is required, so that a loan must be arranged.

When both the pecuniary and non-pecuniary aspects of the proposed change have been set down, it should be possible to make a recommendation on which the farmer or farmers, to whom the partial budget is relevant, may act. Thus, in an extension context, the merits of some proposed new production technology can be assessed to determine whether it should be widely promoted among farmers by the extension service. Similarly, the results of partial budget analysis can be used to answer a policy maker's questions about the effects on farm output, income and resource use of some actual or proposed policy change.

When using partial budget analysis in an advisory or extension context, it is, of course, most important that any recommendation based on the budget results should take account of the farmer's aims and objectives. Where the change is being investigated on behalf of not one, but a group of farmers, a general recommendation might be made, but any individual circumstances predisposing a contrary conclusion should also be noted. If there is only one farmer to be considered, it is always a good idea to discuss the budget with her or him and, if appropriate, with other members of her or his family. The final decision to adopt or not adopt a particular proposal must always rest with the farmer in consultation with her or his family, since it is they, and not the farm management analyst, who have to bear the consequences of the decision.

Finally, at least when working in an advisory context, the analyst may need to do some follow-up work to ensure that a change, which has been recommended in the light of budget results, can be successfully implemented. It may be necessary to monitor the progress of the farm to see that the new system is being correctly introduced. Supplies of new inputs may need to be arranged, or the farmer(s) may need to be instructed in new management skills. If products new to the district are to be produced, marketing channels may need to be established, and so on.

By way of an example of partial budgeting, consider the case of a small farmer in the Cook Islands in the South Pacific who grows about 1 ha of vegetables for the local market and for export to New Zealand. He is considering the purchase of a second-hand imported tractor with basic cultivation implements. The farmer's aim in making the purchase is to avoid having to pay hire charges to a contractor to cultivate his land, and to earn some income by doing contract work for his neighbours. A budget for this proposed change is set out in Table 5.1.

The table includes a definition of the change to be considered, the date of the analysis, the losses and gains in annual income and expenses that it is anticipated would result from the proposed investment, and hence the forecast change in profit. Other considerations of a non-pecuniary nature are also briefly noted. Note that among these other considerations is the fact that, by owning his own tractor, the farmer could perform his cultivations in a more timely manner. If this can be expected to increase yields, the benefits of improved timeliness should have been included in the budget under the heading of extra revenue. In this case, these benefits proved too difficult to quantify and therefore were not included in the main part of the budget.

Table 5.1

A PARTIAL BUDGET FOR PURCHASE OF A TRACTOR

Change under review: Purchase of a second-hand tractor and implements for $ 5 000 to save on contract charges and to earn extra income by doing contract work for neighbours.

Date: May 1992.

Losses[a]	($)	*Gains*[a]	($)
Extra costs:		*Costs saved:*	
Depreciation: $ 5 000/5	1 000	Hire of contractor: 70 hrs at $ 7/hr	490
Interest on average investment: 0.1(5 000/2)	250		
Fuel and repairs: 220 hrs at $ 2.50/hr	550		
Annual licence fee	25		
Revenue foregone:		*Extra revenue:*	
Nil	0	Contract work for neighbours: 150 hrs at $ 7/hr	1 050
Total losses:	1 825	*Total gains:*	1 540

Extra profit = 1 540 - 1 825 = -285, i.e., a loss of $ 285.

[a] Annual basis.

Other considerations:
1. Improved timeliness.
2. Reduced risk of tractor not available when required.
3. $ 5 000 loan required.
4. Farmer must work extra 220 hrs per year.

The recommendation to be drawn from the budget of Table 5.1 obviously depends on the importance the farmer attaches to having ready access to a tractor when he needs it. This consideration would need to carry considerable weight to offset the estimated loss of $ 285 per annum coupled with the extra input of time demanded of the farmer.

A feature to note in the example budget of Table 5.1 is the treatment of the capital costs associated with the purchase of the tractor. Because this capital cost does not occur every year, it does not appear in the budget as an annual cost. Instead, the initial cost of the tractor and implements of $ 5 000 is shared equally over the expected economic life of the equipment, which in this case was five years, leading to an annual depreciation cost of $ 1 000. If it had been anticipated that the equipment would have had any appreciable salvage value at the end of this period, the annual depreciation and interest charges would have been calculated slightly differently according to the formulae:

$$D = (C - S)/L \text{ and } I = i(C + S)/2$$

where D is annual depreciation charge, C is capital cost, S is salvage value, L is economic life in years, I is annual interest charge, i is the relevant annual interest rate and it is assumed that there is no inflation (if there were inflation it would need to be taken into account as outlined in Section 4.7). This contrasts with the depreciation and interest charge calculations of Table 5.1 which assume a salvage value of zero after five years.

In the budget of Table 5.1 the interest charge is calculated on the assumption that the required capital is borrowed at an interest rate of 10 percent per annum calculated on the balance of the loan. Hence an interest charge on the average sum borrowed is included in the budget. If the capital is found from the farmer's own savings, perhaps held in a savings bank, the interest item would appear on the same side of the budget but under revenue foregone, rather than under extra costs. The amount would be calculated as above but using the rate of interest paid by the bank.

It should be noted that the methods of dealing with changes in the capital position of the farm described above are somewhat approximate. If this aspect of the proposed change is considered important, a partial cash-flow budget, as described in Section 5.3 below, may be more appropriate than a partial profit budget.

A second example of a partial budget is given in Table 5.2. This example relates to a possible change in the balance of enterprises on a cropping farm in the Cameron Highlands of Malaysia. The proposed change is to expand the production of Chinese cabbage with a corresponding reduction in the area devoted to tomatoes. A total of five acres (2.02 ha) is involved in the proposed change. It is possible to grow three crops of Chinese cabbage in a year, but only two crops of tomatoes. It is not implied that these crops would be grown consecutively on the same piece of land, but rather that the overall annual farm rotation would be modified to incorporate three five-acre Chinese cabbage crops instead of two five-acre crops of tomatoes.

The extra costs shown in the budget of Table 5.2 are the variable costs of Chinese cabbage production, while revenue foregone is the gross income previously earned from two five-acre crops of tomatoes. On the other side of the budget, costs saved are the variable costs of tomato production, and extra revenue is the gross income which would now be earned from Chinese cabbages.

In this case, the budget shows an increase in annual profit for the proposed change. Although the change implies an increase in the amount of family labour needed, it is assumed that this labour is available, and a recommendation might well be made in favour of the proposal.

5.2 *Gross margin budgets*

It should be reasonably evident that a budget such as the one shown in Table 5.2 above, relating to a change in the levels of the enterprises in a farm plan, can be more simply constructed using gross margins. The budget of Table 5.2 records the gross income foregone and the variable costs saved for the enterprise being reduced in scale (tomatoes), and the extra gross income and additional variable costs for the enterprise being expanded

Table 5.2

A PARTIAL BUDGET FOR A CHANGE IN CROPPING PROGRAMME

Change under review: Replacement in annual rotation of two five-acre plantings of tomatoes by three five-acre plantings of Chinese cabbage.

Date : June 1976.

Losses[a]	(M$)	*Gains*[a]	(M$)
Extra costs:		*Costs saved:*	
5 × 3 acres Chinese cabbage:		5 × 2 acres tomatoes:	
Planting materials, M$ 26/ac	390	Planting materials, M$ 7/ac	70
Fertilizer, M$ 1 132/ac	16 980	Fertilizer, M$ 1 197/ac	11 970
Insecticide, M$ 148/ac	2 220	Insecticide, M$ 182/ac	1 820
Fungicide, M$ 69/ac	1 035	Fungicide, M$ 173/ac	1 730
Weedicide, M$ 27/ac	405	Weedicide, M$ 28/ac	280
Fuel, M$ 44/ac	660	Fuel, M$ 47/ac	470
Revenue foregone:		*Extra revenue:*	
5 × 2 acres tomatoes at M$ 4 200/ac	42 000	5 × 3 acres Chinese cabbage at M$ 4 275/ac	64 125
Total losses:	63 690	*Total gains:*	80 465
Extra profit = 80 465 - 63 690 = M$ 16 775.			

[a] Annual basis.

Other considerations:

1. Increase in family labour input (30 man days).
2. Small reduction in risk.

Source: Based on data given by Chiew (1976).

(Chinese cabbage). A simpler presentation is therefore achieved by deducting the variable expenses from the gross income of each crop. In the example above, the two gross margins would be calculated as shown in Table 5.3 for tomatoes and in Table 5.4 for Chinese cabbage. These tables represent simplified activity budgets for the two enterprises, as outlined in Section 4.3. The partial budget to calculate the extra profit from the change is then simply constructed using the enterprise gross margins as follows:

Losses:	Gross margin foregone: 2 × 5 acres tomatoes at M$ 2 566/acre	M$ 25 660
Gains:	Extra gross margin: 3 × 5 acres of Chinese cabbage at M$ 2 829/acre	M$ 42 435
Extra profit	= 42 435 - 25 660	M$ 16 775

The use of gross margins for calculating the effect of changes in farm organization on farm profit in the manner just illustrated is obviously very convenient. The procedure has already been illustrated in the context of farm programming in Section 4.5. There are some dangers in using gross margin for partial budgeting which must be kept in mind. First, there is an obvious temptation to conclude that farm profit can always be increased by expanding those enterprises showing a high gross margin per unit land area at the expense of those showing a lower return to land. As has been illustrated in Chapter 4, this might not always be so because of resource and other constraints. If the areas of the crops with high gross margin per unit of land are expanded without regard to the constraints, a likely consequence is that fixed expenses will be increased, perhaps to the point where the increase in total gross margin is more than offset. It follows, therefore, that partial budgets should be constructed using gross margins including explicit consideration of the effect of the proposed change on the level of fixed expenses. Thus, the appropriate format for a partial budget using gross margins is as follows:

Losses	$	*Gains*	$
Gross margin foregone	w	Extra gross margin	y
Extra fixed expenses	x	Fixed expenses saved	z
Total losses	A = w + x	Total gains	B = y + z
Extra profit		B - A	

In our gross margin budget example of Tables 5.3 and 5.4, no changes in fixed expenses were anticipated, so that there was no need to set out the budget in this more complete form.

The second danger in the gross margin budgeting approach is the implicit assumption of linearity in gross income and variable expenses. While Chinese cabbage presently being grown on the farm in our example above may indeed yield a gross income of M$ 4 275 per acre on average, with average variable expenses of M$ 1 446 per acre, as set out in Table 5.4, it may not be safe to assume that the additional three five-acre crops will also produce the same gross income per acre with the same level of variable expenses.

Table 5.3

GROSS MARGIN BUDGET FOR TOMATOES

	(M$)	(M$)
Gross income/acre:		
175 piculs/acre at M$24/picul		4 200
Variable expenses/acre:		
Planting matcrials	7	
Fertilizer	1 197	
Insecticide	182	
Fungicide	173	
Weedicide	28	
Fuel	47	
Total		1 634
Gross margin/acre:		2 566
Approximate growing period		5 months
Labour input		154 days

Perhaps the additional area may have to be grown on less suitable land or at a less appropriate stage in the rotation, so that the yield will be less than for the existing area. More fertilizer may be needed to achieve the same yield. Maybe, because a larger proportion of the farm is now devoted to Chinese cabbage, the incidence of pests and disease will be increased, so that spraying expenses may be greater, not only on the additional area, but also on the existing area.

The gross margin budgeting format set out above does not provide a convenient framework for consideration of non-linearities of the types just described. If such non-linearities are thought to be present in a particular case, the more general partial budgeting format, discussed in Section 5.1, is more appropriate. The danger in the gross margin approach is that proper consideration may not be given to possible non-linearities. For this reason, gross margin budgeting should be used with caution. It is not a technique that is recommended for use by inexperienced farm management workers.

5.3 *Partial cash-flow budgets*

Cash-flow budgeting has already been discussed and illustrated with a fairly comprehensive example in the context of development budgeting in Section 4.7. The main purpose here is to emphasize that cash-flow budgets may be constructed on a partial basis, as well as on a whole-farm basis. In partial cash-flow budgeting, only those cash flows which would be changed as a consequence of some proposed change in the farm plan are included in the budget.

Partial cash-flow budgets may be drawn up on a short, medium or long-term basis. A short-term budget would be constructed to show the effects on the seasonal pattern of cash flow of the change under review. It would therefore normally be drawn up on a monthly basis, probably with a planning horizon of one year. A medium-term budget would extend over perhaps two or three years with cash flows typically recorded quarterly, while a long-term budget would extend over several years and the cash flows would normally be reported on an annual basis.

Table 5.4

GROSS MARGIN BUDGET FOR CHINESE CABBAGE

	(M$)	(M$)
Gross income/acre:		
190 piculs/acre at M$22.5/picul		4 275
Variable expenses/acre:		
Planting materials	26	
Fertilizer	1 132	
Insecticide	148	
Fungicide	69	
Weedicide	27	
Fuel	44	
Total		1 446
Gross margin/acre:		2 829
Approximate growing period		4 months
Labour input		106 days

Short and medium-term partial cash-flow budgets are of limited value in most circumstances, since, with these shorter time horizons, the usual purpose of cash-flow budgeting is to establish the feasibility of a particular farm plan in terms of capital and credit. As discussed in Section 4.4, this question can usually best be investigated on a whole-farm basis. However, long-term partial cash-flow budgets do find considerable use for evaluating the profitability of some proposed change in the farm plan using discounting methods. In fact, although the development budget in Section 4.7 above was drawn up on a whole-farm basis, the evaluation of net present value (NPV) and internal rate of return (IRR) was carried out in a partial way, i.e., the proposed development project was evaluated in terms of the changes in net cash flows compared with the existing farm system.

For a further, rather more straightforward example of partial cash-flow budgeting, we turn again to the budget for the purchase of a farm tractor in the Cook Islands. A partial profit budget for this proposal is given in Table 5.1. For a simple investment decision of this kind, where no development phase is involved, an adequate economic appraisal can be made in the way illustrated in Table 5.1. An alternative evaluation, which is theoretically slightly more satisfactory, can be made using a cash-flow budget coupled with the NPV criterion. The relevant calculations are shown in Table 5.5 for the five-year period corresponding to the expected life of the tractor.

The budget of Table 5.5 is set out in a manner which parallels the format of a partial profit budget. Cash flows lost, in the form of extra payments or foregone receipts, are recorded for each year in the planning period. Similarly, gains in the form of payments saved or extra receipts are also enumerated. Subtracting total cash-flow losses from total cash-flow gains indicates the extra net cash flow in each period covered by the budget. These net cash flows can then be discounted to find the NPV or IRR. In the example, the NPV is calculated by discounting using an annual cost of capital or interest rate of 10 percent. It is reassuring to note that the NPV found is negative, implying that the investment would not be profitable. This conclusion conforms with that found in the partial profit budget of Table 5.1.

Table 5.5

PARTIAL CASH-FLOW BUDGET FOR PURCHASE OF A TRACTOR[a]

	Year 0 ($)	Year 1 ($)	Year 2 ($)	Year 3 ($)	Year 4 ($)	Year 5 ($)
Losses						
Extra payments:						
Cost of tractor	5 000	-	-	-	-	-
Fuel and repairs	-	550	550	550	550	550
Annual licence fee	-	25	25	25	25	25
Receipts foregone:						
Nil	-	-	-	-	-	-
Total annual losses	5 000	575	575	575	575	575
Gains						
Payments saved:						
Hire of contractor	-	490	490	490	490	490
Extra receipts:						
Contract work	-	1 050	1 050	1 050	1 050	1 050
Total annual gains	-	1 540	1 540	1 540	1 540	1 540
Extra net cash flow	-5 000	+965	+965	+965	+965	+965
Discount factor [b]	1.0000	0.9091	0.8264	0.7513	0.6830	0.6209
Present value	-5 000	+877	+797	+725	+659	+599
Net present value =	-$ 1 343[b]					

[a] For details of the proposed change, see Table 5.1. Budget prepared in May 1992.
[b] Assuming an annual interest rate of 10 percent, i.e., i = 0.10.

Partial cash-flow budgets of the form illustrated are most appropriate for evaluating changes of a developmental nature, i.e., where costs of making the change are spread over more than one year, and/or where there is a time lag of a few years before the full benefits of the change occur. In this context, if inflation should be a significant factor, it should be taken into account as outlined in Section 4.7.

5.4 *Parametric budgets*

As discussed above, budgeting is concerned with predicting the consequences of alternative courses of action. In this sense, as noted in Section 4.5, budgets constitute perhaps the simplest approach to farm system simulation. However, because the future is always to some degree unpredictable, many of the planning coefficients used in budgets are uncertain. Rates of technical performance may be difficult to predict because they vary from year to year and from farm to farm, and may be inadequately documented. Similarly, prices of inputs and outputs may vary in a largely unpredictable way. Budgets are ordinarily constructed using the best estimates of future rates of performance and prices. A best estimate can be taken as the mean or expected value of the farmer's or analyst's subjective probability distribution for that coefficient or required piece of data. In addition, the term *best estimate* implies that all reasonable steps have been taken to gather relevant information, so that the degree of uncertainty, or variance, surrounding the estimate is as low as practicable. Because the amount of evidence that can be gleaned varies from one planning coefficient to another, the degree of uncertainty will also vary from coefficient to coefficient. The planner will often be well advised to consider the effect on the budget of departures, in uncertain planning coefficients, from the estimates initially adopted.

In some cases, one particular planning coefficient may be regarded as a key source of uncertainty. A useful variant of partial budgeting in such a case is known as *break-even budgeting*. In this method, which is usually applied to partial profit budgeting, the budget is drawn up to establish the value of the selected coefficient at which gains and losses are equal. The value so determined is known as the *break-even value*. The merit of the method lies in the fact that it changes the nature of the assessment that must be made in regard to the uncertain coefficient. Instead of assessing the expected value, the planner or farmer can assess the probabilities that the actual value will be above or below the established break-even level. Thus, the chance that the proposed change will prove profitable can be assessed (subject to all other coefficients taking their expected values). It is usually easier to assess the probability of an uncertain coefficient exceeding or falling below a specified value than it is to assess an expected value for that coefficient. If the break-even value is found to be very high or very low, a conclusion about the likely profitability of the change under review may be drawn with a high degree of confidence.

The break-even budgeting method can be illustrated using the example of the partial profit budget for the purchase of a tractor presented in Table 5.1. The decision in this case can be seen to hinge on the amount of contract work obtained for the tractor. The demand for such contract work in the district might be viewed as highly uncertain, so that it would be useful to establish the break-even value for the number of hours of work obtained. The required break-even budget is shown in Table 5.6.

The procedure in break-even budgeting is to assign some symbol, in this case, h for hours, to the key uncertain variable. The partial profit budget is then drawn up in the usual way except that the expression for extra profit, found as gains minus losses, becomes an algebraic expression involving the variable. The break-even value is then found by setting this expression equal to zero and solving, as illustrated in the lower part of Table 5.6.

The notion of replacing a selected planning coefficient in a budget with a variable symbol can be extended to more than one coefficient. Such budgets are called *parametric budgets* and are designed to show the effect on (extra) profit of variations in the selected planning coefficients. Thus, break-even budgets are really a special category of parametric budgets.

Table 5.6

BREAK-EVEN BUDGET FOR THE PURCHASE OF A TRACTOR

Change under review: Purchase of a second-hand tractor and implements for \$ 5 000 to save on contract charges and to earn extra income by doing contract work for neighbours.

Date: May 1992.

Variable: Let h = hours of contract work performed.

Losses[a]	(\$)	*Gains*[a]	(\$)
Extra costs:		*Costs saved:*	
Depreciation: \$ 5 000/5	1 000	Hire of contractor: 70 hrs at \$ 7/hr	490
Interest on average investment: 0.1(5 000/2)	250		
Fuel and repairs: (70+h) hours at \$ 2.50/hr	175 + 2.5h		
Annual licence	25		
Revenue foregone:		*Extra revenue:*	
Nil		Contract work for neighbours: h hrs at \$ 7/hr	7h
Total losses:	1 450 + 2.5h	*Total gains:*	490 + 7h

Extra profit = 490 + 7h - 1 450 - 2.5h = 4.5h - 960.

Break-even value:
When extra profit is zero, 4.5h - 960 = 0, i.e., h = 213.3 hours.

[a] Annual basis.

Other considerations: As noted in Table 5.1.

Parametric budgeting is best explained using an example, and we turn again to the budget for the purchase of a tractor. Suppose that now we wish to investigate the effects of different assumptions, not only about the amount of contract tractor work obtained, but also about the economic life of the equipment and about the level of fuel and repair costs per hour worked. Each of these planning coefficients can be represented by a variable symbol and a parametric budget can be drawn up as shown in Table 5.7.

As shown in Table 5.7, the expression derived for increase in profit, D, in terms of the three selected parameters, h, t and f, is:

(5.1) $D = 215 + 7h - 5000/t - f(70 + h).$

This expression can now be used and interpreted in a number of ways. One possibility is simply to evaluate the expression for selected values of the parameters. The values used might be those judged relevant to a particular case, so that the parametric budgeting approach provides a means of extending the application of the budget to a number of farms with somewhat different circumstances. For an example of a very extensive parametric livestock budget intended for use in this way, see Byrne (1964.) An extension of this approach is to tabulate the values of D for particular values of h, t and f within the ranges judged relevant. However, perhaps the best way of summarizing the results of such evaluations is in graphical form, as illustrated in Figure 5.1.

The graphs in Figure 5.1 are drawn to permit evaluation of D for given values of h, f and t. Use of the graphs is illustrated for $h = 150$, $f = 2.5$ and $t = 5$, which were the values used in the original partial profit budget of Table 5.1. For these values of the three parameters, Figure 5.1 shows a net loss of -$ 285, as calculated in the original budget.

The construction of Figure 5.1 warrants some explanation. It is developed from a rearrangement of expression (5.1) above into the form:

(5.2) $D = \{215 + 7h - f(70 + h)\} - 5000/t.$

The term $(215 + 7h - f(70 + h)$ is evaluated first and is plotted on the horizontal axis of Figure 5.1 for values of h in the range of interest and for selected values of f. In the lower right-hand quadrant of the figure, the final term incorporating t is introduced. Because the graphs to be plotted are linear, it suffices to find two points on each line, which can then be joined using a ruler to obtain the lines shown.

If the budget is implemented via a computer spreadsheet, the processes of break-even and parametric budgeting are much simplified. There is no need for algebra since the various uncertain values are readily changed by over-typing with a different value. The break-even value of a particular coefficient is easily found with a spreadsheet using a trial and error approach, while the data needed to tabulate or graph the effects of varying two or more uncertain coefficients are readily generated by systematically entering selected combinations of values.

Before leaving the topic of parametric budgets, it should be noted that although the usual application of the method is in the context of partial profit budgets, parametric budgeting can also be applied to other kinds of partial budgets, such as cash-flow budgets. For example, the partial cash-flow budget of Table 5.5 could be constructed using the same parameters as in Table 5.7. The net present value could thereby be found as an expression involving h, f and t, and this expression could be evaluated graphically or in other ways, as described above. The chief difference would be that the parametric cash-flow budget would prove rather more complicated than the parametric profit budget.

The procedures of break-even and parametric budgeting can also be applied to whole-farm budgets. In a break-even context, the value of the coefficient of concern can be determined at which some selected measure of overall farm profit is zero, or is equal

Figure 5.1

GRAPH TO EVALUATE EXPRESSION FOR EXTRA PROFIT IN TRACTOR-PURCHASE PARAMETRIC BUDGET EXAMPLE OF TABLE 5.7

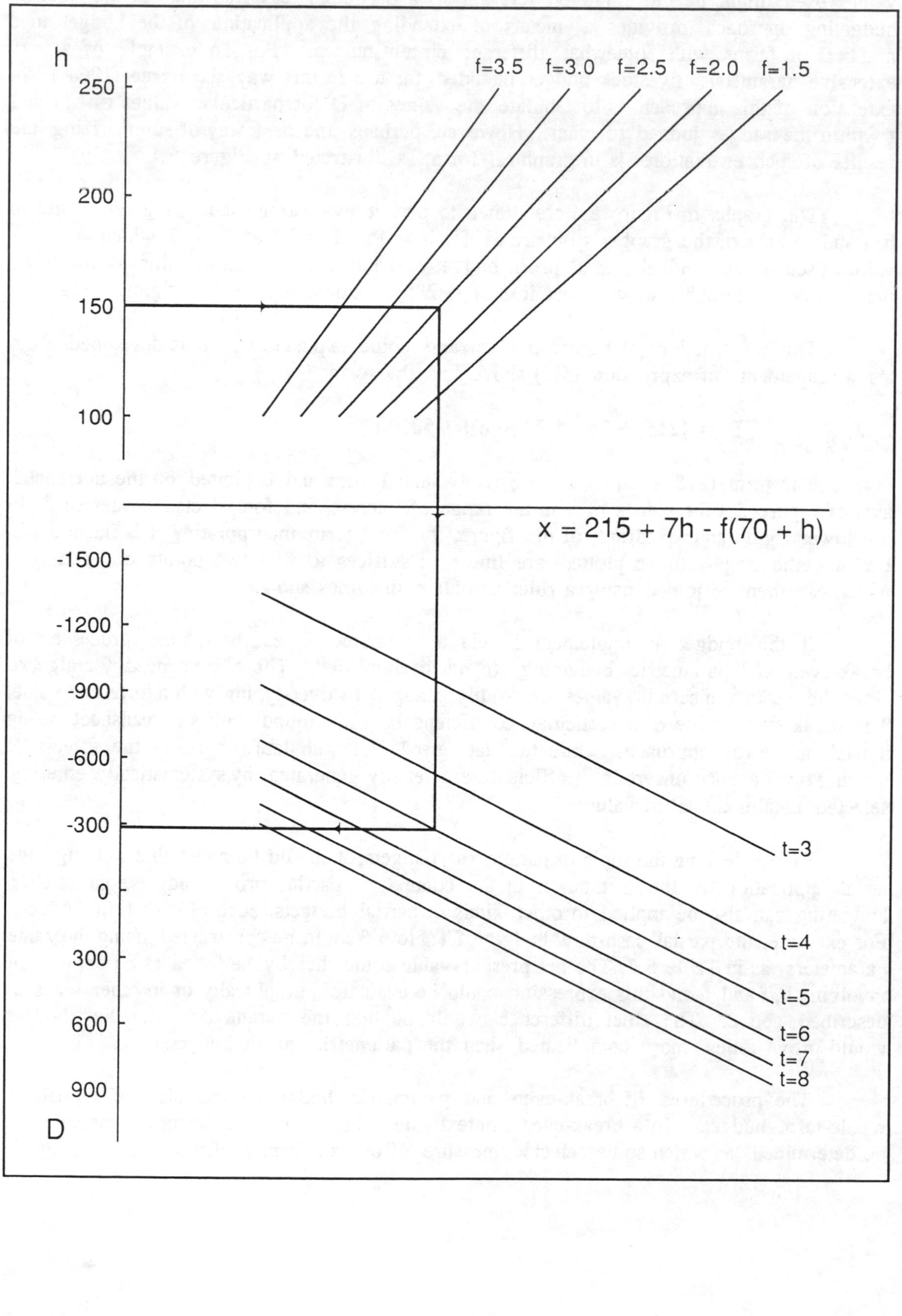

Table 5.7

PARAMETRIC BUDGET FOR THE PURCHASE OF A TRACTOR

Change under review:	Purchase of a second-hand tractor and implements for $ 5 000 to save on contract charges and to earn extra income by doing contract work for neighbours.
Date:	May, 1992.
Parametric variables: Let:	h = hours of contract work performed; t = economic life of machinery; f = fuel and repair costs per hour worked.

Losses[a]	($)	*Gains*[a]	($)
Extra costs:		*Costs saved:*	
Depreciation:	5 000/t	Hire of contractor: 70 hrs at $ 7/hr	490
Interest on average investment: 0.1(5 000/2)	250		
Fuel and repairs: (70 + h) hours at $ f/hr	f(70 + h)		
Annual licence fee	25		
Revenue foregone:		*Extra revenue:*	
Nil	0	Contract work for neighbours:	
		h hrs at $ 7/hr	7h
Total losses:	5 000/t + 275 + f(70 + h)	*Total gains:*	490 + 7h

Extra profit = D = 490 + 7h - 5 000/t - 275 - f(70 + h) = 215 + 7h - 5 000/t - f(70 + h)

[a] Annual basis.

Other considerations: As noted in Table 5.1.

to some chosen critical value. Likewise, parametric procedures can be used to reflect the effects on overall farm performance of variations in a number of planning coefficients.

5.5 Risk budgeting

Risk budgeting is a form of parametric budgeting adapted to the case where probability distributions have been specified for the uncertain coefficients such as yields and prices, and where the aim is to assess the probability distribution of the resulting profit or gross margin. Again, like other forms of budgeting, it is a type of simulation modelling as discussed in Section 4.5.

To give a simple example of risk budgeting, the gross margin per unit area of a cash crop can be defined as:

(5.3) $$g = y(p - u) - v$$

where:
g is gross margin ($/ha);
y is yield (t/ha);
p is price ($/t);
u is those variable expenses that are related to the level of yield ($/t); and
v is those variable expenses not related to the level of yield ($/ha).

In the typical case, both y and p will be uncertain and subjective probability distributions on these uncertain quantities might be assessed. Risk budgeting is concerned with using these distributions, together with estimates of u and v, to find the probability distribution of g.

In some special cases it is possible to calculate statistics of the distribution of g directly from information about the distributions of y and p. For most distributions of y and p likely to be considered, it is straightforward to calculate the mean and variance of g (Anderson and Doran, 1978). If higher-order moments of the distribution of g are needed, such as the third moment which is used to measure the skewness of the distribution, some difficulties may be encountered, especially if the distributions of y and p are not independent. Similarly, if it is desired to obtain the whole distribution of g, perhaps to display in the form of a cumulative distribution function for subjective evaluation of the degree of risk, direct analysis will be applicable only in a few special cases. When direct analysis fails, the best operational approach is by use of simulation based on Monte Carlo sampling as illustrated by Anderson, Dillon and Hardaker (1977, Ch. 8).

The Monte Carlo method applied to risk budgeting involves pseudo-random sampling from the distributions of the uncertain parameters in the budget to obtain a set of planning coefficients. The arithmetic involved in calculating the required gross margin is then performed in the usual way, and the whole process is repeated many times. The resulting distribution of values of the gross margin can then be summarized in some informative way. For example, the distribution might be printed as a cumulative distribution function, or required summary statistics (such as the estimated mean and variance) of the gross margin can be calculated.

Because of the relatively large sample size (i.e., runs of the budget simulation model) needed in applying the Monte Carlo risk budgeting procedure outlined above, a computer is used to implement such analyses. Computer programmes have been designed for such purposes (e.g. the @RISK (Palisade, 1992) add-on to popular spreadsheets). The following illustrative application is taken from an example in Anderson (1976).

The case studied relates to a decision maker interested in a risk evaluation of the gross margin per hectare of barley. Variable expenses for the crop are regarded as being virtually certain at $ 82/ha. It is assumed, largely for the sake of expediency, that uncertainty in the yield and price of barley can be adequately captured using triangular distributions. This form of distribution has the advantage of being completely defined by only three parameters - the highest possible value, the lowest possible value, and the most likely or modal value (Anderson, Dillon and Hardaker, 1977, Ch. 8). These parameters for the assessed distributions of the yield and price of barley are given in Table 5.8. It is assumed that there is no correlation between yield and price, i.e.,that the two distributions are independent.

The above data were processed using the Monte Carlo method of risk budgeting. Summary statistics of the distribution found for the gross margin per hectare are given in Table 5.9. In addition, the results are plotted in the form of a cumulative distribution function in Figure 5.2 which shows, for example, that there is a probability of 0.75 that the gross margin per hectare will be below $ 64. The information in Figure 5.2 and Table 5.9 could be used by the decision maker to assess the riskiness of the barley gross margin.

Figure 5.2

SMOOTHED CUMULATIVE DISTRIBUTION FUNCTION FOR THE DISTRIBUTION OF BARLEY GROSS MARGIN

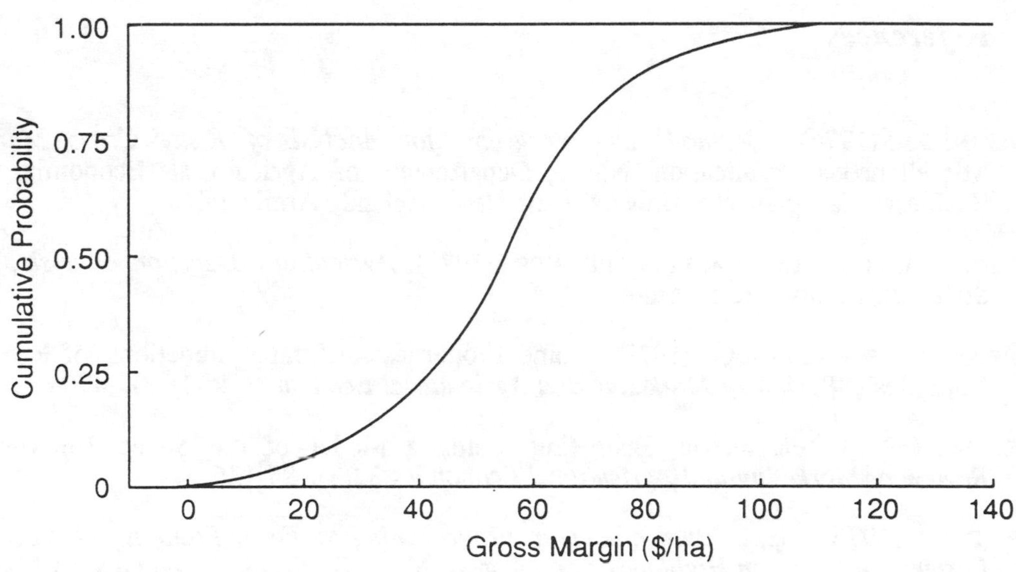

Table 5.8

PERFORMANCE MEASURES FOR BARLEY - RISK BUDGETING EXAMPLE

Yield	(t/ha)
Worst possible yield	1.00
Most likely yield	1.75
Highest possible yield	2.50
Price	($/t)
Worst possible price	60
Most likely price	75
Highest possible price	90

Table 5.9

SUMMARY STATISTICS OF STOCHASTIC GROSS MARGIN

Mean ($/ha)	46.6
Standard deviation[a] ($/ha)	25.1
Coefficient of skewness[b]	0.36

[a] Square root of variance.
[b] Defined as the third central moment divided by the 1.5th power of the variance. The coefficient is positive or negative according as the distribution is skewed positively (long tail above mode) or negatively (long tail below mode).

Similar data for other cash crops could be processed in the same way and would allow the relative attractiveness of barley vis-à-vis other crops to be assessed. A risk-averse farmer might well elect to grow a crop with a lower expected gross margin if the results of risk budgeting showed it to be less risky than the alternatives.

5.6 *References*

ANDERSON, J.R. (1976). *Methods and Programs for Analysis of Risky Gross Margins*, Miscellaneous Publication No. 3, Department of Agricultural Economics and Business Management, University of New England, Armidale.

ANDERSON, J.R., J.L. DILLON & J.B. HARDAKER (1977). *Agricultural Decision Analysis*, Iowa State University Press, Ames.

ANDERSON, J.R. & H.E. DORAN (1978). 'Some Properties of Simple Functions of Random Variables', *Review of Marketing and Agricultural Economics* 46(1): 37-47.

BYRNE, P.F. (1964). 'Parametric Budgeting Using a Model of the Sheep Enterprise', *Review of Marketing and Agricultural Economics* 32(3): 95-136.

CHIEW, E.F.C. (1976). *Application of Linear Programming to Farm Planning of Vegetable Farmers in Cameron Highlands*, unpublished M.Ag.Sc. thesis, University of Malaya, Kuala Lumpur.

6. INPUT-OUTPUT BUDGET ANALYSIS

Much data relating the level of crop yield or output to different levels of inputs are generated via agronomic experiments. This is particularly so for such important inputs as fertilizers, insecticides, fungicides, weedicides, and labour, animals and machinery used in crop production. Likewise, animal feeding experiments often generate data relating feed inputs or stocking rate to livestock output. In Chapter 7, econometric procedures relating to the estimation and economic analysis of input-output relationships (or production functions) based on such data are outlined. Less elaborate and more direct procedures for the economic appraisal of such data and the derivation of farmer recommendations from them are presented in this chapter. The basis of these procedures is partial budget analysis as outlined in Chapter 5. When applied to the analysis of input-output data, such partial budgeting is known as input-output budget analysis. As already intimated, the input-output alternatives being compared will usually relate to the different treatments used in an experiment or set of comparable experiments, including on-farm trials. However, data on differing input-output combinations may also be available from farm surveys and such data may also be appraised via input-output budget analysis.

The aim of input-output budget analysis is to derive recommendations which are consistent with the farmer's desires to increase expected income, to avoid undue risk and to make the best possible use of her or his scarce investment funds.

To illustrate input-output budget analysis, we will use the maize-fertilizer trial data shown in Table 6.1. These data encompass the results of eight trials each with the same set of 12 nitrogen (N) and phosphate (P) fertilizer combinations or treatments. Each of the yield levels listed in Table 6.1 is the average of the three replications run of each treatment in each of the trials. These average yields provide the best estimate of the treatment output that would be obtained on the entire field in which the particular trial was located. Trials 1 to 4 were conducted in one year and, respectively, trials 5 to 8 the next year at the same sites. Thus the data have both a spatial (four different sites) and a time (two different years) dimension.

The data of Table 6.1 are those used by Perrin *et al.* (1976) in their exposition of input-output budgeting which, with their permission, is followed here so that the more thoroughgoing treatment presented in their CIMMYT Manual can be used as a direct supplement to the presentation of this chapter, as can CIMMYT (1988 a, b).

Table 6.1

MAIZE YIELDS (T/HA OF 14 PERCENT MOISTURE GRAIN) BY FERTILIZER TREATMENT IN EIGHT TRIALS

Trial	Fertilizer treatment (kg/ha)											
N:	0	50	100	150	0	50	100	150	0	50	100	150
P_2O_5:	0	0	0	0	25	25	25	25	50	50	50	50
1	0.40	1.24	3.63	3.76	0.79	2.58	4.23	4.72	1.67	2.51	3.28	3.66
2	1.53	2.60	5.14	5.32	1.67	3.79	5.10	6.83	1.41	4.13	5.89	6.27
3	4.15	4.86	4.80	4.87	4.44	5.00	4.97	5.28	5.12	5.66	6.36	6.62
4	2.42	3.82	5.23	4.48	2.36	4.54	6.26	7.17	1.61	4.41	5.38	6.58
5	1.64	1.92	2.08	2.19	2.04	3.21	3.12	2.93	1.44	3.44	3.32	3.62
6	1.61	2.94	4.14	4.34	1.81	3.92	3.61	3.81	1.18	3.89	5.38	4.92
7	4.74	5.41	4.29	4.92	4.91	5.22	5.38	5.14	5.10	4.88	4.54	5.28
8	1.21	2.33	1.97	2.23	1.53	2.78	2.49	2.80	1.37	3.51	3.75	4.35
Avg.:	2.21	3.14	3.91	4.01	2.44	3.88	4.40	4.84	2.36	4.05	4.74	5.16

Source: Perrin et al. (1976).

6.1 Data and analysis requirements

To be successful, input-output budgeting should lead to recommendations that are acceptable to farmers. This implies two things: first, the data used in the analysis must be representative in the sense that they should fit the farmer's production conditions, otherwise the farmer will not obtain the results predicted by the analysis; second, the procedure used in evaluating the data should be consistent with the farmer's goals and with the factors - particularly her or his tenure and resource situation - that influence her or his ability to achieve those goals. Both these requirements imply a farming systems orientation.

DATA REPRESENTATIVENESS

Whether the data used come from experiments or from a farm survey, they must relate to a group of farmers from within an agro-climatic zone whose farms are similar and who use much the same practices. Such a group of farmers constitute a *recommendation domain*. This is the domain or farmer target group to which the data must relate and be relevant, and to which recommendations from the analysis will be directed. The data of Table 6.1 relate to such a recommendation domain. They encompass four representative sites across the region to which they relate, involve two years of results so as to give some account of climatic variability over time, and relate to practices (use of N and P) which are of interest and feasible for farmers in the region.

MEETING FARMER GOALS

It is impossible to conduct experiments on each individual farm and make recommendations tailored to each individual farmer. The best that we can generally do is to make generalized recommendations that are oriented to a particular recommendation domain but with, as need be, some differentiation of recommendations for farmers of different tenure type (such as owners and sharefarmers) within the domain. Individual farmers may then select from and adjust these recommendations to their own unique circumstances as dictated by their resource and tenure situation, goals, and preferences about how best to use available resources to achieve those goals.

As noted in Section 1.5, farmers may have diverse goals and varying constraints on their achievement. To make generalized recommendations from input-output budget analysis, some simplification is necessary. The assumption made is that farmers think in terms of net benefits as they make their decisions. For example, a weed-conscious farmer will recognize that by eliminating weeds from the field, she or he will be likely to benefit by harvesting more grain. On the other hand, the farmer will also recognize that she or he must give up some cash to buy herbicides and then give up some time and effort to apply them, or she or he must give up a lot of time and effort for hand weeding. The farmer will weigh the benefits gained in the form of grain (or other useful products) against the things lost (costs) in the form of time and cash given up. The net result of this weighing up in the farmer's mind we refer to as the *net benefit* from a decision - the value of the benefits gained minus the value of the things given up.

While the farmer can make her or his own judgements about net benefits intuitively by making her or his own judgements about trade-offs between monetary and non-monetary elements, and her or his own judgements and preferences about the risks that may be faced, as an outsider the farm management analyst has to be more systematic. Accordingly, likely net benefits are judged in monetary terms, attaching so far as possible money values to all the elements of the net benefit calculation even though no money transaction may actually occur. This, of course, does not imply that farmers are concerned only with money. It is simply a device to represent the process that goes on in the farmer's mind. For example, if our weed-conscious farmer were quite commercialized, we could attach anticipated market prices to the labour, herbicides and grain in the net benefit calculation. But if she or he were a subsistence farmer, we would have to employ the concept of opportunity cost to represent the values she or he places on labour and grain since there would be no money paid out or received. *Opportunity cost* is the value of any resource in its best alternative use. Consider the opportunity cost of the farmer's time. If she or he has a job off the farm which has to be given up temporarily to weed her or his field, then the opportunity cost of the farmer's time in weeding maize, say, is the wage she or he would have been earning if she or he had worked off-farm. Suppose, however, that the best alternative use of her or his time is working on the tobacco crop, and that a day's work on tobacco will increase the value of the tobacco harvest by $ 6. In this case, the opportunity cost of time spent in weeding maize is $ 6 per day since that is what is given up by weeding maize instead of tending tobacco. But what if the farmer would merely sit in the shade if she or he were not to weed maize? Is the opportunity cost of the farmer's time zero? This is not very likely since most people place some value on relaxation. Still, it is difficult to estimate the value which a farmer places on leisure if that is the highest-valued alternative use of her or his time. Likewise, if the alternative being considered involves a drastic reorganization, say, of the farm cropping pattern, it may be impossible to estimate opportunity cost without a thoroughgoing whole-farm analysis. As in these examples, reliable estimates of opportunity cost may often not be readily available. In such cases the best that can usually be done is to use a judgemental estimate of opportunity cost.

As well as the problem of simplifying the net benefit calculation by using money as a common denominator, there are three other problems to be met in making farmer recommendations from input-output budget analysis. Accommodating resource constraints (particularly scarcity of investment funds) is one and handling uncertainty (arising particularly from price and climatic variation) is another. These two difficulties are respectively considered in Sections 6.4 and 6.6 below. The third problem is that of allowing for differences in the tenure status of farmers. This question is discussed in Section 6.7. Until then it is assumed (unrealistically) that there are no differences in tenure status between farmers in the recommendation domain so that, other things being equal, the budget evaluation of costs and benefits is the same for all farmers.

6.2 Estimating benefits and costs

In applying partial budgeting to sets of yield response data (such as that of Table 6.1) in order to carry out input-output budget analysis, it is useful to define more precisely a number of elements that enter the budget calculations. Assuming that the farmer is an owner operator or a cash renter and not a sharefarmer or landlord, the relevant definitions are as follows:

Net yield is the measured yield per hectare in the field, minus harvest and storage losses where appropriate.

Field price of output is the value to the farmer of an additional unit of production in the field prior to harvest. Farmers who sell part or all of their grain will be concerned with money field price while those who consume the entire crop will be concerned with opportunity field price. *Money field price of output* is the market price of the product minus harvest, storage, transportation and marketing costs per unit. *Opportunity field price of output* is the money price which the farm family would have to pay to acquire an additional unit of the product for consumption.

Gross field benefit is the net yield times field price for all products from the crop. In general, this may include money benefits or opportunity benefits, or both.

Field price of an input is the total value which must be given up to bring an extra unit of input onto the field.

Money field price of an input refers to money values such as purchase price or other direct expenses per unit of input.

Opportunity field price of an input refers to the value of input opportunities which must be given up, i.e., the value of the input in its best alternative use.

Field cost of an input is its field price multiplied by the quantity of that input which varies with the decision. It may be expressed as money field cost or opportunity field cost, or perhaps both, depending on the input.

Total field cost (or variable cost) of the decision is the sum of field costs for all inputs which are affected by the choice. Such variable cost can consist of either money costs or opportunity costs or both.

Net benefits are equal to total gross field benefits minus total field costs.

While the above definitions are expressed in terms of crop production, analogous definitions (on a per animal rather than per hectare basis if desired) apply for livestock production.

Should the farm decision maker be a sharefarmer, appropriate adjustment must be made to the above definitions so that they relate only to the sharefarmer's share of input and output. Likewise, if it is the landlord and not the sharefarmer who is the relevant decision maker, the defined quantities must be in terms of the landlord's share of input costs and output returns.

6.3 A simple example

Assuming that sharefarming considerations are not relevant, partial budget analysis of each of the (N,P) treatment yield averages over the eight trials of Table 6.1 is shown in Table 6.2. The yield curves in Figure 6.1 provide a graphic picture of the average yield response. Both Table 6.2 and Figure 6.1 omit consideration of the yield variability associated with each treatment across locations and across time. This will be considered later.

Table 6.2 shows the alternative choices of fertilizer levels as column headings, then the average yield for each, followed by net yield after adjusting downward 10 percent for assumed harvest and storage losses (this adjustment being judged the appropriate one for the recommendation domain being considered). The market price judged relevant for maize in the area is $ 1 200 per ton, but after making corrections for harvest costs, transportation costs and shrinkages, the field price of additional yield is estimated to be $ 1 000 per ton. Resulting gross field benefit is shown in line 3. Lines 4, 5 and 6 of the table calculate the variable money cost and lines 7, 8 and 9 the variable opportunity costs; total variable costs are calculated in line 10 and the net benefit per hectare of each alternative is given in line 11. The cost items, of course, reflect the cultural practices of the recommendation domain (animal tillage and hand application of fertilizer); likewise fertilizer field prices include transport cost, and labour opportunity cost is a judgement based on discussion with farmers in the area.

The net benefit estimates given in line 11 of Table 6.2 complete the partial budget analysis of the average treatment yields from the experiments of Table 6.1. One might be tempted at this point to choose the (N,P) treatment of (100,50) as the generalized recommendation. However, this would be a hasty choice as no consideration has yet been given to the questions of capital scarcity, yield uncertainty and risk aversion.

Table 6.2

PARTIAL BUDGET ANALYSIS OF TREATMENT YIELD AVERAGES FROM MAIZE TRIALS OF TABLE 6.1

Budget element	Fertilizer treatment (kg/ha)											
N:	0	50	100	150	0	50	100	150	0	50	100	150
P_2O_5:	0	0	0	0	25	25	25	25	50	50	50	50
(1) Average yield (t/ha)	2.21	3.14	3.91	4.01	2.44	3.88	4.40	4.84	2.36	4.05	4.74	5.16
(2) Net yield (t/ha)	1.99	2.83	3.52	3.61	2.20	3.49	3.96	4.36	2.12	3.64	4.27	4.64
(3) Gross field benefit ($/ha @ 1 000/t)	1 990	2 830	3 520	3 610	2 200	3 490	3 960	4 360	2 120	3 640	4 270	4 640
(4) Nitrogen ($8/kg N)	0	400	800	1 200	0	400	800	1 200	0	400	800	1 200
(5) Phosphate ($ 10/kg P_2O_5)	0	0	0	0	250	250	250	250	500	500	500	500
(6) Variable money costs ($/ha) [(4)+(5)]	0	400	800	1 200	250	650	1 050	1 450	500	900	1 300	1 700
(7) Number of applications	0	1	2	2	1	1	2	2	1	1	2	2
(8) Cost per application (2 man-days @ $25)	50	50	50	50	50	50	50	50	50	50	50	50
(9) Variable opportunity cost ($/ha)[(7)×(8)]	0	50	100	100	50	50	100	100	50	50	100	100
(10) Total variable costs ($/ha) [(6)+(9)]	0	450	900	1 300	300	700	1 150	1 550	550	950	1 400	1 800
(11) Net benefit ($/ha) [(3)-(10)]	1 990	2 380	2 620	2 310	1 900	2 790	2 810	2 810	1 570	2 690	2 870	2 840

Figure 6.1

AVERAGE YIELD RESPONSE CURVES FOR NITROGEN
AT THREE LEVELS OF PHOSPHORUS

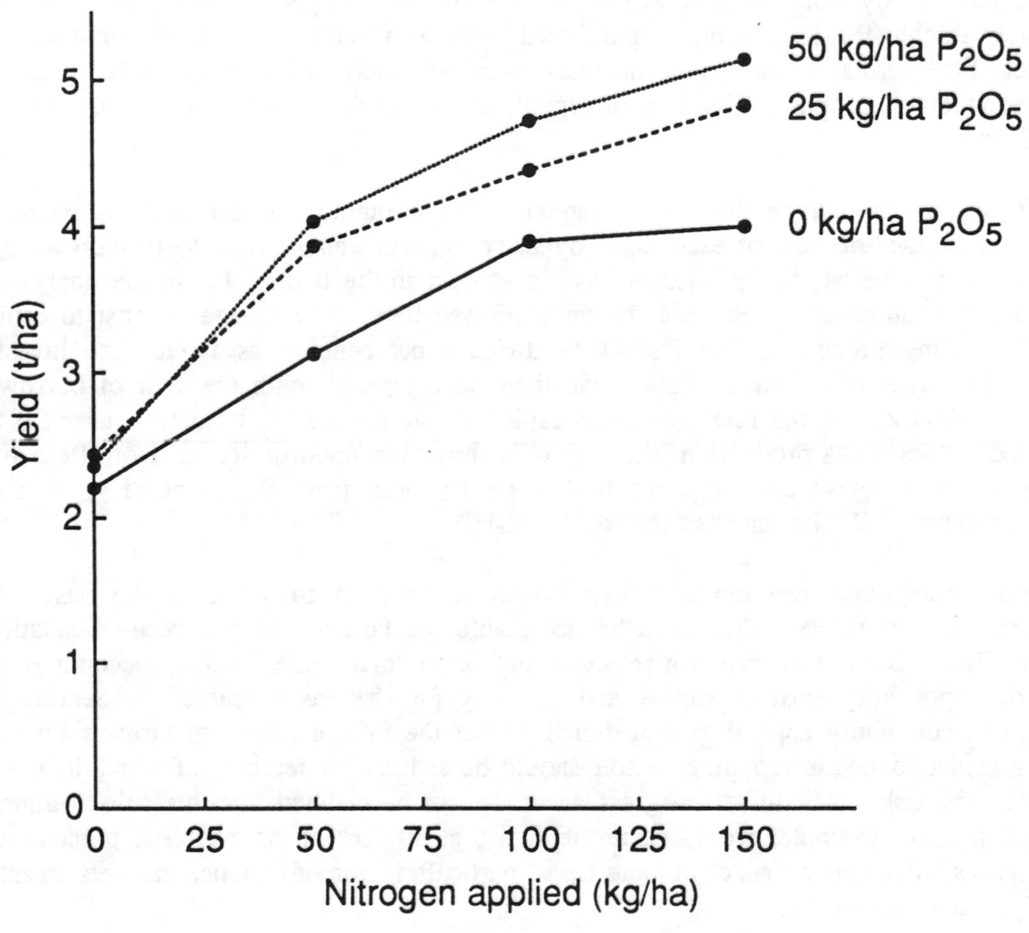

6.4 Allowing for capital scarcity

The analysis of Table 6.2 is simplistic as the cost of capital (and also risk) are not considered. It is important to allow for the cost of capital because shortage of capital is a general feature of small farmers and must be allowed for in deciding on recommendations to be made to them, otherwise the recommendations are unlikely to be acceptable.

By *investment capital* is meant the value of inputs (purchased or owned) which are allocated to an enterprise with the expectation of a return at a later point in time. By the *cost of investment capital* is meant the benefits given up by the farmer through having her or his capital tied up in the enterprise for a period of time. Such *cost of capital* may be a direct cost in the form of an interest charge that has to be paid; or it may be an opportunity cost in the form of earnings given up by not using the funds, or an input already owned, in their best alternative use.

The cost of capital for small farmers in developing countries is generally quite high. Interest charges by moneylenders are often in excess of 100 percent per year. This can effectively double the cost of inputs purchased with such loans. Too, most small farmers have very little capital of their own and want to invest it only in inputs giving high returns. This means that the opportunity cost of capital, as well as the direct cost, is quite high for these farmers.

Two ways to include the cost of capital in input-output budget analysis would be either to increase the cost of each input by an appropriate amount or to include a direct or opportunity interest charge element as a cost item in the budget (as in the analysis of Table 5.1). Another approach, and the one followed here, is to charge no cost to capital in the budgeting procedure, but instead to attribute net benefits as a return to invested capital. This rate of return to capital can then be compared with the cost of borrowed capital, if relevant, and the rate which this capital would realize in alternative uses. If the calculated return for a production alternative is above the opportunity cost or alternative rate of return, then we can judge the first to be desirable from the point of view of the farmer (assuming all alternatives are equally risky).

For generalized recommendations, however, we need to work on the basis of a minimum rate of return which will be acceptable to farmers in the recommendation domain. There is no clear basis for selecting such a minimum rate. Taking account of the direct or opportunity cost of capital and allowing for risk (as discussed in Section 6.6 below), one commonly applied rule-of-thumb is that the rate of return to farmers on their working capital over the cropping season should be at least 40 percent, of which half is an allowance for risk. Of course, no great accuracy can be claimed for this rule-of-thumb. Some people, for example, would place the figure at 50 percent or even 100 percent and these figures will be appropriate in some cases, particularly for subsistence farmers in areas with high yield variability.

6.5 Marginal analysis of net benefits

The series of partial budgets constituting an input-output budget analysis can be evaluated graphically as a *net benefit curve*. This curve shows the relationship between the variable costs of the alternatives and their expected net benefits. The net benefit curve is constructed by plotting each of the alternatives under consideration according to its net benefit and variable cost, and then drawing a graph through the undominated alternatives, as shown in Figure 6.2 for the fertilizer data of Table 6.2. The *dominated alternatives* are those which would never be chosen because relative to them there is at least one other alternative which has a higher or at least an equal net benefit and a lower variable cost. Under normal circumstances we would never expect a farmer to choose a dominated alternative. Thus in Figure 6.2 the only undominated (N,P) alternatives are (0,0), (50,0), (50,25), (100,25) and (100,50).

Figure 6.2

NET BENEFIT CURVE BASED UPON THE PARTIAL BUDGET ANALYSIS OF TABLE 6.2

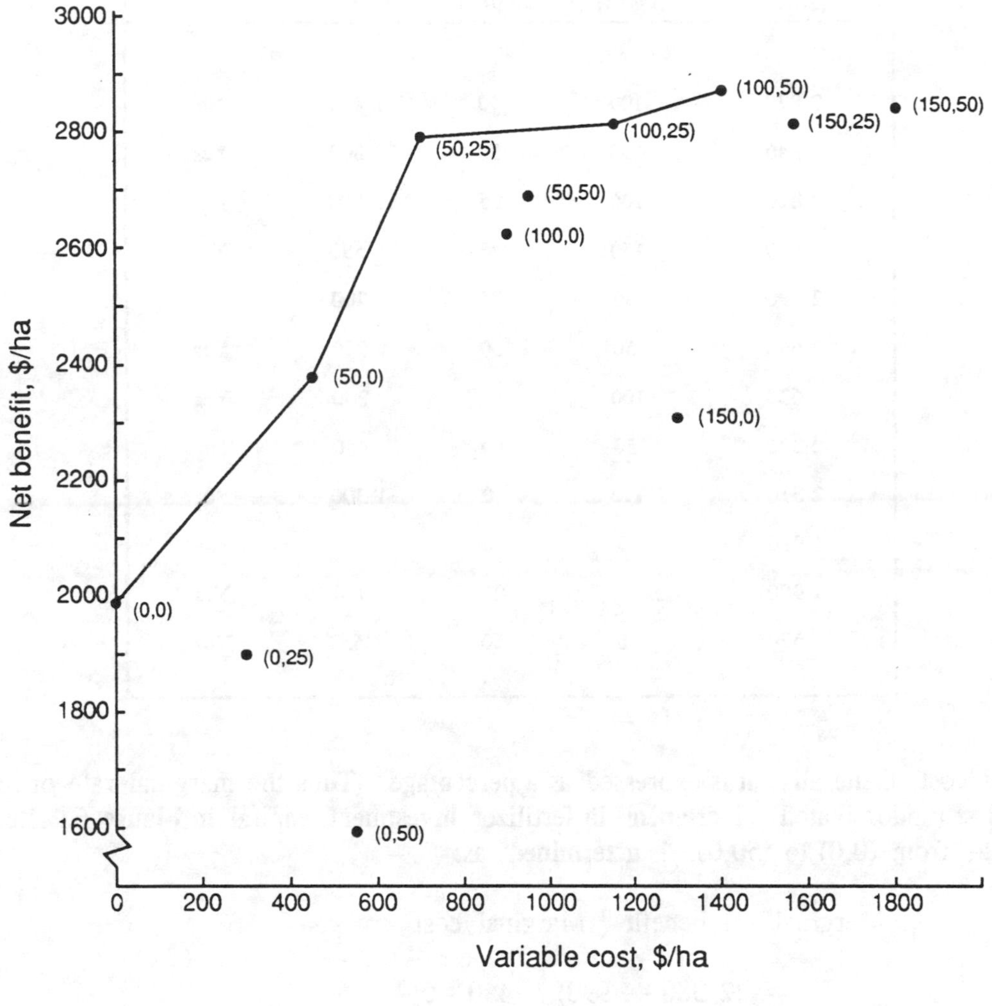

Marginal analysis may now be applied to the net benefit curve of Figure 6.2 (i.e., to the undominated alternatives of Table 6.2) in order to assess just how the net benefits of investment change as the amount invested increases. *Marginal net benefit* is the aspect of significance, i.e., the increase in net benefit obtainable from a given increment of investment. Thus in the example of Table 6.2, the marginal net benefit from investing $ 450 in 50 kg of N and nothing in P is $ 2 380 - $ 1 990 = $ 390. The next possible increment of expenditure is to spend an additional $ 250 for 25 kg of P_2O_5, thereby taking us from the (50,0) to the (50,25) alternative as shown in Table 6.2. The marginal net benefit from this increment in expenditure is $ 2 790 - $ 2 380 = $ 410. The *marginal rate of return* to a given increment in expenditure is the marginal net benefit divided by the

Table 6.3

DOMINANCE ANALYSIS OF FERTILIZER INVESTMENT ALTERNATIVES

Net benefit	Investment alternative		Variable cost	Dominated?
	N	P_2O_5		
($/ha)	(kg/ha)	(kg/ha)	($/ha)	
2 870	100	50	1 400	No
2 840	150	50	1 800	Yes
2 810	100	25	1 150	No
2 810	150	25	1 550	Yes
2 790	50	25	700	No
2 690	50	50	950	Yes
2 620	100	0	900	Yes
2 380	50	0	450	No
2 310	150	0	1 300	Yes
1 990	0	0	0	No
1 900	0	25	300	Yes
1 570	0	50	550	Yes

marginal cost. Generally, it is expressed as a percentage. Thus the marginal rate of return of the first (undominated) increment in fertilizer investment capital in Figure 6.2, i.e., the increment from (0,0) to (50,0), is determined as:

Marginal net benefit / Marginal cost

= (2 380 - 1 990) / (450 - 0)
= 390 / 450
= 87%.

For the second increment of investment, i.e., from (50,0) to (50,25), the marginal rate of return is likewise:

Marginal net benefit / Marginal cost

= (2 790 - 2 380) / (700 - 450)
= 410 / 250
= 164%.

Of course, it is not necessary to construct a net benefit curve to determine the undominated alternatives. This can be done directly, as shown in Table 6.3, by listing the alternatives in order of net benefit and then deleting dominated alternatives by inspection (any alternative which has a variable cost equal to or higher than any alternative above it is dominated). Thus we obtain the five undominated alternatives of Table 6.4, which are of course the same as those making the net benefit curve of Figure 6.2.

Table 6.4 presents the marginal net benefit, marginal cost and marginal rate of return for each input-output investment alternative. Considering the listed rates of return, and applying the general rule-of-thumb that farmers will not want to make an investment

Table 6.4

MARGINAL ANALYSIS OF UNDOMINATED FERTILIZER INVESTMENT ALTERNATIVES

Alternative				Change from next highest benefit		
N (kg/ha)	P_2O_5 (kg/ha)	Net benefit ($/ha)	Variable cost ($/ha)	Marginal net benefit ($/ha)	Marginal cost ($/ha)	Marginal rate of return (%)
100	50	2 870	1 400	60	250	24
100	25	2 810	1 150	20	450	4
50	25	2 790	700	410	250	164
50	0	2 380	450	390	450	87
0	0	1 990	0	-	-	-

unless it returns at least 40 percent per crop season as proposed in Section 6.4, it is obvious that farmers would generally be willing to invest both the first $ 450 for 50 kg of N and the further $ 250 for 25 kg of P_2O_5. With marginal rates of return of 87 and 164 percent respectively, both these increments yield well over the required 40 percent. But farmers in the recommendation domain would in general not want to invest more on N and P than this first $ 700. Thus using the marginal analysis approach and a minimum return criterion of 40 percent per crop season, we could be rather confident in recommending the (50,25) investment alternative. On the other hand, if risks were not great and very cheap credit were available so that farmers were, perchance, happy with a 10 percent return over the crop season, then a recommendation of (100,50) with a total investment outlay of $ 1 400, i.e., $ 700 beyond (50,25), and a marginal rate of return on this additional $ 700 of (2 870 - 2 790) / 700 = 11 percent would be acceptable.

The above analysis has not included specific consideration of risk. This is taken up in Section 6.6 below. First, however, we should note the contrast between the correct (i.e., marginal) analysis we have applied and the incorrect approach of applying a global or average basis of analysis. The rate of return to the extra $ 700 expenditure incurred by using the (100,50) alternative rather than the (50,25) alternative is 11 percent. But the average rate of return to the entire expenditure of $ 1 400 entailed for the (100,50) alternative is (2 870 - 1 990) / 1 400 = 63 percent. On the basis of a 40 percent minimum return criterion, this appears adequate - but that would be an incorrect conclusion since marginal analysis shows that, while the farmer would be earning 63 percent on her or his $ 1 400 outlay, she or he would in fact be earning 114 percent on the first $ 700 and only 11 percent on the last $ 700 invested.

6.6 *Allowing for variability in net benefits*

Particularly for small farmers, risk is an important consideration. This is especially true for farmers near the subsistence level. For them an occasional net loss can have very serious consequences.

Risk due to variability in net benefits from a particular investment can arise from two sources. These are variability in yield and variability in prices or opportunity costs. We consider each of these risk elements in turn.

YIELD VARIABILITY AND MINIMUM RETURNS ANALYSIS

Two major types of yield variability that will occur with any particular level of input use in any recommendation domain are differences across space (i.e., from location to location or site to site) and across time (i.e., between seasons or years). Both spatial and time variability are well illustrated by the net benefit data of Table 6.5 based on partial budget analyses of the fertilizer-trial data of Table 6.1. As previously noted, trials 1 to 4 relate to four different sites in one year, and trials 5 to 8 respectively refer to the same sites in the following year. The net benefits listed are based on constant prices and relate to the average yield of the three replications run of each treatment at each site. While there will be variation in yield at a particular site between replications of the same treatment, we do not need to consider this within-site variation as it simply corresponds to the usual variation faced by farmers within a particular field and for which they automatically allow.

The average net benefits for all eight trials listed at the bottom of Table 6.5 formed the basis of our marginal analysis (without regard to risk) in Section 6.5 above.

Inspection of Table 6.5 shows substantial variability across both space and time. For example, for the (50,25) alternative, net benefits range from a high of $ 4 000 to a low of $ 1 620 with an average net benefit of $ 2 790. More importantly, notice that no single treatment consistently gives the highest net benefit across the trials either overall or across sites or years.

The data of Table 6.5 come from a set of agronomic experiments involving a relatively consistent and careful pattern of management. If the basis of the data were a farm survey, there would also be a further source of variation due to inevitable variations in management practice between sample farmers in any recommendation domain. Such inevitable variation in management practice will also induce variation in the benefits a farmer may expect in applying recommendations based on input-output budget analysis from experiment-based data.

To summarize, there are three sources of yield variability to be recognized in attempting to predict farm performance of alternative input investments. They are:

- ◇ Site-to-site or spatial variability under the same management conditions.
- ◇ Year-to-year or time variability under the same management conditions.
- ◇ Management level variability on a given site in a given year.

Minimum returns analysis provides a method of examining the relative risk of disaster of alternative investment possibilities. In Section 6.4 we suggested adding a 20 percent risk premium onto the direct cost of capital as a rough rule-of-thumb. Minimum returns analysis provides a further refinement to complement such a rule-of-thumb. The procedure of minimum returns analysis is to appraise the worst 25 percent or so of the outcomes of each alternative under study. If the proposed recommended alternative based on marginal analysis appears to be no more risky than current farmer practice, confidence in the proposed recommendation is enhanced. If, on the other hand, the proposed recommendation is found to have worst results which are poorer than the poorest from current farmer practice, then the recommendation needs to be reconsidered.

To carry out minimum returns analysis at least five or six sets of observations on each investment alternative are needed. Too, if experiment-based data are being used, as well as successful trials, they should encompass all those trials which failed or were abandoned because of drought, flood, insects or disease etc., so long as these failures occurred for reasons that might also confront farmers. Failed or abandoned trials should only be excluded if they arose because of factors that would not occur in farm production.

Table 6.6 presents the worst net return from the eight trials for each investment alternative of Table 6.5. For this set of data, the alternative recommended by marginal analysis, i.e., (50,25), is also the investment which has the best worst return ($ 1 620) across the eight situations. Thus a farmer concerned about occasional low returns could not do better than to choose this alternative.

The last line of Table 6.6 shows the average net return for the worst two outcomes of each of the studied alternatives. Again the (50,25) alternative provides nearly the highest average.

Often the alternative selected by marginal analysis will prove to be significantly inferior to others in terms of downside risk or minimum net return. In such cases, account must be taken of the importance attached to risk by farmers in the recommendation domain and a decision made as to whether or not to adjust the recommendation.

PRICE VARIABILITY AND SENSITIVITY ANALYSIS

In assessing net benefits in input-output budget analysis, just as with any whole-farm or partial budgeting, it is generally impossible to be sure of the prices to be used. This is especially true for product prices and labour costs. As with yields, product prices and labour costs will vary both over time and across locations. In particular, different farmers will attach different opportunity costs to their time.

How serious such errors in estimation may be can be ascertained by using *sensitivity analysis*. Under this procedure, the prices judged uncertain or prone to error are changed within likely bounds of the original budget estimate to determine if the ranking of alternatives is affected. Sensitivity analysis in budgeting is thus a particular application of parametric budgeting as outlined in Section 5.4.

To demonstrate the use of sensitivity analysis, consider whether errors in estimating labour cost could have an important effect on our fertilizer recommendation example.

Table 6.5

NET BENEFITS OF ALTERNATIVE FERTILIZER INVESTMENTS BY SITE AND YEAR ($/ha)

Trial	Year	Site	Alternative (N,P) investments											
			(0,0)	(50,0)	(100,0)	(150,0)	(0,25)	(50,25)	(100,25)	(150,25)	(0,50)	(50,50)	(100,50)	(150,50)
1	1	A	360	670	2 370	2 080	2 410	1 620	2 660	2 700	950	1 310	1 550	1 490
2	1	B	1 380	1 890	3 730	3 490	1 200	2 710	3 440	4 600	720	2 770	3 950	3 840
3	1	C	3 740	3 920	3 420	3 080	3 700	3 800	3 320	3 280	4 060	4 140	4 320	4 160
4	1	D	2 180	2 990	3 810	2 730	1 820	3 390	4 480	4 900	900	3 020	3 440	4 120
5	2	A	1 480	1 280	970	670	1 540	2 190	1 660	1 090	750	2 150	1 590	1 460
6	2	B	1 450	2 200	2 830	2 610	1 330	2 830	2 100	1 880	510	2 500	3 440	2 630
7	2	C	4 270	4 420	2 960	3 130	2 120	4 000	3 690	3 080	3 990	3 440	2 690	2 930
8	2	D	1 090	1 650	870	710	1 080	1 800	1 090	970	680	2 210	1 980	2 120
	Average		1 990	2 380	2 620	2 310	1 900	2 790	2 810	2 810	1 570	2 690	2 870	2 840

Table 6.6

MINIMUM RETURNS ANALYSIS OF THE FERTILIZER INVESTMENT ALTERNATIVES OF TABLE 6.5

Net benefit	Alternative (N,P) investiments											
	(0,0)	(50,0)	(100,0)	(150,0)	(0,25)	(50,25)	(100,25)	(150,25)	(0,50)	(50,50)	(100,50)	(150,50)
	($/ha)											
Worst	360	670	870	670	1 080	1 620	1 090	970	510	1 310	1 550	1 460
Second worst	1 090	1 280	970	710	1 200	1 800	1 660	1 090	680	2 150	1 590	1 490
Average of worst two observations	725	975	920	690	1 140	1 710	1 375	1 030	595	1 730	1 570	1 475

From Table 6.2, we see that of the five undominated treatments of Table 6.4, the first two require four extra days of labour, the second two require two extra days of labour, and the last no extra labour. Would a change in labour price affect the ranking of these undominated alternatives? At the previously established field price of labour of $ 25 per day, the (100,50) alternative returns a net benefit $ 80 higher than the (50,25) alternative. However, if we increased the field price of labour to $ 65 per day, both would return the same net benefit, calculated as follows:

	(50,25) ($)	(100,50) ($)
Gross field benefit	3 490	4 270
Variable money costs	650	1 300
Variable labour costs (at $ 65/day)	130	260
Total variable costs	780	1 560
Net benefit	2 710	2 710

Thus for farmers whose opportunity cost for labour approaches $ 65, the (100,50) alternative would give no increase in benefits over the (50,25) alternative. This provides further argument for the recommendation of (50,25) from marginal analysis. Further, comparing the (50,25) and (0,0) alternatives, it can be shown (again using parametric budgeting) that for any labour field price up to $ 212 per day, the (50,25) alternative would still offer a higher net benefit. Thus we can be confident that errors in estimating labour field price will not affect the correctness of our recommending the (50,25) alternative.

Now suppose we were interested in whether maize field price changes of up to plus or minus 20 percent would affect the recommendation to be made. The maize field price range to be considered is thus a low of $ 800 to a high of $ 1 200 per ton. At a field price of $ 1 200 per ton, the question is whether (100,50) should replace (50,25) as the recommendation. At $ 800 per ton, it is whether (0,0) should replace (50,25). Relevant calculations are thus as follows:

	Maize field price of ($):			
	1 200/t		800/t	
	(50,25)	(100,50)	(0,0)	(50,25)
Gross field benefit	4 188	5 124	1 592	2 792
Variable costs	700	1 400	0	700
Net field benefit	3 488	3 724	1 592	2 092
Marginal net benefit		236		500
Marginal rate of return		34%		71%
Marginal rate of return at $ 1 000/t		11%		114%

Thus at the higher maize price, the (100,50) alternative becomes nearly high enough to warrant recommendation (assuming a minimum return criterion of 40 percent). If there was a good chance of a maize field price of more than $ 1 200, this alternative would need to be seriously considered. However, the calculations show that, even if the maize price were as low as $ 800, the (50,25) recommendation is still sustained since even though the marginal rate of return falls from 114 percent to 71 percent, it is handsomely above 40 percent.

6.7 *Allowing for tenure differences*

Often the recommendation domain of interest will involve significant groups of farmers having different types of tenure but of a relatively common form within each group. If these tenure types are such that each implies a different relative relationship between enterprise costs and benefits, a single generalized recommendation from input-output budget analysis may often be inappropriate. In particular, this is likely to be the case if the recommendation domain includes, as one of its significant tenure types, sharefarming situations where the proportionate share of costs of the farm decision maker (whether she or he be the landlord or the sharefarmer) is not the same as her or his proportionate share of benefits. The appropriate recommendation for such decision makers will not necessarily be the same as it would for an owner operator, a cash renter or the decision maker in a sharefarming arrangement where all costs and returns are shared in the same proportion.

In using input-output budget analysis to derive a recommendation for sharefarmer decision makers rather than owner operators or cash renters, exactly the same principles apply relative to allowing for capital scarcity and risk as outlined in the previous sections of this chapter. The only difference is that the partial budget analysis along the lines of Table 6.2 must be made in terms not of total enterprise costs and returns but in terms of the decision maker's share of these costs and returns.

To illustrate the above considerations, suppose the recommendation domain to which the data of Table 6.1 relate contains significant groups of (a) owner operators, (b) sharefarmers on an arrangement whereby the sharefarmer is the decision maker and all costs and returns of the crop are shared between the sharefarmer and the landlord in the respective proportions of 60 percent and 40 percent, i.e., a 60:40 share agreement, and (c) sharefarmers on an arrangement whereby the landlord is the decision maker and receives 75 percent of the crop and provides all the purchased non-labour inputs while the sharefarmer receives 25 percent of the crop and provides all the required labour. Taking appropriate account of these tenure arrangements, the net benefits for each fertilizer alternative can be calculated in similar fashion to that of Table 6.2; they are as listed in Table 6.7. Note that the net benefits for the owner-operator decision maker are the same as in Table 6.2 since that table assumed the farmer to be an owner operator or cash renter. Note also that the relative net benefits of the different alternatives to the 60: 40 sharefarmer follow the same pattern as for the owner operator because this sharefarmer shares to the same degree (60 percent) in all costs and benefits; consequently the sharefarmer's net benefits are 60 percent of the owner's net benefits. For the sharefarming situation where the landlord is the decision maker, however, the differential sharing of costs and benefits causes the relative relationship between the net benefits of the alternatives to be altered.

Table 6.7

AVERAGE NET BENEFIT OF ALTERNATIVE FERTILIZER INVESTMENTS BY TENURE SITUATION OF RELEVANT DECISION MAKER

	Alternative (N,P) investments											
Decision maker	(0,0)	(50,0)	(100,0)	(150,0)	(0,25)	(50,25)	(100,25)	(150,25)	(0,50)	(50,50)	(100,50)	(150,50)
	($/ha)											
Owner operator[a]	1 990	2 380	2 620	2 310	1 900	2 790	2 810	2 810	1 570	2 690	2 870	2 840
Share-farmer[b]	1 194	1 428	1 572	1 386	1 140	1 674	1 686	1 686	942	1 614	1 722	1 704
Landlord[c]	1 492	1 722	1 840	1 507	1 400	1 967	1 920	1 820	1 090	1 830	1 902	1 780

[a] As in Table 6.2.
[b] Having a 60 percent share of all enterprise costs and benefits.
[c] Receiving a 75 percent share of benefits and paying all purchased non-labour inputs.

Table 6.8

MARGINAL ANALYSIS OF LANDLORD DECISION MAKER'S UNDOMINATED FERTILIZER INVESTMENT ALTERNATIVES

Alternative				Change from next highest benefit		
N (kg/ha)	P_2O_5 (kg/ha)	Net benefit ($/ha)	Variable cost ($/ha)	Marginal net benefit ($/ha)	Marginal cost ($/ha)	Marginal rate of return (%)
50	25	1 967	650	245	250	98
50	0	1 722	400	230	400	57
0	0	1 492	0	-	-	-

Table 6.8 presents marginal analysis of the average net benefits of undominated alternatives for the landlord decision maker. For the owner-operator and cash-renter tenure situations, the undominated alternatives and their marginal rates of return are as shown in Table 6.4. Comparing Tables 6.4 and 6.8, it can be seen that the landlord's three undominated alternatives are the same as the last three for the owner-operator and cash-renter situations, but that the landlord's tenure arrangements with her or his sharefarmer are such as to delete the (100,50) and (100,25) alternatives from consideration. However, comparing the marginal rates of return in Tables 6.4 and 6.8, it is apparent that on the basis of a 40 percent minimum return criterion and without taking account of risk, the appropriate recommendation for the landlord decision maker would be the (50,25) alternative. Perchance, this is the same as suggested by Table 6.4 for the owner-operator and cash-renter situations. It must be emphasized that such coincidence of preferred alternatives is by no means always to be expected. This being so, input-output budget analysis needs to be carried out for each significant tenure group in the recommendation domain.

As outlined in Section 6.6 above, risk analysis to take account of yield and price variability could also be applied to the data of Table 6.7 from the point of view of the landlord decision maker.

6.8 Summary

The procedures of input-output budget analysis may be summarized as follows:

I. Define the recommendation domain of interest and ascertain the extent to which it contains significant groups of farmers having different tenure, or other, status.

II. For each significant group, calculate average net benefits to the farmer decision maker for each investment alternative.

A. Estimate benefits for each alternative as follows:

- ◇ Calculate average farm yields for each alternative.
- ◇ Estimate the field price of products. For sellers, this will be the local farmer market price less cost of harvest, shelling/threshing, storage, transportation and marketing. These costs will generally total at least 10 percent of the market price, sometimes much more. For subsistence farmers, local market price plus transportation and marketing costs may be more appropriate.
- ◇ Multiply field price per unit by the decision maker's share of average farm yield for each product and sum to obtain gross field benefit for each alternative.

B. Estimate variable costs for each alternative as follows:

- ◇ Identify the variable inputs, i.e., those items which are affected by the choice of alternative. Include chemicals, seed, labour, equipment, etc. as appropriate depending on the decision maker's tenure situation. Estimate the quantity of each of these inputs used for each alternative. To estimate the quantity of labour and equipment required under farmer conditions, familiarity with farmers' practices is required.

- ◇ Estimate the field price of each input. Normally this will be retail price plus transportation costs for purchased inputs. Field price of labour will normally be an opportunity cost. Start with the farm-labour wage rate and adjust appropriately if the labour is needed at a very busy season or a very slack season.

- ◇ Multiply the field price of each relevant input by its quantity and sum over inputs to obtain the variable cost for each alternative. This will include a money cost component and an opportunity cost component.

C. Subtract the decision maker's variable costs from her or his gross field benefit to obtain the net benefit for each alternative.

III. Using marginal analysis, choose a recommended treatment for each significant farmer group as follows:

A. Array treatments from high to low net returns. Eliminate dominated alternatives. Calculate the rate of return to each increment in capital. Graph the net returns curve if several alternatives are involved.

B. Select as the recommendation the alternative which offers the highest net benefit and a marginal rate of return of at least 40 percent (or some other critical level judged appropriate) on the last increment of capital expenditure.

IV. Check the suitability of the recommendation for each significant farmer group from the point of view of yield and price variability as follows:

A. Use minimum returns analysis to compare the minimum returns from the selected alternative to those from all other alternatives. If it compares unfavourably, a different recommendation may be more consistent with local farmers' circumstances.

B. Use sensitivity analysis to determine whether the choice of recommendation is sensitive to product or input prices which are particularly subject to estimation error. If the recommendation is sensitive to these changes, consider changing the recommendation or obtaining more information about the price in question.

6.9 References

CIMMYT (1988a). *From Agronomic Data to Farmer Recommendations*, Completely Revised Edition, CIMMYT, Mexico City.

CIMMYT (1988b). *From Agronomic Data to Farmer Recommendations: An Economics Workbook*, CIMMYT, Mexico City.

PERRIN, R.K., D.L. WINKELMANN, E.R. MOSCARDI & J.R. ANDERSON (1976). *From Agronomic Data to Farmer Recommendations: An Economics Training Manual*, Information Bulletin 27, CIMMYT, Mexico City.

7. PRODUCTION FUNCTION ESTIMATION AND ANALYSIS

7.1 Introduction

Small farmers generally have little control over the climatic, economic and social environments in which they have to work. Nonetheless, they must decide what products to produce, how they will produce them (i.e., what technology to use), and how much of them to produce.

These questions are all interrelated. As shown in Chapters 4, 5 and 6, budget analysis can provide guidelines. Linear programming analysis, as outlined in Chapter 4, also answers these questions but in a more complete way. In particular, it takes more direct account of the resource constraints facing the farmer. Another approach is that of production function analysis. It is more analytical than budgeting and based on more complicated theory than linear programming. And while budgeting and linear programming can readily be applied to the individual farm, production function analysis is not so useful for the individual farm. Its main application is to the analysis of sets of sample data from experiments or groups of farms. From such sample data, production function analysis can be used to give guideline suggestions about recommendations to farmers. It gives a more overall view which can facilitate the appraisal of government policies affecting farm production.

Because of the influence of climate, pests and disease, the small farmer cannot decide exactly how much of a product to produce. She or he can, however, decide how to allocate the limited resources of land, labour, power, cash, etc. available to the farm family. Apart from the effect of climate and other uncontrolled factors, this allocation of resources will determine how much the farm family produces. Thus, though she or he cannot exercise full control, the farmer can certainly influence how much of a crop to produce by deciding how much seed, manure, chemical fertilizer, labour, land, etc. to use for the crop.

The quantitative relationship between inputs and outputs is known as a *production function*. The estimation and analysis of such relationships are known as production function analysis. In its fullest forms, such analysis can be very complicated. We shall make no attempt to cover such complications here, nor will we try to explain all the theory involved. Our interest is to introduce the basic essentials of how to use production function analysis in farm management research. For more detail, reference must be made to such texts as Beattie and Taylor (1985), Debertin (1986), Dillon and Anderson (1990), Heady and Dillon (1961), Kmenta (1971), Leftwich (1970) and Singh (1977, Ch. 2). At the same time, the nature of production function analysis is such that our exposition necessarily covers more complicated material than that presented in other chapters of this bulletin.

7.2 Cautions

The production function is a physical relationship. Taking account of all the input factors (soil, fertilizer, climate, labour, etc.) influencing output, it defines the production possibilities open to the farmer. Suppose we knew this production function. In an ideal world we could then combine this information with information on prices and opportunity costs (a) to judge what combination of inputs would be best for the farmer to use and (b) to study the effects on production and input use of alternative government policies influencing prices and the quantity of resources available to the farmer.

But, the world is never ideal. Information from production function analysis can never be perfect. First, there will always be uncertainty about the effect of such uncontrolled factors as weather and disease. Second, the production function has to be estimated statistically from data which may be imperfect. Third, the estimated production function can only be interpreted as an average relationship across some set of (hopefully representative) observations. Fourth, prices and opportunity costs may not be known with certainty. Fifth, every farm and farmer is unique. Resource qualities and amounts vary between farms. Farmers vary in their managerial skill, their opportunity costs, their assessment of uncertainty and their reactions to it, and in their preferences about the possibilities they see as open to them.

For the above reasons, information based on production function analysis must be interpreted with caution and judgement. It can be very useful for both extension and policy purposes, especially when supplemented with macro and other micro economic analyses. But it should never be regarded as perfect. This is especially so relative to small farms involving a subsistence component and having to operate in a delicate balance with their physical, economic and social environments.

7.3 Notation

As a convenient shorthand in production function analysis, output is usually denoted by Y and the amount of the i-th input factor by X_i. Thus we can say, in words, that:

Y depends on the input quantities $X_1, X_2, X_3, \ldots, X_m$;

or, more briefly in algebraic shorthand, that output and inputs are related by the function

$$Y = f(X_1, X_2, \ldots, X_m). \quad (7.1)$$

Since this function involves m input variables, it is termed an *m-factor production function*.

Equation (7.1) says that the amount of output Y is determined by the quantities of the m input factors $X_1, X_2, \ldots, X_m$, the precise algebraic form of the production function being unspecified. If Y were rice production, the set of X variables would be all those factors such as available soil nutrients, climate, fertilizer, labour, etc. which influence rice yield. While we can usually specify the more important of these factors, we could hardly list all of them.

The input factors $X_1, X_2, \ldots, X_m$ may be classified in various ways. Some will be under the farmer's control, others not. Some will be variable, some fixed. Some will be uncertain, others not. Some will be very important, others of little significance. Usually the production function will be estimated in terms of some small number of important input factors, say $X_1, X_2, \ldots, X_n$ which are variable (i.e., not fixed in size) and are under the farmer's control. The remaining (m - n) input factors $X_{n+1}, X_{n+2}, \ldots, X_m$ are all those that are either fixed or not under the farmer's control, or so unimportant in their influence that we can regard them as fixed. In these terms, the production function is generally written

$$(7.2) \quad Y = f(X_1, X_2, \ldots, X_n | X_{n+1}, \ldots, X_m)$$

or, more briefly, as the n-variable input function

$$(7.3) \quad Y = f(X_1, X_2, \ldots, X_n).$$

For example, we might estimate rice yield per hectare (Y) as a function of the amount of nitrogen fertilizer applied (N), pesticide used (P) and labour used (L). This implies

$$(7.4) \quad Y = f(N, P, L)$$

and it is assumed that all the other factors influencing rice yield per hectare (such as water available, solar energy, soil type, etc.) are held fixed or are unimportant. This assumption can never be fully true so that the estimated function corresponding to equation (7.4) can only be approximately correct. In general, such approximations will be reasonable enough, so long as we remember that they are only approximations. As discussed by Dillon and Anderson (1990, Ch. 5), they relate (in a rough sense) to some set of average conditions for all those input variables left out of the estimated production function.

If appropriate data are available, the set of input factors included in the production function may be extended to include some of the factors not under the farmer's control. For example, equation (7.4) might be extended to include solar energy (S) so as to give an estimated function

$$(7.5) \quad Y = f(N, P, L, S).$$

Since the level of solar energy that will be available to a future crop can only be predicted probabilistically, as shown by Dillon and Anderson (1990, Ch. 7) the analysis of such production functions becomes more complicated.

7.4 *Shape of the production function*

Agricultural input-output relationships follow the law of diminishing returns. As additional units of an input are used, each extra unit causes a smaller increase in output and, beyond some level of use, extra units of an input may cause output to fall. In other words, the *marginal product* of the i-th input factor (i = 1, 2,...,n), denoted MP_i and calculated as the first derivative dY / dX_i of the production function, decreases as X_i increases. This implies that if we graph the single-variable input production function $Y = f(X_i)$, it will have a shape as in Figure 7.1. Likewise, the production surface corresponding to the two-variable production function $Y = f(X_1, X_2)$ will have a shape as in Figure 7.2 where the height of the surface above any point in the (X_1, X_2)-plane tells us the level of output corresponding to that combination of X_1 and X_2. For more than two inputs, we cannot draw the production function but have to rely on algebraic representation.

From an economic efficiency point of view, we are only interested in that part of the production function (i.e., region of the production surface) where each input factor has a diminishing but positive marginal product. This implies that for meaningful economic analysis, any estimated production function must have positive first derivatives, i.e., $dY / dX_i > 0$, and negative second derivatives, i.e., $d^2Y / dX_i^2 < 0$ within the relevant range of interest.

7.5 *Algebraic form of the production function*

By algebraic form we mean the specific algebraic representation of the production function. While equations (7.4) and (7.5) depict possible production functions for rice, they do not imply a specific form of function. As already noted, within the relevant range of input levels for economic analysis, the only requirements on the algebraic form of the production function are that its slope relative to increased use of any particular input factor (i.e., dY / dX_i) be positive and that this slope be diminishing (i.e., d^2Y / dX_i^2 be negative). These requirements should hold for all the variable factors involved. Many algebraic forms meet these requirements. The choice of a particular algebraic form, however, is delimited by three further considerations. First, the functional form used must adequately represent the production process it is meant to represent. Essentially, this is a matter of subjective judgement based on how well the estimated function fits the data on which it is based and how well it fits our prior judgements about the physical and economic logic of the production process under study. Various criteria can assist in making this judgement as we discuss below in Section 7.8. Second, the algebraic form should preferably be one which is easily estimated by statistical procedures. Third, it should be easily manipulated in terms of economic analysis.

While a variety of algebraic forms meet the above requirements - see Dillon and Anderson (1990, Ch. 2) and Jauregui and Sain (1992) - three forms stand out as being of most general usefulness. They are the quadratic polynomial, the square-root quadratic polynomial, and the power (or Cobb-Douglas) function. We shall restrict our discussion to these three types of production function. Experience indicates that they serve adequately and that, except for special purposes, there is little if anything to gain from investigating other more elaborate functional forms.

QUADRATIC POLYNOMIAL

With a single variable input, the quadratic polynomial production function is written:

(7.6) $$Y = a_0 + a_1X_1 + a_{11}X_1^2.$$

Figure 7.1

SHAPE OF THE SINGLE-VARIABLE PRODUCTION FUNCTION $Y = f(X_1)$

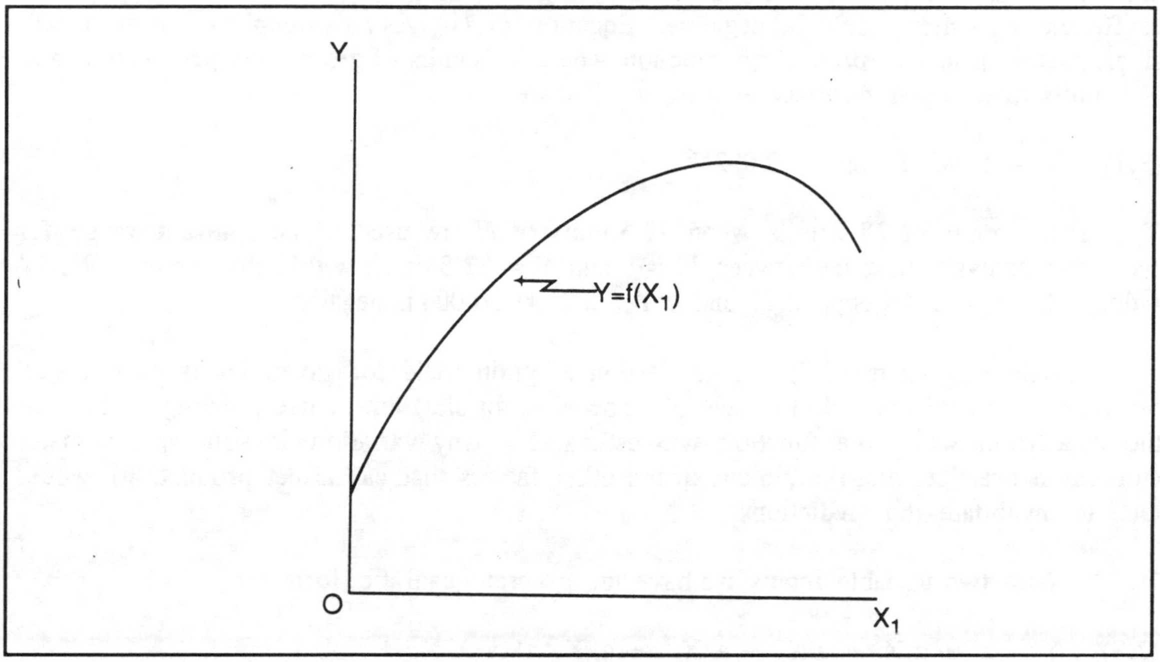

Figure 7.2

PRODUCTION SURFACE CORRESPONDING TO $Y = f(X_1,X_2)$

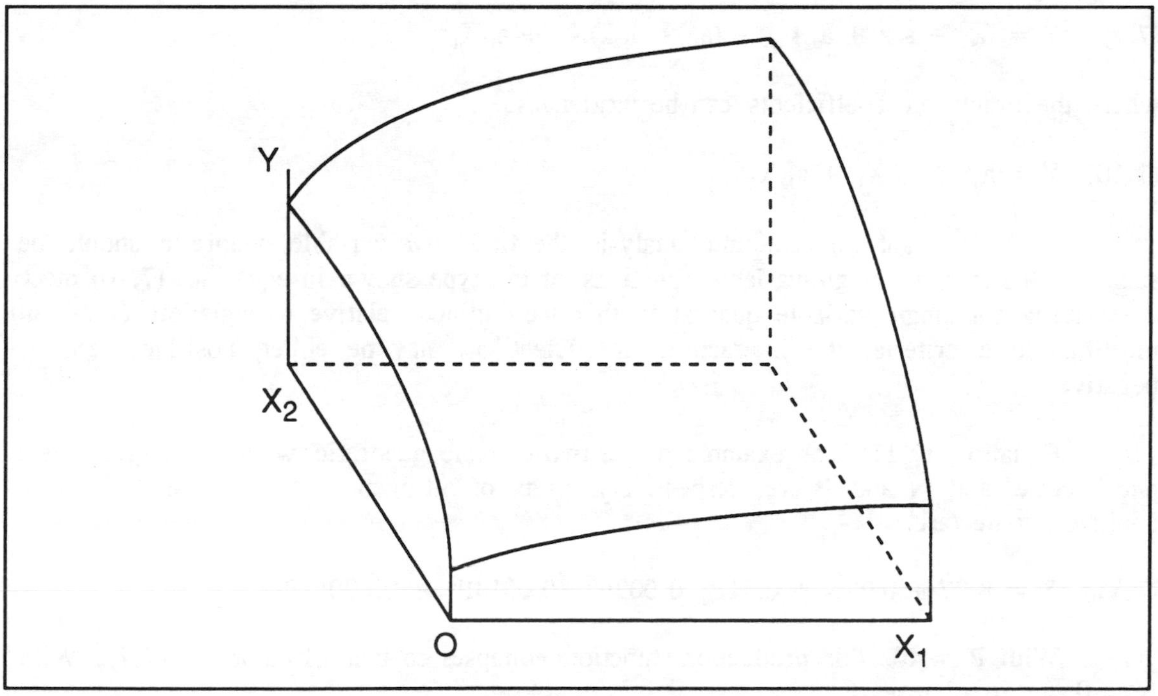

In this equation, a_0, a_1 and a_{11} are coefficients to be estimated statistically. To be relevant for economic analysis, any such fitted function should have the general shape shown in Figure 7.1. This implies that output is a maximum when X_1 equals $-a_1 / 2a_{11}$ and that the linear coefficient a_1 is positive and larger in absolute terms than the quadratic coefficient a_{11} which should be negative. Equation (7.7) gives an example of an estimated single-factor quadratic production function where Y is units of grain yield per hectare and N is units of nitrogen fertilizer applied per hectare.

(7.7) $Y = 18.43 + 0.29N - 0.002N^2$.

Y is a maximum of 28.9 units when 72.5 units of N are used. The relevant range for economic analysis must lie between N = 0 and N = 72.5 since, within this range of N, $dY / dN = 0.29 - 0.004N$ is positive and $d^2Y / dN^2 = -0.004$ is negative.

Using equation (7.7), we can estimate grain yield for given levels of nitrogen fertilizer. We could only do this sensibly, however, for situations corresponding to that for the data from which the function was estimated. Any variation in soil type, climate, cultivation practice, etc. (i.e., in any of the other factors that can affect production) would tend to invalidate the predictions.

With two variable inputs we have the general quadratic form:

(7.8) $Y = a_0 + a_1X_1 + a_2X_2 + a_{11}X_1^2 + a_{22}X_2^2 + a_{12}X_1X_2$

which is exactly analogous to equation (7.6) except for the addition of a term involving the interaction coefficient a_{12}. If either of the input factors is taken as fixed at a particular level, the two-variable quadratic collapses to a single-variable quadratic in the other factor. Thus if X_2 is fixed at some level, say k, we have:

(7.9) $Y = (a_0 + a_2k + a_{22}k^2) + (a_1 + a_{12}k)X_1 + a_{11}X_1^2$

where the bracketed coefficients can be written as:

(7.10) $Y = a_0' + a_1'X_1 + a_{11}X_1^2$.

To be relevant for economic analysis, the fitted two-variable quadratic should be such that its implied single-variable functions of the type shown in equation (7.10) meet the criteria for single variable quadratics that we outlined relative to equation (7.7). In meeting these criteria, the interaction coefficient a_{12} may be either positive, zero or negative.

Equation (7.11) is an example of the two-variable quadratic where Y is grain yield per hectare and N and P are, respectively, units of nitrogen and phosphate fertilizer applied per hectare.

(7.11) $Y = 8.27 + 0.27N + 0.31P - 0.002N^2 - 0.0014P^2 + 0.0006NP$.

With P = 40, this production function collapses to that of equation (7.7). With N = 0 say, it collapses to:

(7.12) $Y = 8.27 + 0.31P - 0.0014P^2$.

Equation (7.11) implies a maximum yield of 40 units of Y when N = 86.9 and P = 129.3. So long as the relevant range of fertilizer levels does not exceed these values, the function is appropriate for economic analysis (assuming, of course, that it fits the data satisfactorily).

With three variable input factors, the quadratic becomes:

(7.13) $$Y = a_0 + a_1X_1 + a_2X_2 + a_3X_3 + a_{11}X_1^2 + a_{22}X_2^2 + a_{33}X_3^2 + a_{12}X_1X_2 + a_{13}X_1X_3 + a_{23}X_2X_3 .$$

With one of the factors fixed at some level, it collapses to a two-variable function; with two factors fixed, it collapses to a single-variable function. For economic relevance, these implied single-factor functions for each factor must meet the criteria already outlined. As equation (7.13) shows, three-variable quadratics are messy. If we have three or more variable factors, it is generally best to use a power function rather than either the quadratic or square-root quadratic form.

SQUARE-ROOT QUADRATIC POLYNOMIAL

Square-root quadratic polynomials are exactly analogous to the ordinary quadratic functions discussed above except that X_i is replaced throughout by its positive square-root $X_i^{½}$. Thus for a single factor X_1 we have:

(7.14) $$Y = a_0 + a_1X_1^{½} + a_{11}X_1,$$

and for two factors X_1 and X_1:

(7.15) $$Y = a_0 + a_1X_1^{½} + a_2X_2^{½} + a_{11}X_1 + a_{22}X_2 + a_{12}X_1^{½}X_2^{½}$$
$$= a_0 + a_1Z_1 + a_2Z_2 + a_{11}Z_1^2 + a_{22}Z_2^2 + a_{12}Z_1Z_2$$

where $Z_i = X_i^{½}$. In other words, a square-root transformation is applied to the input variables. Compared to the shape of the ordinary quadratic, the effect of the square-root transformation is to make the production surface more gently sloped and nonsymmetrical when plotted against X_i levels. As discussed by Dillon and Anderson (1990, Ch. 2), other transformations or mixtures of transformations might also be used.

The conditions for square-root quadratics to be relevant for economic analysis are analogous to those for the ordinary quadratic. When plotted, the (implied) single-variable functions should have the general shape of Figure 7.1 with (in terms of $X_i^{½}$) the linear coefficient a_i being positive and the quadratic coefficient a_{ii} being negative. The interaction coefficient a_{ij} of equation (7.15), if relevant, can be positive or negative.

Like the ordinary quadratic, square-root functions are generally not as convenient to use as the power function when there are three or more variable factors to be considered.

Equation (7.16) gives an empirical illustration of the two-variable square-root quadratic. Again Y is grain units per hectare and N and P are units of nitrogen and phosphate fertilizer per hectare. The function is based on the same set of data as our quadratic examples of equations (7.7) and (7.11).

(7.16) $Y = 8.31 + 1.66N^{1/2} + 1.84P^{1/2} - 0.13N - 0.035P + 0.1N^{1/2}P^{1/2}$.

POWER OR COBB-DOUGLAS FUNCTION

The power or Cobb-Douglas production function has the following algebraic form:

(7.17) one variable input: $Y = a_0X_1^{a1}$

(7.18) two variable inputs: $Y = a_0X_1^{a1}X_2^{a2}$

(7.19) n variable inputs: $Y = a_0X_1^{a1}X_2^{a2}...X_n^{an}$.

where the exponents ^{a1}, ^{a2},..., ^{an}, respectively, denote exponent coefficients $a_1, a_2, ..., a_n$.

As equations (7.18) and (7.19) indicate, with two or more variable factors, the power function is multiplicative. When the input and output quantities are transformed to logarithms, the resultant function is linear in the logarithms, e.g., with n variable inputs we have:

(7.20) $\log Y = \log a_0 + a_1 \log X_1 + a_2 \log X_2 + ... + a_n \log X_n$.

If all factors except one are held constant at non-zero levels, the multi-variable power function collapses to a single-variable function as in equation (7.17). To be relevant for economic analysis, the power function must have each estimated a_i coefficient positive and less than one. This ensures diminishing returns to each factor. As well, none of the X_i values can be zero since this implies zero output. Another difference to the quadratic and square-root quadratic functions is that the power function does not have a maximum; it increases indefinitely.

The power function estimate based on the same set of grain-fertilizer response data used to illustrate the polynomial function is:

(7.21) $Y = 7.55N^{0.097}P^{0.244}$.

7.6 *Economic analysis*

Given an estimate of a multi-variable production function, we can estimate the level of output for given quantities of input, the marginal physical productivity of each input factor, and the isoquant equation for any specified level of output. From the isoquant equation, which specifies the locus of all input combinations yielding a specified level of output, we can estimate the rate of technical substitution between factors. These substitution rates can then be equated to the inverse factor-price ratios to determine the

Figure 7.3

MARGINAL PRODUCT OF NITROGEN FERTILIZER FROM ESTIMATED ALTERNATIVE CROP-FERTILIZER PRODUCTION FUNCTIONS

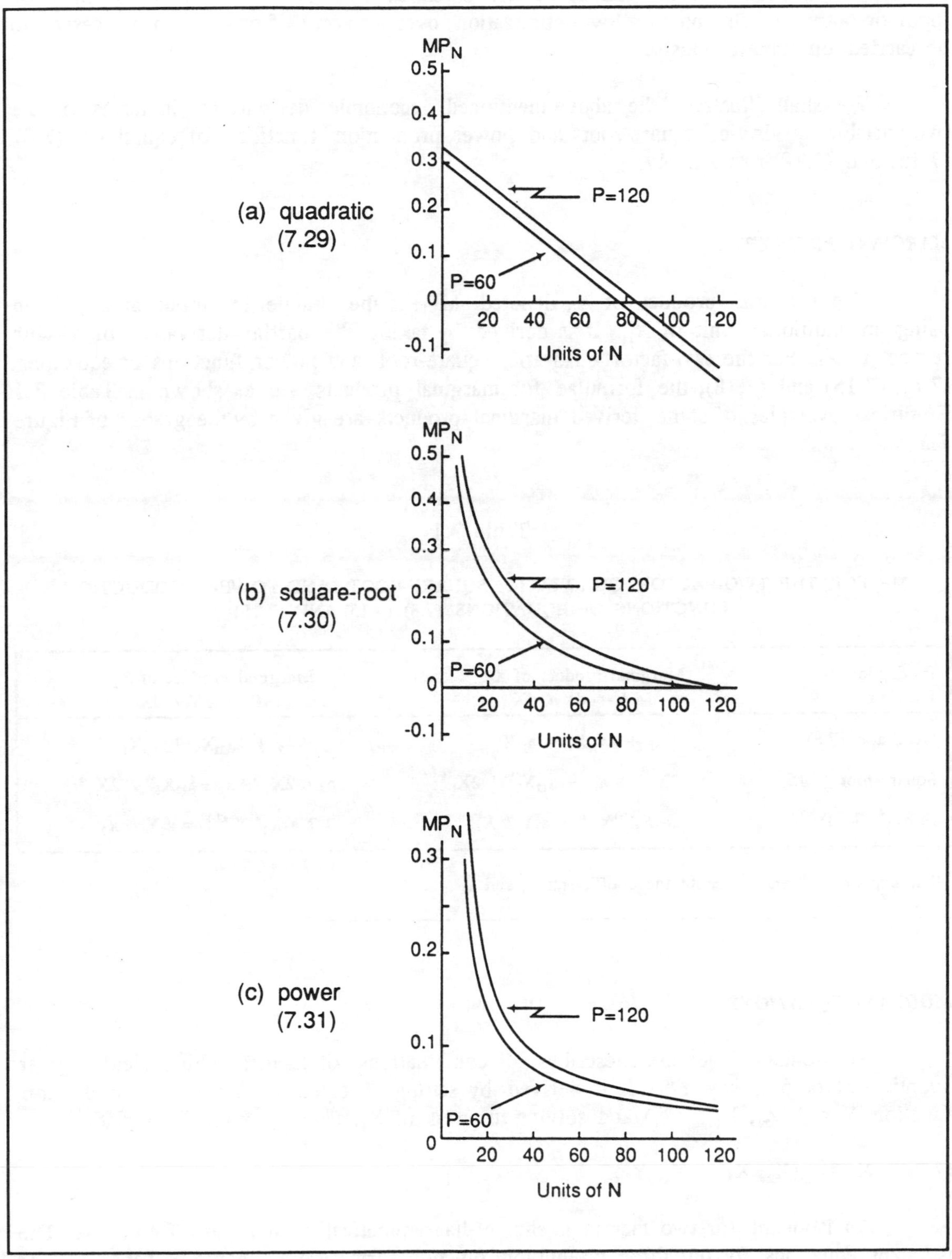

isocline equations specifying the least-cost combination of input factors for any feasible level of output. Finally, the profit maximizing set of inputs can be determined by simultaneously solving the set of equations equating the marginal product of the i-th factor with the factor/product price ratio. As shown by Dillon and Anderson (1990, Ch. 3), production function analysis can be further extended to take account of constraints on input or output levels and to allow optimization over an array of production processes to be carried on simultaneously.

We shall illustrate the above-mentioned economic derivations in terms of the two-variable quadratic, square-root and power production functions of equations (7.8), (7.15) and (7.18) respectively.

MARGINAL PRODUCT

The marginal product of X_i, denoted MP_i, is the change in output arising from using an additional unit of X_i. It is derived by taking the partial derivative of Y with respect to X_i. For the two-factor quadratic, square-root and power functions of equations (7.8), (7.15) and (7.18), the formulae for marginal products are as shown in Table 7.1. Empirical examples of some derived marginal products are given by the graphs of Figure 7.3.

Table 7.1

MP_i FOR THE TWO-FACTOR QUADRATIC, SQUARE-ROOT AND POWER PRODUCTION FUNCTIONS OF EQUATIONS (7.8), (7.15) AND (7.18)

Production function	Marginal product of X_1 $MP_1 = dY / dX_1$	Marginal product of X_2 $MP_2 = dY / dX_2$
Quadratic (7.8)	$a_1 + 2a_{11}X_1 + a_{12}X_2$	$a_2 + 2a_{22}X_2 + a_{12}X_1$
Square-root (7.15)	$a_1 / 2X_1^{½} + a_{11} + a_{12}X_2^{½} / 2X_1^{½}$	$a_2 / 2X_2^{½} + a_{22} + a_{12}X_1^{½} / 2X_2^{½}$
Power[a] (7.18)	$a_0a_1X_1^{a1-1}X_2^{a2} = a_1Y / X_1$	$a_0a_2X_1^{a1}X_2^{a2-1} = a_2Y / X_2$

[a] The exponents ^{a1} and ^{a2} denote the coefficients a_1 and a_2.

ISOQUANT EQUATIONS

An isoquant equation describes all combinations of factors which yield a given quantity of output, say Y*. It is derived by setting Y equal to Y* in the production function $Y = f(X_1, X_2, \ldots, X_n)$ and solving in terms of X_1, say, to obtain the equation:

(7.22) $X_1 = g(X_2, X_3, \ldots, X_n, Y^*)$.

An isoquant for two factors is shown diagrammatically in Figure 7.4 below. The isoquant equations for our three production function forms are as shown in Table 7.2. As these equations indicate, the polynomial forms are more computationally tedious than the power form.

Figure 7.4

ILLUSTRATION OF OPTIMAL INPUT DETERMINATION FOR THE CASE OF AN OUTPUT CONSTRAINT (POINT A) AND AN OUTLAY CONSTRAINT (POINT B) BASED ON THE QUADRATIC PRODUCTION FUNCTION ESTIMATE OF EQUATION (7.29)

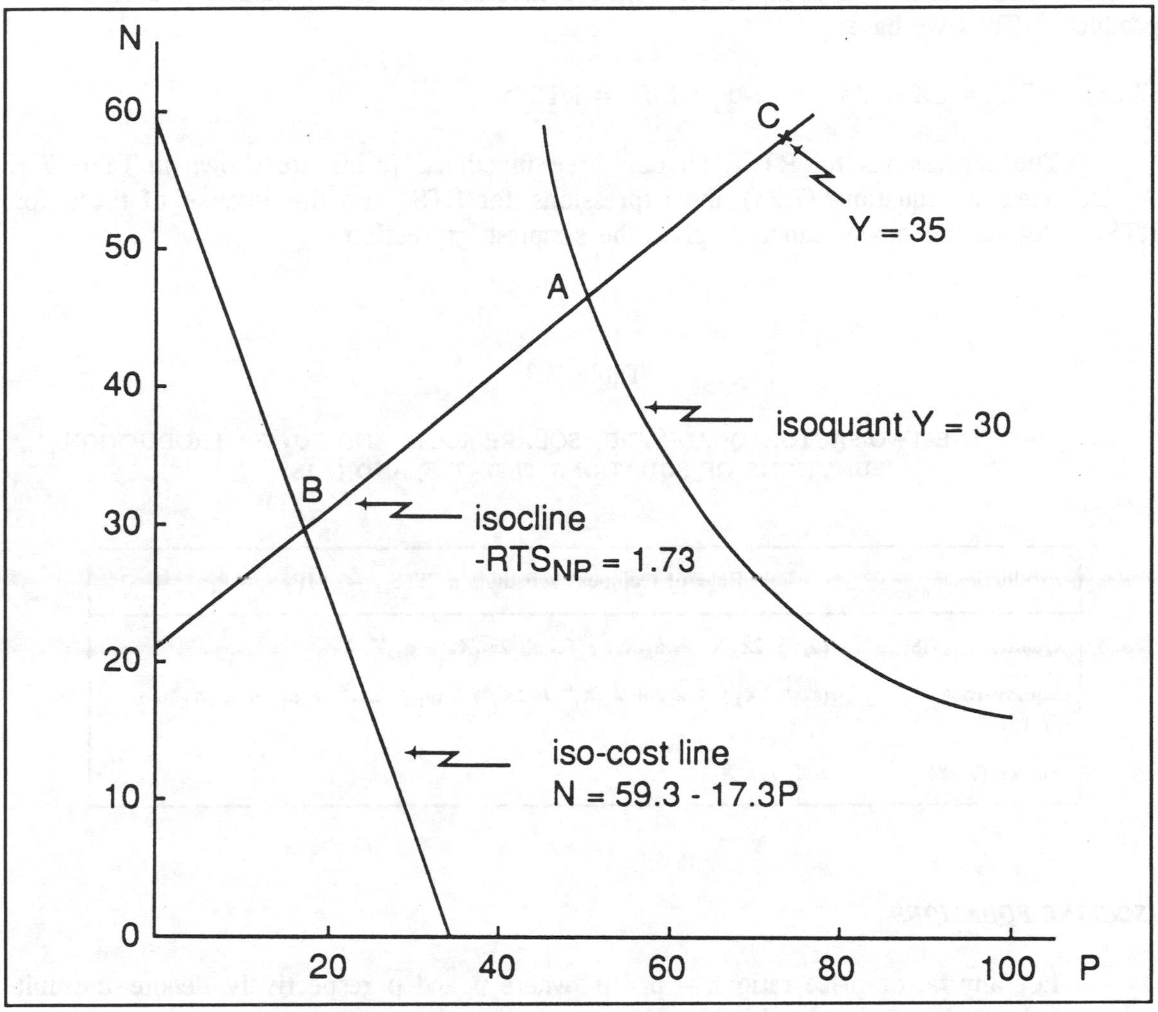

Table 7.2

ISOQUANT EQUATIONS FOR THE TWO-FACTOR QUADRATIC, SQUARE-ROOT AND POWER PRODUCTION FUNCTIONS OF EQUATIONS (7.8), (7.15) AND (7.18)

Production function	Isoquant equation $X_1 = g(X_2, Y^*)$
Quadratic (7.8)	$X_1 = \{-(a_1 + a_{12}X_2) \pm [(a_1 + a_{12}X_2)^2 - 4a_{11}(a_2X_2 + a_{22}X_2^2 + a_0 - Y^*)]^{½}\}/2a_{11}$
Square-root (7.15)	$X_1 = \{-(a_1 + a_{12}X_2^{½}) \pm [(a_1 + a_{12}X_2^{½})^2 - 4a_{11}(a_2X_2^{½} + a_{22}X_2 + a_0 - Y^*)]^{½}\}^2/4a_{11}^2$
Power[a] (7.18)	$X_1 = (Y^*/a_0 X_2^{a2})^{1/a1}$

[a] The exponents ^{a1} and ^{a2} denote the coefficients a_1 and a_2 .

RATE OF TECHNICAL SUBSTITUTION

The rate of technical substitution of factor X_i for factor X_j, denoted RTS_{ij}, specifies the amount by which X_i must be increased if X_j is decreased by one unit and the level of production is to remain unchanged. RTS_{ij} is equal to the slope of the isoquant which in turn is equal to the negative inverse ratio of the factors' marginal products. Thus we have:

(7.23) $RTS_{ij} = dX_i / dX_j = - MP_j / MP_i = RTS_{ji}^{-1}$.

The expressions for RTS_{12} for our three functional forms are shown in Table 7.3. As indicated by equation (7.23), the expressions for RTS_{21} are the inverse of those for RTS_{12}. Again, the power function gives the simplest expression.

Table 7.3

RTS_{12} FOR THE TWO-FACTOR QUADRATIC, SQUARE-ROOT AND POWER PRODUCTION FUNCTIONS OF EQUATIONS (7.8), (7.15) AND (7.18)

Production	Rate of technical substitution $RTS_{12} = -MP_2 / MP_1$
Quadratic (7.8)	$-(a_2 + 2a_{22}X_2 + a_{12}X_1) / (a_1 + 2a_{11}X_1 + a_{12}X_2)$
Square-root (7.15)	$-(a_2 / 2X_2^{½} + a_{22} + a_{12}X_1^{½} / 2X_2^{½}) / (a_1 / 2X_1^{½} + a_{11} + a_{12}X_2^{½} / 2X_1^{½})$
Power (7.18)	$-a_2X_1 / a_1X_2$

ISOCLINE EQUATIONS

For any factor price ratio $k = p_j / p_i$, where p_i and p_j respectively denote the unit price of X_i and X_j, the isocline equation specifies the least-cost expansion path or combination of the pair of factors X_i and X_j for production of any specified quantity of output. It is assumed that in small farm situations, the unit prices of X_i and of Y (denoted p_i and p_y respectively) are given and not influenced by the farmer. Hence the price ratio k can be treated as a constant independent of Y. At every point along the least-cost isocline the rate of technical substitution of X_i for X_j is inversely equal to the negative ratio of their prices, i.e.,

(7.24) $-RTS_{ij} = p_j / p_i = k$.

Solution of this equation gives the least-cost isocline equations for our three functional forms as listed in Table 7.4. The relative simplicity of the power function is again obvious. Note that with n factors there will be n(n - 1) / 2 isocline equations, one for each of the possible pairs of factors. Diagrammatic illustration of isoclines is given in Figures 7.4 and 7.5.

Table 7.4

LEAST-COST ISOCLINE EQUATIONS WITH $p_2/p_1 = k$ FOR THE TWO-FACTOR QUADRATIC, SQUARE-ROOT AND POWER PRODUCTION FUNCTIONS OF EQUATIONS (7.8), (7.15) AND (7.18)

Production function	Least-cost isocline equation for $p_2 / p_1 = k$
Quadratic (7.8)	$X_1 = [ka_1 - a_2 + (ka_{12} - 2a_{22})X_2] / (a_{12} - 2ka_{11})$
Square-root (7.15)	$X_1 = \{(2(ka_{11} - a_{22})X_2^{½} - a_2 \pm \{[a_2 - 2(ka_{11} - a_{22})X_2^{½}]^2 + 4ka_{12}(a_1X_2^{½} + a_{12}X_2)\}^{½}\}^2 / 4a_{12}^2$
Power (7.18)	$X_1 = ka_1X_2 / a_2$

OPTIMAL INPUT COMBINATION

If there are no constraints on the quantity of output to be produced or on the quantity of inputs available, the profit-maximizing combination of inputs is given by simultaneous solution of the set of equations equating the marginal product of each input with its factor/product price ratio. Thus with n variable inputs there is a set of n equations:

$$(7.25) \quad MP_i = p_i / p_y$$

to be solved simultaneously for the set of optimal X_i values. For each of our three two-variable functional forms, these equations are as shown in Table 7.5. As noted in the table, for the power function to imply finite optimal input amounts, we must have the sum

Table 7.5

EQUATIONS TO BE SOLVED SIMULTANEOUSLY TO OBTAIN OPTIMAL INPUT QUANTITIES FOR THE TWO-FACTOR QUADRATIC, SQUARE-ROOT AND POWER PRODUCTION FUNCTIONS OF EQUATIONS (7.8), (7.15) AND (7.18)

Production function	$MP_i = p_i / p_y$
Quadratic (7.8)	$X_1 = (p_1 / p_y - a_1 - a_{12}X_2) / 2a_{11}$
	$X_2 = (p_2 / p_y - a_2 - a_{12}X_1) / 2a_{22}$
Square-root (7.15)	$X_1 = [(a_1 + a_{12}X_2^{½}) / 2(p_1 / p_y - a_{11})]^2$
	$X_2 = [(a_2 + a_{12}X_1^{½}) / 2(p_2 / p_y - a_{22})]^2$
Power[a] (7.18) with $a_1 + a_2 < 1$	$X_1 = [p_1 / p_ya_0a_1X_2^{a2}]^{1 / (a1-1)}$
	$X_2 = [p_2 / p_ya_0a_2X_1^{a1}]^{1 / (a2-1)}$

[a] The exponents ^{a1} and ^{a2} denote the coefficients a_1 and a_2 .

of the exponent coefficients (in this case $a_1 + a_2$) less than one. This sum indicates, for the power function, the type of returns to scale that are implied to prevail. Respectively, if this sum is less than one, equal to one or more than one, we have decreasing, constant or increasing returns to scale.

CONSTRAINTS TO PRODUCTION

Typically, a farmer's supply of resources will be constrained in that she or he faces an outlay constraint. In this case the optimal level of production is specified by simultaneous solution of the set of least-cost isocline equations:

(7.26) $-RTS_{ij} = p_j / p_i$

and the iso-cost locus:

(7.27) $X_1 = [C - (p_2X_2 + p_3X_3 + \ldots + p_nX_n)] / p_1$

where C is the farmer's total possible expenditure on the factors $X_1, X_2, \ldots, X_n$. Thus for each of our three functional forms with two variable factors we have a pair of equations (equation (7.27) plus the appropriate one from Table 7.4) to solve for X_1 and X_2. It then remains to check that greater profit cannot be obtained for an outlay of less than C. If it can, the outlay constraint is not effective and unconstrained best operating conditions must be calculated as per Table 7.5. The appropriate check is to calculate the ratio p_yMP_i / p_i for one of the input levels calculated from equations (7.26) and (7.27). As shown by Dillon and Anderson (1990, Ch. 3), if this ratio is greater than one, the constraint is effective. An example of an iso-cost line is shown in Figure 7.4.

Sometimes there may be a constraint on the quantity of output that a farmer is allowed to produce. In this case the optimal input quantities are given by simultaneous solution of the least-cost isocline equations of equation (7.24) (or Table 7.4) and the isoquant equation (7.22) (Table 7.2). Figure 7.4 provides a diagrammatic illustration.

Farmers will also often be constrained by the cost of credit or by profit possibilities available to them from alternative products. Suppose the cost of credit or the net return per unit of outlay available from other production processes is denoted by r. Outlay on X_i in the process under study should then be restricted to the level which yields a marginal profit of r. The optimal resource quantities are then given by simultaneous solution of the set of n equations:

(7.28) $MP_i = p_i(1 + r) / p_y$.

As illustrated by Bay and Schoney (1982), the advent of computers has greatly facilitated the conduct, graphical representation and interpretation of all of the above elements of production function analysis.

7.7 *Empirical example*

To illustrate production function analysis we shall use the grain-fertilizer functions used to exemplify the quadratic, square-root and power functions in Section 7.5. With Y,

N and P respectively denoting units of yield, nitrogen and phosphate fertilizer per hectare, the equations are:

Quadratic (R^2 = 84%):

$$(7.29)\quad Y = 8.27 + \underset{***}{0.27N} + \underset{***}{0.31P} - \underset{***}{0.002N^2} - \underset{***}{0.0014P^2} + \underset{*}{0.0006NP}$$

Square-root quadratic (R^2 = 87%):

$$(7.30)\quad Y = 8.31 + \underset{***}{1.66N^{1/2}} + \underset{***}{1.84P^{1/2}} - \underset{***}{0.13N} - \underset{*}{0.035P} + \underset{*}{0.1N^{1/2}P^{1/2}}$$

Power (R^2 = 88% of log Y):

$$(7.31)\quad Y = 7.55\underset{**}{N^{0.097}}\underset{***}{P^{0.244}}.$$

These equations were each estimated by ordinary least-squares regression as discussed in Section 7.9 below. The R^2 values indicate how much of the variation in the yield data (or logarithms of the yield data for the power function) is explained by the fitted functions; the asterisks under the coefficients indicate their level of statistical significance (*** = 1%, ** = 5%, * = 10%) as discussed in Section 7.8. The data on which the functions are based are listed in Table 7.6. Some predicted yields based on the estimated functions are shown in Table 7.7.

Table 7.6

CROP-FERTILIZER DATA USED TO ESTIMATE THE TWO-FACTOR QUADRATIC (7.29), SQUARE-ROOT (7.30) AND POWER (7.31) PRODUCTION FUNCTIONS

Units of phosphate (P) as P_2O_5	Units of nitrogen (N)					
	0	20	40	60	80	120
	(units of grain produced)					
0	7.8	9.6	13.2	16.0	12.2	9.0
20	20.2	22.1	27.2	26.2	23.4	23.1
40	18.8	26.0	29.0	38.0	26.4	29.3
60	15.3	22.1	26.9	28.9	28.7	32.1
80	23.2	27.9	33.0	37.9	37.0	31.7
120	27.5	31.9	37.0	40.2	44.0	33.6

Source: Yeh (1962).

The marginal products of N and P are given for our three functional forms by the respective equations shown in Table 7.8. Estimated values of MP_N at P levels of 60 and 120, calculated from the formulae of Table 7.8, are listed in Table 7.9 for each of our three estimated functions. Analogous calculations could be made for other levels of P, and likewise for MP_P at various levels of N. The MP_N data of Table 7.9 are graphed in Figure 7.3.

Table 7.7

PREDICTED GRAIN YIELDS FOR SOME LEVELS OF FERTILIZER BASED ON THE QUADRATIC (7.29), SQUARE-ROOT (7.30) AND POWER (7.31) PRODUCTION FUNCTION ESTIMATES

Estimated function	Units of phosphate (P)	Units of nitrogen (N)			
		0[a]	40	80	120
		(predicted units of grain produced)			
Quadratic	0[a]	8.3	15.9	17.1	11.9
Square root		8.3	13.6	12.8	10.9
Power		7.6	10.8	11.5	12.0
Quadratic	40	18.4	27.0	29.2	24.9
Square-root		18.6	27.9	28.7	28.1
Power		18.6	26.6	28.4	29.5
Quadratic	80	24.1	33.6	36.8	33.5
Square-root		22.0	32.9	34.4	34.3
Power		22.0	31.5	33.6	35.0
Quadratic	120	25.3	35.8	39.9	37.6
Square-root		24.3	36.5	38.5	38.9
Power		24.3	34.7	37.1	38.6

[a] Taken as one unit in the case of the power function.

Table 7.8

EXPRESSIONS FOR MARGINAL PRODUCTS OF N AND P DERIVED FROM THE ESTIMATED QUADRATIC (7.29), SQUARE-ROOT (7.30) AND POWER (7.31) PRODUCTION FUNCTIONS[a]

Estimated function	$MP_N = dY / dN$	$MP_P = dY / dP$
Quadratic (7.29)	$0.27 - 0.004N + 0.0006P$	$0.31 - 0.0028P + 0.0006N$
Square-root (7.30)	$0.83 / N^{1/2} - 0.13 + 0.05P^{1/2} / N^{1/2}$	$0.92 / P^{1/2} - 0.035 + 0.5N^{1/2} / P^{1/2}$
Power (7.31)	$0.73P^{0.244} / N^{0.903}$	$1.84N^{0.097} / P^{0.756}$

[a] Note that for the power function, MP_i may also be expressed as a_iY / X_i where Y is the estimated yield.

Table 7.9

MP_N AT P = 60 AND P = 120 FOR THE TWO-FACTOR QUADRATIC (7.29), SQUARE-ROOT (7.30) AND POWER (7.31) PRODUCTION FUNCTION ESTIMATES

Level of N	MP_N with P = 60			MP_N with P = 120		
	Quadratic	Square-root	Power	Quadratic	Square-root	Power
1	0.30	1.09	1.99	0.34	1.25	2.36
20	0.23	0.14	0.13	0.26	0.18	0.16
40	0.15	0.06	0.07	0.18	0.09	0.08
60	0.07	0.03	0.05	0.10	0.05	0.06
80	-0.01	0.01	0.04	0.02	0.02	0.04
100	-0.09	-0.01	0.03	-0.06	0.01	0.04
120	-0.17	-0.02	0.03	-0.14	0.00	0.03

The isoquant equations derived from our three estimated functions are presented in Table 7.10. These equations give all the combinations of N and P required to produce specified levels of Y. Some such equal-product combinations and the associated rates of technical substitution of N for P are shown in Tables 7.11, 7.12 and 7.13 based respectively on our quadratic, square-root and power function estimates. The respective numerical formulae (corresponding to the algebraic formulae of Table 7.3) on which these RTS_{NP} values are based are given in Table 7.14. As would be expected from the logic of production, increasing quantities of N are required to replace a unit of P as the level of P decreases, if production is to be maintained unchanged. Thus in the quadratic case of Table 7.11 with Y = 20, 0.73 units of N can replace one unit of P when P = 40, but when P = 10, 3.89 units of N are required.

Table 7.10

ISOQUANT EQUATIONS BASED ON THE QUADRATIC (7.29), SQUARE-ROOT (7.30) AND POWER (7.31) PRODUCTION FUNCTION ESTIMATES

Quadratic:	$N = \{-(0.27 + 0.0006P) \pm [(0.27 + 0.0006P)^2 + 0.008(0.31P - 0.0014P^2 + 8.27 - Y^*)]^{½}\} / (-0.004)$
Square-root:	$N = \{-(1.66 + 0.1P^{½}) \pm [(1.66 + 0.1P^{½})^2 + 0.52(1.84P^{½} - 0.035P + 8.31 - Y^*)]^{½}\}^2 / 0.068$
Power	$N = (Y^* / 7.55P^{0.244})^{10.309}$

Table 7.11

RTS$_{NP}$ FOR Y = 20 AND Y = 30 WITH VARIOUS LEVELS OF N AND P BASED ON THE QUADRATIC PRODUCTION FUNCTION ESTIMATE (7.29)

Y = 20			Y = 30		
Units of N	Units of P	-RTS$_{NP}$	Units of N	Units of P	-RTS$_{NP}$
5	40	0.73	16	100	0.15
14	30	1.01	21	80	0.42
26	20	1.51	34	60	0.96
49	10	3.89	59	45	3.60

Table 7.12

RTS$_{NP}$ FOR Y = 20 AND Y = 30 WITH VARIOUS LEVELS OF N AND P BASED ON THE SQUARE-ROOT PRODUCTION FUNCTION ESTIMATE (7.30)

Y = 20			Y = 30		
Units of N	Units of P	-RTS$_{NP}$	Units of N	Units of P	-RTS$_{NP}$
1	35	0.13	11	90	0.30
3	25	0.34	15	80	0.45
10	15	1.26	24	70	0.84
20	10	3.59	31	60	1.35

Table 7.13

RTS$_{NP}$ FOR Y = 20 AND Y = 30 WITH VARIOUS LEVELS OF N AND P BASED ON THE POWER PRODUCTION FUNCTION ESTIMATE (7.31)

Y = 20			Y = 30		
Units of N	Units of P	-RTS$_{NP}$	Units of N	Units of P	-RTS$_{NP}$
1	50	0.05	9	120	0.19
4	30	0.34	24	80	0.76
12	20	1.51	50	60	2.10
68	10	17.14	137	40	8.63

Table 7.14

FORMULAE FOR CALCULATING RTS_{NP} (= 1 / RTS_{PN})
DERIVED FROM THE ESTIMATED QUADRATIC (7.29), SQUARE-ROOT (7.30) AND POWER (7.31) FUNCTIONS

Estimated function	$RTS_{NP} = - MP_P / MP_N$
Quadratic (7.29)	$-(0.31 - 0.0028P + 0.0006N) / (0.27 - 0.004N + 0.0006P)$
Square-root (7.30)	$-(0.92 / P^{½} - 0.035 + 0.05N^{½} / P^{½}) / (0.83 / N^{½} - 0.13 + 0.05P^{½} / N^{½})$
Power (7.31)	$- 2.52N / P$

Least-cost isocline equations are derived as per equation (7.24). These equations, based on our three estimated functions and with a price ratio of $k = p_P / p_N = 14.0 / 8.1 = 1.73$ are given in Table 7.15. As shown in Figure 7.4, for the quadratic function the intersection of this isocline with the isoquant for $Y = Y^*$ (i.e., simultaneous solution of the isoquant and isocline equations) gives the least-cost combination of N and P for production of Y^* under the given input price ratio. This corresponds to a constraint on output. The example shown at point A in Figure 7.4 is for Y = 30. For a constraint on outlay as specified by equation (7.27), the optimal input combination under the given price conditions is specified by the intersection of thc least cost isocline and the iso-cost line. This also is illustrated in Figure 7.4 at point B for the case of outlay being constrained to 480 money units per hectare.

To determine the optimal level of Y and the associated combination of N and P if there are no constraints on output or outlay, we need also to know p_y. Calculation of these optimal quantities is as per equation set (7.25). Thus, if the price of Y is 100 per unit, setting $MP_N = p_N / p_y$ and $MP_P = p_P / p_y$ for the case of the quadratic equation (7.29), we have the two equations:

(7.32a) $0.27 - 0.004N + 0.0006P = 0.081$

(7.32b) $0.31 - 0.0028P + 0.0006N = 0.14.$

Simultaneous solution of these equations indicates optimal input quantities of N = 58.2 and P = 73.2 units per hectare. Substituting into production function equation (7.29), these input quantities imply an expected yield of 35 units of Y per hectare (as shown at point C in Figure 7.4). Analogous calculations for the estimated square-root and power production functions give the optimal quantities shown in Table 7.16.

If the opportunity cost of funds is r per unit of outlay, equation (7.28) provides the optimal quantities. Thus if r is 0.15 (i.e., an opportunity cost of funds of 15 percent), we have for the quadratic case:

(7.33a) $0.27 - 0.004N + 0.0006P = 0.093$

(7.33b) $0.31 - 0.0028P + 0.0006N = 0.161.$

Simultaneous solution of this pair of equations indicates that, under the given price and opportunity cost conditions, the optimal input quantities are N = 54.0 units per hectare and P = 64.8 units per hectare. The implied optimal level of output is 33.3 units per hectare.

7.8 Choice between alternative estimates

Choice between alternative production function estimates is a matter of subjective judgement, guided by consideration of: (a) goodness of fit; (b) *a priori* economic and physical logic; (c) ease of analysis; and (d) judgement about the economic implications drawn from the production function estimates. We shall illustrate these considerations using the alternative crop-fertilizer functions of equations (7.29), (7.30) and (7.31). Though not specifically oriented to production function estimates, good discussion of these questions is provided by Rao and Miller (1971, Ch. 2).

GOODNESS OF FIT AND STATISTICAL SIGNIFICANCE

Goodness of fit to the data on which a function is based can be judged by: (a) visible inspection of either predicted outputs against the data output values or of implied single-variable functions plotted against the corresponding data observations; and (b) statistical measures relating the fitted function to the data on which it is based.

The two major statistical measures are the coefficient of multiple determination or R^2 value which measures the amount of variation in the data explained by the fitted equation, and tests of significance (t tests) on the estimated individual coefficients. For example, the quadratic estimate of equation (7.29) has an R^2 value of 0.84 indicating that this equation explains 84 percent of the variation in the yield data of Table 7.6. The corresponding figure for the estimated square-root function (7.30) is 87 percent. The estimated power function of equation (7.31) is based on a logarithmic transformation of the data of Table 7.6. Its R^2 value refers to this transformed set of data. As a result the R^2 value for the power function is not strictly comparable with those for the quadratic and square-root functions, only roughly so - see Rao and Miller (1971, Ch. 2) who also discuss the use of the adjusted coefficient of multiple determination, denoted adj. R^2, which adjusts R^2 for the number of coefficients being estimated relative to the number of sets of observations available.

As usually conducted, tests of significance on the individual regression coefficients indicate the probability that a coefficient of that size could have arisen by chance from the sample data if the true value of the coefficient were zero. Thus, as shown in equations (7.29), (7.30) and (7.31), most of the coefficients of the estimated functions are significant at the 1 percent level, i.e., there is one chance or less in a hundred that a coefficient of that size would have been estimated if its true value were zero. Traditionally, significance levels of 5 percent or less have been regarded as highly satisfactory and 10 percent as satisfactory. However, these levels are quite arbitrary. They are based on notions of scientific objectivity and caution, and may bear no relation to the farmer's decision problem. For example, as discussed by Dillon and Anderson (1990, Ch. 5), in terms of expected profit it may still be very profitable for a farmer to base decisions on an estimated function which has no coefficients significant at the traditional arbitrary levels.

ECONOMIC AND PHYSICAL LOGIC

Different functional forms have different implications about the general shape of the production surface and about such derived quantities as marginal products, isoquants, rates of technical substitution and isoclines, all of which are important components of economic analysis. Figure 7.5 shows such differences schematically for the quadratic, square-root and power functions with two variable input factors. For the square-root and power forms, isoclines emanate from the origin; for the quadratic and square-root functions the isoclines converge to a point where output is maximized and MP_i is zero; for the power and quadratic functions the isoclines are straight lines. Thus if it is judged that the isoclines should be curved and pass through the origin, this would suggest the use of a square-root function for the production process under study. In general, however, little such prior information will be available except from previous studies of a relevant nature.

More generally, use may be made of particular physical logic about the way input factors interact. Thus it is generally regarded as logical that input factors interact multiplicatively at the whole-farm level. This suggests the use of power functions for whole-farm analysis rather than polynomial-type functions which are rather more additive in nature. At the same time, polynomial (e.g., quadratic and square-root) functions can be justified as approximating functions to the unknown true production function (Heady and Dillon, 1961, p. 204). Similarly, in deciding on whether or not to include interaction terms in the chosen function, e.g., the NP term in equation (7.29), we should be guided by whether or not we believe such interaction is physically logical and not simply by whether or not such a term has a statistically significant coefficient. Such decisions can be of real economic significance, e.g., if the quadratic and square-root functions do not include interaction terms, MP_i depends only on X_i and is not influenced by the level of other input variables.

EASE OF ANALYSIS

The more complicated or extensive the production function, the more difficult analysis becomes and, if hand calculation rather than a computer is being used, the more likely the chance of making errors in calculation. This consideration is most important from a practical point of view. Thus we have stressed the use of the quadratic, square-root and power forms because of their relative ease of estimation and analysis. Comparing these three forms, the power function is by far the simplest in terms of deriving isoclines, isoquants, factor substitution rates and economic optima. With more than two variable inputs the quadratic and square-root functions become messy, though with only one or two input factors they generally serve well.

JUDGEMENT AND IMPLICATIONS

The final important criterion that contributes to the choice between alternative estimates is judgement based on their derived implications. Thus, comparing the empirical quadratic, square-root and power function estimates of equations (7.29), (7.30) and (7.31), we might note that they all have a reasonably high R^2 value, have signs on their coefficients that are as dictated by physical and economic logic (as discussed in Section 7.4), and have coefficients that are all statistically significant. Nor is there any overriding physical logic

Figure 7.5

ISOQUANTS AND ISOCLINES FOR TWO-VARIABLE PRODUCTION FUNCTIONS OF (a) QUADRATIC, (b) SQUARE-ROOT AND (c) POWER FORM

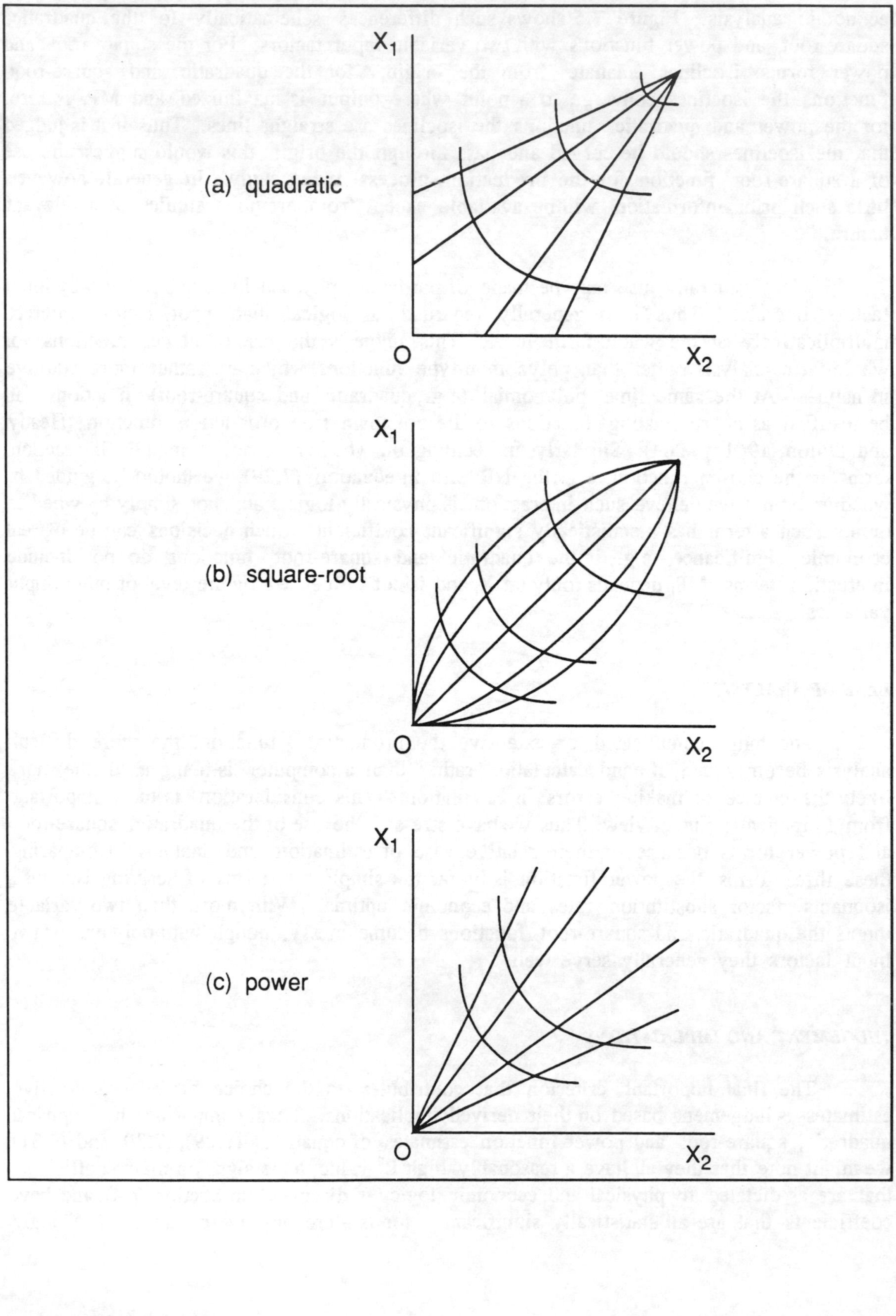

that would cause us to choose one of these functions rather than another. All three appear to fit the data adequately. As Table 7.16 shows, however, there are real differences between the unconstrained optimal input rates implied by the three functions. Though the judgement can only be subjective, our choice between the three functions would be for the square-root function - largely influenced by the fact that experience indicates it generally serves satisfactorily (Heady and Dillon, 1961, Ch. 14).

Table 7.15

LEAST-COST ISOCLINE EQUATIONS FOR THE ESTIMATED QUADRATIC (7.29), SQUARE-ROOT (7.30) AND POWER (7.31) FUNCTIONS WITH p_p / p_n = 1.73

Estimated function	Least-cost isocline equation ($-RTS_{NP}$ = 1.73)
Quadratic (7.29)	$N = 20.89 + 0.51P$
Square-root (7.30)	$N = \{-(0.92 + 0.19P^{1/2}) \pm [(0.92 + 0.19P^{1/2})^2 + 0.29P^{1/2} + 0.017P]^{1/2}\}^2 / 0.01$
Power (7.31)	$N = 0.686P$

Table 7.16

UNCONSTRAINED OPTIMAL LEVELS OF N, P AND Y BASED ON THE QUADRATIC (7.29), SQUARE-ROOT (7.30) AND POWER (7.31) PRODUCTION FUNCTION ESTIMATES WITH P_N = 8.1, p_p = 14 AND p_y = 100

	Optimal quantity		
Estimated function	N	P (units per hectare)	Y
Quadratic (7.29)	58.2	73.2	35.0
Square-root (7.30)	30.8	46.8	28.3
Power (7.31)	32.5	47.2	27.1

7.9 *Estimation*

Given an appropriate set of data on output with various input combinations either at the whole-farm level or at the technical unit (i.e., per hectare or per animal) level, production functions are typically estimated by least-squares regression procedures. This is a standard statistical method for fitting continuous functions involving a single dependent variable (Y) and one or more independent variables (the X_i's). Procedures for hand calculation of the estimated regression function and its associated R^2 and significance test values are outlined in most standard statistical texts such as Draper and Smith (1966). Sometimes more sophisticated econometric procedures may be worthwhile (Kmenta, 1971) but they are hardly relevant to this introductory outline.

Good discussion of the practicalities of least-squares regression is provided by, e.g., Heady and Dillon (1961) and Rao and Miller (1971). Today there is no need to carry out regression estimation by hand. Standard software packages are available for use with computers (including personal computers) and for programmable pocket calculators. What is still necessary is to have an appreciation of the data to be used and to organize them appropriately for production function estimation. An appreciation of the data is best obtained in a practical sense by tabular analysis and by graphical appraisal of the observations on input factors one at a time against the output observations. By gaining a feel for the data in this way, any general tendencies they exhibit or peculiar (perhaps erroneous) observations can be picked up. Computer software to expedite this graphical analysis is also widely available.

Given that a set of relevant data is to be (or has been) collected from farms or experiments, its organization in appropriate form for estimation purposes is most important. Just what form this organization might best take depends on the nature of the data and the proposed analysis. Broadly speaking, a useful distinction can be made between (a) data collected by means of controlled experiments for purposes of fitting production functions to technical units (e.g., yield-fertilizer relations per hectare, animal-feed relations per head), and (b) data collected from farm surveys for purposes of whole-farm analysis. Accordingly, we shall discuss data collection and organization under these two headings. But whatever the type of data - from experiments or from farm surveys - the estimation will be better (a) the more homogeneous is the sample in terms of the factors not included in the estimation (e.g., climate and soil); (b) the larger the sample size or number of observations; and (c) the greater the number of input combinations included in the observations.

7.10 Data from controlled experiments

To generate experimental data best suited to production function analysis on a technical unit basis (i.e., per hectare or per animal), experiments need to be designed accordingly. Traditionally, agricultural scientists have been interested in whether significant differences exist between treatment means; for example, "Which fertilizer treatment gives the highest yield?". Normally such a *Yes/No?* type of research aim implies statistical analysis via analysis of variance. In turn this implies an approach to experimentation involving fewer treatment levels (i.e., factor combinations) and more replication. In contrast, economic analysis based on the estimation of a continuous production function implies more factors at more levels, a systematic arrangement of factor levels into treatment combinations, and less emphasis on replication.

EXPERIMENTAL DESIGN

The essence of the experimental design problem in cooperative research between economists and physical scientists is, first, to obtain as much beneficial information as possible within the research budget constraint while, second, achieving a satisfactory compromise between the aims of the different researchers. For a given amount of experimental resources, a balance has to be struck between experimental unit size (field plot area or number of animals), number of input factors to be studied, number of treatments (i.e., combinations of factor levels) and number of replications. For example, with 27 experimental plots of a given size, a great many choices are possible. These could range from 27 replicates of a single factor at a single level (i.e., one treatment) to a single replicate with three factors each at three levels (i.e., 27 treatments). For estimation of a curvilinear production surface, there must be at least three levels of each factor. But beyond this requirement, choice between more or less treatments and replications is a matter of subjective judgement. The actual choice of treatment levels (i.e., ranges of the input factors to be studied) is a matter of judgement aimed at centering the experiment about where we think the economic optima will be. If little is known about the location of the optimum, input levels should be chosen with a fairly wide span to minimize the risk of having an optimum located beyond the experimental data.

Though several designs are appropriate for production function analysis, as outlined by Dillon and Anderson (1990, Ch. 5), the most appropriate are complete or fractional factorials. A *factorial design* is one in which each level of each factor appears in combination with each level of each other factor. Thus a complete two-factor six-level factorial (as in Table 7.6) involves $6^2 = 36$ factor-level combinations or treatments. A complete three-factor five-level factorial would involve $5^3 = 125$ treatments, each on a separate experimental unit (plot or group of animals). Obviously with more than three factors and three levels, complete factorials become quite large. The way round this difficulty is to use a *fractional factorial design*. This consists of some convenient fraction of a full factorial, the omitted treatments being as evenly distributed as is feasible across the range of factor combinations. Thus one fifth of a three-factor five-level factorial would involve $5^3 / 5 = 25$ treatments. Two thirds of a two-factor six-level factorial would have 24 treatments. If possible (i.e., if research resources permit), the fractional factorial should be such as to have each factor appearing at least once at each of the levels it would have in the complete factorial. There should also be at least one replication of the experiment so that at least two observations are available for each treatment.

IMPORTANT FACTORS

Bio-economic farm management research should be aimed at identifying those factors to which production and profit are most sensitive, i.e., the most economically relevant variables. Initially, for example, this may imply fertilizer experiments. However, consideration should also be given to other aspects of crop culture so as to enable identification of improved packages of technology and the constraints that must be relieved to facilitate their adoption. Thus, in the early stages of a research programme, many management alternatives may be broadly assessed in a *yes/no* or *with or without* framework, e.g.,two levels each of fertilizer, weeding, disease control, planting date, plant density, etc. For this work of picking out the more important factors, two-level n-factor factorials are best. For example, with two levels of fertilizer, late and early planting, low and high plant density, with and without weeding, and with and without insecticide, there would be five factors giving a total of $5^2 = 25$ treatments per replicate. Such two-level experiments do not yield data suitable for production function (i.e., marginal) analysis. But they can greatly assist in the development of improved packages of technology and help identify the important factors to be studied in more detailed experiments. This later work can emphasize questions of optimality as opposed to the earlier work aimed simply at identifying improved economic input combinations.

Some broad rules-of-thumb to apply (in consultation with cooperating scientists) in choosing experimental designs for obtaining data for production function analysis are as follows (Dillon and Anderson, 1990, Ch. 5):

- ◇ on the basis of prior two-level n-factor experiments or other knowledge, make a priority listing of the potential factors to be studied;
- ◇ assess available experimental resources to see the number of experimental units (plots or animal groups) of different sizes that could be allocated between treatments and replicates with different designs involving alternative numbers of factors moving down the priority listing;
- ◇ check that there are not analogous experiments from previous years or in other relevant places with which the results of the proposed experiment could be combined; if so, think of arranging the experiment so that combined analysis is feasible - this way far more reliable information is possible and research efficiency enhanced;
- ◇ in terms of design, minimal guidelines to aim for relative to the number n of factors involved might be along the lines:

if $n = 1$,	use at least six or seven levels with at least one replication;
if $n = 2$,	use at least three fifths of a five-level factorial and if possible a complete five-level factorial with at least one replication;
if $n = 3$,	try to have at least five levels of each factor in a fractional factorial with at least one replication;
if $n \geq 4$,	aim to have at least four levels of each factor in a fractional factorial with at least one replication.

In general, as discussed by Dillon and Anderson (1990, Ch. 5) and Heady and Bhide (1984), as well as often being more expensive, livestock experiments are more complicated to run and analyze than crop experiments. There are two reasons for this: first, animals can exercise free will and, second, the sequencing of inputs over time is more influential in animal production than in crop production.

ENVIRONMENTAL FACTORS

Inevitably there will be variations in such factors as soil characteristics (e.g., available nutrients, pH, organic matter), weather parameters (e.g., rainfall, temperature, solar energy), disease effects, etc. across experimental units in space (i.e., from location to location) and in time (i.e., from year to year). As exemplified by Barker (1978), these variations cause substantial variations in output over space and time. Accordingly, so far as possible, information should also be collected on relevant environmental variables. If this is done, as discussed by Anderson, Dillon and Hardaker (1977, Ch. 6) and Dillon and Anderson (1990, Ch. 8), it then becomes possible to fit more comprehensive production functions of the form:

Y = f (decision variables, soil characteristics, weather parameters, disease parameters, etc.)

covering results from different locations and years. Such functions provide a better basis for extrapolation to other locations and also provide a sounder basis for farmer recommendations with allowance made for response variation over space and time.

FARM VERSUS EXPERIMENTAL RESULTS

Because of more intensive management, use of sole cropping and the generally smaller areas involved, experimental yields are inevitably better than farm yields (Dillon and Anderson, 1990, Ch. 8). As discussed in Section 1.5 and by Barker (1978) and De Datta *et al.* (1978), the size and causes of this yield gap are a topic requiring research relative to different types of crops and farmers in different regions. In particular, experimental research on crops has not yet adequately recognized that crop production on small farms is frequently based on multiple cropping systems with strong complementary and competitive effects between crops.

Whatever its causes, the existence of the difference between farm and experimental yields must be taken into account when we are drawing either farmer recommendations or policy implications from production function analysis based on on-station experimental data - and, unless we have additional knowledge, subjective judgement must be exercised about how big the difference is likely to be.

Though we have covered the major considerations involved in production function analysis based on experimental data, there are many other aspects of possible relevance. These are variously discussed by Anderson (1967), Anderson, Dillon and Hardaker (1977, Ch. 6) and Dillon and Anderson (1990).

7.11 Farm survey data for whole-farm production function analysis

Farm surveys may be organized specifically to obtain data for the estimation of technical unit production functions. For example, data on crop yields and associated fertilizer use may be collected from a sample of farms to estimate crop-fertilizer response functions. The important considerations in such work are to ensure (a) that there is as little variation as possible in factors not included in the analysis (e.g., soil type, cultivation practices, climate, etc.), (b) that there is plenty of variation in the input combinations under study (e.g., that not all the farmers are using the same levels of fertilizer) and (c) that sample size is adequate - say of at least 40 or so.

More usually, farm survey data are collected or used for the estimation of whole-farm production functions. These are functions relating total farm output to the use of land, labour and capital on a whole-farm basis. In collecting data for estimating such functions it is important that standardized procedures be used so far as possible, as discussed in Chapter 2, and that - if possible - sufficient data be collected to allow for the analysis of output variation over space and time as discussed by Dillon and Anderson (1990, Ch. 8).

CLASSIFICATION OF FACTORS

Because whole-farm production functions usually involve more than two factors and because factor interrelationships are generally assumed to be multiplicative at the whole-farm level, the power function is indicated as the simplest appropriate functional form for whole-farm analysis. Experience indicates that it generally works satisfactorily.

The use to which an estimated whole-farm production function can be put depends on the way in which inputs and output are defined and measured. The broad resource categories involved are land, labour, capital and management. As yet, there is no satisfactory way of measuring management so we will assume that it is not included in the function. The other factors - land, labour and capital - can be disaggregated in various ways to give a more specific set of factors, e.g.,land of different types, different categories of capital expenditure, etc. If a high degree of aggregation is used, the implications of the resultant function may be of little relevance to farmer decision making. For example, knowledge that the marginal return to capital exceeds its cost on the average sample farm may be of little use to a particular farmer who needs to know just what type of capital expenditure to make. On the other hand, such general information may be very useful to a policy maker who has to decide on credit policy.

Ideally, input and output variables should be measured in homogeneous physical units. This, however, is impossible, especially for capital items and also for output if multiple products are involved. The practical basis of aggregation has to be in value terms. Consequently, the distinction between a physical production function and a value of production function is generally blurred in whole-farm analysis. Also, the generality of the fitted function is reduced since it strictly applies only to the particular price regime on which value aggregation is based.

CAPITAL

Capital may be disaggregated in various ways into a number of separate input categories. The rule is that the particular specific inputs within an individual category should be as nearly perfect substitutes (RTS_{ij} = 1) or perfect complements (RTS_{ij} = 0) as possible. As well as being theoretically correct, this rule is functional in that it tends to specify the production problem in a way meaningful to farmers.

Heady and Dillon (1961, p. 220) indicate some of the ways in which capital has been disaggregated. Some of these examples of disaggregation of capital encompassing a variety of types of farms are:

◇ into: farm improvements (depreciation cost on buildings, levees, etc.); liquid assets (bullocks, feed, seed, fertilizer, etc.); working assets (machinery, breeding livestock, equipment, etc.); and cash operating expenses (repairs, fuel, oil);

◇ into: machinery and equipment (depreciation, maintenance and running costs); livestock and feed expenses; miscellaneous operating expenses;

◇ into: depreciation on machinery; feed purchase; fertilizer; miscellaneous operating expenses (fuel, repairs, etc.).

Thus a variety of categories has been used. In general, two broad categories may be distinguished: (a) items lasting longer than a single production period (e.g., tools and equipment); and (b) items virtually completely used up in a single production period (e.g., insecticide). Long-lived items should be entered in the production function in terms of their annual depreciation and maintenance costs; single-period items in terms of their cost delivered to the farm. Note also that any cash operating expense items (such as harvesting costs and freight on output) whose size is directly determined by the volume of output should be excluded from the analysis.

LABOUR

Two factors must be borne in mind in measuring the input of labour. First, what is needed is the amount of labour actually used in production, not the amount of labour available, some of which may not have been used. Second, so far as possible, account must be taken of variations in labour quality by calculating the total labour used in terms of some standard unit such as Adult Male Equivalents.

LAND

If possible, the sample observations should be confined to farms that are relatively homogeneous in land quality. If so, area can be used as a measure of land services used. If not, standardization in market value terms is necessary. If there are distinct differences in land type (e.g., flat versus hilly, arable versus non-arable, irrigated versus non-irrigated, eroded versus non-eroded), land should also be disaggregated in terms of type. Of course, land not used should not be included in the analysis.

OUTPUT

Most farms produce more than one type of product. For whole-farm analysis, therefore, the various types of output have to be aggregated to a single measure. Sometimes it may be possible to allocate a farm's input use between crop and livestock products. If so, separate functions can be fitted, one for crop products and one for livestock production.

The most logical way to aggregate different products is in value terms. In consequence, nothing can then be said relative to resource allocation in individual crop enterprises. And, as previously noted, aggregation in value terms implies that product prices have already been specified and cannot be varied in analysis without re-estimating the production function for each set of product prices to be investigated.

USING THE POWER FUNCTION

Economic analysis of whole-farm production functions follows the procedures presented in Section 7.6 and exemplified in Section 7.7. However, two particular things need to be done in using the power function. First, some observations will usually involve zero levels of one or more input factors. The power function implies that each factor must be at a non-zero level. To overcome this difficulty, the zero observations should be replaced by some arbitrary amount of small size. Second, analysis of the fitted power function to estimate the value of marginal product of an input relative to its price should be carried out with each input at the level equal to its geometric mean level in the sample. For each input factor this level is the antilog of the mean of the logarithms of the sample observations.

As in the case of experimental data, there are many other considerations that may be taken into account in whole-farm production function analysis. Discussion of such points is to be found in Heady and Dillon (1961, Chs 4 to 7).

SUBSISTENCE CONSIDERATIONS

As with any farm management research involving farms with a subsistence component, care must be exercised in using production function analysis with such farms. In particular, the measurement of output should include production used for subsistence and other non-commercial purposes. Judgement must also be exercised about the prices and opportunity costs to be used for economic appraisal. This will be increasingly difficult the greater the degree to which input transactions are not commercialized. Indeed, with pure subsistence farming it may be impossible to decide on any objective set of prices (barter values) or opportunity costs on which economic analysis can be based.

7.12 References

ANDERSON, J.R. (1967). 'Economic Interpretation of Fertilizer Response Data', *Review of Marketing and Agricultural Economics* 35 (1): 2-16.

ANDERSON, J.R., J.L, DILLON & J.B. HARDAKER (1977). *Agricultural Decision Analysis*, Iowa State University Press, Ames.

BARKER, R. (1978). 'Yield and Fertilizer Input', in IRRI, *Interpretive Analysis of Selected Papers from Changes in Rice Farming in Selected Areas of Asia*, International Rice Research Institute, Los Baños, pp. 35-66.

BAY, T.F. & R.A. SCHONEY (1982). 'Data Analysis with Computer Graphics: Production Functions', *American Journal of Agricultural Economics* 64 (1):289-97.

BEATTIE, B.R. & C.R. TAYLOR (1985). *The Economics of Production*, Wiley, New York.

DE DATTA, S.K., K.A. GOMEZ, R.W. HERDT & R. BARKER (1978). *A Handbook on the Methodology for an Integrated Experiment-Survey on Rice Yield Constraints*, International Rice Research Institute, Los Baños.

DEBERTIN, D.L. (1986). *Agricultural Production Economics*, Macmillan, New York.

DILLON, J.L. & J.R. ANDERSON (1990). *The Analysis of Response in Crop and Livestock Production*, Pergamon Press, Oxford, 3rd edn.

DRAPER, N.R. & H. SMITH (1966). *Applied Regression Analysis*, Wiley, New York.

HEADY, E.O. & S.BHIDE (1984). *Livestock Response Functions*, Iowa State University Press, Ames.

HEADY, E.O. & J.L. DILLON (1961). *Agricultural Production Functions*, Iowa State University Press, Ames.

JAUREGUI, M.A. & G.E. SAIN (1992). *Continuous Economic Analysis of Crop Response to Fertilizer in On-Farm Research,* CIMMYT, Economics Paper No.3, CIMMYT, Mexico City.

KMENTA, J. (1971). *Elements of Econometrics*, Collier-Macmillan, London.

LEFTWICH, R.H. (1970). *The Price System and Resource Allocation*, Dryden Press, Hinsdale, 4th edn.

RAO, P. & R.L. MILLER (1971). *Applied Econometrics*, Wadsworth, Belmont.

SINGH, I.J. (1977). *Elements of Farm Management Economics*, East-West Press, New Delhi.

YEH, M.H. (1962). *Application of Curvilinear Equations to Economic Problems*, Department of Agricultural Economics, University of Manitoba, Winnipeg.

8. RISKY DECISION ANALYSIS

Because of their lack of control over climate, the markets in which they sell and the institutional environment in which they operate, farmers always face uncertainty and the consequent risks of production and income variability generated by this uncertainty. For small farmers, and especially subsistence farmers, this uncertainty can frequently involve calamitous consequences. In Chapter 6 we outlined some general procedures (conservative rules-of-thumb for investment appraisal, minimum returns analysis and sensitivity analysis) for taking account of risk in a general way relative to any particular recommendation domain. In this chapter our orientation is to the individual farmer rather than to the group of farmers constituting a recommendation domain.

Dealing with an individual farmer, it is possible to take account of that individual's personal beliefs about the risks she or he faces and her or his personal preferences for the possible consequences associated with any risky decision that might be under consideration. To do this we use *decision theory analysis* which provides a procedure for ensuring that an individual makes decisions which are consistent with her or his personal beliefs and preferences, and - given these beliefs and preferences - that these decisions are the best possible given the information available to that individual. Of course, decision analysis does not guarantee that, with hindsight, the decision will be seen to be correct in the sense of having given the best possible result. That would only be possible with perfect foresight (i.e., in the absence of uncertainty) or, stated another way, if we could remember the future. All that decision analysis ensures is that good decisions are made relative to the uncertainty perceived by the decision maker and her or his risk preferences.

In outlining the procedure of decision analysis, we shall first specify the component elements of any decision problem, discuss the concepts of degrees of belief (probability) and degrees of preference (utility), and then illustrate the application of decision analysis by way of a decision tree. The approach outlined is very pragmatic and oriented to the situation of a farm management specialist assisting an individual farmer in decision making. No concern is given to the finer details or possible extensions of decision theory. For such fuller elaboration, reference should be made to Makeham, Halter and Dillon (1968), Anderson, Dillon and Hardaker (1977), or Anderson and Dillon (1992).

8.1 Components of a risky decision

To solve a risky decision problem, it must first be adequately specified in terms of the relevant acts, possible states and their probabilities as seen by the decision maker, and the possible consequences associated with each act-state pair. A choice criterion must also be specified. These components are discussed in turn below.

ACTS

Acts are the relevant actions available to the decision maker. They constitute the set of alternative decisions among which a choice must be made. We shall denote the j-th act by a_j. The acts $a_1, a_2, \ldots a_j, \ldots$ must be defined to be mutually exclusive and should be exhaustive in the sense of covering all possible alternatives. Obviously a decision can be no better than the best of the options the decision maker considers, so good decision analysis must be based on skilful definition of the available acts. One act that must always be considered is to do nothing or to defer action. Decision problems featuring a continuous variable, such as fertilizer rate, may sometimes require specification of an infinite set of possible acts but typically can be represented approximately but adequately by a small finite set of discrete acts.

In practice, giving explicit consideration to every possible act would make many decision problems too complicated to handle and some simplification is necessary. Perhaps restricting formal consideration to only the half dozen or so most important options will be enough to capture the essence of the problem, although for important decisions, many more options can be considered if appropriate.

STATES

The possible events or *states of nature* which may occur and influence the outcome of whatever decision is taken are denoted $\theta_1, \theta_2, \ldots \theta_i, \ldots$ These states must also be defined in such a fashion as to be mutually exclusive and exhaustive. The essence of a *risky decision problem* is that the decision maker does not know for certain which state will prevail. Some state variables are intrinsically continuous (e.g., rainfall) but generally a discrete representation of such variables (such as good, average, or poor for rainfall) will prove adequate. Skill, experience and judgement are each important in specifying states in optimal detail. States may be of simple or compound description. For example, a particular state of nature might be defined in terms of some combination of rainfall during the growing season, rainfall at flowering, disease incidence, and prices after harvest so as to account for the several elements of uncertainty impinging on a decision.

As with acts, formal consideration of every possible state of nature that could impinge on choice will usually make analysis too difficult and simplifications will have to be made. Again, such simplification is a subjective process to produce a model of the decision problem that is at once tractable and yet plausible.

PROBABILITIES

The *probabilities* relevant to decision making correspond to the degrees of belief held by the decision maker about the chance of occurrence of each of the possible relevant states. Thus they are subjective probabilities. The probability of the i-th state occurring is denoted by P_i. As usual with probabilities for mutually exclusive and exhaustive events such as the set of states, the probability P_i must lie between 0 and 1 (i.e., $0 \leq P_i \leq 1$), the probability of either the i-th or the k-th state occurring is $P_i + P_k$, and the probability of at least one of the states occurring is 1 (i.e., $\sum_i P_i = 1$).

CONSEQUENCES

Depending on which of the uncertain states occurs, choice of an act leads to some particular *consequence*, outcome or payoff. The consequence associated with the i-th state and the j-th act is denoted c_{ij}.

Consequences may be monetary or non-monetary, or both. Whenever convenient, they should be measured in money terms either on the direct basis of market values or indirectly on the basis of equivalent money payoffs as specified by the decision maker. If money values cannot be used, then the consequences should be specified by the decision maker on the basis of some subjective rating scale such as from 0 to 100. However, problems involving consequences which are measurable either directly in money terms or indirectly in money equivalents constitute the most common type of risky decisions encountered in farm management. These monetary consequences should be specified in net terms, i.e., as the net money payoff available after all the costs associated with the decision are subtracted from the gross revenue received from the decision. In essence, therefore, the calculation of consequences in money terms involves doing a partial (or sometimes a whole-farm) budget for each act-state pair. If the act-event sequences of a decision extend over a year or more and there are significant differences between alternative acts in their time pattern of expenditures and revenues, then discounting should be applied and the consequences measured in present value terms.

CHOICE CRITERION

In choosing between alternative acts, some *criterion of choice* is necessary in order to compare the set of possible consequences of any act with the set of possible consequences of any other act. Decision theory implies that the appropriate choice criterion is *expected utility* and that the best act to choose is the one which maximizes the decision maker's expected utility (Anderson, Dillon and Hardaker, 1977, Ch. 4). Expected utility is calculated as the probability weighted average of the decision maker's relative preferences for consequences, where the probabilities used are the decision maker's personal probabilities. This corresponds to choosing the act which best meets the decision maker's personal preferences about consequences while at the same time taking account of her or his personal perception of the risks associated with the decision. The utility of the consequence c_{ij} is denoted $U(c_{ij})$ and thus the expected utility of the j-th act, denoted $U(a_j)$, is given by:

$$(8.1) \quad U(a_j) = \sum_i P_i U(c_{ij}) = P_1 U(c_{1j}) + P_2 U(c_{2j}) + \ldots + P_i U(c_{ij}) + \ldots$$

As we shall show in Section 8.4 below, it is not always necessary to formalize the choice criterion in terms of utility as an equivalent procedure is available which can generally be used in assisting farmers in their risky choices.

8.2 *Depiction of risky decision problems*

Decision problems may be displayed in either matrix or tree form. Table 8.1, for example, depicts in symbolic form the *payoff matrix* for a decision problem involving two possible states of nature and three possible acts or decision alternatives. The expected utility of each act would be calculated as:

(8.2a) $U(a_1) = P_1U(c_{11}) + P_2U(c_{21})$

(8.2b) $U(a_2) = P_1U(c_{12}) + P_2U(c_{22})$

(8.2c) $U(a_3) = P_1U(c_{13}) + P_2U(c_{23})$

and the optimal act would be the one with the largest expected utility.

Table 8.1

MATRIX REPRESENTATION OF A DECISION PROBLEM WITH TWO STATES AND THREE ACTS

θ_i	P_i	a_1	a_2	a_3
θ_1	P_1	c_{11}	c_{12}	c_{13}
θ_2	P_2	c_{21}	c_{22}	c_{23}

Figure 8.1 shows the decision problem of Table 8.1 in the form of a *decision tree* where the available acts are depicted as branches from *decision nodes*, conventionally denoted by squares, and states are shown as branches from *chance* or *event nodes* denoted by circles. An essential feature of decision trees is that they be drawn so that the sequence in which decisions are taken and events occur is reflected as we move from left to right across the decision tree. Thus in the simple problem of Table 8.1 as shown as a decision tree in Figure 8.1, the decision maker chooses an act and, only thereafter, one of the possible states of nature eventuates and determines the consequence or outcome of the chosen action.

An empirical example of a risky decision problem involving three states and two acts is shown in Table 8.2 and Figure 8.2. The alternative acts are for the farmer either to spray or not spray a crop for disease control. The possible states of nature are that the season will be good, fair or poor. Consequences are measured as the net return to the farmer after taking account of all the costs involved (including the cost of spray, if used). As in any risky decision, these consequences reflect the interaction between the decision taken and the state of nature which occurs.

Figure 8.1

DECISION TREE REPRESENTATION OF THE RISKY DECISION PROBLEM OF TABLE 8.1

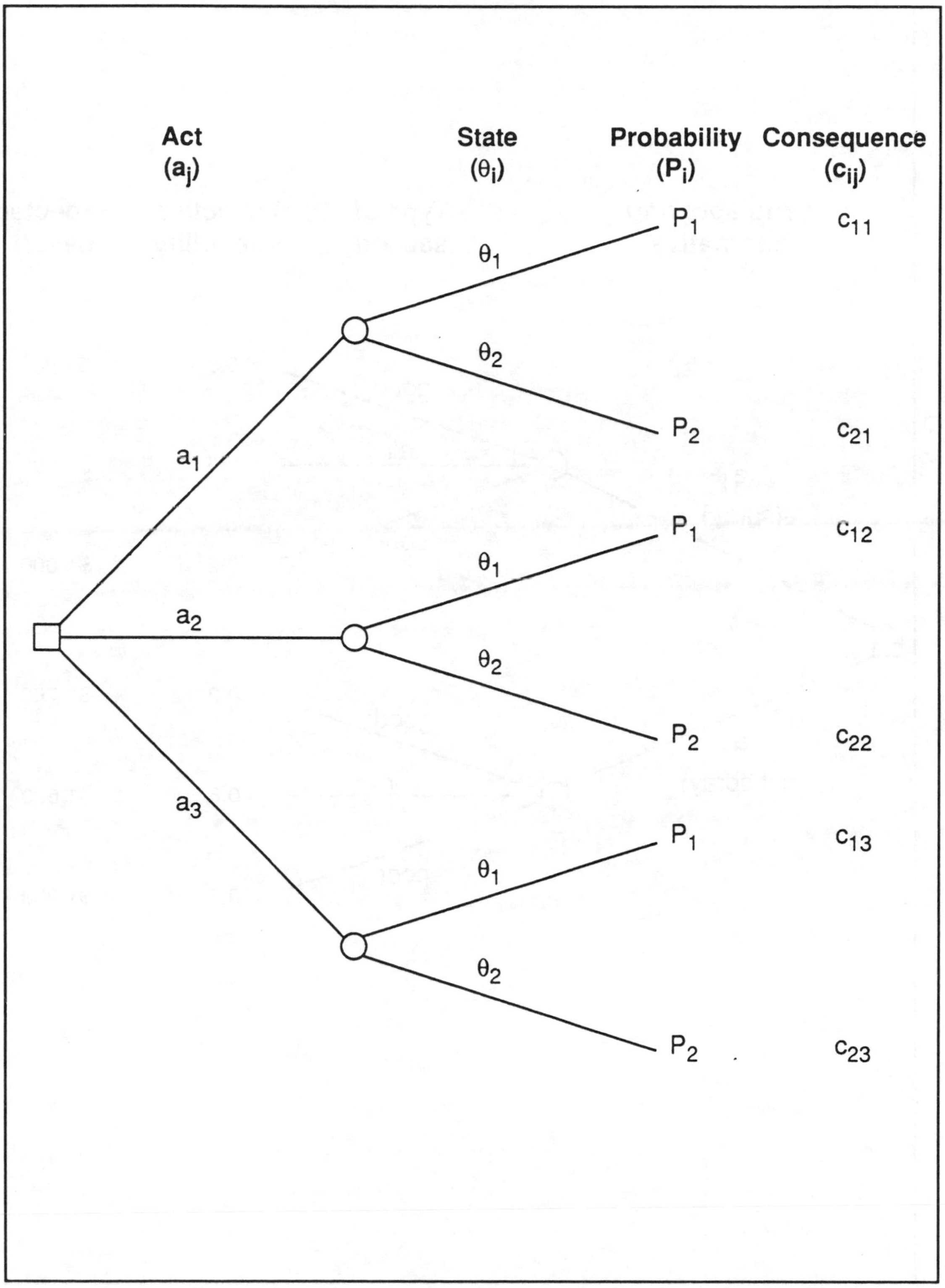

Figure 8.2

DECISION TREE REPRESENTATION OF THE CROP DECISION PROBLEM OF TABLE 8.2

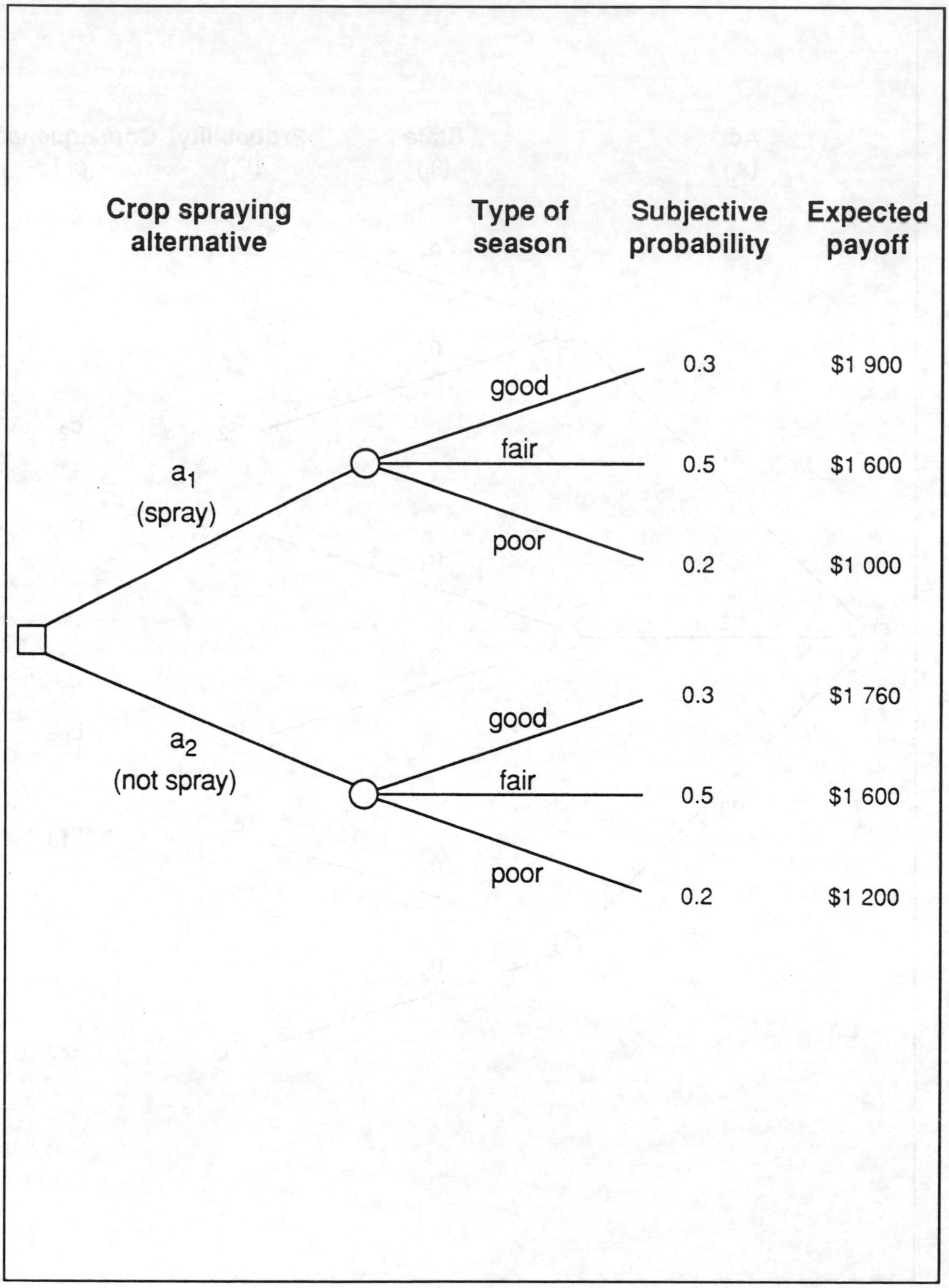

Table 8.2

EMPIRICAL EXAMPLE OF A PAYOFF MATRIX FOR A RISKY DECISION PROBLEM

Type of season	Probability	Alternative actions ($)	
		Spray	Not spray
Good	0.3	1 900	1 760
Fair	0.5	1 600	1 600
Poor	0.2	1 000	1 200

8.3 *Empirical treatment of probabilities*

Farmers, like the rest of us, must bear the consequences of any risky decisions they take. Hence the decision taken should be based on the decision maker's own personal degrees of belief about the likelihood of the different states that might occur. These degrees of belief correspond to the decision maker's *subjective probabilities* for the possible events. In making these probability judgements, of course, farmers will be guided by their own experience and any other information which they judge to be relevant (such as historical records, natural signs and advice from experts or wizards). Thus there is no reason why two farmers in otherwise identical circumstances facing the same states and consequences should not hold differing degrees of belief about the occurrence of the states (and thus reach different decisions even if their choice criteria are the same). Further, such personal probability judgements cannot be right or wrong, although a rational person would wish to refine her or his degrees of belief, eliminating as far as possible any biases arising from misconceptions or misinterpretations of the available data.

BIASES IN PROBABILITY JUDGEMENTS

The most important sources of bias likely to occur in making probability judgements relate to the phenomena of *representativeness* and *anchoring*. We shall look at each of these sources of bias in turn.

Many probability judgements require an assessment of the chance that A is a member of the set B. For example, a farmer may need to evaluate the probability that a spell of dry weather is the start of a prolonged drought. Typically, such judgements are made by assessing the extent to which the object of occurrence under review is representative of the class to which it is to be related. So our farmer might judge how representative the current dry spell is of the first few weeks of droughts experienced in the past. While representativeness is obviously a relevant clue in forming probability judgements, there is a danger of placing too much reliance on it to the neglect of other kinds of evidence. For example, the farmer might assign a high probability to the possibility of a drought starting because the present dry spell is just like the start of the last big drought, disregarding the fact that few spells of dry weather actually develop into long droughts. Likewise, our farmer might misconceive chance by misguidedly saying that, because on average one year in five in the area is a drought year, and because the last four years have been wet, there is sure to be a drought this year.

Anchoring is the second source of bias and is of particular importance in the context of the probability elicitation methods described below. Most people find the introspective effort required to make probability judgements quite difficult. In consequence, once some particular value occurs to them or is suggested by someone else, they tend to anchor on this value. For this reason care must be taken to try and avoid bias due to anchoring on the first values considered. For example, because there is a general tendency for people to make their subjective probability judgements too tight, it is a good idea to start the elicitation with considered estimates of the upper and lower limits, i.e., of the range, of a distribution.

ELICITATION OF PROBABILITIES FOR DISCRETE STATES OF NATURE

As outlined by Anderson, Dillon and Hardaker (1977), various methods are available to elicit a decision maker's degrees of belief for the events judged relevant to whatever risky decision problem is faced. For work with small farmers, and particularly for problems involving discrete states of nature, the *visual impact method* is probably best.

With this procedure a chart or form is prepared on which discrete values or class intervals of the random variable being considered (e.g., rainfall), or the specified states of nature (e.g., high, medium or low prices), are identified along with respective spaces for counters. A reasonable number of counters (say 50 matches) are then allocated over the spaces by the decision maker according to her or his degrees of belief. Once an initial allocation has been made, the decision maker can review it visually and make any desired adjustments to the distribution across the cells corresponding to the set of states. Probabilities are then given as the ratios of observed cell frequencies to total counters. For example, if twelve out of 50 counters are allocated to the space for the fourth possible state, $P_4 = 12 / 50 = 0.24$.

As well as for simple events such as the type of season that may occur, the visual impact method can also be used to elicit probabilities for more complicated states of nature based on compound events. For example, if the consequences of a decision depend on both the type of season (which may be good, fair or poor, say) and the level of product price (which may be high, medium or low, say), there will be a total of nine possible states each consisting of some type of season in conjunction with some price level. The required chart for the visual impact procedure would thus, in this case, involve a total of nine cells, one for each of the possible combinations of season and price.

ELICITATION OF CONTINUOUS PROBABILITY DISTRIBUTIONS

In the case of a state of nature that is best measured as a continuous variable, then at least in principle, if sufficient divisions of the scale for the variable are made, and sufficient counters used, the results of the visual impact elicitation procedure will approximate the *probability density function* (PDF). (A PDF often has the familiar bell-shape. PDFs have the property that the area under the curve between any two values of the uncertain variable is proportional to the likelihood that the outcome will in fact lie in that range.) However, in practice, such an approach would be very cumbersome and there are better ways of dealing with such continuous cases.

The easiest way to elicit a decision maker's probability judgements for a continuous uncertain variable of interest is in terms of cumulative probabilities. Suppose the variable is denoted by X. Then the *cumulative distribution function* (CDF) for X is defined as the curve showing the probability that X may be less than or equal to some particular level of X, say X^*, i.e., it specifies $P(X \leq X^*)$. Such functions can be depicted graphically with $P(X \leq X^*)$ plotted on the vertical axis and X^* on the horizontal axis, as shown in Figure 8.3 which, for example, indicates that the elicited subjective probability of there being at least 2000 mm of June-October rain in Hissar next year is 0.75.

The visual impact method can be adapted to the elicitation of the probability distribution of a continuous random variable. The range of the variable is first determined and divided into a convenient number of mutually exclusive and exhaustive class intervals. The decision maker then allocates counters to the classes as before, the probability for each class being calculated as the ratio of the class frequency to the total counters. These probabilities are then added up to specify points on the cumulative distribution curve. As in Figure 8.3, a curve can then be smoothed through these points permitting values of $P(X \leq X^*)$ to be read off for any selected values of X^*.

A second method of determining the cumulative distribution curve is that known as the *judgemental fractile method*. This method proceeds by direct questioning of the decision maker via a series of questions such as:

1. For what value of X^* is it just as likely X will be above X^* as it is likely it will be below it? This X^* value corresponds to $P(X \leq X^*) = 0.5$. It may be denoted $X_{0.5}$.

2. For what value of X^* is it just as likely X will be above X^* as it is likely it will be below it but above $X_{0.5}$? This X^* value corresponds to $P(X \leq X^*) = 0.75$. It may be denoted $X_{0.75}$.

3. For what value of X^* is it just as likely X will be below X^* as it is likely it will be above it but below $X_{0.5}$? This X^* value corresponds to $P(X \leq X^*) = 0.25$. It may be denoted as $X_{0.25}$.

4. For what value of X^* is it just as likely X will be below X^* and above $X_{0.75}$ as it is likely it will be above X^*? This X^* value corresponds to $P(X \leq X^*) = 0.875$. It may be denoted $X_{0.875}$.

5. For what value of X^* is it just as likely X will be below X^* and above $X_{0.5}$ as it is likely it will be above X^* but below $X_{0.75}$? This X^* value corresponds to $P(X \leq X^*) = 0.625$. It may be denoted $X_{0.625}$.

A further two questions analogous to questions 4. and 5. above but respectively referring to the equal probability intervals above and below $X_{0.25}$ would provide $X_{0.375}$ and $X_{0.125}$. With these seven questions, seven points are provided for plotting the cumulative distribution curve which can be smoothed through the elicited points. Such an approach

Figure 8.3

SUBJECTIVE CUMULATIVE DISTRIBUTION FUNCTION ELICITED FOR NEXT YEAR'S JUNE-OCTOBER RAINFALL IN HISSAR

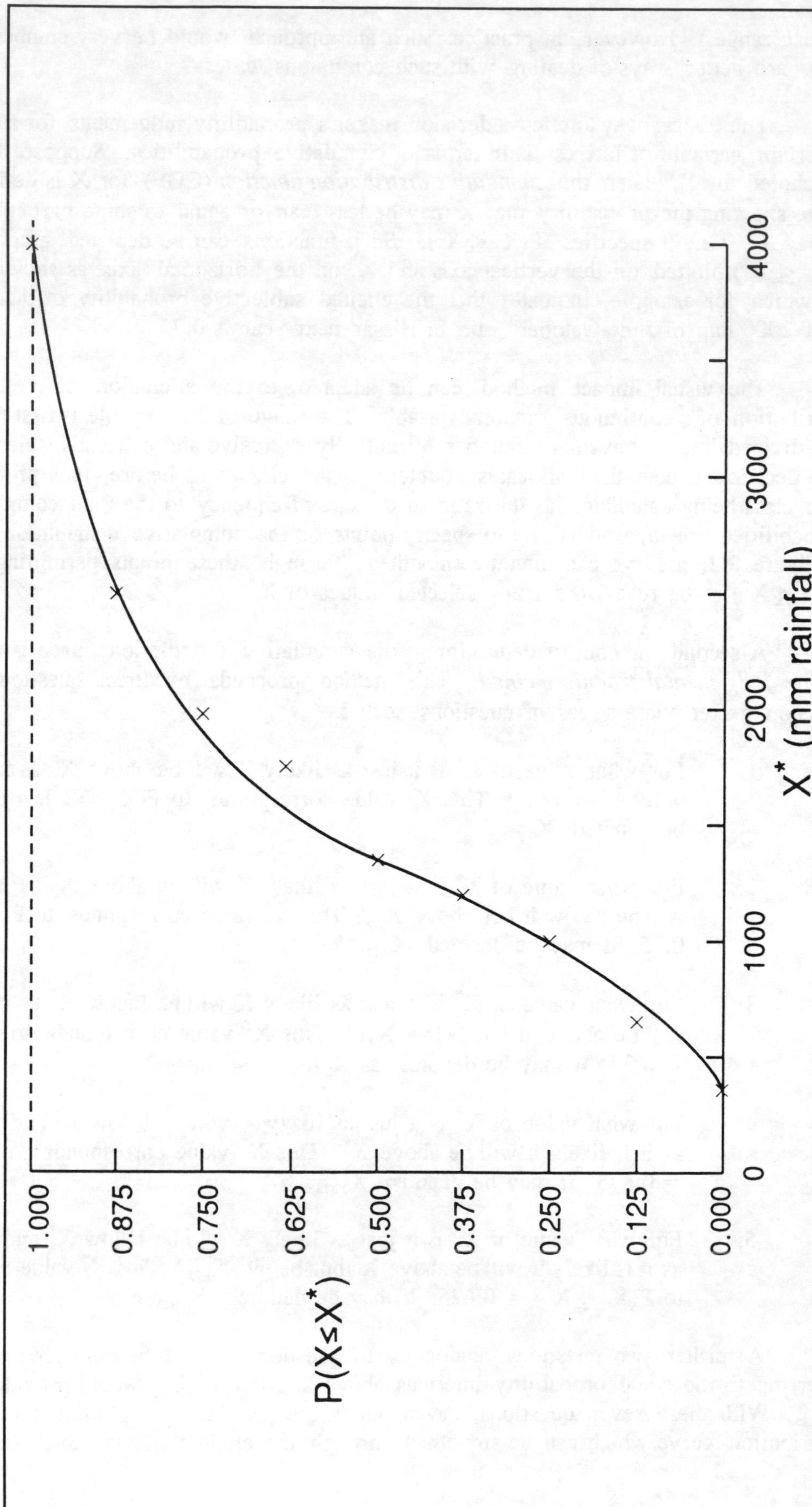

was used in eliciting the cumulative distribution curve of Figure 8.3. Of course, the above questioning procedure will actually proceed in an iterative fashion. Thus, for example, question 1. might proceed in the form: "Consider the value X^*. Is X more likely to be above or below X^*?" Several X values may be tried before the decision maker declares that some particular value equals $X_{0.5}$.

USE OF STANDARD DISTRIBUTIONS

In some analyses it is convenient to approximate a subjective probability distribution for some uncertain quantity of relevance by one of the standard probability distributions developed by statisticians. Such representation makes calculations easier since moments of the standard distributions, such as mean, variance (or its positive square root, the standard deviation) and the third moment (a measure of skewness), are usually readily calculated once the distribution has been specified. These measures may be directly useful in the decision analysis. Similarly, if a distribution is one of the standard ones, it is possible to generate random deviates to use in such procedures as stochastic budgeting or Monte-Carlo simulation as outlined, respectively, in Chapters 4 and 5. Both the calculation of moments and the generation of random deviates are considerably more cumbersome if, instead of using a standard distribution, the elicited distribution is treated as wholly arbitrary and unique.

The distribution-fitting task is facilitated by the fact that the elicited distributions for many uncertain quantities turn out to be unimodal, i.e. there is some *most likely* value and probability declines the further one moves away from this modal point. Such unimodal distributions have S-shaped cumulative distribution functions.

Perhaps the best-known unimodal distribution is that known as the *normal distribution*, which is also symmetrical, so that its mode and mean are identical. Despite the frequent use of this distribution by statisticians, it proves to be rather rare in the real world. Elicited distributions (or historical observations bearing on them) often turn out to be skewed. Theory suggests that a random variable will approximate the normal distribution if it is derived as the sum of the influences of a large number of other random variables. For example, it might be adequate to regard farm profit as approximately normal, but the evidence is that phenomena such as crop yields and annual rainfall are typically non-normal.

The normal distribution is wholly defined by just its mean and standard deviation. Partly for this reason, it also proves rather convenient to use in some types of decision analysis. Analysts will therefore often use the normal approximation so long as the implied approximation is judged to be reasonable. There are statistical tests that can be used when working with sample data to assess the adequacy of the normal distribution as an approximation. However, probably the best approach, consistent with the subjective philosophy of decision analysis, is to plot the cumulative distribution function of the elicited distribution on special graph paper known as normal probability paper. The paper is drawn up so that the CDF of a true normal distribution will plot as a straight line. The analyst, or the decision maker, can therefore eyeball the plotted curve and decide whether the normal approximation is acceptable.

When the normal approximation is not acceptable, some other distribution has to be found. A distribution that has great advantages of ease of elicitation and use, and that in consequence has been widely used in decision analysis, is the ***triangular distribution***. The PDF, depicted as f(y), and corresponding CDF, depicted as F(y), for a typical triangular distribution for a variable y having a possible range from y = a (minimum) to y = b (maximum) are shown in Figure 8.4. Despite the rather implausible shape of the PDF, the fact that the CDF comprises two spliced quadratic functions $F_1(y)$ and $F_2(y)$ allows sufficient flexibility to give a good approximation to many arbitrary S-shaped CDFs.

Only three estimates are needed to define a triangular distribution: the upper and lower limits and the mode or most likely value. If a is the minimum value, b the maximum and m the mode (see Figure 8.4), the first two moments of the distribution, the mean and variance, may be calculated as:

$$(8.3) \quad E[X] = (a + m + b) / 3$$

$$(8.4) \quad V[X] = [(b - a)^2 + (m - a)(m - b)] / 18.$$

Several other types of distribution find application in decision analysis. A useful review of some of the alternatives is provided by Pouliquen (1970).

SPARSE DATA SITUATIONS

Often only limited data may be available in situations in which it is desired to apply decision analysis. In such cases, as long as the judgements are made carefully, the appropriate procedure is to subjectively estimate the required probabilities for prices, yields or whatever. For probability estimation with sparse data, use can also be made of what is known as the fractile rule (Anderson, Dillon and Hardaker, 1977, Ch. 3). This says that if n observations are available on a continuous random variable, then when these observations are arranged in ascending order of size, the k-th observation is a reasonable estimate of the k / (n + 1) fractile. This implies that a reasonable estimate of the probability of a randomly drawn value of the variable being less than or equal to the k-th observed value is k / (n + 1). Fractile estimates made in this way can be plotted and a cumulative distribution function can be smoothed through the plotted points. In sketching such a function, account should be taken of any other relevant knowledge about the distribution. For example, it is obvious that a distribution of the yield of a crop cannot extend to negative values.

8.4 Empirical treatment of preferences

UTILITY OR DEGREES OF PREFERENCE

Once the acts, states, state probabilities and act-state consequences of a risky decision problem have been specified, it only remains to choose the optimal act on the basis of maximizing the decision maker's expected utility. Expected utility is a quantitative measure of a decision maker's preference for the set of possible consequences associated with a risky act. Comparing the expected utility of the alternative acts is equivalent to a comparison of the decision maker's degrees of preference for these alternatives and enables the most preferred act to be selected. As shown by Anderson, Dillon and

Figure 8.4

PDF (at top) AND CDF (at bottom) FOR A TRIANGULAR DISTRIBUTION

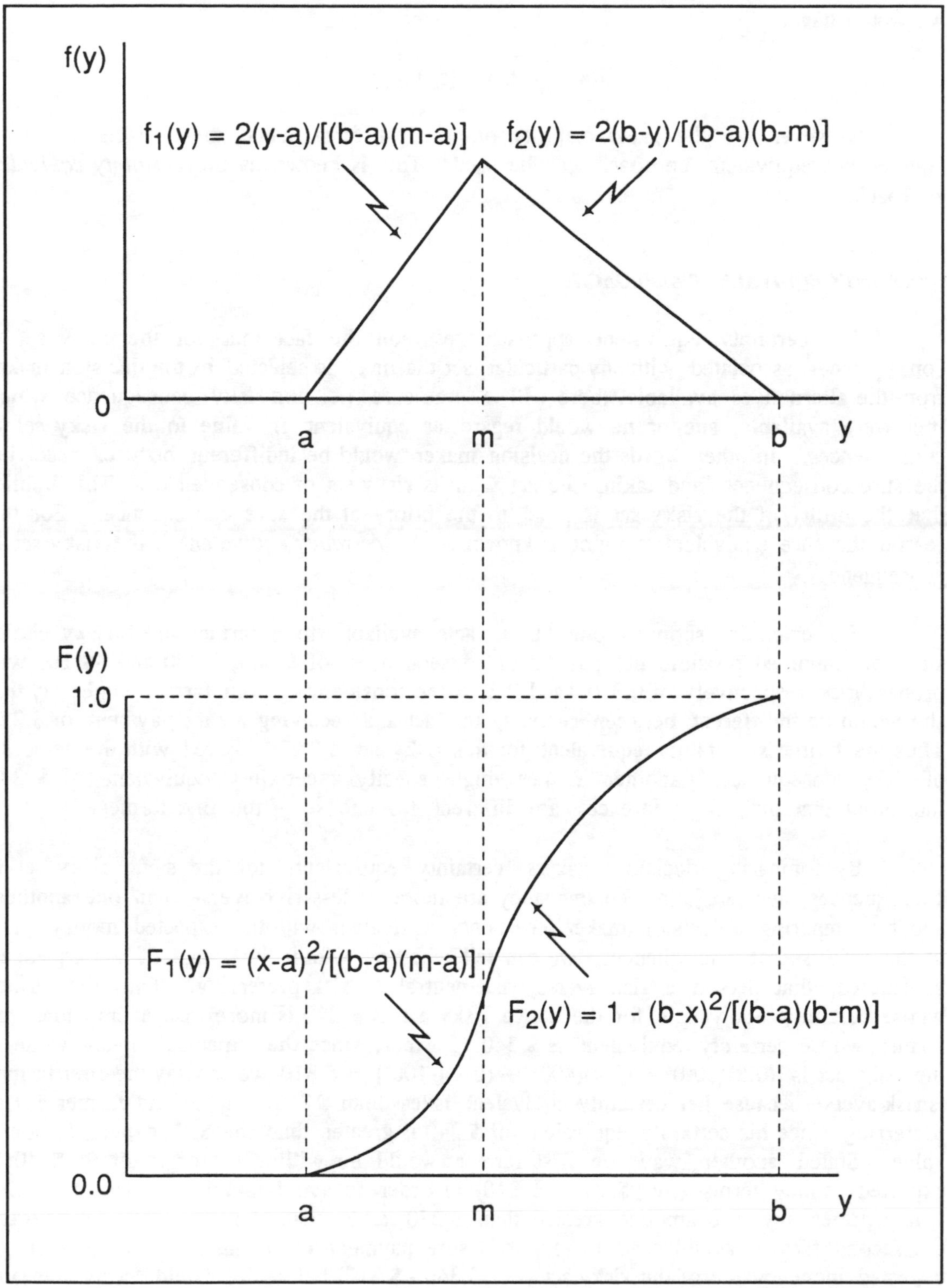

Hardaker (1977, Ch. 4), it is possible to elicit the utility curve or utility function for any individual decision maker and use this to read off her or his utility value for any particular consequence. Then, applying the decision maker's probabilities for the states of nature, the expected utility of each alternative act may be calculated. For example, for the j-th act we would have:

$$U(a_j) = \sum_i P_i U(c_{ij}).$$

However, for the great majority of practical farm management decisions, a far simpler but equivalent approach can be used. This is known as the *certainty equivalent* approach.

CERTAINTY EQUIVALENT APPROACH

The certainty equivalent approach rests on the fact that for the risky set of consequences associated with any particular act that may be selected by the decision maker from the alternatives available, there will be some sure (i.e., non-risky) consequence which, if it were available, she or he would regard as equivalent in value to the risky set of consequences. In other words the decision maker would be indifferent between receiving the sure consequence and taking the act with its risky set of consequences. This implies that the utility of the risky act is equal to the utility of the sure consequence. For this reason the sure equivalent amount is known as the *certainty equivalent* of the risky set of consequences.

For example, suppose one of the acts available to a farmer in a risky choice situation involved possible net payoffs or consequences of \$ 600, \$ 400 and -\$ 100 with probabilities respectively of 0.3,0.4 and 0.3. After consideration our farmer might say that she would be indifferent between choosing this act and receiving a sure payment of \$ 270. Thus the farmer's certainty equivalent for this risky act is \$ 270. Faced with the same set of risky consequences, another farmer might specify a certainty equivalent of \$ 340, indicating that his risk preferences are different from those of the first farmer.

By comparing decision makers' certainty equivalents for the same risky set of consequences, we can judge whether they are more or less risk averse than one another; and by comparing a decision maker's certainty equivalent with the expected money value of the risky set of consequences, we can tell whether, within the range of consequences considered, that person is risk averse, risk neutral or risk preferring. Thus the farmer whose certainty equivalent for the above risky act is \$ 270 is more risk averse than the farmer whose certainty equivalent is \$ 340. Further, since the expected money value of the risky act is [(0.3)(600) + (0.4)(400) + (0.3)(-100)] = \$ 310, we can say the first farmer is risk averse because her certainty equivalent is less than \$ 310. The second farmer is risk preferring since his certainty equivalent of \$ 340 is greater than the act's expected money value. Stated another way, the first farmer would be willing to forgo up to \$ 40 in expected money terms (i.e., \$ 270 - \$ 310) in order to avoid taking the risky act. She would prefer any sure amount greater than \$ 270 rather than the risky act. In contrast, the second farmer would need to receive a sure payment of at least \$ 30 more than the expected money value of the risky act (i.e., \$ 340 - \$ 310) before he would accept the sure consequence rather than the risky act. Only if a decision maker's certainty equivalent for a risky act is equal to its expected money value is she or he risk neutral.

To use the certainty equivalent approach to solve risky decision problems, all we have to do is get the decision maker to nominate (by introspection) her or his certainty equivalent for each alternative risky act. The act with the highest certainty equivalent is then the best choice because it corresponds best with that person's preferences, taking into account the uncertainties present in the decision situation.

Decision trees provide the most convenient way of applying the certainty equivalent approach to solving risky decision problems. The reason for this is that, compared to a payoff matrix, the decision tree representation provides a far more readily comprehended model of the decision problem. In particular, unlike a payoff matrix, a decision tree shows clearly the time sequencing of acts and events.

Application of the certainty equivalent approach via a decision tree model of risky choice involves the following five steps:

◇ Draw the decision tree in chronological sequence from left to right with acts branching from decision nodes denoted by squares and events branching from event or chance nodes denoted by circles.

◇ Assign the relevant subjective probabilities to event branches, checking that the probabilities are consistent with the logic of probability.

◇ Attach net dollar payoffs to the terminal branches, making sure that account has been taken of all the costs and revenues of preceding branches. If the time span involved is sufficiently long, the terminal payoffs should be measured in present value terms.

◇ Working back leftward from the terminal branches, replace the chance events at each event node by their certainty equivalent; then choose between antecedent acts on the basis of their certainty equivalents, the act with the highest certainty equivalent being the preferred alternative at each decision node. This process is known as *backward induction*. As backward induction proceeds, write the certainty equivalent at each event node to make the whole process clearly explicit.

◇ Mark off or delete inferior acts as they are located so that when the base of the tree is reached, the optimal path through the tree (i.e., the optimal act) is clearly evident.

8.5 Risk efficiency analysis

There are obvious limits to the applicability of the certainty equivalent approach. Unless the farmer has been trained to use the approach, it demands that the farmer be consulted at every stage in a decision analysis when risky outcomes must be resolved. It would clearly be desirable if the farmer's risk preferences could be encoded in some way that would obviate this. And, indeed, as noted above, this is possible in principle by means of a utility function. By eliciting a few certainty equivalents in a particular structured fashion, it is possible, in principle, to derive a function that effectively encodes that person's risk preferences. In practice, however, there are some problems.

First, the degree of introspective capacity needed to give consistent answers in the questioning procedure is considerable, and experience shows that many people are simply unable to cope with the task. Moreover, administering the procedure is no simple task. It is time-consuming and requires considerable sensitivity on the part of the interviewer. Inadequately prepared investigators can easily derive responses that are meaningless. It seems clear that the derivation of utility functions from small-scale farmers to encode their individual risk preferences is unlikely to be practicable.

This view is reinforced when it is noted that many farm management decision analyses are not performed with just one farmer client as the intended beneficiary. Usually the purpose has to be to produce general recommendations that can be extended to large numbers of small-scale farmers in some recommendation domain or target area. Since it can be expected that these target farmers will have different attitudes to risk, whose utility function is to be used?

The methods of *stochastic dominance* (SD) analysis go some way to resolving these difficulties. If it is possible to say something about the range of risk attitudes to be expected among the majority of the clients of any analysis, at least a partial ordering of alternative decision options may be possible. For example, it is to be expected that most small-scale farmers are averse to risk - by and large, they are too poor to be otherwise. Making this assumption, we might decide to rule out any decision option that is more risky than another, unless it has benefits in terms of a higher expected return. SD methods formalise this process.

The aim in SD analysis is to segregate the set of possible decision options into two: a preferred or dominant set, amongst which any farmer whose risk attitudes conform with the assumptions will find her or his most preferred option; and a dominated set that is of no interest to that same group of farmers. Clearly, this approach is *second best* in that it leads only to a simplification of farmers' risky decisions and not their complete resolution. The stronger the behavioural assumptions that can be made, the smaller, in general, will the set of dominant options be. Yet the stronger the behavioural assumptions, the smaller the proportion of farmers whose risk attitudes match those assumptions. Clearly, the more we know, or can safely assume, about risk preferences, the better.

The methods of SD analysis are applied to probability distributions of consequences, described by their CDFs. From a set of such distributions corresponding to a set of decision options, a series of pair-wise comparisons is made. Distribution A is matched against distribution B and , using one of the rules to be described below, it may be found that A dominates B, B dominates A, or there is no dominance. In the first two cases, the dominated distribution is of no further interest and is dropped from the prospective dominant set. But in the third case, both A and B must be retained, at least for the time being. The procedure continues with the introduction of a third distribution, say C, and again all pair-wise comparisons are made to eliminate any dominated distributions, and so on.

The rules for SD analysis are presented below in increasing order of the strength of the behavioural assumptions involved. The illustrations are in terms of continuous distributions, but the methods apply identically to both discrete and continuous cases.

FIRST-DEGREE STOCHASTIC DOMINANCE (FSD)

FSD analysis is based on the generally plausible behavioural assumption that, for some appropriate measure of decision consequences Y (e.g., profit), decision makers will always prefer more Y to less. Such behaviour translates into a rule that the (cumulative) distribution F(y) dominates the (cumulative) distribution G(y) in the FSD sense if F(y) lies to the right of G(y) for all values of consequences Y. This is equivalent to saying that, if F(y) is FSD over G(y), the probability of getting less than any given value of Y, say Y^*, is greater for G(y) than for F(y) for all values of Y^*.

FSD is illustrated in Figure 8.5. Distribution A dominates distribution B in the FSD sense. However, in the other cases illustrated there is no FSD because the distributions cross.

Figure 8.5

CDFs ILLUSTRATING FSD OF DISTRIBUTION A OVER DISTRIBUTION B FOR AN UNCERTAIN VARIABLE Y

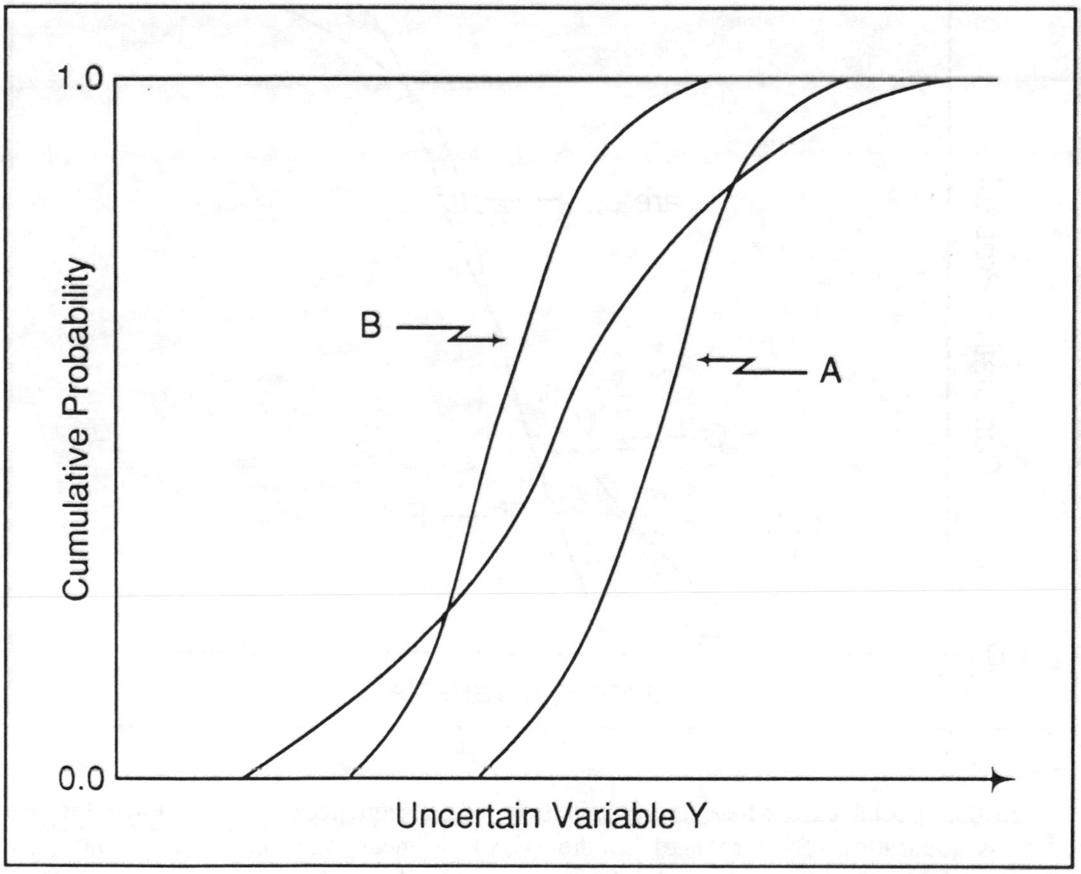

Empirically, the FSD rule is not very useful because very few acts (distributions) can be dismissed in this way. Therefore, a more stringent rule is needed to prune the feasible actions to a smaller set.

SECOND-DEGREE STOCHASTIC DOMINANCE (SSD)

If the additional behavioural assumption that the decision makers are risk averse is made, the FSD set can often be considerably reduced in size. An intuitive interpretation can be gained from Figure 8.6. Because the illustrated distributions F and G cross, neither can dominate the other in the FSD sense. But if the cumulative difference in area between the two curves is always positive as we move from left to right, there is SSD. In this case, since area α is greater than area β, F dominates G in the SSD sense. Note that the rule means that a distribution with a negative tail lying to the left of another distribution can never dominate it.

Figure 8.6

CDFs ILLUSTRATING SSD OF DISTRIBUTION F OVER DISTRIBUTION G FOR AN UNCERTAIN VARIABLE Y

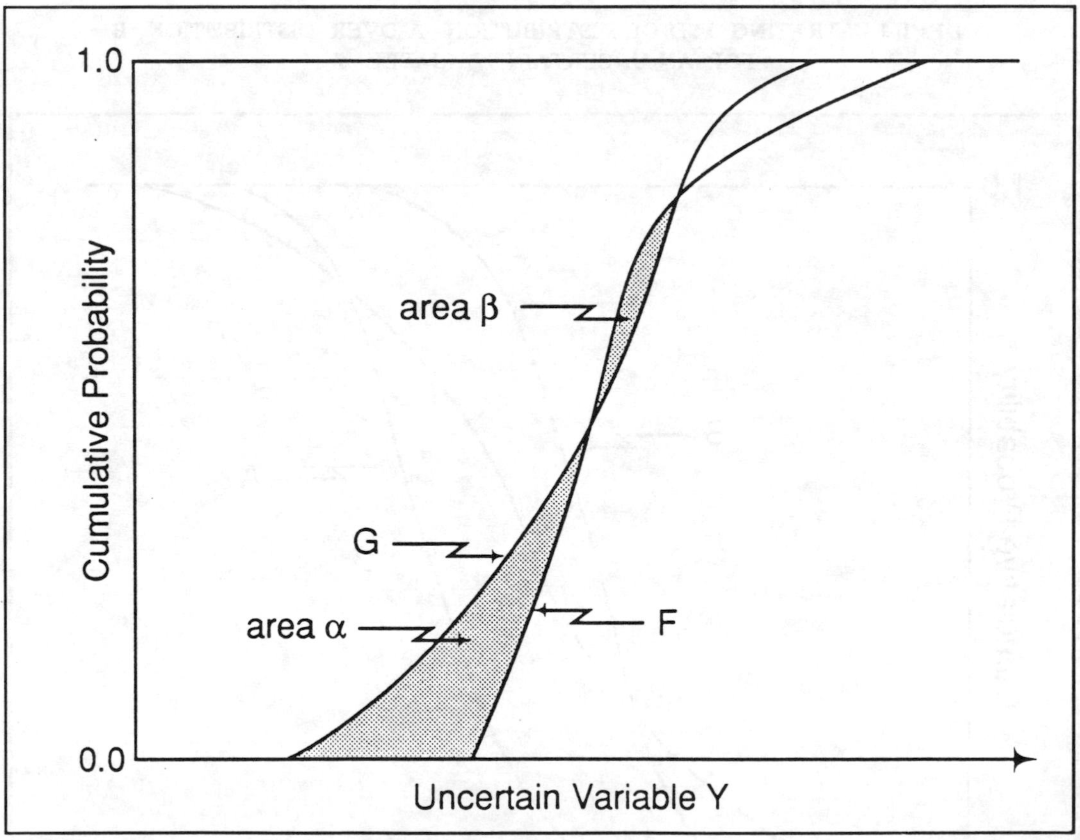

In the special case where the distribution of consequences is normal (or the utility function is quadratic), SSD reduces to the (E,V) or mean-variance rule. That is, one distribution dominates another in the (E,V) sense if it has a higher mean payoff for any level of variance or, equivalently, it has a lower variance at any feasible level of payoff. Although the conditions for exact application of the (E,V) rule are rather demanding, it is often used as an approximate means of ranking non-normal distributions. However, with the increased ease of use of other forms of stochastic dominance analysis, such as those to be described next, such approximate methods are less justifiable.

OTHER FORMS OF STOCHASTIC DOMINANCE

By making the further plausible assumption about behaviour that most farmers are decreasingly risk averse as their wealth increases, a still more discriminating rule, known as third-degree stochastic dominance is obtained. But unfortunately, experience shows that this rule will usually cull rather few acts from the SSD set. Searching for a better approach, analysts realised that it will often be possible to set limits on the degrees of risk aversion likely to be found in any target group of farmers. In particular, it is often held, on the basis of some empirical evidence, that most farmers have *coefficients of relative risk aversion*[1] between about 1.0 and 4.0. Prosperous commercial farmers might be nearer the lower limit and poor semi-subsistence farmers near the upper limit of this range.

From this generalisation, and knowing something about the levels of total wealth of farmers in the target area, a method of *stochastic dominance with respect to a function* (SDRF), also known as *generalised stochastic dominance*, can be used that usually turns out to reduce considerably the SSD set. SDRF is based on setting upper and lower bounds on the *coefficient of absolute risk aversion*, another measure of risk aversion that can be derived from the coefficient of relative risk aversion of any individual by dividing by that person's wealth. As compared to SSD, the advantage of the SDRF method is that, when two CDFs cross, the one with the lower tail can dominate the other provided that its advantage over the second distribution at higher levels of consequences are sufficiently large, given the specified range in absolute risk aversion.

APPLICATION OF STOCHASTIC DOMINANCE METHODS

As already noted, SD analysis involves pair-wise comparisons of all the distributions associated with the full set of decision alternatives. To apply the method other than by eyeballing the graphed CDFs requires that each pair of distributions must be compared at a large number of levels of payoff. In other words, the process is very time consuming. Fortunately, however, computer software is available, adapted for use on PCs, that makes the task much quicker and more practicable - see, for example, Raskin and Cochran (1986).

8.6 Some illustrative examples

CERTAINTY EQUIVALENT APPROACH

A simple example is given by applying the certainty equivalent approach to the decision tree of Figure 8.2. This tree already shows all the relevant information. It only remains to determine the decision maker's certainty equivalent for each of the two event nodes and then apply backward induction - which in this case is very simple since there is only a single decision node. Suppose that on the basis of our questioning and her or his introspection, the farmer specifies a certainty equivalent of $ 1 510 for the set of risky consequences branching from event node A and a certainty equivalent of $ 1 550 for those

---

[1] The coefficient of relative risk aversion is a measure of how averse to risk a person is. The measure is dimensionless, meaning that comparisons between individuals are valid regardless of the units in which the consequences (income or wealth) are measured.

at event node B. The decision problem of Figure 8.2 may then be replaced by the equivalent but simpler decision problem of Figure 8.7 which involves the original single decision node but no chance nodes. It is immediately apparent that the preferred choice is action a_2, i.e., not to spray, and we can cross off the alternative a_1. Thus, although the alternatives of spraying or not spraying have expected money values that are very nearly equal ($ 1 570 and $ 1 568, respectively), we have ascertained that the farmer's preferences for money outcomes and attitude to risk are such that she or he would clearly be better served by choosing not to spray.

Figure 8.7

APPLICATION OF CERTAINTY EQUIVALENT APPROACH TO RISKY DECISION PROBLEM OF FIGURE 8.2

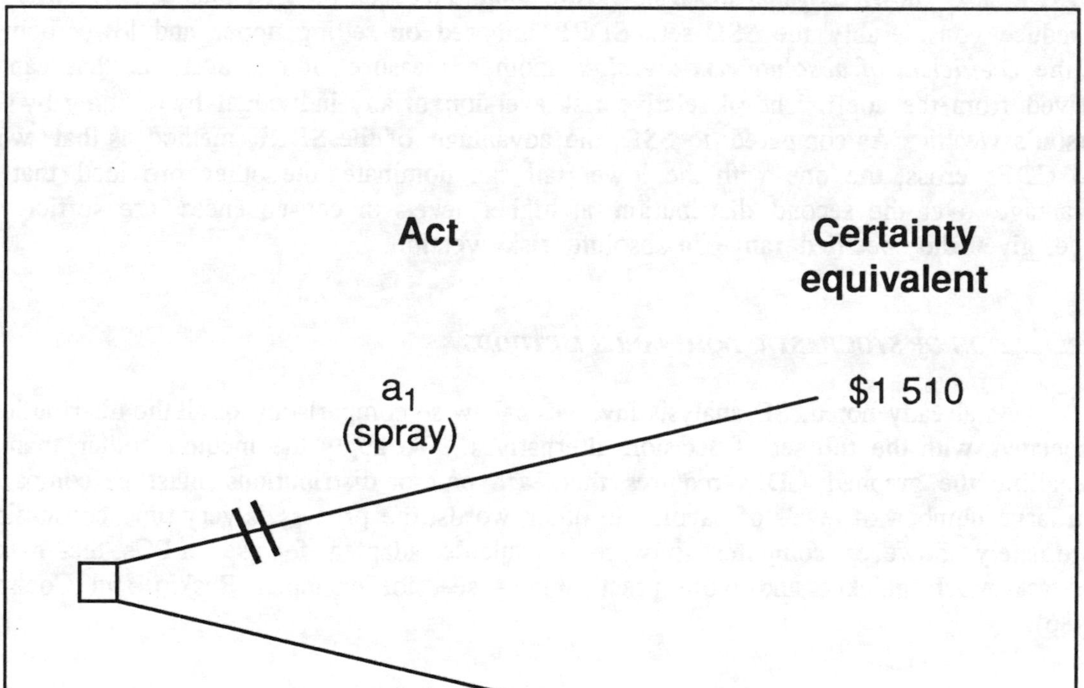

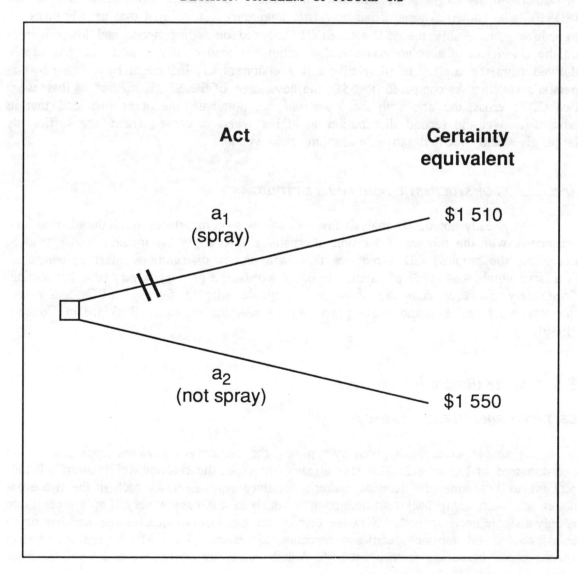

Conceptually there is no reason why the certainty equivalent approach could not be applied to risky decision problems depicted in matrix form. Thus it would be an easy matter in the case of the matrix presentation of Table 8.2 to add a row at the bottom of the matrix in which elicited certainty equivalents could be inserted and the act with the largest certainty equivalent selected. As a practical matter, however, most real-world farm decisions would involve a larger payoff matrix than that of Table 8.2 and the elicitation of a farmer's certainty equivalents would proceed more easily in the context of the decision tree format.

As an example of a more complicated risky decision problem we present a problem analyzed by Singh (1978) based on data collected by Singh and Choudhry (1977). The problem relates to that of a farmer in Haryana, India, who has grown 5 ha of potatoes. He has to decide whether to harvest and sell the crop now in November while it is still making some growth, or to harvest in January when the crop will be mature. If he harvests in January, he may either sell immediately or store the crop until October. The uncertainties in the situation relate to the prices that will prevail in January and October, although yield uncertainty could also be included in the analysis if it were relevant.

Relevant information as elicited from the farmer for detailing the decision tree is as follows:

Harvest in November:

Yield:	150 q/ha.
Price:	Rs 60/q.
Harvest cost:	Rs 287/ha.
Payoff:	Rs (150)(5)(60) - (5)(287) = Rs 43 565.

Harvest in January and sell immediately:

Yield:	190 q/ha.
Price:	0.5 chance of Rs 50/q and 0.5 chance of Rs 40/q.
Harvest cost:	Rs 287/ha.
Payoff:	Rs 46 065, if price is Rs 50/q. Rs 36 565, if price is Rs 40/q.

Harvest in January and store for October sale:

Yield after storage (4.21 percent loss): 182 q/ha.

Price:	0.6 chance of Rs 75/q and 0.4 chance of Rs 62/q.
Harvest cost:	Rs 287/ha.

Storage preparation cost (grading, etc.): Rs 86/ha.

Storage cost:	Rs 12.50/q.
Payoff:	Rs 55 010, if price is Rs 75/q. Rs 43 180, if price is Rs 62/q.

It is important to emphasize that all the above information is as agreed by the farmer and that, in particular, the price levels and probabilities reflect his personal judgement of the relevant parameter values. Given this information, the decision tree can be drawn as in Figure 8.8. Note that it involves a sequence with two act nodes and two event nodes. From left to right, these nodes reflect the chronological order of deciding whether or not to harvest in November, the chance determination of prices in January, the decision of whether or not to sell or store if harvest is in January, and the chance determination of price in October.

Figure 8.8

DECISION TREE REPRESENTATION OF PATATO HARVEST PROBLEM

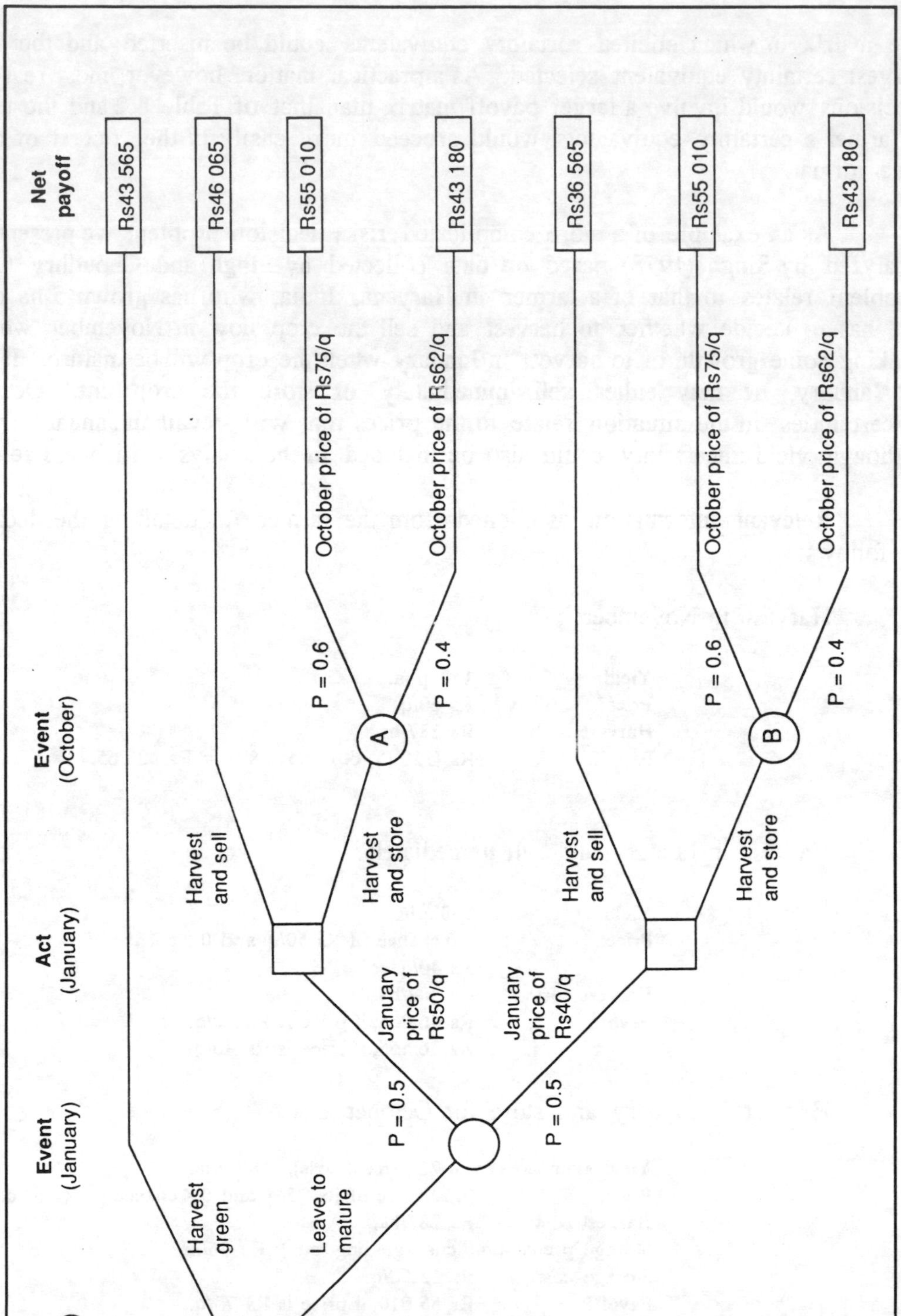

Guided by the potato farmer's introspection, backward induction based on certainty equivalence can be used to solve the decision tree of Figure 8.8. We begin with the event forks furthest to the right in the tree. There are two of these, labelled A and B, and by the nature of the present problem, they are identical (having the same risky consequence set with the same probabilities of occurrence). Based on introspection, suppose the farmer nominates a sure payment of Rs 45 000 as his certainty equivalent for event node A, and hence for event node B also. With this information, we can replace Figure 8.8 with the simpler but equivalent tree of Figure 8.9. Inspection of Figure 8.9 indicates that if the crop is harvested in January and the January price should turn out to be Rs 50/q, it would be best to harvest and sell (giving Rs 46 065) rather than to store (with a certainty equivalent payoff of Rs 45 000). Accordingly, the harvest and store act at decision node C can be eliminated from further consideration. Conversely, if the January price should be Rs 40/q, the best act at decision node D would be to store for October sale. In consequence, should the optimal act for the farmer in November be to leave his crop for January harvest (as we show is the case below), he can plan to assess the price situation in January and act accordingly. If the January price is Rs 50/q, he should harvest and sell for a payoff of Rs 46 065. If the January price is Rs 40/q, he should store to October for a payoff with a certainty equivalent of Rs 45 000.

Continuing with the backward induction, we can replace decision nodes C and D with their payoffs from the preferred decisions at those nodes. This reduces the decision tree of Figure 8.9 to that of Figure 8.10 in which there is a single event node E to be evaluated. Suppose the decision maker nominates Rs 45 400 as his certainty equivalent for the risky consequences at E. Again, the decision tree can be simplified by backward induction to give Figure 8.11. As this simplified tree shows, the decision problem has now been reduced to a choice between a sure payoff of Rs 43 565 for harvesting in November and a sure equivalent payoff of Rs 45 400 for harvesting in January. Obviously, the optimal decision is to harvest in January and to then decide whether to sell in January or in October depending on whether the January price is Rs 50/q or Rs 40/q. Note that this solution applies only to the particular farmer we have been considering. Another farmer, because of her or his personal degrees of belief and preferences (as reflected by her or his personal probability judgements and certainty equivalents) could reach a different conclusion as to her or his optimal decision.

Exactly the same procedures as illustrated above would apply for more complicated problems involving lengthier act-event sequences, acts with larger numbers of alternatives, and events with more possible outcomes. The secret of such analyses is to model the decision problem in such fashion as to capture its important elements in terms of decisions and events without making the decision tree so bushy that it is incomprehensible. Only if the tree is comprehensible will a farmer be able to adequately specify the required certainty equivalents for backward induction.

USE OF SPARSE DATA AND STOCHASTIC EFFICIENCY ANALYSIS

To illustrate the fractile rule described in Section 8.3 above, suppose we wish to apply decision analysis to the fertilizer investment data of Table 6.5. Since there are eight observations for each investment alternative, we can apply the fractile rule to estimate the net benefit value corresponding to the 1/9, 2/9, 3/9, 4/9, 5/9, 6/9, 7/9 and 8/9 fractiles of the cumulative distribution function corresponding to each investment alternative.

Table 8.3

FRACTILES FOR THE DISTRIBUTION OF NET BENEFITS ($/ha) FROM EACH OF THE ALTERNATIVE FERTILIZER INVESTMENTS OF TABLE 6.5

Fractile	Alternative (N,P) investments											
	(0,0)	(50,0)	(100,0)	(150,0)	(0,25)	(50,25)	(100,25)	(150,25)	(0,50)	(50,50)	(100,50)	(150,50)
0.111	360	670	870	670	1 080	1 620	1 090	970	510	1 310	1 550	1 460
0.222	1 090	1 280	970	710	1 200	1 800	1 660	1 090	680	2 150	1 590	1 490
0.333	1 380	1 650	2 370	2 080	1 330	2 190	2 100	1 880	720	2 210	1 980	2 120
0.444	1 450	1 890	2 830	2 610	1 540	2 710	2 660	2 700	750	2 500	2 690	2 630
0.555	1 480	2 200	2 960	2 730	1 820	2 830	3 320	3 080	900	2 770	3 440	2 930
0.667	2 180	2 990	3 420	3 080	2 120	3 390	3 440	3 280	950	3 020	3 440	3 840
0.778	3 740	3 920	3 720	3 130	2 410	3 800	3 690	4 600	3 990	3 440	3 950	4 120
0.889	4 270	4 420	3 810	3 490	3 700	4 000	4 480	4 900	4 060	4 140	4 320	4 160

Figure 8.9

FIRST-STAGE BACKWARD INDUCTION OF POTATO HARVEST PROBLEM OF FIGURE 8.8

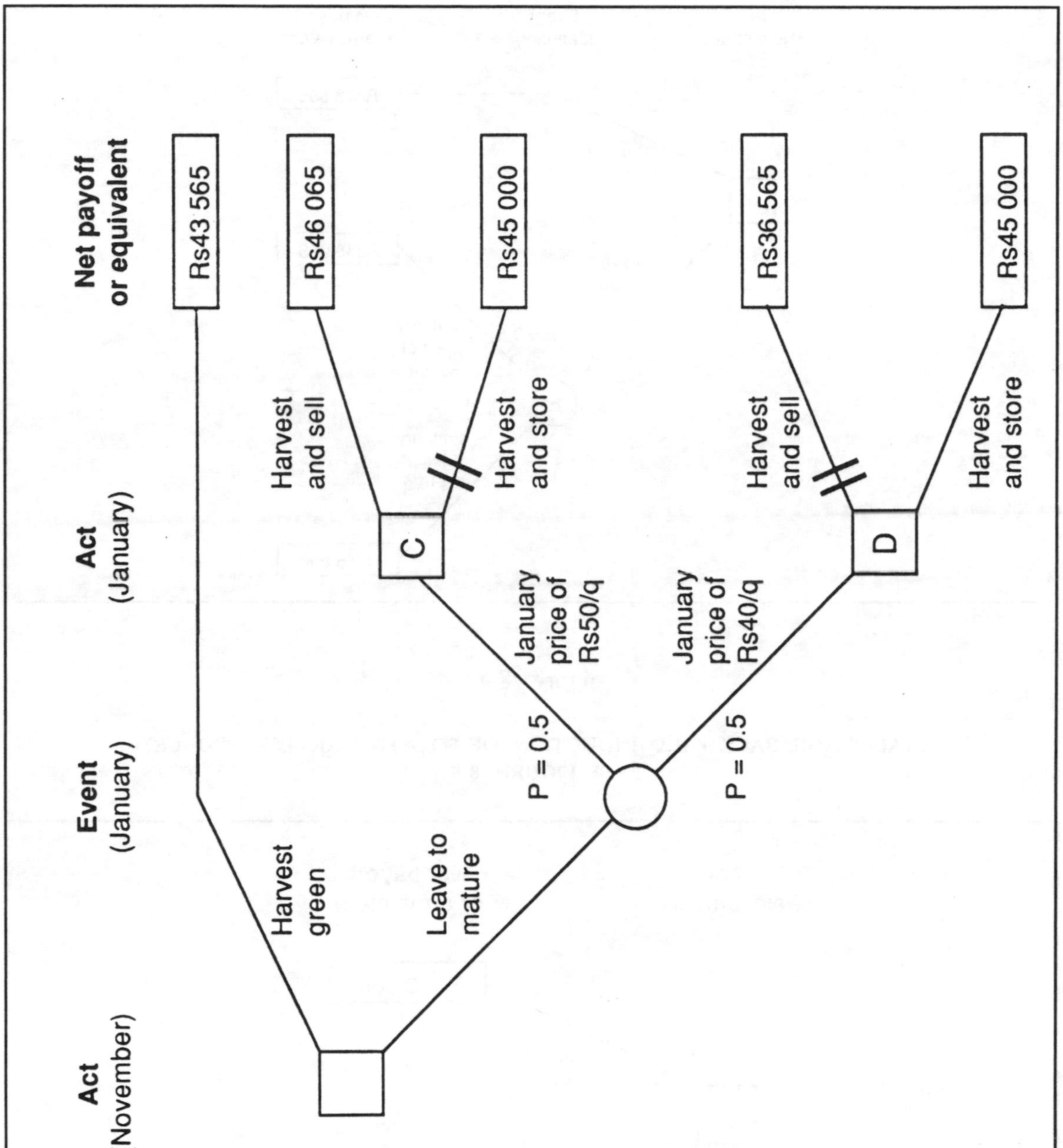

Figure 8.10

SECOND-STAGE BACKWARD INDUCTION OF POTATO HARVEST PROBLEM OF FIGURE 8.8

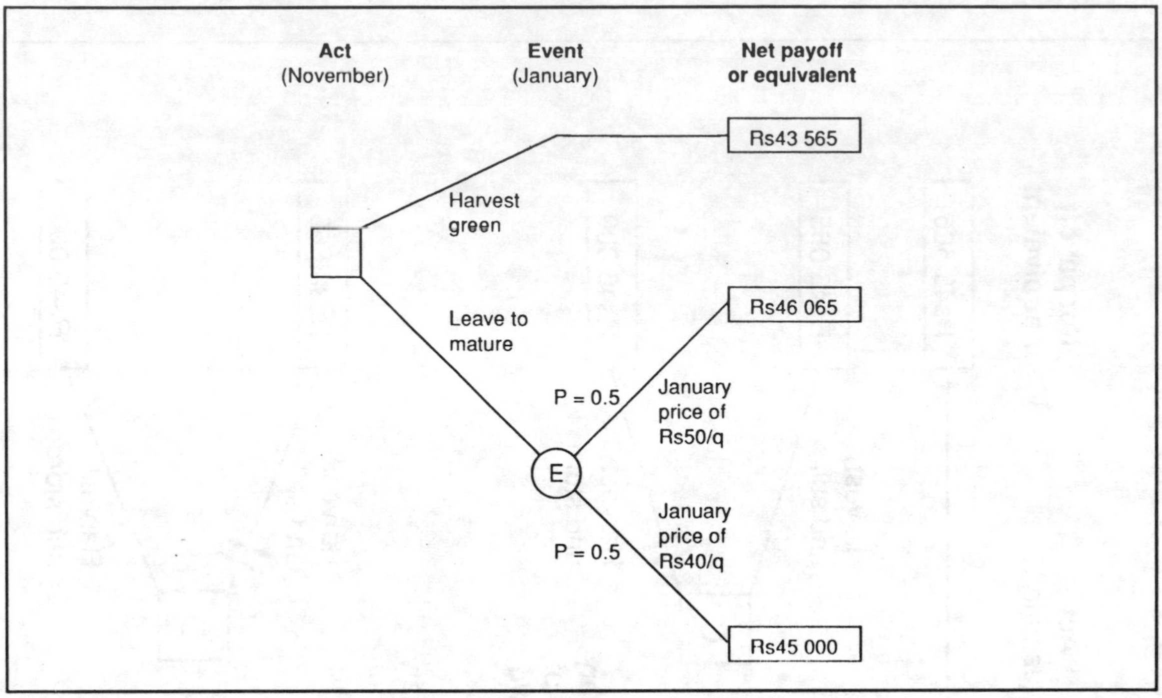

Figure 8.11

FINAL-STAGE BACKWARD INDUCTION OF POTATO HARVEST PROBLEM OF FIGURE 8.8

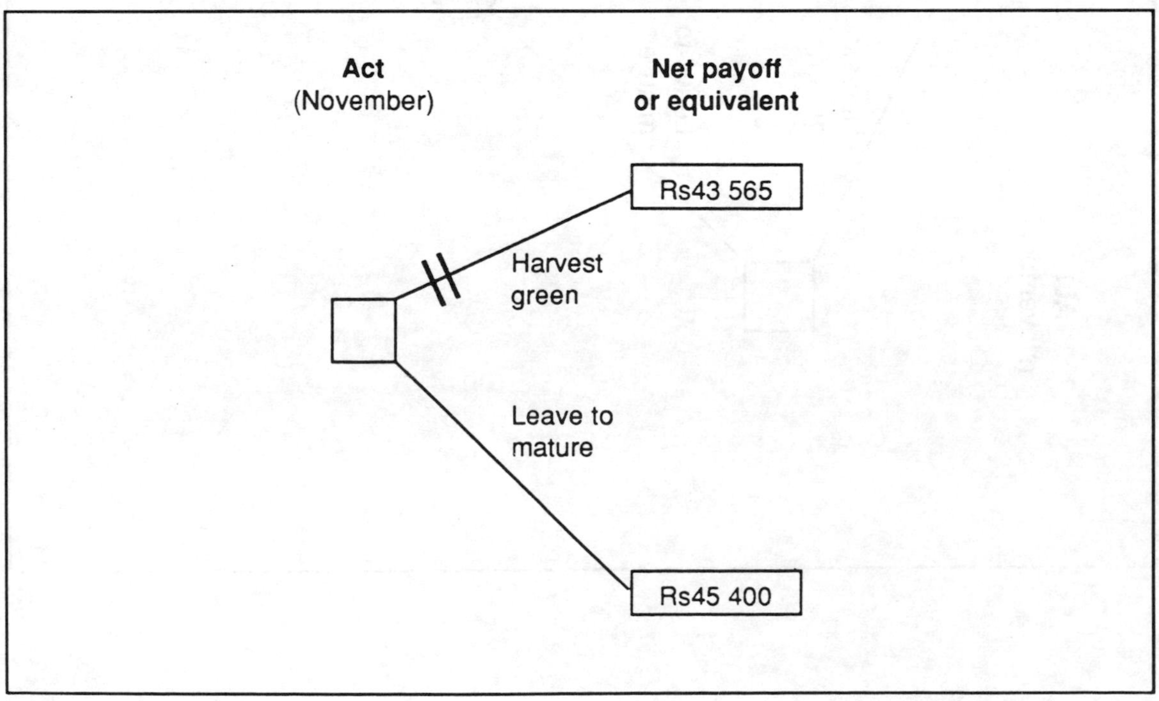

These fractiles are shown in Table 8.3 from which we see, for example, that for the (100,25) alternative, there is an estimated probability of 0.444 that a net benefit of $ 2 660 or less will be received.

Based on the fractile data of Table 8.3 (or smoothed cumulative distribution curves drawn from these data), we may estimate event probabilities for decision analysis of the fertilizer investment problem. Thus suppose we decide to model the problem by considering three levels of net benefit for each alternative. Suppose these are high, medium and low, where these correspond to the central values of the top, middle and lower thirds of the net benefit probability distribution. From Table 8.3 (or more accurately from the smoothed cumulative distribution curves if we drew them), we can estimate the central value of net benefit within the high, medium and low class intervals. Our estimates of these values are as shown in Table 8.4 which, of course, constitutes a payoff matrix for this risky decision problem.

Inspection of the payoffs listed in Table 8.4 shows that the first five alternatives and the ninth are dominated. For each of these, one of the other alternatives always gives a greater net benefit. Accordingly these dominated alternatives can be dropped from further consideration and we are left with the reduced decision matrix of Table 8.5. For each of the alternatives listed in Table 8.5, certainty equivalents could then be elicited for each individual farmer and her or his optimal investment choice ascertained. Whether or not the expected utility of this investment is greater than the utility she or he would gain from other (i.e., non-fertilizer) investment opportunities, if available, is something the individual farmer would have to decide.

The dominance among the decision options mentioned above can be extended using the methods of stochastic dominance introduced earlier. The data in Table 8.3 were analyzed using a computer program developed by Raskin and Cochran (1986). Tests of FSD, SSD and SDRF were applied. For the latter, a plausible guess was made about the likely range of absolute risk aversion in a typical community of small-scale farmers.

For FSD, the efficient set included (50,0), (100,0), (50,25), (100,25), (150,25), (50,50), (100,50) and (150,50). These (N,P) combinations dominated the remaining four of (0,0), (150,0), (0,25) and (0,50). These latter fertilizer combinations are inefficient because they would not be preferred by any farmer who likes more income rather than less.

For SSD, it is assumed that farmers are risk averse. Making this assumption reduces the stochastically efficient set from eight under FSD to three: (50,25,), (50, 50) and (100,50). It can be seen that, in this application, SSD proves to be a much more discriminating rule than FSD.

In an attempt to further reduce the number of dominant options, SDRF was used. The range of coefficients of absolute risk aversion was specified as 0.0001 to 0.001. The result was the elimination of a further option, leaving in the efficient set only the (50,25) and (100,50) alternatives. Note that the choice between these two can only be made with still more exact information about farmers' risk preferences. It is likely that some farmers in the target population would prefer one and others the second option.

Table 8.4

ESTIMATED NET BENEFITS ($/ha) AND ASSOCIATED PROBABILITIES FOR DECISION ANALYSIS OF THE FERTILIZER INVESTMENT PROBLEM

Probability	Alternative (N,P) investments											
	(0,0)	(50,0)	(100,0)	(150,0)	(0,25)	(50,25)	(100,25)	(150,25)	(0,50)	(50,50)	(100,50)	(150,50)
1/3	725	975	920	690	1 140	1 710	1 375	1 030	595	1 730	1 570	1 475
1/3	1 465	2 045	2 895	2 670	1 680	2 770	2 990	2 890	825	2 635	3 065	2 780
1/3	4 005	4 170	3 770	3 310	3 055	3 900	4 085	4 750	4 025	3 790	4 135	4 140

Table 8.5

PAYOFF MATRIX FOR FERTILIZER DECISION PROBLEM ($/ha)

Probability	Alternative (N,P) investments					
	(50,25)	(100,25)	(150,25)	(50,50)	(100,50)	(150,50)
1/3	1 710	1 375	1 030	1 730	1 570	1 475
1/3	2 770	2 990	2 890	2 635	3 065	2 780
1/3	3 900	4 085	4 750	3 790	4 135	4 140

8.7 Concluding comment

In this chapter we have sketched decision theory analysis in the context of a farm management specialist assisting farmers, either individually or as a target group, in their risky decision making. For that reason we have emphasized the practical analytics of decision theory and not considered elaborations of the theory. For such further extensions, reference should be made to such texts as Anderson, Dillon and Hardaker (1977). For further discussion of stochastic dominance methods in agriculture, see, for example, Eidman (1983), King and Robison (1984) or Anderson and Dillon (1992).

8.8 References

ANDERSON, J.R., J.L. DILLON & J.B. HARDAKER (1977). *Agricultural Decision Analysis*, Iowa State University Press, Ames.

ANDERSON, J.R. & J.L. DILLON (1992). *Risk analysis in dryland farming systems*, Farm Systems Management Series 2, Food and Agriculture Organization of the United Nations, Rome.

EIDMAN, V.R. (1983). 'Cash Flow, Price Risk and Production Uncertainty Considerations', in K.H. Baum and L.P. Schertz (eds), *Modeling Farm Decisions for Policy Analysis*, Westview, Boulder, pp. 159-80.

KING, R.P. & L.J. ROBISON (1984). 'Risk Efficiency Models', in P.J. Barry (ed.), *Risk Management in Agriculture*, Iowa State University Press, Ames, pp. 68-81.

MAKEHAM, J.P., A.N. HALTER & J.L. DILLON (1968). *Best-Bet Farm Decisions*, Professional Farm Management Guidebook No. 6, A.B.R.I., University of New England, Armidale.

POULIQUEN, L.Y. (1970). *Risk Analysis in Project Appraisal*, World Bank Staff Occasional Paper No. 11, Johns Hopkins University Press, Baltimore.

RASKIN, R. & M.J. COCHRAN (1986). *A User's Guide to the generalized Stochastic Dominance Program for the IBM PC*, Department of Agricultural Economics and Rural Sociology, University of Arkansas, Fayetteville.

SINGH, I.J. (1978). *Decision Trees and Farmers' Decision Making under Uncertainty*, Department of Economics, Haryana Agricultural University, Hissar.

SINGH, I.J. & K. CHOUDHRY (1977). *Economic Analysis of Potato Production and Marketing in Haryana*, Research Bulletin No. 2, Department of Economics, Haryana Agricultural University, Hissar.

9. FARM MANAGEMENT RESEARCH AND AGRICULTURAL POLICY

Many rural development interventions are designed to increase farm production and hence rural incomes. Depending on the structure of agriculture in the country or region of interest, production decisions may be made by a few large-scale, commercial farm operators, often these days the managers of plantations or other farming enterprises owned by government or quasi-government agencies. More commonly, however, the decisions are made by large numbers of independent small-scale farmers. In either event, the success of the agricultural policy or project will usually hinge on whether anticipated improvements in farm output or productivity are achieved. The generally rather poor performance of rural development projects implemented or funded by international agencies such as the World Bank may be attributed, in large part, to over-optimism on the part of the project designers about the willingness or ability of producers to change (World Bank 1988).

In this chapter the use of farm management research results for agricultural development is discussed with particular reference to project planning and management, and the policy analysis matrix.

9.1 Project planning and management

With the exception of centrally-planned economies, rural development projects designed to raise agricultural productivity depend on the responses of producers to incentives, supposedly created or improved by the project itself. For example, a new rural road may be designed to increase access of rural producers to markets, a research and extension programme may be intended to develop and spread to farmers improved methods of production, a rural credit scheme may be intended to break a perceived constraint on the capacities of poor farmers to buy the inputs needed to raise production and income. Yet, predicting just how farmers will respond to such changes is fraught with difficulty, as past performance too often proves. Aggregate historical production data, if they exist at all and are reasonably reliable, may provide a very poor basis for predicting the responses of producers under what are intended to be quite different circumstances, once the project has been implemented. The farm management economist has both the tools and the micro-level focus to contribute useful insights to this and other project-related tasks, as discussed below.

The stages in project planning and management are often thought of as forming a cycle, as illustrated in Figure 9.1.

Figure 9.1

THE PROJECT PLANNING AND MANAGEMENT CYCLE
(after Goodman and Love, 1979, p.3)

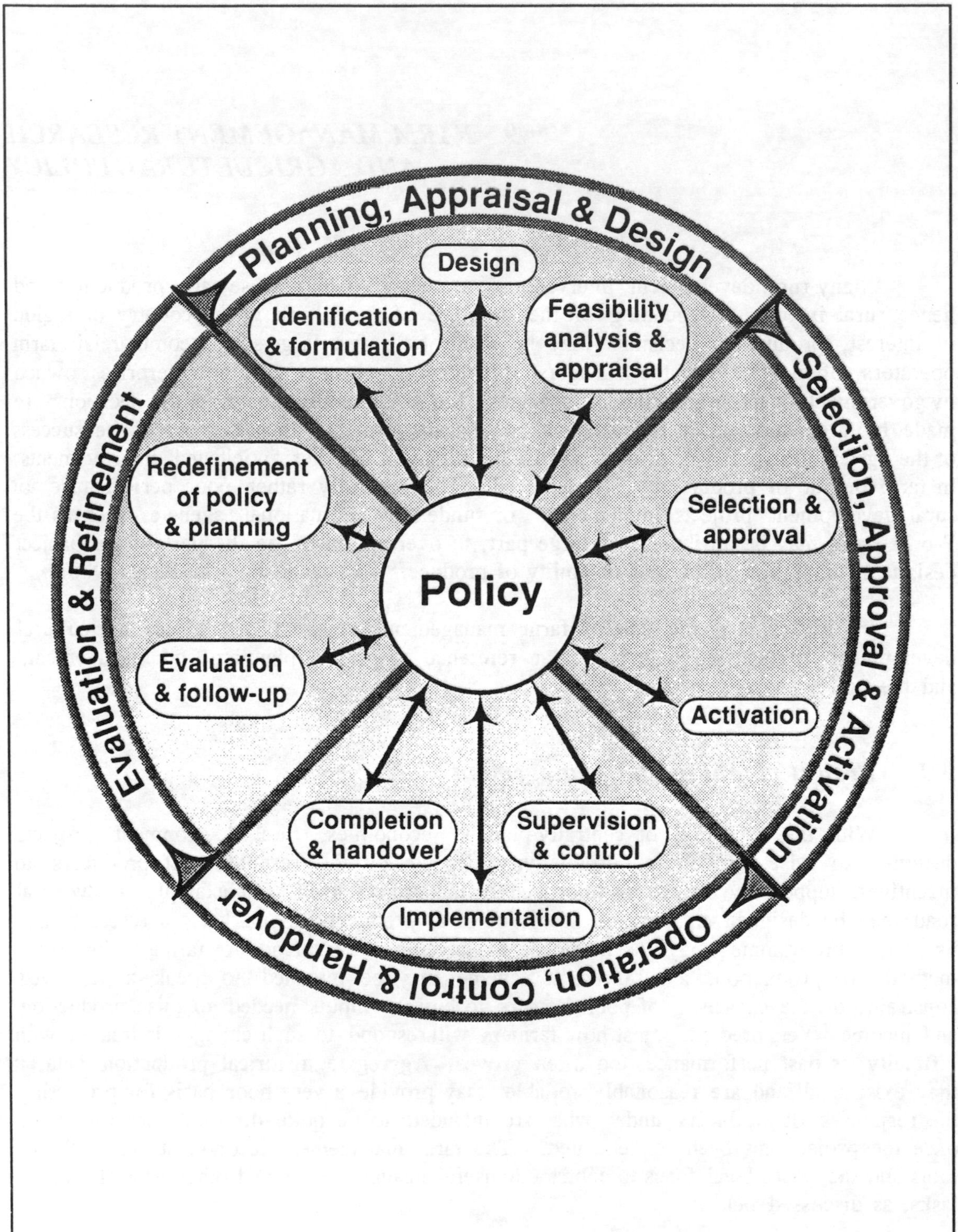

The initial phases for a given project relate to project planning, appraisal and design. First of all, within this group of activities, is project identification. The importance of this phase cannot be over-emphasised; there is an unfortunate tendency for project ideas to develop a momentum that can be difficult to halt, even though the project may be unsuitable. Once a project proposal has reached a certain stage, vested interests can make it difficult for an objective appraisal to be undertaken. It is therefore crucial that only proposals with good chances of success are allowed to reach the stage of being formulated as projects.

For agricultural development projects, the identification phase is one to which farm management analysis can contribute substantially. Such development projects are usually designed to break some important production constraints, or to exploit some new opportunity, in order to expand output and raise incomes. But a project will be ill-conceived, and likely to fail, if the wrong constraints have been identified, or what was perceived as a new opportunity turns out to be nothing of the sort.

Clearly, a detailed and reliable knowledge of the actual circumstances faced by farmers can minimise the risk of such errors. Moreover, the methods of farm management analysis are well suited to analyzing just such questions. Whole-farm planning methods, such as linear programming, give clear and explicit indications of which constraints are important for representative case farms. The same methods, or the partial and input-output budgeting methods described in Chapters 5 and 6 above, allow the merits of new technologies to be assessed. Moreover, the methods of farming systems research, and in particular the on-farm testing of prospective technologies, as discussed in Chapters 1 and 2, provide reliable indications of the chances of available new technologies being taken up.

Farm management analysis can also be valuable in the project design phase. It is here that the details of the project are decided. Getting the design right means knowing exactly what needs to be done to produce the intended benefits. Farm planning methods can be directly useful in project design. The design of a rural credit package, for example, to meet the credit needs of producers expected to take up some new technology, will be best completed after a proper assessment of the likely credit needs and capacities to repay of the target groups of farmers, performed using cash-flow budgeting methods for representative farm situations. Budgeting, combined with data on the numbers and sizes of farms in the project area, will allow estimation of the aggregate levels of inputs such as seeds and fertilizer that will be needed, and the aggregate levels of output that will be produced. Such estimates can be vital for planning important project components for expansion of input delivery or output marketing services.

Good project design also means being able to predict the response of farm families to the new or improved incentives and opportunities created under the project. Farm surveys may provide necessary data for the analysis of likely responses of producers to changed circumstances such as higher prices for outputs or reduced cost and availability of inputs.

In judging project feasibility, experience shows that it is easy for project planners to over-estimate the capacity of farm families to take on extra work. There is a widespread perception that the rural areas of the developing world are characterised by surplus labour. But this is by no means always the case - in most farming systems there are times of the year when labour is scarce. If the new initiatives that are to be introduced under a project compete for labour at these peak times, they may well be doomed to failure. The construction of seasonal labour budgets, with peak periods identified, as described in Chapter 4, may avoid such mis-judgement by project designers. Similar feasibility considerations may apply to other resources, such as land or farm capital, and again the budgeting methods described in Chapter 4 are relevant.

Even if the proposed changes to the farming system are feasible, in terms of the demands that will be placed on farm-household resources, the question of the effect on profitability also has to be assessed. If people are to be expected to work harder, and probably to bear increased risks, they will need the promise of an adequate reward. Whole-farm profit budgeting can be used to assess whether the required incentive should eventuate under the conditions expected to be created by the project.

Such farm profit budgets for representative farm situations will be valuable building blocks in the project appraisal phase. Here methods of economic and social cost-benefit analysis are used to estimate and judge the worth of the project. The normal approach (Gittinger 1982) is first to undertake a *financial appraisal* of the project, in which the predicted costs and returns to the various participants in the project, including government, are assembled. Costs and returns are assessed at prevailing prices for the financial appraisal. Since most rural development projects involve farmers, farm-level budgets will form the basis of a major part of the financial appraisal. Not only will they show the project's expected impact on production but, as noted above, they also provide a basis for estimating needed changes in input delivery and output marketing, as well as possibly needed changes in infrastructure.

Assessing the impact of a project on the national economy is known as *economic appraisal*. It requires the *shadow pricing* of project inputs and outputs. Shadow prices are prices that reflect more appropriately than prevailing prices the worth to the economy as a whole of inputs and outputs. They are used because, in many developing countries, the prevailing prices are distorted by government interventions or by various forms of market failure. The use and estimation of shadow prices are described later in this chapter. Sometimes, a further step may be taken with the carrying out of a *social appraisal*, wherein judgements are made about the relative values to be placed on project benefits going to different income groups within the society. The use, for example of *poverty weights* is described by Squire and van der Tak (1975). Both economic and social project appraisals take as their starting point basic input-output data used in the financial appraisal, much of which, as noted, must be generated by farm management analyses.

In both project supervision and control, and also in the subsequent *ex post* evaluation and refinement phases, the farm management economist again can contribute by assessing the impacts of the project on representative farms. Methods of farm management data collection described in Chapter 2, and the methods of processing and presenting those data described in Chapter 3, are relevant to project monitoring and appraisal. Usually, budgets will have been prepared during project preparation to indicate the nature and magnitudes of the changes expected to be induced by the project. The methods of *budgetary control* can be valuable in the monitoring phase, whereby actual performance is matched against budgeted performance on a regular basis, say quarterly (usually using cash-flow measures), and reasons for departures from budgetary expectations are analyzed. Regular monitoring is important in order to identify problems soon enough for corrective action to be taken during the life of the project.

In post-project evaluation, on the other hand, the aim is to learn from the successes and failures of a project, so as to guide decision making about future projects of a generally similar nature. In this evaluation phase, comparative analysis of budgeted and actual farm performance can be used, again including an analysis of the reasons for differences between expected (or predicted) and actual outcomes. Only when such differences have been correctly diagnosed will it be possible to judge what refinements to policy or project design are needed in order that similar projects executed in future will be more successful.

9.2 Outline of the policy analysis matrix

In many developing countries government policies have significant impacts on prices, and hence on the profitability of farming operations. Recently there has been a growing interest in assessing the impacts of such price distortions and in measuring the comparative advantage of groups of farmers in the production of various commodities, with and without the effects of price distortions. Such calculations are intended to show whether the expansion of production of particular commodities would be privately and socially profitable.

Pearson and Monke (1987) have described a method of investigating such questions called the Policy Analysis Matrix (PAM) that is based heavily on the types of micro-level data that farm management analysts commonly produce. The PAM approach is outlined below. The treatment here is necessarily superficial, and readers seeking more detail are referred to the more comprehensive descriptions of Pearson and Monke (1987), Gotsch (1989) and Monke and Pearson (1989).

A PAM is an accounting table for a given agricultural commodity system that is compiled from farm budgets and other information to provide a comprehensive picture of the policy environment for that commodity system. This may be done on a national or on a regional basis. A PAM embodies two types of accounting identity - one defining profitability as the difference between revenues and costs, and the other measuring the effects on these costs, revenues and profitabilities of price distortions and market failures.

The structure of a PAM is shown in Figure 9.2. In the first row, the private profitability of the commodity system is found by deducting from the value of outputs the costs of all inputs and factors used, i.e., $D = A - (B + C)$. For this calculation the outputs, inputs and domestic factors are all valued at prevailing prices.

In the second line of the matrix the same calculation is performed but this time with outputs and inputs valued at their social or shadow prices, i.e., $H = E - (F + G)$. The determination of these social or shadow prices is explained in more detail below, but the prices used are intended to represent the real value to the society of the outputs, inputs and factors after correcting for price distortions created by government policies or by market imperfections.

Finally, the third line of the matrix shows the differences between the private and social profitability calculations, reflecting the policy or market failure effects. Thus $I = A - E$ measures the transfers through policies affecting output prices, $J = B - F$ measures the transfers through policies affecting input prices, and $K = C - G$ measures the transfers through policies and market failures affecting the prices of domestic factors of

Figure 9.2

SCHEMATIC POLICY ANALYSIS MATRIX
(after Gotsch, 1989, p.8)

	Tradeables				Domestic		
	Outputs		Inputs		factors		Profits
Private	A	-	B	-	C	=	D
Social	E	-	F	-	G	=	H
Policy effects	I	-	J	-	K	=	L

production. The net transfers are shown as L = I - (J+K). As is evident from this outline, a PAM permits a comparison of private and social profitability of the commodity system under review, and also highlights the sources of these differences, whether caused by government interventions or by market failure. A completed matrix thus indicates those areas in which policy reforms (including measures to make markets more effective) are required to improve the efficiency of the agricultural system.

Private profits (D) are an important result in a PAM because they show the competitiveness of the system under prevailing prices. In other words, they are an indication of the private comparative advantage of the given group of farmers in the production of the commodity (or commodities) in question. Policy makers seeking to provide incentives for the production of particular commodities or to particular groups of producers need to be assured that an adequate, but not excessive, rate of profit can be obtained. On the other hand, social profitability (H) measures the comparative advantage from the viewpoint of the nation in the production of that commodity (or group of commodities). Policies that will stimulate production in areas of comparative advantage are generally to be preferred.

If private and social profitabilities diverge, and particularly if the two profitability measures are of opposite signs, there is an indication to policy makers that they need to reconsider the nature and levels of their interventions. The last row in the PAM is relevant here since it allows the cause of such differences to be dissected. It becomes possible, therefore, to judge whether corrections are needed to prices in tradeable outputs, tradeable inputs, or whether failures in markets for domestic factors of production need attention.

As explained below, from the PAM it is possible to calculate various measures of the degree of protection (positive or negative) implied by the differences between private and social costs, returns and profitability. These measures are useful indicators of the extent of price distortions.

The PAM analysis may be performed for a single commodity production system, or for a whole-farm system. The former is often of most interest to policy makers since many important policy settings, such as levels of subsidies on inputs or taxes on outputs, are commodity-based. The difficulty with a commodity-based PAM analysis, however, is that there are problems in the proper allocation and valuation of joint costs of producing just one commodity that is actually part of a multi-commodity farming system. Methods of apportioning joint costs may be used, but tend to be very arbitrary.

A solution to this problem can be found using a whole-farm linear programming (LP) model to value the inputs to single commodities at their appropriate opportunity costs. As explained in Chapter 4, such information about the marginal values of resources is a standard part of the solution generated by LP. For the purposes of PAM analysis, these valuations are needed for two models, one formulated using prevailing prices, and one using social prices. For further details, see Gotsch (1989).

For the purposes of this introductory outline of the PAM approach, it is assumed that the analysis is to be for a single commodity and that the problem of cost apportionment has been solved by one means or another.

9.3 Construction of a policy analysis matrix

DATA NEEDS

The basic data needed for construction of a PAM are, first, detailed input-output information about the commodity system of interest. These data are the same as the input-output information needed for farm budgeting. They include the levels of yields, the variable inputs used, and the demands the commodity system places on farm resources. These inputs and outputs need to be valued at prevailing prices for the private profitability analysis. Where such prices do not exist, as for example in cases where there is no effective market for land, estimates of the opportunity costs of those items must be made. Thus, land may be valued in terms of return from its next most profitable use.

Second, social shadow prices must be obtained for the social profitability calculation. The procedures to follow vary according to whether the commodities are traded internationally, are non-traded inputs or outputs, or are non-traded primary factors (land, labour, and capital).

SOCIAL PRICES FOR TRADED INPUTS AND OUTPUTS

For traded commodities, social shadow prices are based on international prices in appropriate world markets, correctly converted to domestic prices, and adjusted to farm-gate prices by adding (for inputs) or subtracting (for outputs) cost of transport and handling. If the exchange rate is distorted, the conversion to domestic currency units should be done using the shadow exchange rate (see Gittinger 1982, pp. 247-50). In adjusting world prices to shadow prices at the farm gate, all transfer payments, such as taxes or subsidies are excluded. Domestic transport and handling cost must be valued in shadow prices, according to their composition in terms of tradeables and non-tradeables.

For commodities that could be traded but are not (perhaps because government measures make such trade impossible or unprofitable), the same shadow pricing procedures should be used as for traded commodities.

SOCIAL PRICES FOR NON-TRADED INPUTS AND OUTPUTS

Some inputs (and perhaps some outputs) are not normally traded internationally. Examples are electricity, irrigation water and domestic transport services. An accurate assessment of shadow prices for such non-tradeables requires that they be decomposed into their traded components and their non-traded primary factors. For example, transport services may be decomposed into imported trucks, fuel, etc., and non-traded land, labour and capital factors. Clearly this procedure can be quite data-intensive and difficult. However, the task can sometimes be simplified, at least for minor inputs and outputs, using standard conversion factors that may have been estimated by some national or international organization concerned with such matters.

PRICES FOR NON-TRADEABLE DOMESTIC RESOURCES

Estimating private and social prices for land, labour and capital is often the most difficult step in a PAM analysis. Domestic markets for these factors are often very imperfect - land sale or renting may be illegal or highly regulated, wage rates may be regulated and provide a poor measure of the value of family labour, and capital and credit markets may also be highly distorted. Whilst estimating the private prices of these factors is therefore often hard, even more problems exist in deriving realistic social prices. These factors cannot, of course, be obtained from world markets, yet, as noted, prevailing domestic prices may be substantially distorted by government measures or market failure. Attempts to use prevailing prices as a starting point and then correcting for the distortions to obtain social prices is usually fraught with difficulties.

In the case of land (which will also embody land-based improvements such as irrigation), the shadow price may be taken as the value in the next most profitable use, calculated at prevailing prices for the estimate of the private value of land, and at social prices for estimating the social value. Estimates of these opportunity costs may be made if the PAM is developed for a single commodity - the opportunity cost of land for crop A is the profit that could be earned from the next best alternative, say crop B. (Of course, this approach assumes that labour and capital inputs are first appropriately valued.) However, the method fails if the PAM relates to a whole farming system. In this case, unless there is a realistic alternative to farming, such as forestry or urban development, it will be best to show returns to land as a residual, thereby limiting the conclusions that can be drawn about social profitability and comparative advantage.

For labour, prevailing wage rates may be distorted by regulations such as for minimum wages, although these are not widely found relative to agriculture in developing countries. Where there is evidence of unemployment or under-employment of labour in the rural areas of interest for the PAM (perhaps only on a seasonal basis), it may be appropriate to discount the prevailing wage rates to better reflect the private and social opportunity costs of this factor. Commonly, planning agencies responsible for rural development projects will have considered these matters and there may be acceptable estimates of the shadow prices of various categories of labour that can be used for construction of the PAM.

The private price of capital may be indicated by prevailing interest rates. The rates in the informal markets will usually be a better guide than those in the formal sector for private profitability calculation - formal credit is often subsidised but rationed. Because distortions in almost any domestic markets tend to affect market interest rates, and because the manipulation of official interest rates is a widespread form of government intervention, the best indication of the social rate of return may come from a review of rates calculated across a number of development projects or from estimates from other similar countries. Often, such reviews have been conducted, and estimates of the appropriate rates made, by the government central planning office or by international organizations such as the World Bank. If no such estimates are available, rates estimated for other broadly similar countries may be used as a guide.

AN EXAMPLE

An example of a simple PAM for rice grown in an irrigated mixed farming area "somewhere in that vast arid and semi-arid region extending from the Middle East to Bangladesh" is taken from Gotsch (1989). He shows how the required data for the PAM can be organized using a PC spreadsheet, and develops all the calculations needed to generate the final PAM presentation table in a logical step-by-step way. Only his final presentation table for the rice crop is shown here as Table 9.1. This PAM has been calculated including private and social shadow prices for land based on the next best alternative crop. On this basis, it may be deduced from the table that rice in this farming system is socially profitable but privately unprofitable. The difference is explained mainly by lower private than social returns, indicating an actual or implied substantial tax on output. Higher private than social costs for land also affect farmers negatively, although tradeable inputs and capital are apparently subsidized and are available to farmers at lower prices that their social opportunity costs, somewhat off-setting the negative impact of the output tax on private profitability.

Table 9.1

ILLUSTRATIVE SINGLE COMMODITY PAM FOR RICE

	Tradeables		Domestic Factors			Profit
	Outputs	Inputs	Capital	Labor	Land	
Private	363.2	149.2	8.1	150.5	122.4	-66.9
Social	504.6	180.0	16.2	150.5	63.4	94.6
Policy effects	-141.4	-30.8	-8.1	0.0	59.0	-161.5

Source: After Gotsch (1989).

9.4 *Interpretation of a policy analysis matrix*

Using the PAM of Table 9.1, a number of measures useful for policy analysis can be calculated. These are discussed here in relation to the schematic PAM presented in Figure 9.2 above.

MEASURES OF PROTECTION

Nominal protection coefficients (NPCs) are measures of the impact of interventions on the value of output or on the costs of tradeable inputs. While they are important indicators in their own right of the degree of protection, it is also often useful to compare NPCs across commodities.

The NPC on output, calculated as A / E in terms of the elements of Figure 9.2, is a measure of the effects of policy intervention on output prices. For the example PAM in Table 9.1, the NPC on output of 363.2 / 504.6 = 0.72 is less than 1.0, indicating that a substantial output tax applies. (Outputs earn less at prevailing domestic prices than world prices.) Similarly, the NPC on tradeable inputs, defined as B / F with respect to Figure 9.2, is 0.82 in this case. Again, the figure is less than 1.0, this time implying a subsidy on inputs. (Inputs are cheaper than they would have been at world prices.)

The *effective protection coefficient* (EPC) is defined as the ratio of the value added at prevailing prices to the value added at social prices, i.e., (A - B) / (E - F) in Figure 9.2. In the example illustrated in Table 9.1, the EPC is (363.2-149.2) / (504.6-180.0) = 0.66, which, since it is less than 1.0, shows that, despite the subsidy on inputs, the overall effect of the government-induced distortions in output and input prices is to reduce net returns to farmers to below what they would have been had there been no interventions.

MEASURES OF COMPARATIVE ADVANTAGE

The *private profitability coefficient* (PPC) is a measure of the comparative advantage farmers have in producing a particular commodity. The PPC is calculated as C / (A - B)

(Figure 9.2), i.e., the ratio of the domestic resource cost to value added, both valued at prevailing prices. In the example of Table 9.1, the PPC of (8.1+150.5+122.4)/ (363.2-149.2) = 1.31 is greater than 1.0, indicating that rice is not a profitable crop for the farmers to grow. (The resource cost is more than the value added.) Hence, the indication is that policy makers would need to reduce the tax on output, or increase the input subsidies, if they wished to create opportunities for the farmers to substitute rice for other crops.

The *domestic resource cost coefficient* (DRC) is a measure of the comparative advantage in production of the particular commodity judged from the point of view of the nation. In terms of Figure 9.2, it is calculated as G / (E - F), i.e., the ratio of domestic resource cost to value added, both valued as social prices. A DRC ratio of less that 1.0 implies that positive social profits are earned from production of that commodity. Since the DRC ratio in the example is 230.1 / 324.6 = 0.71 (i.e., < 1.0), there is an indication of comparative advantage - an expansion of rice production would improve agricultural efficiency from the national viewpoint.

9.5 Advantages and limitations of policy analysis matrices

The PAM approach has a number of advantages for use in policy analysis in a developing country setting. Commodity-based budgets showing estimates of costs of production and profit for groups of farmers are widely used in marketing boards and agriculture ministries in many developing countries in discussions about the setting of output and input prices. The necessary data for these calculations are often readily available from special-purpose or routine surveys. Adding to these calculations of private profitability some measures of the impacts of government-induced distortions of commodity prices therefore constitutes a readily-understood extension of a familiar approach.

Although the underlying logic of a PAM analysis is quite sophisticated, the calculations required are fairly simple and not too data demanding. As Gotsch (1989) shows, the whole process from the construction of the required data base, through the processing of these data, to the production of the final presentation table, can be done using any one of a number of readily-available spreadsheet packages on an ordinary personal computer.

Last but not least, the results of a PAM analysis are reasonably easily understood by policy makers (perhaps after some suitable explanation). Although conceptually simple, the information provided can be quite insightful. Inconsistencies between declared policy objectives and actual policy settings are highlighted, and needed remedial actions clarified.

The main limitation of the PAM method is that supply and demand responses to policy changes affecting prices are not indicated. While there are market-level approaches that overcome this limitation (e.g., Josling and McCalla 1985), they are more complex and data-demanding. They use as their starting point not the micro-level commodity budgets used in PAM analysis, but estimates of supply and demand curves, putting their method beyond the scope of this manual.

A further limitation of PAM analysis has already been alluded to and relates to the strong assumptions involved in single-commodity analysis - the most widely used form of

PAM. There are usually serious problems in assigning (private and social) prices to factors and commodities such as family labour or animal power, the markets for which are very imperfect. Nevertheless, in situations where a quick, perhaps rather approximate, yet often still insightful analysis is needed, making good use of commonly available micro-level data, the PAM is a valuable approach.

9.6 *References*

GITTINGER, J.P. (1982). *Economic Analysis of Agricultural Projects*, Johns Hopkins University Press, Baltimore.

GOODMAN, L.J. & R.N. LOVE (1979). 'The Integrated Project Planning and Management Cycle (IPPMC)', in L.J. Goodman and R.N. Love (eds), *Management of Development Projects*, Pergamon, New York, Ch.1.

GOTSCH, C. (1989). *Agricultural Policy Analysis on Electronic Spreadsheets: Commodity and Farming Systems Models*, Farm Management and Production Economics Service, Agricultural Services Division, Food and Agriculture Organization of the United Nations, Rome.

JOSLING T.E. & A.F. McCALLA (1985). *Agricultural Policies and World Markets*, Macmillan, New York.

MONKE E.A. & S.R. PEARSON (1989). *The Policy Analysis Matrix for Agricultural Development*, Cornell University Press, Ithaca.

PEARSON, S.R. & E.A. MONKE (1987). *The Policy Analysis Matrix: A Manual for Practitioners*, Pragma, Stanford.

SQUIRE, L. & H.G. VAN DER TAK (1975). *Economic Analysis of Projects*, Johns Hopkins University Press, Baltimore.

WORLD BANK (1988). *Rural Development: World Bank Experience, 1965-86*, Operations Evaluation Department, World Bank, Washington, D.C.

GLOSSARY

This glossary contains definitions of the main farm management research terms used in this bulletin. No attempt has been made to provide a comprehensive listing of general farm management terms. Such a listing is provided by: FAO, *Farm Management Glossary*, FAO Agricultural Services Bulletin No. 63, FAO, Rome, 1985.

Cf. : *confer* (= compare).
q.v.: *quod vide* (= which see).

Accidental sampling - a method of *non-probability sampling* (q.v.) in which the sampled individuals or units are selected by chance.

Activity - a particular method of producing some specified type of *output* (q.v.). See *farm activity*.

Activity budget - a summary of the technical and economic characteristics of a *farm activity* (q.v.). Used in farm *budgets* (q.v.) and *programming* (q.v.).

Activity gross income - the value of the *output* (q.v.) of a *farm activity* (q.v.) over some accounting period (usually a year), whether that output is sold or not.

Activity gross margin - *activity gross income* (q.v.) minus the *variable expenses* (q.v.) attributable to that *activity* (q.v.).

Acts - the actions available to a decision maker among which she or he must choose.

Adjusted coefficient of multiple determination (*adj.* R^2) - the *coefficient of multiple determination* (q.v.) of a function estimated by *least-squares regression* (q.v.), such as a *production function* (q.v.), adjusted for the number of coefficients estimated.

Aggregation bias - the bias resulting from the aggregation to a population level of results based on a *case-study* (q.v.), *representative-farm* (q.v.) or *sample survey* (q.v.) approach. Bias occurs because such approaches do not necessarily reflect population values exactly.

Agricultural policy - the policy framework specified by government for the operation of agriculture. It may have dimensions relating to aspects such as economics, health, welfare and the environment.

Agro-economic zones - zones which are defined in terms of common features. For different purposes these features will differ but may involve such dimensions as climate, soil resources, topography, land use, ethnic groupings, market access, etc.

Anchoring - a form of bias in *probability* (q.v.) elicitation whereby judgements tend to be excessively centred on a particular value.

Ancillary activity - an *activity* (q.v.) which is conducted to provide *input* (q.v.) to another activity or to transform the product of another activity prior to sale or other end use.

Area familiarization - see *field study*.

Assets - anything of value in the possession of the farmer or claims of the farmer on anything of value held by others. May be clasified as *current assets* (q.v.) or *fixed assets* (q.v.).

Backward induction - the procedure followed in solving a *risky decision problem* (q.v.) depicted as a *decision tree* (q.v.).

Bar chart - a figure in which the size of different classes within a set of data is represented by bars of fixed width but of height or length proportional to the magnitude to be represented.

Break-even budget - a *budget* (q.v.)(usually a *partial profit budget* (q.v.)) drawn up to establish the value of a selected planning coefficient for which gains and losses are equal.

Budget - a quantitative assessment of future needs and outcomes. Generally a financial statement of the expected performance of an *activity* (q.v.), *enterprise* (q.v.), project or farm showing expected costs and revenues for a future period. May be in physical units as in a *labour budget* (q.v.), *livestock feed budget* (q.v.) or *water-balance budget* (q.v.). See also *break-even budget, cash-flow budget, development budget, finance budget, gross margin budget, parametric budget, partial profit budget, profit budget, whole-farm budget.*

Budgetary control - the process of matching the recorded progress of a project or of selected aspects of farm production against a *budget* (q.v.).

Cash flow - the sequence over time of payments or receipts in the form of cash (including transactions conducted through a bank).

Cash-flow budget - a statement of projected *farm payments* (q.v.) and *farm receipts* (q.v.) associated with a particular farm plan.

Case study - the detailed study of a particular individual unit such as a farm, *enterprise* (q.v.), *activity* (q.v.) or household.

Case-study approach - the approach to *farm management research* (q.v.) via farm *case studies* (q.v.) rather than *representative-farm* (q.v.) or *sample survey* (q.v.) methods.

Census - see *farm census.*

Certainty equivalent - that sure *consequence* (q.v.) which, if it were available, the decision maker would regard as equivalent to a particular set of risky *consequences* (q.v.).

Certainty equivalent approach - a method of resolving a *risky decision problem* (q.v.) using *certainty equivalents* (q.v.).

Chance-constrained programming - a form of *risk programming* (q.v.) in which risky *constraints* (q.v.) are satisfied at some prescribed *probability* (q.v.) level.

Chance node - see *event node.*

Choice criterion - a measure adopted as a basis for comparing the *consequences* (q.v.) of alternative *acts* (q.v.).

Cluster sampling - a form of *multistage sampling* (q.v.) in which all the individuals or units at the last stage are sampled.

Cobb-Douglas function - a commonly used algebraic form for *production function analysis* (q.v.); for the general case $\log Y = \log a_o + \Sigma_i a_i \log X_i$, where Y is estimated output quantity, X_i is the i-th input quantity, and a_o and a_i are estimated coefficients.

Coefficient of absolute risk aversion - a personal measure of risk aversion derived by dividing a decision maker's *coefficient of relative risk aversion* (q.v.) by her or his wealth.

Coefficient of multiple determination (R^2) - a statistic measuring the proportion of the variation in a set of data explained by a *least-squares regression* (q.v.) equation fitted to the data.

Coefficient of relative risk aversion - a dimensionless (and thus interpersonally comparable) measure of how averse a decision maker is to *risk* (q.v.).

Coefficient of skewness - the statistic α_3 computed as $\alpha_3 = M_3/V^{1.5}$ where M_3 is the *third central moment* (q.v.) and V is *variance* (q.v.); the coefficient is positive or negative according as the distribution is positively (long tail above the mode) or negatively (long tail below the mode) skewed.

Commercial farming - farming in which the majority of the farm *output* (q.v.) is sold, usually also involving appreciable use of purchased *inputs* (q.v.).

Comparative advantage - see *principle of comparative advantage.*

Comparative analysis - comparison of the performance of a particular farm with some standard such as the average performance of a group of broadly similar farms.

Competitive enterprise - an *enterprise* (q.v.) the production of whose *output* (q.v.), over the relevant range, is competitive with that of another enterprise. Cf. *complementary enterprise.*

Complementary enterprise - an *enterprise* (q.v.) which, over some range, enhances the level of *output* (q.v.) of another enterprise. Cf. *competitive enterprise.*

Component research - research aimed at the development of improved components for use in a *farming system* (q.v.). Most often carried out on experiment stations.

Compound interest rate - the rate of interest used in *compounding* (q.v.) or *discounting* (q.v.). Depending on the context it may be a market rate or an *opportunity cost* (q.v.) rate.

Compounding - calculation of the future value of a present sum on the basis of the rate of *compound interest* (q.v.). It is given by $C_n = C_0(1 + i)^n$ where i is the interest rate per period (usually per year), n is the number of periods, C_0 is the present sum and C_n is the value after n periods. Note that this formulation assumes i is the same in each period.

Consequence - the outcome or payoff a decision maker receives or suffers when she or he adopts a particular *act* (q.v.) and a particular *state of nature* (q.v.) occurs.

Constraint - something which limits the achievement of an objective. It may be of a biological, economic, social, cultural, personal, resource or other nature.

Cost analysis - see *principles of cost analysis.*

Cost of capital - benefits given up by the farmer through having *investment capital* (q.v.) tied up in an *enterprise* (q.v.) for a period of time.

Cropping pattern - the distribution of crops over time and space on a farm during one production cycle.

Cross tabulation - the organization of data in tabular form in terms of two or more dimensions of classification.

Cumulative distribution function (CDF) - a function representing the *probability* (q.v.) that an *uncertain variable* (q.v.) X takes a value less than or equal to some particular value X*, defined for all values of X.

Cumulative frequency curve - a *graph* (q.v.) depicting on the vertical axis the relative frequency of some *uncertain variable* (q.v.) X cumulated for all values of X less than or equal to any given value on the horizontal axis.

Current assets - the total of physical working *assets* (q.v.) and liquid assets such as cash in hand or at the bank.

Debt servicing capacity - *farm net cash flow* (q.v.) less cash needed for family living expenses.

Decision analysis - a procedure for ensuring that a decision maker makes decisions that are consistent with her or his personal beliefs about the *risk* (q.v.) she or he faces and her or his personal preferences for possible consequences from the decision.

Decision node - a point in a *decision tree* (q.v.) where a choice must be made.

Decision theory - see *decision analysis*.

Decision tree - a diagrammatic representation in tree form of a *risky decision problem* (q.v.).

Degree of belief - see *subjective probability*.

Degree of preference - see *utility*.

Depreciation - the cost of wear and obsolescence associated with *fixed assets* (q.v.) such as implements, machinery and structures over time.

Development budget - a *budget* (q.v.) used when planning changes in farm methods or organization that will take some considerable time to implement.

Development programme - a schedule used in a *development budget* (q.v.) and showing anticipated *inputs* (q.v.) and *outputs* (q.v.) in dated sequence.

Development target - the selected end position for a *development budget* (q.v.).

Diminshing returns - see *principle of diminishing physical and economic returns*.

Discount factor - the value by which the elements of a future *cash flow* (q.v.) must be multiplied to calculate its *present value* (q.v.). Specified as $(1 + i)^{-n}$ where i is the relevant rate of interest and n is the number of periods over which *discounting* (q.v.) is to occur.

Discounting - calculation of the *present value* (q.v.) of a future sum on the basis of the rate of *compound interest* (q.v.). It is the converse of *compounding* (q.v.) and is given by $C_o = C^n(1 + i)^{-n}$ where i is the interest rate per period (usually per year), C_n is the sum to be received at the end of period n in the future and C_o is the present value. Note that this formulation assumes that i is the same in each period.

Discrete stochastic programming - a form of *risk programming* (q.v.) in which a relatively small number of possible outcomes of risky coefficients are considered.

Domestic resource cost coefficient (DRC) - a measure of the *comparative advantage* (q.v.) in production of a particular commodity from a societal view. Calculated as the ratio of input cost to value added, both valued at *shadow prices* (q.v.). Cf. *private profitability coefficient*.

Dominance - a term used in various contexts (e.g., in *farm programming* (q.v.), *input-output budget analysis* (q.v.) and *decision analysis* (q.v.)) to indicate that one alternative is superior to another in the sense of producing higher benefits with equal or lower costs.

Economic appraisal - assessment of the costs and benefits of an activity on the basis of *shadow prices* (q.v.). Cf. *financial appraisal, social appraisal.*

Economic principle of marginality - see *principle of marginality.*

Effective protection coefficient (EPC) - a measure of the impact of policy intervention defined as the ratio of value added at prevailing prices to the value added at *shadow prices* (q.v.). Cf. *nominal protection coefficient.*

Enterprise - see *farm enterprise.*

Enterprise choice - see *principle of enterprise choice.*

Enterprise gross income - the value of the *output* (q.v.) of a *farm enterprise* (q.v.) over some accounting period (usually a year), whether that output is sold or not.

Enterprise gross margin - *enterprise gross income* (q.v.) minus the *variable expenses* (q.v.) attributable to that *enterprise* (q.v.).

Equity - see *farm equity capital.*

Equity ratio - *farm equity capital* (q.v.) divided by *total farm capital* (q.v.); it is a measure of the level of indebtedness and is usually expressed as a percentage.

(E,V)-analysis - the appraisal of *risky choices* (q.v.) on the basis of their mean or *expected value (E)* (q.v.) and their *variance (V)* (q.v.).

(E,V)-efficient plans - farm plans that have the lowest possible *variance (V)* (q.v.) of income for all levels of expected income *(E)* - see *expected value*; such plans may be generated by *quadratic risk programming* (q.v.).

Event node - a point in a *decision tree* (q.v.) where uncertainty exists as to which of a number of events or *states of nature* (q.v.) will occur.

Ex ante evaluation - evaluation undertaken before implementation of some course of action of its likely costs and benefits.

Expansion path - see *isocline equation.*

Expected utility - a criterion for *risky choice* (q.v.) computed as the *subjective probability* (q.v.) weighted average of the *utilities* (q.v.) of the possible *consequences* (q.v.).

Expected value (E) - the probability-weighted average of all possible values of an *uncertain variable* (q.v.).

Ex post evaluation - evaluation after implementation of some course of action of its actual costs and benefits.

Factor - see *factor of production, input factor*.

Factor of production - an *input* (q.v.) used in a production process.

Factorial design - an experimental design in which each level of each *factor* (q.v.) appears with each level of each other factor.

Family earnings - *net farm earnings* (q.v.) plus other household income; it represents the total income available to the farm family for all purposes.

Farm activity - a specified method of producing a crop or operating a livestock enterprise. For a particular *enterprise* (q.v.), a farmer will have the choice between a number of *activities* (q.v.) on which production may be based.

Farm case study - the detailed study of an individual farm.

Farm cash surplus - *farm net cash flow* (q.v.) adjusted for loans received and interest and principal payments; it represents the amount of cash generated by the farm and available for household use.

Farm census - collection of selected information from all the farms comprising some population.

Farm development budget - see *development budget*.

Farm enterprise - the production of a particular commodity or group of related commodities for sale or domestic use.

Farm equity capital - *total farm capital* (q.v.) less farm borrowings.

Farm-household - the family *household* (q.v.) associated with a farm or the farm and its associated household taken as an integrated unit.

Farm-household analysis - study of the farm and its *household* (q.v.) as an integrated unit.

Farm management - the process by which resources and situations are manipulated by the farmer in trying, with less than full information, to achieve her or his goals.

Farm management research - research aimed at understanding and/or improving the process of *farm management* (q.v.) so as to assist the farmer or policy maker.

Farm net cash flow - *farm receipts* (q.v.) minus *farm payments* (q.v.).

Farm net worth - see *farm equity capital*.

Farm payments - cash (or its equivalent in kind) paid for goods and services purchased for farm use.

Farm plan - a statement of the *activities* (q.v.) to be carried out on the farm over a specified period of time.

Farm programming - see *programming approach.*

Farm receipts - the value of cash received from sale of agricultural *output* (q.v.).

Farm survey - data collection from a sample of farms from a given population.

Farm system - see *farming system.*

Farm system simulation - the mimicking of the operation of a farm via some type of *model* (q.v.).

Farmer - the principal decision maker involved in the management of a farm. Usually but not always will be the head of the *farm-household* (q.v.).

Farming system - the *system of production* (q.v.) used by a farmer as specified by the technology used, resources available, preferences held and goals pursued within a given agro-ecological and socio-economic environment.

Farming systems research (FSR) - research of a multidisciplinary nature conducted with a *farming system* (q.v.) perspective.

Field cost (of an input) - the *field price of an input* (q.v.) multiplied by the quantity of the *input* (q.v.) which varies with the decision.

Field price (of an input) - the total value which must be given up to bring an additional unit of *input* (q.v.) onto the field.

Field price (of an output) - the value to the farmer of an additional unit of *output* (q.v.) in the field, prior to harvest.

Field study - informal study of a particular area or problem, often conducted as a preliminary to more formal study.

Finance budget - a *budget* (q.v.) constructed to show the extent of necessary borrowings and the manner in which interest and principal payments on loans advanced are to be met.

Financial appraisal - assessment of the financial costs and benefits of an *investment* (q.v.) either *ex ante* (q.v.) or *ex post* (q.v.) under expected or prevailing actual prices. Cf. *economic appraisal, social appraisal.*

First-degree stochastic dominance (FSD) - for a decision maker who prefers more rather than less of a good such as income, one *risky choice* (q.v.) dominates another in the sense of FSD if its *cumulative distribution function* (q.v.) always lies to the right of the other.

Fixed assets - durable *assets* (q.v.) that are used for more than one production cycle. They are subject to *depreciation* (q.v.).

Fixed costs - see *fixed expenses.*

Fixed expenses - those components of *total farm expenses* (q.v.) that do not satisfy the definition of *variable expenses* (q.v.).

Fixed input - an *input* (q.v.) whose level remains unchanged during the production process.

Fractile - the j-th fractile ($0 \leq j \leq 1$) is the value of a *random variable* (q.v.) such that the probability of a randomly drawn value of the variable being less than the fractile value is j.

Fractile rule - if only n observations are available on a continuous *random variable* (q.v.), then when these observations are arranged in ascending order of size, the k-th observation is a reasonable estimate of the $k/(n + 1)$ *fractile* (q.v.).

Fractional factorial design - a *factorial design* (q.v.) in which selected combinations of *factors* (q.v.) are omitted.

Frequency distribution - a table, *graph* (q.v.) or mathematical function indicating the frequency of occurrence of particular values of a *random variable* (q.v.).

Gender analysis - the study of farm and household responsibilities, activities and rewards relative to men, women and children in terms of who does what, who has access to or control of resources and who has access to or control of benefits.

Gender task allocation - the allocation of farm and household activities and responsibilities between men, women and children.

General purpose table - a table constructed to present a summary overview or to present a large amount of *primary data* (q.v.) or *secondary data* (q.v.) in a convenient form.

Generalized stochastic dominance - see *stochastic dominance with respect to a function.*

Goal tradeoff - see *principle of goal tradeoff.*

Government failure - misallocation of resources from a societal point of view because of inappropriate government policy intervention in the market.

Graph - a figure drawn on two axes representing two variables with points representing paired values of the two variables connected by a line or curve.

Gross farm income - the value of the total *output* (q.v.) of a farm over some accounting period (usually a year), whether that output is sold or not.

Gross field benefit - *net yield* (q.v.) times *field price* (q.v.) for all products from a crop.

Gross margin - see *activity gross margin* or *enterprise gross margin.*

Gross margin budget - a *partial profit budget* (q.v.) drawn up using *enterprise gross margins* (q.v.).

Gross margins planning - a version of *simplified programming* (q.v.) in which *activities* (q.v.) are selected on the basis of only one key *constraint* (q.v.), usually land.

Histogram - a figure composed of a number of rectangles drawn adjacent to each other such that the area of each rectangle is equal to or, more generally, is proportional to the frequency of observations in the class interval represented by the width of the rectangle.

Household - a person or group of persons normally living in the same house or compound, usually sharing a community of life and bound together by a shared economy. See *farm-household*.

Household net cash income - *farm cash surplus* (q.v.) plus other *household* (q.v.) receipts; it represents the cash available to the farm family for all payments not relating to the farm.

Hypothesis - an "if.....then....." statement which is aimed to be tested by research.

Input - see *input factor*.

Input factor - a resource which is used in a production process. Relative to a given time span, may be classified as a *variable input* (q.v.) or a *fixed input* (q.v.) and according as to whether or not its level of use is under the farmer's decision making control.

Input-output budget analysis - *partial profit budgets* (q.v.) applied to the analysis of *input-output data* (q.v.).

Input-output coefficients - technical coefficients specifying the quantity of some particular *input* (q.v.) per unit of *output* (q.v.) or the amount of output produced per unit of input.

Input-output data - data relating the level of crop or livestock *output* (q.v.) to (different) levels of *input* (q.v.) use.

Integer programming - a form of mathematical programming related to *linear programming* (q.v.) in which selected variables are constrained to whole-number values.

Internal rate of return (IRR) - that *rate of compound interest* (q.v.) which makes the *net present value* (q.v.) of an *investment* (q.v.) exactly zero.

Investment - the purchase of *assets* (q.v.) with a view to possible future advantage.

Investment appraisal - an evaluation of the profitability of some *investment* (q.v.). Commonly involves *net present value* (q.v.) or *internal rate of return* (q.v.) calculations.

Investment capital - value of *inputs* (q.v.) (purchased or owned) which are allocated to an *enterprise* (q.v.) with the expectation of a return at a later point in time.

In vitro analysis - analysis carried out in abstract.

In vivo analysis - analysis carried out under actual conditions.

Iso-cost locus - equation specifying all *input* (q.v.) combinations corresponding to a particular level of expenditure.

Isocline equation - the equation specifying the least cost combination of a set of *input factors* (q.v.) for production of any specified quantity of *output* (q.v.).

Isoquant equation - an equation describing all combinations of *input factors* (q.v.) which yield a given quantity of *output* (q.v.).

Judgemental fractile method - a method of eliciting a *subjective probability distribution* (q.v.) by assessing *fractiles* (q.v.) of the distribution.

Key constraint - a *constraint* (q.v.) selected as potentially limiting choice of a *farm plan* (q.v.) and hence used as a basis for *activity* (q.v.) selection in *simplified programming* (q.v.).

Labour budget - a *budget* (q.v.), usually based on standardized labour units such as *person-day* (q.v.), *man-day* (q.v.) or *man-year* (q.v.) *equivalents*, comparing labor requirements with labour available, usually constructed on a seasonal basis.

Labour chart - a form of *labour budget* (q.v.) constructed as a figure with a calendar of working days recorded on the horizontal axis and with number of workers recorded on the vertical axis; the chart shows the number of workers required for each task and the duration of that task.

Labour day - a unit of labour input or requirement, usually assumed to represent the work accomplished in eight hours.

Labour profile - the seasonal pattern of labour requirements for a given *farm activity* (q.v.).

Law of diminishing returns - the physical law that applies to all production processes such that the *marginal product* (q.v.) of a *variable input* (q.v.) eventually declines as more of the factor is used relative to a given amount of *fixed inputs* (q.v.).

Least-squares regression - a standard statistical method for fitting continuous functions involving a single dependent variable and one or more independent variables; it is used in *production function analysis* (q.v.).

Linear programming (LP) - a computer-based procedure used for solving allocation problems such as farm planning and formulation of livestock diets.

Livestock equivalents - units used in *livestock feed budgeting* (q.v.) such that the feed (energy) requirements of different categories of livestock are expressed in terms of a single standardized type of livestock. There are no commonly agreed standards of equivalency though most assessements would approximate the relationship that one livestock equivalent equals one large animal (cow, bullock, horse, mule) equals six sheep or goats equals three pigs, with appropriate adjustments made for lactating, pregnant and young animals.

Livestock feed budget - a *budget* (q.v.) comparing feed requirements of farm livestock with feed available from a farm's crops and pastures, etc.; it is usually drawn up on a seasonal basis.

Livestock gross income - the value of livestock production in the form of animals and produce, adjusted for inventory changes and net of the value of any livestock purchased or obtained as gifts.

Livestock unit - see *livestock equivalents*.

Long-term cash-flow budget - a *cash-flow budget* (q.v.) constructed for a planning horizon of ten years or so with intermediate cash balances normally calculated at annual intervals.

Management performance criteria - set of technical, economic and/or financial measures, expressed in ratio, percentage or absolute terms, that enable an analyst or the farmer to assess managerial performance. For example, *equity ratio* (q.v.), *return to family labour* (q.v.) and *return to total capital* (q.v.). *Comparative analysis* (q.v.) will normally involve such criteria.

Man-day equivalent - a unit of measurement of labour availability or requirement, usually assumed to represent the work accomplished by an adult male worker in eight hours.

Man-year equivalent - the work of a *man-day equivalent* (q.v.) over one year.

Marginal cost - the increase in *variable cost* (q.v.) which occurs in changing from one production alternative to another; it is often measured relative to adding a marginal unit of an *input* (q.v.).

Marginal net benefit - the increase in *net benefit* (q.v.) which can be obtained by changing from one production alternative to another; it is often measured relative to adding a marginal unit of an *input* (q.v.).

Marginal opportunity cost - the foregone value of not including a marginal unit of a given *farm activity* (q.v.) in the farm plan.

Marginal principle - see *principle of marginality*.

Marginal product (of an input) - the change in *output* (q.v.) arising from using an additional unit of the *input* (q.v.).

Marginal rate of return - the *marginal net benefit* (q.v.) divided by the *marginal cost* (q.v.).

Marginal value product (MVP) - the *opportunity cost* (q.v.) of a marginal unit of a resource.

Market failure - misallocation of resources from a societal view because the market does not work.

Medium-term cash-flow budget - a *cash-flow budget* (q.v.) extending over three or four years with the intermediate cash balances calculated at quarterly or half-yearly intervals.

Minimum returns analysis - a procedure for assessing risky production alternatives by examining their worst possible *net returns* (q.v.) and selecting that alternative whose worst return or whose average return for its worst possibilities is highest among the alternatives being considered.

Mixed activity - two or more *activities* (q.v.) that are in such close association that separate economic analysis is not meaningful.

Model - a simplified representation of reality built to reflect those features of a farm, enterprise, process, etc. that are of most importance in the context of a particular study.

Money field price (of an input) -- the purchase price of a unit of an *input factor* (q.v.) plus other direct expenses (such as transportation costs) per unit of input incurred in using the input factor.

Money field price (of an output) - the market price of a unit of product minus harvest,storage, transportation and marketing costs, and quality discounts.

Monte Carlo budgeting - *risk budgeting* (q.v.) based on *random sampling* (q.v.) of some coefficients.

Monte Carlo programming - a *programming approach* (q.v.) to *farm system simulation* (q.v.) based on *random sampling* (q.v.) of some coefficients.

MOTAD programming - a form of *risk programming* (q.v.) based on Minimization Of Total Absolute Deviation of *total gross margin* (q.v.).

Multiphase sampling - a sampling scheme involving collection of different categories of information from different subsamples.

Multiple cropping - the growing of more than one crop on the same land in the one year.

Multistage sampling - a *probability sampling* (q.v.) method involving two or more steps, e.g., sampling of villages and then sampling of households within the sampled villages.

Multivariable production function - a *production function* (q.v.) involving more than one *variable input* (q.v.).

Net benefit - the value of the benefit gained less the value of the things given up in achieving the benefit, e.g., total *gross field benefit* (q.v.) minus total *variable cost* (q.v.).

Net benefit curve - a curve showing the relationship between *variable costs* (q.v.) of alternatives and their expected *net benefits* (q.v.).

Net cash flow - see *farm net cash flow.*

Net farm earnings - *net farm income* (q.v.) less interest paid on borrowed capital; it represents the reward to all family-owned resources used in farm production.

Net farm income - *gross farm income* (q.v.) minus *total farm expenses* (q.v.); it is the reward to the farm family for their labour and management together with the return on all the capital invested in the farm, whether borrowed or not.

Net present value (NPV) - the net total of the discounted values of the payments and receipts associated with a given project or farm plan. See *discounting*.

Net return - see *net benefit.*

Net worth - see *farm equity capital*.

Net yield - the measured yield per hectare in the field, minus harvest losses and storage losses where appropriate.

Nominal protection coefficient (NPC) - a measure of the impact of policy intervention on the value of *output* (q.v.) or cost of a purchased *input* (q.v.) as measured in terms of prevailing prices. Cf. *effective protection coefficient.*

Non-probability sampling - a method of sampling in which the probability of a particular individual or unit being included in the sample is not known. Cf. *probability sampling*.

Normative studies - studies aimed at how best to achieve some target.

Objective function - a statement, often expressed algebraically, of the objective to be maximized and the variables on which it depends.

On-farm trials (OFT) - trials or experiments conducted on a farm rather than on an experiment station. Usually specified as either farmer or researcher managed.

Opportunity cost - the economic principle that the cost of any choice is measured by the value of the best alternative foregone; thus the opportunity cost of a resource is its value in its best alternative use.

Opportunity field price (of an input) - refers to the value of the *input* (q.v.) in its best alternative use.

Opportunity field price (of an output) - the money price which the farm family would have to pay to acquire an additional unit of the product for consumption.

Outcome - see *consequence*.

Output - any physical product or service generated by an *activity* (q.v.).

Parametric budget - a *budget* (q.v.) (usually a *partial profit budget* (q.v.)) drawn up using algebraic symbols for selected planning coefficients and used to appraise the consequences of variations in those coefficients. A form of *sensitivity analysis* (q.v.).

Parametric programming - a form of *linear programming* (q.v.) in which selected coefficients are varied over some chosen range.

Partial budget - see *partial profit budget*.

Partial cash-flow budget - a *cash-flow budget* (q.v.) showing only those *cash flows* (q.v.) that would be changed as a consequence of some proposed change in the *farm plan* (q.v.).

Partial profit budget - a *budget* (q.v.) drawn up to estimate the effect on some measure of farm profit of a proposed change in farm organization or methods affecting only part of the farm.

Payments - see *farm payments*.

Payoff - see *consequence*.

Payoff matrix - a table representing the *acts* (q.v.), *states of nature* (q.v.), *subjective probabilities* (q.v.) and *consequences* (q.v.) of a *risky decision problem* (q.v.).

Person-day - see *man-day*.

Pie chart - a figure in the form of a circle that is divided into segments such that the size of each segment (angle) is proportional to the magnitude or frequency of that class.

Policy analysis matrix (PAM) - an accounting table for a given commodity system, either on a regional or national basis, which allows assessment of the effects of price and/or income policies or *market failures* (q.v.) in terms of the difference between private and social benefits and costs.

Positive studies - studies aimed at understanding actual behaviour.

Power function - see *Cobb-Douglas function*.

Present value - the value now of some money amount or *cash flow* (q.v.) to be paid or received in the future, adjusted for differences in the value of money over time arising from the *opportunity cost* (q.v.) of capital. See *discounting*.

Primary data - data obtained directly from the study of an entity or situation. Cf. *secondary data*.

Principle of comparative advantage - the economic principle implying that various crops and livestock should, other things being equal, be produced in those areas where the physical and other resources are best suited to their production.

Principle of diminishing physical and economic returns - the economic principle that *variable inputs* (q.v.) should be added to *fixed inputs* (q.v.) so long as the added return expected from the last unit of variable input used is just sufficient to cover the added cost of that unit.

Principle of enterprise choice - the economic principle that *enterprises* (q.v.) and the associated *activities* (q.v.) on which they are based should enter the *farm plan* (q.v.) so long as their expected contribution to *net farm income* (q.v.) exceeds the *opportunity cost* (q.v.) of the resources they use.

Principle of goal tradeoff - the economic principle that a farmer should trade off competing goals so long as the gain in satisfaction from the goal receiving increased emphasis is greater than the loss in satisfaction incurred by decreasing emphasis on the other goal or goals.

Principle of marginality - the economic principle that choices about the use of resources should be made such that the marginal gain from the slightest possible change in resource use is equal to the marginal loss implied by the change.

Principle of substitution - the economic principle that, in substituting one method for another, the saving in the method replaced must be greater than the cost of the technique added.

Principles of cost analysis - the division of costs into *fixed costs* (q.v.) and *variable costs* (q.v.).

Private profitability - the profitability to individual producers of an activity. Assessment is in terms of actually prevailing or expected prices. Cf. *social profitability*.

Private profitability coefficient (PPC) - a measure of the *comparative advantage* (q.v.) farmers have in producing a particular commodity. Calculated as the ratio of input cost to value added, both valued at prevailing prices. Cf. *domestic resource cost coefficient*.

Probability - a measure of the chance of occurrence of an event. It may range between zero and unity. See *subjective probability, probability distribution*.

Probability density function (PDF) - an algebraic function giving the *probability* (q.v.) of occurrence of possible values of an uncertain continuous bariable. This function has the property that the area underneath it between any two values of the *uncertain variable* (q.v.) is proportional to the likelihood that the value of the variable will lie in that range.

Probability distribution - a specification in verbal, diagrammatic or algebraic form of the *probability* (q.v.) of occurrence of all possible values of a *random variable* (q.v.).

Probability sampling - a method of drawing a sample such that the *probability* (q.v.) of a particular individual or unit being included in the sample is known or can be estimated with reasonable precision.

Production function - the quantitative relationship between *inputs* (q.v.) and *outputs* (q.v.) for some production process.

Production function analysis - a method of assessing production decisions by estimation and analysis of *production functions* (q.v.).

Profit budget - a *budget* (q.v.) drawn up in terms of some measure of farm profit such as *net farm earnings* (q.v.).

Profit motive - the aim of seeking maximum (financial) profit. Often assumed to be the objective in commercial farm *enterprises* (q.v.).

Programme planning - see *simplified programming*.

Programming approach - approaches to farm planning based on *linear programming* (q.v.) or its variants, such as *simplified programming* (q.v.).

Project appraisal - assessment via *economic appraisal* (q.v.), *financial appraisal* (q.v.) or *social appraisal* (q.v.) of the costs and benefits of a development project.

Project cycle - the sequential phases of a project in terms of: (1) planning, appraisal and design; (2) selection, approval and activation; (3) operation, control, monitoring and handover; and (4) evaluation and refinement.

Project evaluation - the evaluation of a project to assess whether, *ex ante* (q.v.), planned objectives can be achieved or, *ex post* (q.v.), have been achieved.

Purposive sampling - a method of *non-probability sampling* (q.v.) in which a sample is drawn to illustrate or represent some particular characteristic in the population.

Quadratic polynomial - a commonly used algebraic form for *production function analysis* (q.v.); for the general case $Y = a_o + \Sigma_i a_i X_i + \Sigma_i a_{ii} X^2{}_i + \Sigma_{i<j} a_{ij} X_i X_j$ where Y is estimated output quantity, X_i or X_j is the i-th or j-th input quantity, and a_o, a_i and a_{ij} are estimated coefficients.

Quadratic risk programming - a method of *farm programming* (q.v.) permitting *risk* (q.v.) in *activity gross margins* (q.v.) to be taken into account.

Quota sampling - a method of *non-probability sampling* (q.v.) in which individuals or units with defined characteristics are selected until specified quotas have been filled.

Random sampling - a method of *probability sampling* (q.v.) in which the *probability* (q.v.) of any individual or unit being included in the sample is constant.

Random variable - a variable whose value in any particular future instance is not sure but follows some *probability distribution* (q.v.).

Rapid rural appraisal - see *field study*.

Rate of compound interest - see *compound interest rate*.

Rate of technical substitution of factor i for factor j (RTS_{ij}) - the amount by which factor i must be increased if factor j is reduced by one unit and the level of production is to remain unchanged.

Receipts - see *farm receipts*.

Recommendation domain - a group of farmers within an *agro-economic zone* (q.v.) whose farms are sufficiently similar and who follow sufficiently similar practices that a given recommendation is applicable to the entire group.

Reconnaissance study - see *field study*.

Relative frequency curve - a figure derived as (or equivalent to) a smoothed *relative frequency polygon* (q.v.).

Relative frequency polygon - a line *graph* (q.v.) obtained by connecting the mid-points of the tops of the rectangles of a *histogram* (q.v.) of relative frequencies.

Representative farm - a farm chosen as representative of some class of farms.

Representativeness - a source of bias in *probability* (q.v.) elicitation whereby too much weight is attached to the extent to which a particular event is representative of a particular class of events.

Resource endowment - the amount and quality of resources, in the forms of land, labour, etc., available in a particular region or to a particular group of farms or to an individual farm.

Return per man - a measure of labour productivity; when applied to family labour it is calculated as *return to family labour* (q.v.) divided by the number of family members (measured as "adult male equivalents") working on the farm.

Return per person - see *return per man*.

Return to family labour - *net farm earnings (q.v.)* less an imputed interest charge on *farm equity capital* (q.v.); it may be expressed on a "per adult male equivalent" basis.

Return to farm equity capital - *net farm earnings (q.v.)* minus the value of family labour used on the farm, usualy expressed as a percentage of *farm equity capital* (q.v.).

Return to total capital - *net farm income* (q.v.) less the value of family labour used on the farm, usually expressed as a percentage of *total farm capital* (q.v.).

Risk - a situation with uncertain *consequences* (q.v.).

Risk attitude - extent to which a decision maker seeks to avoid (i.e., risk aversion) or is willing to face (i.e., risk preference) *risk* (q.v.). Measured quantitatively by the *coefficient of relative risk aversion* (q.v.) or *coefficient of absolute risk aversion* (q.v.).

Risk budgeting - a form of *parametric budgeting* (q.v.) adapted to the case where *probability distributions* (q.v.) of uncertain coefficients have been obtained, and where the aim is to assess the distribution of the selected profit measure.

Risk efficiency analysis - the comparison of alternative *risky choices* (q.v.) on the basis of *stochastic dominance analysis* (q.v.), *(E,V)-analysis* (q.v.) or related methods.

Risk premium - an amount, often given as a percentage, by which a decision maker discounts the *expected value (E)* (q.v.) of a risky income or other uncertain *consequence* (q.v.).

Risk programming - the generic term for methods of accounting for *risk* (q.v.) in *farm programming* (q.v.).

Risky choice - choice among *acts* (q.v.) whose *consequences* (q.v.) are not certain; or an *act* (q.v.) whose *consequences* (q.v.) are not certain.

Risky decision problem - a decision problem in which the *consequences* (q.v.) of alternative *acts* (q.v.) are uncertain.

Rural development - the general development of the rural community in terms of such attributes as income, health, education, culture and infrastructure.

Sample survey - a survey of a sample drawn from a population of interest. See *probability sampling* and *non-probability sampling.*

Sampling frame - a list of those members of a population from whom a sample is to be drawn.

Scatter diagram - a figure drawn on two axes representing two variables with paired values of the two variables plotted to show the distribution of observations.

Seasonal labour profile - see *labour profile*.

Second-degree stochastic dominance (SSD) - for a decision maker who is risk averse, a method of discriminating between *risky choices* (q.v.) whose *cumulative distribution functions* (q.v.) cross.

Secondary data - data obtained indirectly, often from publications or records, rather than directly from the study of an entity or situation. Cf. *primary data.*

Semi-subsistence farming - farming in which both domestic use and sale of *output* (q.v.) account for significant proportions of the farm output or farm income.

Sensitivity analysis - a process which features changing a planning coefficient within reasonable bounds of the original estimate to determine if the original ranking of alternatives is affected.

Shadow price - a price that reflects more appropriately the value of an *input* (q.v.) or an *output* (q.v.) than does the prevailing price.

Short-term cash-flow budget - a *cash-flow budget* (q.v.) normally constructed over a twelve-month planning horizon with the intermediate cash balances calculated at monthly or bimonthly intervals.

Simplified programming (SP) - a method of selecting a *farm plan* (q.v.) in which the required calculations are performed without the need for access to a computer.

Small farmer - a farmer having only limited resources, low income in cash or kind and often producing on a *subsistence* (q.v.) or *semi-subsistence* (q.v.) basis.

Social appraisal - assessment of the distribution across society of the costs and benefits of an activity. Cf. *economic appraisal*, *financial appraisal*.

Social price - see *shadow price*.

Social profitability - the profitability to society of an activity undertaken on a private basis by its members. Assessment is in terms of *shadow prices* (q.v.). Cf. *private profitability*.

Sparse data analysis - *decision analysis* (q.v.) based on relatively few observations. generally making use of the *fractile rule* (q.v.).

Special purpose table - a table drawn up to illustrate some specific point or points about a set of collected data.

Spreadsheet analysis - the use of a computerized tabular format in which the effect of changes in basic entries to the table are automatically carried through to other entries. Often used in budget-type analyses.

Square-root quadratic polynomial - a commonly used algebraic form for *production function analysis* (q.v.); identical to a *quadratic polynomial* (q.v.) in which every input variable is replaced by its positive square root.

State of nature - an event outside of the control of the decision maker which may occur and influence the outcome of a decision.

Stochastic dominance - the *dominance* (q.v.) of one *risky choice* (q.v.) by another by virtue of the latter having preferable risk characteristics as determined by *stochastic dominance analysis* (q.v.).

Stochastic dominance analysis - the ordering of alternative *risky choices* (q.v.) through comparison of their *cumulative distribution functions* (q.v.) under the assumption of the decision maker having some particular *risk attitude* (q.v.). See *first-degree stochastic dominance* and *second-degree stochastic dominance*.

Stochastic dominance with respect to a function (SDRF) - a method of *stochastic dominance analysis* (q.v.) based on the setting of upper and lower bounds on the decision maker's *coefficient of absolute risk aversion* (q.v.).

Stochastic programming - see *risk programming*.

Stochastic variable - an *uncertain variable* (q.v.) whose value occurs at random on the basis of some *probability distribution* (q.v.).

Stock equivalents - see *livestock equivalents*.

Stratified sampling - a *probability sampling* (q.v.) method in which the population is first divided into groups or strata on the basis of one or more characteristics of interest.

Structural model - a *model* (q.v.) showing the structure of an entity or process of interest.

Subjective probability - a probability reflecting a decision maker's degree of belief about the chance of occurrence of a given *state of nature* (q.v.) or value of a *random variable* (q.v.). See *probability distribution*.

Subjective probability distribution - a *probability distribution* (q.v.) based upon the decision maker's *subjective probability* (q.v.) judgements.

Subsistence farming - farming in which the majority of the *output* (q.v.)is used by the farm family, contrasting with *semi-subsistence farming* (q.v.) and *commercial farming* (q.v.).

Substitution - see *principle of substitution*.

Survey - see *farm survey*.

Sustainability - the capacity to continue undiminished over time.

Sustainable development - as defined by the FAO Council in 1988, the management and conservation of the natural resource base, and the orientation of technological and institutional change in such a manner as to ensure the attainment and continued satisfaction of human needs for present and future generations. Such sustainable development (in the agriculture, forestry and fisheries sectors) conserves land, water, plant and animal genetic resources, is environmentally non-degrading, technically appropriate, economically viable and socially acceptable.

System of production - the technology used in an *activity* (q.v.) or set of activities. In relation to the set of activities constituting all the *enterprises* (q.v.) of a farm, the overall set of technologies specifies the farm's production system.

Systematic sampling - a method of *probability sampling* (q.v.) involving the selection of every k-th member from a list, working backward and forward from a random starting point.

Systems simulation - see *farm system simulation.*

Tabular analysis - preparation of summaries of collected data in the form of tables.

Third central moment (M_3) - the expected value of the third power of the deviations from the mean, denoted by E(X), of a *probability distribution* (q.v.). $M_3 = E(X-E(X))^3$.

Total farm assets - see *total farm capital.*

Total farm capital - the total value of all the *assets* (q.v.) of the farm whether or not owned by the farmer.

Total farm expenses - the value of all *inputs* (q.v.) used up or expended in farm production.

Total field cost - the sum of *field costs* (q.v.) for all *inputs* (q.v.) which are affected by a choice; also called *variable cost* (q.v.).

Total gross margin (TGM) - the sum of all the *enterprise gross margins* (q.v.) or *activity gross margins* (q.v.) on a farm.

Total household net income - see *family earnings.*

Two-phase sampling - a form of *multiphase sampling* (q.v.) involving data collection from two subsamples.

Uncertain variable - see *random variable.*

Utility - a numerical measure of a decision maker's relative preference for possible *consequences* (q.v.).

Utility function - a mathematical function that relates different levels of goal satisfaction with *utility* (q.v.) levels. Because net money benefit is an easily measured goal, the utility function is frequently expressed in terms of this variable.

Variable costs - see *variable expenses, total field cost.*

Variable expenses - those components of *total farm expenses* (q.v.) that are specific to a particular crop or livestock *enterprise* (q.v.) and that vary more or less in direct proportion to the scale of the enterprise.

Variable input - an *input* (q.v.) whose level is variable. The level used may or may not be under the control of the decision maker.

Variance (V) - the probability-weighted average or *expected value* (q.v.) of the square of the deviations of a random variable from its mean. $V = E(X-E(X))^2$.

Village studies - a form of data collection in which some information is typically gathered on a full village basis and other information is obtained from a sample of village households.

Visual impact method - a method of eliciting *subjective probabilities* (q.v.) based on allocation of counters over possible classes.

Water-balance budget - a *budget* (q.v.) of the irrigation water needs of a crop or combination of crops.

Whole-farm budget - a *budget* (q.v.) drawn up to show the anticipated *consequences* (q.v.), in terms of selected measures of performance, of some actual or proposed *farm plan* (q.v.).

Whole-farm planning - planning involving consideration of the *farm system* (q.v.) as a whole, as distinct from a *partial budgeting* (q.v.) approach to planning.

Whole-farm production function - a function relating total farm output to the use of land, labour and capital on a whole-farm basis.

Working capital - capital needed for the day-to-day running of a farm as distinct from longer term *investment capital* (q.v.).

Yield constraint research - research into the causes of *yield gap* (q.v.).

Yield gap - the difference between actual farm yields and either potential farm yiclds or experiment station yields.

SUBJECT INDEX